TRYST
with
DIGNITY
and
HONOUR

Brigadier Dinesh Mathur (Retired)

© BRIGADIER DINESH MATHUR (RETIRED) 2021

All rights reserved

All rights reserved by author. No part of this publication may be reproduced, stored in a retrieval system or transmitted in any form or by any means, electronic, mechanical, photocopying, recording or otherwise, without the prior permission of the author.

Although every precaution has been taken to verify the accuracy of the information contained herein, the author and publisher assume no responsibility for any errors or omissions. No liability is assumed for damages that may result from the use of information contained within.

First Published in September 2021

ISBN: 978-93-5472-269-1

BLUEROSE PUBLISHERS

www.bluerosepublishers.com

info@bluerosepublishers.com

+91 8882 898 898

Cover Design:

Ms Ritika Mathur

Distributed by: BlueRose, Amazon, Flipkart

Table of Contents

In Memoriam .... *v*

Acknowledgements .... *vi*

Foreword .... *viii*

Prologue .... *xii*

NDA & Pre-Commission Training 1
    Off to the NDA 1
    Now, the cynosure of all eyes – The one and only
    Twenty Third 35
    Behind every great Twenty Thirder is a wonderful lady . 41
    Training at the IMA 46
    Training at The School of Artillery, the Alma Mater 50

Life in the Regiment of Artillery 56
    The Fledgling Years Including Operations 56
    Learning to Fly and Operations 105
    To Himachal Pradesh and Back to Agra 131
    The Flood Gates to Nilgiris 143
    Back to Gwalior 149
    The Unforgettable Years at Helm 155
    Back to Alma Mater Once Again 171
    The Amritsar Sojourn and Alma Mater Once Again 177

Outside Regiment of Artillery 197
    The Alluring Jungles of Mizoram 197
    The First Post at Mhow 212
    The Nilgiris Invitation 218
    The Ladakh Sojourn 230
    The Desert Safari 236
    The Last Post at Mhow 251
    The Hanging Up of Boots & Uniform 259
    The Birds have Flown 284
    Joys of Imperfection 286

Post Retirement Experiences 290
- Kutch Revisited at Bhuj 290
- Entry into Corporate World 309
- Assignment Celebrity Homes 330
- Corporate Sector & Solid Waste Management 339
- Reunions, Get-togethers and Jubilees 346

The Soliloquy 356
- Random Thoughts 356
- Dignity & Honour 358
- Art of Command 359
- Sycophancy 360
- Loyalty & Integrity 361
- Strategic/Tactical Wisdom 362
- *Nam, namak aur nishan* 363
- Moral Courage 364
- The Working of the Military Secretary's Branch 364
- Quest for Equivalence with Bureaucracy 372
- Gunners and General Cadre 373
- Concept of Artillery Support in Future Operations 375

Contributions to Various Publications 378
- Kutch Revisited 381
- Chinese Perceptions on Border Territorial Disputes and Their Relevance in Indian Context 388
- Of Chinese Diplomacy and War 410
- Sino Indian Standoff – What Next? 420
- Grappling with the Dragon 426
- Afghanistan, its sectarian divisions, and international stakeholders 431
- Inside Afghanistan 438

Social & Spiritual Aspects 443

Epilogue 455

In Memoriam

This book is dedicated to the memory of Lt. Col. (later Maj. Gen) Harjit Singh Talwar, the finest Commanding Officer I ever served and who taught me professional ethics and reinforced my moral values. I also tried to emulate his example throughout my service.

I also dedicate this book in memory of my loving parents who taught me to lead a simple, austere and uncomplicated life without fears or favours from anyone.

Acknowledgements

My grateful acknowledgements are due to the great Indian Army for strengthening my resolve to write this book. I have immense pride in the fact that very early in life, I made the finest and my only career choice without reservations. It was a great privilege to have served for 37½ years in the olive green of which 11 years were in the same rank as a Brigadier.

My next acknowledgement is to the loyal, trustworthy and tough jawans on whose stout shoulders and high sense of duty, I overcame my fears (the inborn instinct of self-preservation) as a subaltern. They were my true witnesses to my performance in actual combat and I hold their mutual acceptance, support and camaraderie very dearly, even now. My officer colleagues and superiors were all outstanding, supportive excellent to work with. In the generation next, I am certain the values of moral courage, dignity and honour would have already permeated and imbibed, by now. There is no need for me to pontificate because, the results on the ground at my level, are very palpable and heartwarming.

I am grateful to my first instructor gunnery, Maj Gen YK Kapoor, AVSM (Retired), whose guidance and sound advice has helped me fulfil the aim of writing this book for posterity without bitterness or rancour. I do hope my experiences invigorate the generation next in making correct decisions /mid-course corrections in life.

I am grateful to my spouse, Manju, for her invaluable support and for allowing me endless hours in my study. Having spent all but six years in service with me, she too, felt the need for me to put down my experiences to writing.

Finally, my deep gratitude to my dear niece Aruna and her lawyer cum English don husband Akhileshwar who spent a lot of time proofreading the script and making invaluable suggestions.

Foreword

It gives me great pleasure to write a Foreword, to this so beautifully written book, "Tryst with Dignity and Honour" by Brigadier Dinesh Mathur (Retired). It speaks of his thoroughness and keenness, for being able to reproduce and present this mass of information in a clear, logical and concise manner. Thanks to his photographic memory.

Going back a little, as a Captain (Instructor Gunnery), at the School of Artillery Devlali, I had the opportunity to train cadets straight from the IMA, on the Young Officers course. This was probably the one and the only time that such a course was run, during the emergency in 1963. We just provided the basics of gunnery and dispatched them as YOs to their respective units. It is my firm conviction that the future of an officer is governed primarily by the grooming he receives in the unit that he is posted to first. My unit, 17 Para Field Regiment, is one such regiment that has nurtured many such budding youngsters and groomed them for higher command. I can say with pride that I had sent five YOs to my regiment then, who had the good fortune to receive their initial grooming in this great regiment. Brig Dinesh Mathur was one of them.

A thoroughbred professional, Brigadier Dinesh Mathur, is amongst the few in service, who acquired the best qualifications, both professional and academic. This has been possible through sustained hard work and dedication. He has rich and varied experience, having served in plains, deserts, mountains and jungles of the NE. He has been selected for prestigious career courses like the Staff Course, Senior and Higher Command Courses, based on his competitive merit, in the peer group. In his staff profile, he has been posted as BM in the NE and a Deputy Commander of an Infantry Brigade in Ladakh. The organisation selected him for posting as a Directing Staff at DSSC Wellington and at War College, which again, would be based on some criterion. His selection for transfer to the general cadre on his merit, after the successful command of an artillery brigade, was again, approved by the hierarchy. I am sure, he could not have been selected for these positions of responsibility unless he met the Army's strict prescribed yardsticks. I also have my doubts, if any relaxations in qualifications or experience can be made in all such appointments.

As an organisation, the Army has always identified youngsters who have leadership potential to bloom, takes great pains to nurture their talent and spend a good deal of time and money, to prepare them to shoulder higher responsibilities. Over time, the organisation must continue to be transparent, maintain continuity in policies of career management and gain lasting trust and confidence from those, it serves. In such a healthy environment, a subordinate with moral courage can afford to disagree with the way of thinking of the superior. However, once a decision has been taken by the superior to overrule the subordinate, the subordinate has no choice but to accept the decision, however, unpalatable it may be. I agree that some superiors have an 'inbuilt bias' but it is also, up to the subordinate to show his calibre, which can change the attitude of the superior.

This is the life story of an officer, who despite having the best of qualifications, was denied his due. I will not hesitate to say that something was amiss, when Brig Dinesh Mathur, did not make it to the next rank, in the general cadre. Would it not have been more prudent on the part of the organisation, to analyse what went wrong, rectify matters and save careers. Instead, the organisation chose to heap indignities, one after another on the officer. It is very apparent, that the powers that be, for some unknown reasons, went out of their way to damage his career prospects and also went to the extent of denying him the privilege of the last posting to his home town, on retirement. I will always say to his credit that he maintained his cool, continued to work with utmost zeal and dedication, for his Dignity and Honour, inculcated over the years. His success in the corporate sector bears testimony to his professional acumen and experience, acquired from the same very Army which did not approve him, beyond the rank of a Brigadier.

The professional reputation you build up is well known to all those you have the opportunity to serve or interact with, during your service. A life lived as per your principles gives the satisfaction of having lived by your principles, even after you retire. I believe these to be the correct principles, akin to natural laws and the ultimate source of our conscience. In my opinion, what counts more, is what others say after you shed your uniform. It is not rare to find officers retiring at a lower rank getting more respect after retirement, than even the ones who reached the highest pinnacle in the Army.

The book seeks to invigorate amongst the generation next, the spirit and quality for the very best, in the pursuit of excellence. It seeks to delve deep into the conscience of the reader, provoking him into seeking a system that is based on the principles of natural justice and fair play. Sometimes, the risk to a career far outweighs the gains of exercising moral courage.

The book would provide an interesting read to his peer group and the uniformed community. I wish him all success in this endeavour.

Maj. Gen. YK Kapoor, AVSM (Retired)

New Delhi

Feb 2021

Prologue

Tryst with Dignity and Honour is honest to God account of the varied situations that came my way in the four decades of my very eventful life in uniform. It is not meant to be a memoir that many generals write, after a successful campaign or on their illustrious and dedicated service to the nation. Everyone does his duty in war and peace; some get recognition and some don't. I have not rendered service where I have displayed extraordinary valour and bravery. I only completed the tasks assigned to me by my superiors. I can never match the valour, competence and intellect of my seniors and my peers in higher ranks who were obviously better than me. It is a narration of events, some very pleasant and some not so pleasant. It is in no way a justification of the decisions I made when I was faced with unforeseen developments, unfamiliar environment and professional challenges during my service and later. I am responsible for whatever they were, whether right or wrong. All of us face hard choices in life. I faced more than my share. It was an anathema to some antagonists in my organisation that an unknown gunner underdog with no "pedigree", could aspire for the turf which is their exclusive preserve. From them, I "learnt to live life on my terms".

I must confess that life in the armed forces moves at such a frenetic pace that there is hardly any time to introspect when faced with these situations. At best, you can reflect on the immediate past events to modify or change track, if permitted and move on in life. You are faced with live situations every day and you do your best. Sometimes your best is not good enough, or it is not noticed or is misunderstood. However, I maintain that I have performed to the best of my abilities.

I have tried my best to explain in my 'Soliloquy' that destiny plays a big role in one's life and nobody can change that. Time, place and personalities do matter. In the armed forces it matters, who you serve under, at which place and at what time in your career. Decisions of seniors, both sound and sometimes impulsive, determine destiny. If you are fortunate to have godfathers in your service, you stand to benefit immensely. If you are not that fortunate, you will again benefit from the self-confidence and experience you gain, by going it unaided. There are always human aberrations in the form of impulsive decisions, extraneous influences and organisational lapses at work, which can upset even the person equipped with the "best destiny". I can claim to have this best destiny because what was taken away by the above three, has been given back by God in some other form.

What matters more is not the ranks you achieve in your service; it is also the respect and reverence you enjoyed in service and what you did during the actual combat. As a front-line soldier, I can say with pride that I overcame fear and did not run away from combat or feign sickness. Earning gallantry or distinguished service awards on fake reports and recommendations of relatives/contacts was like blasphemy for me. It also matters how well you have shaped the lives of your progeny, while in service. I have every reason to feel proud of my children's achievements. These are my personal opinions and like every one of us has an unfettered right to his own, I have to mine.

I have learnt some useful lessons in life which I would like to submit to the generation next for all it is worth. Some may find my views tainted or biased but these are straight from my hip (heart) and may need to be adapted suitably from time to time.

- In a highly competitive environment as in the armed forces, there is no place for second best. You have to be the best. Be passionate about your job. Have a clear-cut aim and a firm resolve to adopt honest & fair means to achieve it through sustained hard work, without expecting any returns. Everyone plans for success, you must also plan for failures, as I did.

- Not only must you be the best in your profession, but the environment and your spoken reputation must also speak for the same. No point being the best, unknown to the people who matter. If required, you may have to tailor your reputation with better public relations and display results that stand out prominently and be seen or heard properly by your superiors. Nobody will do that for you, except yourself.

- With the benefit of hindsight, I can say putting things in the right perspective and prioritizing what is most important in the allotted time frame would carry the day for you. Time management is the whole essence of success.

- You need to listen and follow both your head and heart while dealing with your men, and your head alone while serving your boss, the nation and any professional dilemma. First acquire the wisdom to make the best choice initially, try not to make the same mistake twice and learn from the mistakes of others. The opportunity to correct your past mistakes comes with a price tag.

- A famous quote comes to my mind "Lord grant me the serenity to accept things I cannot change, courage to do things I can, and wisdom to know the difference". This is what helped me to keep working at the same pace, as a highly motivated Brigadier for eleven years from Feb 1990 to Dec 2000".

I have no pretensions to belong to a breed of military writers. They are a class apart and rightfully enjoy patronages, which I don't. I did try to pen down some critical observations from time to time. There are some excerpts from articles submitted to various journals which are based either on my personal experience and study during my service and may need to be updated in the present scenario, on our borders. Some of these written for posterity; are informative, interesting and authentic, and merit attention even now.

Brigadier Dinesh Mathur (Retired)
Gurgaon

NDA & Pre-Commission Training

Off to the NDA

After my Senior Cambridge results, my father, an academician, wanted me to continue in academics and try for civil services or enter the teaching profession like him. He always considered the teaching profession as the noblest profession and was visibly hurt when I haughtily told him about the meagre salaries, which his highly qualified professors were drawing. I will always remember what he said:

"We think our fathers fools, so wise we grow;
Our wiser sons, no doubts, will think us so?"

He then reminded me that the President of India, Dr Radhakrishnan was also a teacher. He too started on a low salary and look where he is now. I expressed my desire to follow my second cousin, Sushil into the Army. Father was initially very reluctant to even allow me to fill up the forms to appear for the NDA exam in May 1959 but later relented. It is quite possible that he realized that, with two sons in Engineering Colleges, and one to follow and two daughters now doing MA/MSc, my applying for the defence services was quite justified. While at DAV College Dehradun, Father had trained a lot of AEC officers from the Army for BT/B Ed in his college, so he knew enough about the Army.

We were all underage for St Stephen's College which was considered another route by my father, for higher studies. However, the lure of the uniform was very pronounced those days. We had elitist schools like Doon School, Lawrence School Sanawar, Mayo Ajmer, Sherwood Nainital, Bishops Cotton Shimla and many others vying for a place in NDA Khadakwasla. We were keen for selection in the armed forces not because of the patriotic fervour but the fact that most girls fell for the smartly dressed and polished gentleman cadets from IMA, located at Dehradun. Defence services were adored for their good living conditions and exclusivity; anyone who was selected for training at NDA/IMA must be dreaming for the cream of the society. We were also the No 1 service in the preferred choice of vocations, higher than doctors, engineers and the civil services those days. It is only later that the successive governments degraded the exalted status of the defence services, very systematically.

In our joint family of first, second and even third cousins all lived on the New Road and each time anyone came on leave, it was 'kind of' obligatory on my parents to call them over for a simple meal. I had the privilege of interacting with two brothers, our second cousins in Dehradun whose names were always quoted by the family as those who had done well by getting through in the NDA in their very first attempt. Whenever they came on leave, we did meet but it was only after my Senior Cambridge that I seriously started thinking of the armed forces as a career. Dehradun had both JSW and whenever we went to town, the cadets from JSW and the gentleman cadets from IMA, clearly stood out and were the toast of the young generation. They conducted themselves with dignity and poise and were most sought after by young girls. These two brothers Sushil from the Artillery and Sudhir from 3 Gorkha Rifles were well known in the family. When Sushil stayed with us once he explained to me how an air observation post of artillery functioned. The glamour of being an Army pilot made him my role model at that time. He had just qualified as an Air OP pilot from AF Flying College and joined a select band of army flyers. His striking persona was something I always admired and I followed him around whenever he came home.

When I asked him how I could get into the exclusive band of army flyers, he just gave me a grin and said "You've got a long way to go, young man. First get into NDA and complete your training and then opt for Artillery in the IMA. After that you have to work hard to merit a selection for Air OP". To this day, I still remember his advice. Coming from such an outstanding sportsman/athlete of his time I did not possess even 10% of his qualities and hence I knew, I would have to make up for this deficiency by persistent hard work. He won an MVC in 1965 and had retired later as a Major General. I will always hold him in high esteem and his photograph is etched in my memory.

I also had my cousins, who due to the generation gap, were parents of those of our age groups, like Col. Vijay Narain of Artillery, son of my uncle, Rai Saheb Raj Bahadur and Brig. Satish of the Armoured Corps, whose father Shri Gopi Narain, my second cousin, who was even senior to my father in age. I respected Col. Vijay Narain a lot, his wise counsel and sagacious advice prompted me to opt for the Regiment of Artillery. Satish was very annoyed at my 'timidity' in showing total lack of interest in the Armoured Corps in general and Deccan Horse, in particular. I had nothing against him but the *showsha* of the Risala was something I thought, I would never be able to emulate, like him.

I appeared for the NDA written exam sometime in June 1959 and qualified in the very first attempt. In August, I was interviewed by the Services Selection Board, Meerut, headed by one Capt. Claudius of the Indian Navy. Physical endurance tests and medical followed, which were cleared without any difficulty. I remember my name figured quite high in the overall merit list. Others with me in the SSB were Bobby Mehta, Robin Deans, Mahalwar and Jyotinder Singh. The reminiscences of school days and my small foray into DAV Inter College as a part-time student now closed the chapter of student life, once for all. The indelible mark of character qualities and self-confidence imbibed in school left no doubts in my mind that in this highly competitive world of today, there is no substitute for honest and sustained hard work. My thoughts, actions and lifestyle were channelized from a very young age of 15 years by my teachers, mentors and my parents. I knew I had to fend for myself in this vast world around, untraversed and unknown. My father, a giant amongst intellectuals, had this to say as his parting words of advice, "If you want to succeed in life, be the best in your profession and do the best in everything you do. Don't worry about the results, that's not your problem".

My mother, a simple lady who was deeply religious, spent most of her time reading Hindu scriptures including the Ramayan and the Bhagavad Gita, and observing all the rituals in the family for our benefit A respectful daughter in law, she also taught us to respect our elders including my two older brothers. She gave me a lifelong possession of a gutka version of Gita, which I carry and read to this date. She taught me *Om Namo Bhagwate Vasudev*, Gayatri Mantra and Hanuman Chalisa, which I learnt to recite regularly. Her views on philosophy of karma were *Karam achche hone chahie, Ek hath de aur dusre hath lay*. (You must do good karma. You will reap as you sow in this life). Words still resonate in my mind. To me, whatever you do in life you will get your retribution for your actions in this life only. How very true!

Most of December 1959 was spent in the preparations for NDA Khadakvasla as per Joining Instructions received by father, who ensured every point was complied with to the last full stop. A black steel box with my name painted, purchased from Paltan Bazar, matching the specifications was half empty after the civilian clothes sets, undergarments, kerchiefs, some shirts and trousers and one lounge suit stitched to specifications were placed inside. A bank draft, for Rs 1200 in a carefully stitched pocket inside the centre of my vest so that it could not be misplaced, was inserted at the last moment by my mother. This draft for Rs 1050 included Rs 900 for the outfit/ kit to be issued at the Academy and Rs 150 for pocket money for one term of five months. There was a canvas holdall for the light bedding which consisted of a thin mattress, one pillow and a bedsheet with a light *razai*, carried on the insistence of Mother. This was only meant for the journey to Pune and back. The suitcase culture wasn't there, in any case, what was permitted was a steel box and a holdall for everyone, irrespective of where you came from.

There was a military warrant issued in my name which I presented to the RTO (now MCO) at the railway station. A special first-class vestibule bogie with reserved seats for NDA cadets was arranged on 04 January 1960, attached with the Bombay Express. I thought that was great as I had never had the good fortune of having travelled anything more than the second or inter-class of that time. Our batchmates started arriving in ones and twos with parents in tow. I showed no hesitation in touching my father's feet before entraining to obtain his blessings. Pravin Badhwar, I already knew, came in with Prakash Suri, Naresh Chand and Jaskiran Malik of Jimmy Kitchen fame. SL Chadha arrived later, Madhav Arren joined us from

Saharanpur, Sushil Sharma from Ghaziabad and Richard Clarke from Meerut. There was a whole lot of our batch from Delhi. By the time we reached Dadar, it was quite a crowd of freshers collected enroute from Agra Cantt, Jhansi and Baroda. All of us excited youngsters introduced ourselves on the train, ordered our meals, mostly chicken curry and rice from the railways, costing ten bucks. We arrived at Dadar at 5.30 am on 6 Jan 1960 to a waiting NDA Reception Centre and were helped in hiring coolies to take us to the platform, where Bombay Poona Express was waiting to depart at 7.45 am. It was touch and go but the extra ten bucks tip paid to coolie ensured that you were on the train. On arrival at Poona station, we were received again by NDA Reception Centre established on the platform. Our luggage was taken by the coolies to the waiting trucks, in which we were to travel, perched on our luggage The last leg of our journey to Khadakvasla via Pashan Gate had commenced. There was pin-drop silence all around. It was like sheep being led to slaughter!

3593 DINESH MATHUR / ARMY

As a 15-year-old cadet in Jan 1960

Our great XXIII course of 218 youngsters, all looking very fit and smart, aged between 15 and 17 years, enthusiastic, some flamboyant and some shy and reserved, had reported for training. We arrived in front of Cadets Mess and were promptly marshalled by our JCO/NCO instructors into our squadron lots, based on the names being called out on the PA system. Everything was proceeding smoothly like clockwork. Our room bearers were there to take charge of your baggage which was then placed in the squadron wise trucks. Our Charlie Squadron has been located in Mysore Block since it arrived from Clement Town. An announcement made on the PA was that we were expected to enter the mess properly dressed, through the side doors, to have lunch first. And my, what a lunch arranged by the Catering Officer, Maj. Verma. Chicken curry, *malai kofta* and mixed vegetables with fresh salad, rice, *dahi burras* and *naans* added. As 15-year-olds, it was a feast and we gobbled up whatever came on the table. And the grand finale was tipsy pudding with no embargo on the number of helpings. NDA certainly knew the way to the hearts of the youngsters!

We were chaperoned by our *ustads* in proper threes, commenced our march to our new home for three years, Charlie Squadron in Mysore Block, uniquely poised, facing the drill square and the Presidency Drive. Amazingly, we found our room bearers waiting for us with our baggage. Well taped up drills, I suppose. Room numbers were already allocated by the office. Our seniors present were only reading out the allotments. We learnt later; these guys had come for a retest. They allowed us to rest before they commenced their so-called "ragging". Everything was so cordial and friendly; their only demands were for some songs or jokes/anecdotes or some mimicry which was more in the form of entertainment. None of us can complain that there was bullying. We had stalwarts like RS Bedi who were instant finds for musical evenings and SVS Gahlot for instant humour (sometimes inadvertent!) in the anterooms. We met promising guys like RC Nanda, who wanted to be a Bollywood star but later settled for the Artillery, Llyod Moses Sassoon, a Bombay Jew, on retest for failing Hindi, a lovable senior, a fighter pilot, shot down in 1971 during the Karachi bombing raid and KKR Kumar from the south, again for flunking Hindi and a few others who became our good friends later. We became good friends with Mohan Rupchand Daryani (later Dar) again from our division, who was also a very quiet and mature senior. We were a mixed lot from good public English medium schools from all parts of the country. RIMC known then PWMC guys stood out along with the KG and Sainik Schools lot, who also hailed from well-known families. There were a few who were a few wards of serving JCOs/OR who adjusted well with us, as scholarship cadets. Pocket money was capped at Rs 30 per month and nobody could violate the rules, not even the Maharaja of Patiala, whose son, Amarindar, was our batchmate. I presume they aimed to inculcate the spirit of oneness and remove the disparity in entrants to NDA, so that it did not affect the performance of cadets and encouraged those who then were thought privileged, to receive scholarships.

We were taken around the Academy on a conducted tour, not in buses but on foot, jogging all the way, under Corporal KKR Kumar, a moustachioed, an easy-going young man and a good soul, who was loved by everyone. Our squadron mates who were arriving now were the bulk who had been promoted to the next term based on their results at the end of the term. Kit issued by QM store was a major event which followed next as also the measurement parade at Phelps & Co at Gole Market. I remember the numbers called by Phelps with "3593 please" when we went to collect our stitched dresses and uniforms. Within a few days of arrival, we were issued bicycles by the MT, the preferred means of conveyance. Within a week Kumar had set us 'on course' for our course. Oh yes, the black steel box with the holdall inside and all the civvies were consigned to the box room, to be collected at the end of term.

With the opening of the Academy after winter vacation, the first official function to take place was the welcome address by the Commandant, Rear Admiral BA (Chippy) Samson in the Assembly Hall. His charismatic personality, command of the language and powerful oratorical skills, punctuated with a great sense of humour, was exceptional. What followed next was a series of opening tests in Science, Math & English to assess our basic skills and assignment to classes. I was nominated for the ABC group of classes with Science B and Arts C. I had listened to the wrong advice from a senior from my school not to do well in the opening test, otherwise, you would be placed in a class where the instructors' expectation level would be as high as the ceilings of your class. You would sail through in a class of average credentials. How wrong was this presumption, was proved much later?

We had a very hectic schedule in the first term. I used to get up at 5.45 am when reveille was sounded by a bugler followed by the siren from the Science Block which could be heard for miles. We walked up to the central tea room, collected our morning cup of tea and biscuits, went through morning rituals including shave before getting ready in our cabins 15x15 feet, which were identical & without fans, space just enough for one bed with a mosquito net frame, a coir mattress and a big locker with a large mirror, half hanging space on one side and the four shelves on the other. All items of clothing including mufti fitted in neatly on the shelves and hanging space. The towel rack and a shoe rack, fitted one below the other on the wall, were covered by a single full-length beige coloured curtain. On the bedside was a small locker for placing the tea mug. A window with venetian blinds was alongside the bed and to its side was the study table with a chair and a table lamp. Another easy chair was to the right of the study table. Apart from the table lamp, there was another hanging light in the centre of the cabin.

Prominently displayed on the wall to the left was the poem "If" by Rudyard Kipling, nicely framed. We knew it by heart, staring at it on the study table in front. The last four lines still resonate, "If you can fill the unforgiving minute with sixty seconds worth of distance run, yours is the earth and everything that's in it, and what is more, you'll be man, my son". We were bound by an Honour Code, a kind of self-discipline, which we observed very meticulously. Loyalty to the nation, the Academy and your fellow cadets came in itself. Truthfulness, honesty, trustworthiness and being forthright under all circumstances was impressed upon. To all of us, it was taboo to lie, cheat or steal. There was a small booklet issued which we kept with us. No pledges or prayers or sermons were ever delivered by our instructors. They were our role models.

We generally got ready by about 6.20 am in our cabins for the outdoors programmed for the day. It was invariably riding or drill, followed by PT or a permutation/combination where the commuting on bikes was the least. Having checked ourselves in the full-length mirror in the corridor outside, inspected by the flight corporals, we all responded to calls of a first termer, "Squadron Fall in" meaning thereby to reach the squadron parade ground for muster fall in immediately (6:30 am). After another inspection by senior cadet appointments, we marched or cycled to our places of training. We returned at about 8.10 after going outdoors, rushing to the showers. The toilets were at either end of each floor of the squadron building and all of us showered without a stitch on, with our bath towels hanging on the pegs nearby. It was against the academy culture to shower with underwear on. Anyone doing that was considered a "sissy". I now understand that cubicles with proper shower curtains have now been provided. After getting ready for breakfast, we marched off to the Cadets Mess and got back by 9:05 am just in time for our fall in for academic classes either in Sudan or Science Blocks. Of the two, the majestic Sudan Block was the hub of the Academy and its imposing red sandstone architecture, amidst the grandeur of the imposing Presidency Drive in front, is something to be admired always.

Two functions are still etched in my memory bank. The first was our introduction morning with the whole squadron in attendance in our anteroom, one Sunday morning. A kind of fancy dress with all kinds of regional attires and costumes came on display with individual performances on mimicry, songs or cracking of jokes. An interesting function where Mone's impromptu song "Once in China" evoked peals of laughter and of course, RS Bedi's credentials as our Pat Boone was fully established. The other function was at the battalion level, the Inter Squadron Novices Boxing which had a humorous start, a Black and White boxing match between two PT *ustads*, the demonstration of how not to box. My opponent was our dear ole Partho Sen from Dog

Squadron, who gave me a tough time. We could then make out who had boxed before in school and tap him for the squadron team.

I must make a mention of the Drill Square which faces our Mysore Block, where we incubated. We assembled at the rear of the Drill square in front of the QM Store, which had adequate space. Nobody could enter the Drill Square for a stroll, just like that. We were led inside this sacred institution in proper squads by our drill instructors, for foot and rifle drills, which are the essential part of our training. They are the foremost pillars on which a military personality is developed. Subedar Major Bora of the Assam Regiment, a diminutive but imposing figure, was the worthy replacement of the last of the Brits, Sergeant Major Collins. His short stature belied the booming voice, in his words of command. Our squadron drill instructors were Subedar Naunihal Singh of Grenadiers and the recently promoted Naib Subedar Bhaktavatsalam from Madras Regiment, both very dedicated, highly energetic and devoted to their jobs of grooming the young boys into military officers. Each instructor carried a measuring stick which was to correct positions, distances and angles between feet at attention, at ease and marching. We went through drill practices marching up and down the tarmac, banging our feet, shouting "Rajaram Sitaram" sometimes "one two three one", in perfect step, swinging our arms up and down to shoulder level.

At first, it was quite an ordeal, but we got used to it in time. In front of the Drill Square was the main entrance which opened into a ship's quarterdeck with rope ladders leading to the mast. On the sides were the seating and in front was the podium for the VIP or the Inspecting officer to stand and take the salute. The passing out parade was held here, and we used to dream of the day when we, too, would pass out through the quarter deck. We were drilled day in and day out in readiness to appear for our drill square test in the presence of Subedar Major Bora. His team of smart and impeccably turned out JCO Instructors struck terror in our hearts, on the drill square. Bora was the only JCO who was to be, justifiably addressed as "Sir". He made us slog for the drill square test, without which we could not proceed on liberty or the mid-term break. The smarter ones like Bedi, BM, Clarke and Nagra passed first followed by others in quick succession. Liberty meant a trip by bus to Poona on a Sunday or a holiday, see a movie in West End or Empire Theatre and return by late evening by the last bus. Most of us frequented the movie halls and preferred a bite there. Others would like a hot dog at Kwality's or Three Coins or a hot cross bun at the Kayani or some minced cutlet at Poona Coffee House or the delicious brain curry at the Irani *dhaba* next to it.

We had a very highly qualified academics staff, comprising our veteran Principal Mr TN Vyas ex Mayo College, Reader in Science Mr RB Mathur and Reader in Social Studies Dr VK Verma, accomplished English Instructors like Mr ND Rao, an Oxford don with blue in boxing, brilliant academicians like Mr BK Paradkar, AN Passi, KS Bhatnagar, PNK Rayan, DS Maini, MK Malhotra, SS Shandilya, NS Khare and many more carefully handpicked from the best public schools in India. There was another instructor, a six-footer, who was referred to as the "civilian adjutant" by all of us, I think it was Mr Sawantnekar. Dear old Mr Jouravlov, a Russian émigré taught us the Russian language for a long time. Monsieurs Pal and Kandhari taught us French, God help you if you addressed these two as Mister instead of Monsieur. They were all entitled to a salute having the salary, accommodation and status ranging from Captain (Instructor) to Colonel (Principal). While at Dehradun, JSW during its formative years, at Clement Town, offered the post of Reader in Science to father, who declined and suggested his subordinate Mr RB Mathur's instead. Almost everyone in the science faculty knew father from Dehradun days as Head of BT Department in DAV College. There were also his students, the Education Corps officers who were freshly commissioned from IMA like Lt. Chitranjan Sawant, the well-known TV commentator of yesteryears, a post-graduate in Physics. Nobody from our course will forget our first term prescribed English book 'The Card' by Arnold Bennet. This novel chronicle the rise from rags to riches of a country bumpkin Denry Machin in Staffordshire in the UK. His luck, initiative and audacity from his early years, won him the reputation of "The Card". Every cadet had this story in mind and hoped for such miracles to happen in his life. The writing of DLTGH (days left to go home) in white chalk, along with the date in every classroom showed how homesick some of us were, especially at the beginning of each term. It is amazing how cadets from varied cultural, ethnic and religious backgrounds, hailing from all parts of the country, gravitated to a common institution and enjoyed each other's company. This explains why the NDA is considered the greatest example of national integration and cohesiveness.

On the services side, Rear Admiral Samson had a terrific tri-service set up with Col. George Bharat Singh as his Deputy and Col. Hoshiar Singh as the Colonel IC Administration. The latter became the Deputy Commandant with the rank of a Brigadier in our fifth term, before leaving for NEFA in Nov 1962 for the war. We had the Adjutant Maj. FS Sondhi from the Brigade of the Guards, a GSO 2 Training Sq. Ldr. LM Katre, Catering Officer Maj. Verma/Randhir Singh, Equitation

Officer Capt. Kanuga, Methods Officer Capt. AB Singh, PT Officer Capt.Nair and a full-fledged accounts officer from IDAS. There were three experienced training teams from each service, to advise the Commandant on the conduct of training. The cadets and their administration were organized into three battalions during our time. No 1 Battalion (ABGK Sqns) commanded by Cdr. Kripal Singh IN, No. 2 (CDH Sqns) commanded by Lt. Col. Piara Singh, VrC, MC and No 3 (EFI sqns) Battalion commanded by Wing Cdr. PC Khanna/later Kirloskar. Our Squadron Commander Charlie Squadron was Lt. Cdr. S Chatterji and three Division Officers Flt. SG Phansalkar, Capt. RK Sood and Capt. KK Bhatia. In the second term Lt. Cdr. RV Arte joined and remained till we passed out. Capt. AC D'Silva, Bhim Singh, EN Vishwanath and Flt. Lt. SK Anand joined later, towards the end of our last term. Most of us cadets would remember the excellent riders, Maj. Thakur Govind Singh of Easy Squadron, and Capt. Virendra Singh of Golf Squadron well, both were from Risala and had charming wives. That's how you remembered your great instructors!

I must mention the old-timers of JSW Dehradun, who were still working for us in NDA, like the cadet orderlies, dhobis and barbers. Muni Lal was my orderly, shared between us four, and he had very juicy tales about his days in JSW. He had served under Gen. Habibullah, Sqn Ldrs Chandan Singh, IH Latif and my cousin, Capt. Satish from Deccan Horse when they were posted as Squaddies/Division Os and how they dealt with troublesome cadets and how they brought back the cadet who ran away to River Tons to commit suicide. The whole Wing was in a flap after the suicide note was found. He was found later sleeping in the abandoned barrack nearby. A similar incident took place when one of our cadets sent the whole Academy to Peacock Bay but was found sleeping on the second-floor balcony. Our dhobi Muqadam from Majra, Dehradun, the 'suspect bootlegger' or the 'conduit' for the supply of hooch to cadets, invariably boarded the Dehradun bogie with us, to visit his family, every end of term. Atma Ram was the head barber now, whose claim to fame was his being the favourite of the balding Gen. Habibullah, who he gave regular head massages. His crib was that the present Commandant, with a good crop of hair, had no time for head massage. He was very choosy and rank conscious; he gave haircuts to senior cadets only and not to first termers. Mohan Lal, the other barber from Dehradun, was very humble and looked after everyone.

In Charlie Squadron (later Echo Squadron), we started with a batch of 22 cadets in Jan 1960. My coursemates all got nicknames, BK Kohli, RS Bedi, IK Gupta, HL Banerji, SK Sharma, VK Kapoor, PMS Bayas, Harish Anthony Khare, Romesh Chugh, BM Kapur, VK Sodhi, RS Nagra, Preet Deep Singh, RM Pherwani, BB Ghai, Bhibhu Mohanti, Santosh Mone, Jyotinder Singh, Vikram Gahlot, Richard Clarke, Ravish Malhotra and of course me. Two others who joined later were MR. Dar and HS Sangha, while IK Gupta and VK Kapoor dropped a term. Bayas and Jyotinder Singh, looking for greener pastures outside the services, decided to call it a day, in our third term, Sushil Sharma went to J Squadron in our fourth term and Ghai to M Squadron in our sixth term. We were a happy go lucky lot, majority from good English schools, each with varied backgrounds and different value systems, not very unusual for the youth of our age group. The Academy laid the foundation for the strong bonds of friendship and camaraderie. I realized that some of our batchmates were from PWMC who had already worn the uniform earlier, for five years, were street smart with a high instinct of self-preservation. The greatest fraternity in the armed forces today is the Rimcollians which ensures the opening of the flood gates of advancement right from the NDA onwards. Next, were the university/college postgraduates, like Banerji, a first-year MSc student, who had fast-tracked their way to NDA in his final attempt at the age of 17 years.

Echo Squadron – first term 1960

The last few were the ones like me, who had just finished schooling and had to put in great effort in academics. Everything taught was new for us. The educational standards at NDA were way below their graduation degrees, the 'already educated' guys amongst us, used to clarify our doubts, in their spare time. When you have daily outdoors followed by academics, you tend to doze off in class and miss the essentials in instructions. This had a very telling effect on the majority of us and the few graduates (Banerji M.Sc. & Ghai B.Sc.) along with Pre-University types, (Kohli, SK Sharma and Ravish Malhotra) fared better in academics.

During our first term, for the first few months, most of the ragging was in the form of collective punishments like front rolling from the Assembly Hall to the Cadets Mess. Sometimes, instead of riding your bikes, your bikes rode on you, carried on shoulders for short distances, as punishment. All these were toughening up exercises which we accepted as a part of life. In Squadron too, there never was any unreasonable ragging or attempt to humiliate any fresher. Some seniors would spend time on weekends to organize singing songs and chatting sessions which were very essential for personality development. Amongst the seniors, agreed there were some bolshy types, but most were friendly. We participated in inter squadron games like hockey, cricket and football, basketball, swimming, athletics and boxing. There was the more talented lot, the singers/musicians who skipped the punishments meted out to all and sundry. Puttee parades were held sometimes to ensure that you were correctly dressed, even if the time to change was at a premium. We had a Pune lot from Wadia College and St Vincent's School who were the best of pals and could gang up against anyone without any reason, just for some "healthy fun".

As the course senior of my squadron batch, I had duties that were laid down by the Academy and explained to me by my seniors. It was my call it bad luck to be given this responsibility of ensuring all of us were on time, checking who was present or absent and reporting the absences if any. I do not remember being unreasonable or unkind to anyone to elicit a negative response. Certain problems with the Pune lot started in the first term itself, immediately after the term commenced. The events which followed were the turning points in my life at the NDA. In all sincerity, I tried to take my responsibilities seriously and perform to the best of my abilities. It is quite possible that my looks, demeanour and manners were misunderstood by the trio, Kohli, Mone and VK Kapoor. They did not appreciate my passage of instructions on behalf of seniors and tried to heckle me whenever an opportunity presented itself. Whenever any slip up took place and was found out by our appointments, I was branded the "informer", as they said. I admit I lacked tact and might have told the truth inadvertently. I looked up to other steady coursemates like Bedi, Ranjit Nagra and Clarke for their support but they would not commit one way or the other. The retaliation came during the study period in the form of deliberate disturbances, which one could ignore. Then came the biggest weapon in their armoury on Sunday evening, just before the cabin's inspection on Monday morning. A carefully planted time bomb went off under the bed which left tell-tale marks on the floor and a lot of muck to clean. One thought was to leave everything as it was, for the inspecting officer to see. I chose not to report and went scrubbing the floor and removed all traces of the bomb because it would have antagonized the trio more, a report being tantamount to squealing. The regular frequency with which these bombs were carefully planted in my cabin, on the plea of healthy pranks, had a very unsettling effect on me.

I spoke to Ranjit, Bedi and Richard again. They advised me not to report to the Div. Officer, as it would escalate matters and create more problems. Our seniors, one who knew me from Dehradun, Kailash Dhingra and Sukhwinder Bhangu, the CSM advised me to accept everything with a smile. I was so demoralized that it continued to affect my overall performance in academics and outdoors. I cleared all the first term tests without any difficulty but I could have fared better, had I the mental resilience to take the regular ragging from the ring leaders of my course. Towards the end of the first term, I met Mr RB Mathur at his residence and spoke to him expressing my desire to quit. He was stunned and took it very seriously and said, "You cannot drop out. I need to speak to your father first thing tomorrow". I was summoned to the Readers Office the next day during the tea break. He quoted my father's message to be strong and take things in their stride. He also quoted him verbatim, "If you are planning to quit, don't come back home". I never spoke to anyone about this, though it was contrary to my expectations from my father. I then changed track, became more tolerant, accepted the ridicule and the regular silly pranks very reluctantly for the next three terms. I got so thick-skinned that whenever there were no pranks played by the duo, I used to remind Mone & Kohli why it is that they have forgotten me, so soon. With my newfound tact and patience, they too eventually gave in and I had a peaceful time thereafter.

I still fail to understand what were the reasons for their hostility towards me. I had met both for the first time. Mone, the son of Collector Pune, had studied in Wadia College in pre-degree before NDA. Kohli who had his schooling in Pune may have been under peer pressure, nursing some imaginary threats from me, God alone knows for what. Kohli and I have worked together later and we are very good friends now. I thank both of them for taking me to the limits of my tolerance, to tell me that it must improve. I met Mone last in Bidar in 1969 when I was ferrying a Krishak aircraft to Sulur from Nasik, where I was posted. Mone was teaching Air Force cadets how to fly and was ferrying an HT2 to Sulur. His flamboyance and aggressive ways hadn't changed much, his warmth and cordiality were very effusive. We headed together to Coimbatore, in our respective aircraft and got stuck there due to bad weather. Mone insisted on taking me out for dinner in town and forced me out of my room. On a borrowed motorcycle we had good drinks and dinner in one of the places he knew. After dinner, he said, "Let's have some fun". He drove, with me on the pillion, to some secluded corner of Coimbatore, famously known as the red-light area. All I heard were the police whistles, beckoning us to stop for a check. Mone shot past the barrier and headed straight to Redfields Officer's Mess with the IAF police in hot pursuit. Mone dodged them within the city somewhere and gained time to reach my room in the mess. Very cleverly, he pushed the bike out towards the rear verandah, told me to change immediately and pretend to sleep. IAF police can be expected and sure enough, there were sounds of a bike being switched off, followed by heavy footsteps and a knock on the door. I opened the door rubbing my eyes a bit to make it appear that I had been woken up from the slumber. After a lot of explaining that I knew nothing of the bike registered number MYX 2787, they left. The next day again a rainy one, I was summoned by the Security Officer, who said that he was not prepared to believe that, firstly, I was not riding this motorcycle seen in the city, and secondly, how come, it was found parked in the rear verandah of my room the next day with a flat tyre. The owner swore that the bike, indeed, was off-road for the last three days. I was given the benefit of the doubt, being from a different service but the beauty was that Mone's name never figured at all. He wanted to entertain his old squadron mate he had met after seven years and kept apologizing for the mess we got in but handled it well to get me out.

Mone was the life of the course and was very popular. Once I returned from liberty at Pune quite late and then realized that I needed a haircut and was sure to get checked and be punished by the drill instructor, Bhakto. Mone was my division and I mentioned my predicament. He lost no time in suggesting that he would trim the hair from the neck and sides and nobody would even know about it. I could later go to the barbershop and get my normal haircut. I fell for his suggestion and he pulled out his Philishave. He asked me to sit on a study chair, donning the beret as I would do for drill. He started and by the time he finished what was outside the beret was completely removed and clean. When I took off my beret, I panicked. The bald patches looked so horrible that I just didn't know what to do next. Mone told me there was nothing wrong and I was being thankless. Somehow, I managed to dupe the drill instructor Bhakto and got away without being punished but when I attended Mr Shandilya's class in Social Studies, taking my beret off, I was a sight. Our civilian instructor was no fool but he advised me to get clean-shaven immediately, maybe even skipping lunch, which I did. Mohan Lal also refused me the haircut, for fear of being checked for the shoddy & patchy job on the neck and sides but a tip of ten bucks helped. Never again, will I get into this situation. The live, vibrant and warm-hearted person he was, Mone lived life on his terms and did everything with finesse. Sadly, Mone passed away sometime back, and couldn't make it for our Pune rendezvous, last year.

In our second term, the squadrons were re-designated. In No. 1 Battalion, Able, Baker, George and King became Alpha, Bravo, Charlie and Delta. In our No 2 Battalion Charlie, Dog and Howe became Echo, Fox and Golf. No 3 Battalion which had Easy, Fox and

Item became Hotel India and Kilo Squadrons. In essence, only A, B and I retained their original designations. Easy landed up in No 2 Battalion as Hotel in our third term when Juliet was raised in its place. We used to run regularly on our cross-country route from the squadron to Gole Market, then to Pashan Gate, turning left towards staff quarters, then following the ridgeline to Officers D3 area to end up in the PT gym. Normal PT runs were sometimes on the Presidency Drive up to the Kondhwa Gate and back to the PT gym. Enroute were the nearby cultivated sugar cane fields, too attractive to be missed out for regular "gunna raids". Our PT ustads were Sgt Moorthy and Petty Officer Verma, who kept us very fit, trained us on mat work, beam, rope and horse. We passed all our PT & Swimming tests, in front of the PTO, somewhat akin to the drill square. Our riding classes twice a week for two periods were not fun, if the instructor found you coming in late, your disregard for riding instructions or bad posture. Excuses like cycle got punctured enroute to Riding School, did not work with riding instructors. Our equestrian training at NDA is one of the finest in the world. Our squadron ustad, an outstanding Services rider Naik Balbir Singh (later a Regiment of Artillery polo player) took the lives out of us. Tauntingly he would say, "So, you want to pass your spur test". He would get after you, to see that you at least fit into the category called reasonable riders. We hated his guts when he ordered, crossed stirrups and bumping trots, which hurt you badly in the crotches. The bareback riding we did ceased to be fun if he ordered continuous trot and no canter. We began to love riding with Balbir, our instructor for three terms. The NDA facility contains Polo Grounds, dressage grounds, jumping course and miscellaneous arenas and various stables that sheltered more than 180 finest bred horses of the Indian Army. Nobody can forget dear old Nagin, a vicious kicker. We got used to the temperamental Badal, who had the reputation of bucking on the slightest pretext, throwing you off and walking you back, 5kms to the stables. Of course, Gulabi, the white irrepressible but steady mare, was the NDA Adjutant's prize mount for the passing out parades and no cadet could ride her. Based on my NDA training, I developed a love for horses and re-commenced riding at Wellington as a Colonel, sometimes accompanied by my son Rohit for hack rides on his favourite Mahshuk, in the Nilgiris downs.

During the mid-term breaks, we went on hikes to Mahabaleshwar, Lonavala, Bombay and Kirkee and enjoyed the hospitality of various service establishments, all courtesy NDA, the cradle of the armed forces. Each establishment made it a prestige issue to look after you. Some hikes went to Goa and Bangalore. A visit to Sinhagad Fort in the first term with your packed lunch was very much on the cards, volunteered or otherwise. I had the pleasure of a mid-term stay at CME with my cousin Suresh Endley (later Lt. Gen) during his degree course. I caught up with sleep, generally enjoyed myself and made full use of the facilities, which the mess offered.

The cafeteria was our favourite haunt whenever we got the time away from our action-packed schedule. It was always well patronized by the cadet fraternity, especially on weekends. Our favourite fare was the *samosa*, *bonda*, and a *paneer pakoda* with Duke's mangola or a milkshake. Sometimes, when you were grubby you ordered an omelette or french toast, samosas and barfi. It was on a self-help basis and you served what you wanted yourself and went to the tables laid out for us. From my pocket money of thirty bucks, you paid your orderly four and a half bucks for boot polish and blanco, the remaining 25 plus was for the toiletries, trips to the Gole Market for and odd dosa idli sambhar, fifty paise each for regular movies in the Assembly Hall on Saturdays. There used to be Sunday morning cartoons, which was a hit for a few of us who didn't want the morning snooze. A trip to Pune on liberty for a movie followed by some eats could be accommodated as well. Things were so cheap those days and we managed very well within the amount. You couldn't get extra money from home, even if you tried because it was banned. As far as I am concerned, my father being a strict disciplinarian you could only expect a rocket, as he would never disobey Academy orders. When I bought a squash racquet, it was on three tranches of 10 buck notes sent by my older brother in his monthly moral lectures, administered by post. To quote my father, reply to my request for additional money to be borrowed from Mr RB Mathur, "I have already forbidden him to loan you any money. So, learn to cut your coat according to the cloth".

We saw movies on a 70 mm screen every Saturday at 6.30 pm in the Assembly Hall (now called Habibullah Hall), which used to cost us 50 paise on the ground floor and the second floor, with the first floor reserved for officers. Some movies I remember seeing were not so old, like North by Northwest, Casablanca, National Velvet, Mardi Gras, Ben Hur, The One That Got Away, To Chase a Crooked Shadow, Dr Zhivago, The Great Escape and Guess Who's Coming to Dinner, etc. It was after the movies that the senior appointments got going. They would hold you responsible for minor infringements like coming in late, murmuring or chatting during the movies or clapping unnecessarily. A lot of self-discipline was enforced and rightly so. A bit of exercise resulted in the whole Academy doing a two-mile run on the Presidency Drive before dinner. As youngsters, smartly attired in shirt and tie, for the movie, we accepted it with a smile. There were also musical evenings in the same hall in which leading artists from Bollywood were invited. I remember the immortal CH Atma singing Preetam Aan Milo, Kamla Seesta *singing Chunri Samal Ke* and *Jab Pyaar Kissi se Hota Hai*, Kamal Barot and Mahendra Kapoor in a booming voice. singing other hit songs. There were plays both in Hindi and English and some of our talented cadets took part with the officers and their wives. Our social calendar, as speLt. out, was hectic but we enjoyed every moment of it.

My fascination for golf started in the second term at NDA. It was routine that hobbies and extra-curricular activities were on Wednesdays every week, when we sacrificed our afternoon siesta, to learn new skills like riding and polo, shooting hiking, aeromodelling, martial arts, golf and literary clubs. I was forced into the Literary Club which met in Valmiki anteroom, the library, every Wednesday afternoon when book reviews were presented by each cadet. I had to give a book review on Old Man and the Sea written by Ernest Hemmingway which I had to read twice to come to levels with Mr ND Rao, an Oxonian who had speed-read the book only once. Anyway, the review was appreciated purely for the fact that the first termer wrote and spoke well. I also listened to very fascinating and masterpiece reviews by our seniors Dabir and Oberoi, both of whom had literary talents. Someone told me that the finest club was the Golf Club because Mr Juaralov, the Russian Instructor who was in charge never sent any absentee reports if you skipped. That was great I thought, I willingly threw my hat in the ring. We learnt a lot from the great Mr Juaralov who took so much pains to teach a newcomer. To this day I remember his coaching on the grip, short game and putting. I found the game so fascinating that I never skipped any of his coaching sessions. Imagine being coached by a single handicapper without any charges, a golf set and equipment is provided free of cost. Juarolav took us to watch various tournaments in RSI Pune where we all enjoyed at the cost of the NDA Golf Club. In my third term, I thought it would be great to join the aero modellers club because I wasn't allowed to continue with the golf club. I also wanted to enjoy all the thrills of making model aeroplanes and flying them in the glider drone. I found a very keen aeromodeller, a cadet RB Menon who was so devoted that he put all his previous experience in RIMC, to reach a reasonable standard in aeromodelling. My model did fly thanks to Menon's tips on the model. I learnt later that Menon, an Air Force cadet, did not get cleared for solo flying and was suspended. Gutsy that he was, he surreptitiously took out an HT2 without permission and ATC clearance. He took off and left the airfield area for a jaunt, despite messages from everyone to return. He even flew below the Sangam Bridge in Allahabad before landing safely at Bamrauli. He proved his instructor wrong that he did not have the capability to fly solo. Maybe his dignity and honour too had been touched by his unfair grounding. The next three terms, the clubs I opted for, were Riding & Polo, Shooting and Hiking. We enjoyed what the Academy organized for us. We were provided with the best possible facilities at state expense. Today, when I look back, I am overwhelmed with gratitude to this great institution, NDA, for this incredible job of tapping our dormant basic instincts into talent.

At the beginning of the first term, the Cadets Mess held a detailed briefing in which the mess etiquette expected from us cadets were explained. The use of various forks and knives, the correct method of holding them, serviettes and their correct usage are explained. The crested crockery, how to place it in front of you and which particular plate or fork would be used for what, all new to most of us. Drinking of toasts with decanters of water being passed from one end to the other was explained. Mess etiquette and table manners in the services do not change and these basics helped all of us tremendously in the Regiments we joined. A guest or dinner night those days were quite regular, where our officers dined with us. We wore closed collar white monkey jackets with a red silk cummerbund and black shoes and socks. Our officers were attired in their impressive regimental mess kits, well-polished silver and spurs. Side caps were worn which were removed and neatly placed outside the mess entrance. The seating plan was displayed outside for officers, but we sat in our division lots. Generally followed was a proper dinner night procedure. The waiters who served us were very well trained and had done this job for ages. The soup was first served along with soup sticks and buns, to be eaten and not drunk, followed by the small course of the mixed grill and mashed potatoes. The main course of chicken mayonnaise and fried fish with vegetables in white sauce came next. The finale was the NDA pudding which was either tipsy, caramel custard, trifle, apple pie or jelly custard. We were served coffee in small cups. After all this, depending on the dignitary, two decanters of water were passed from opposite ends and we filled our wine glasses with water. When the toast was announced we stood up with glasses in our hand, at attention when the national anthem was played and drank the toast to the President or the dignitary as applicable. In short, the NDA groomed you for everything. I remember very vividly, the dinner night in honour of the Chinese Premier, Chou En-Lai during his visit to NDA in late 1961, just a few days before the Sino Indian talks had failed at Delhi.

I must make a mention of our friends and well-wishers amongst the Squadron and coursemates, who played a very important role in my life then and now. First, with the squadron, Sukhwinder Bhangu, our 18th course CSM and an air OP flight mate, was a very spirited gunner who lost his life in a flying accident in Mizoram. Kailash Dhingra, the CQMS, again from the same course who later was a colleague of mine at DSSC Wellington. Our families were very close to each other, they were unfortunate victims of an assault by their domestic help after he retired from service. Arun Phatak, our boxing captain and seasoned gunner who took premature retirement in the eighties continues to be a good friend, trained me in light flyweight for the second and third terms. Manjit Singh and Amarjit Grewal were the rock-solid seniors from the 19th Course alongside whom we fought the 1965 war in Rann of Kutch and Lahore Sector. Then there were others like Darshan Khullar FRGS, a seasoned mountaineer and a gunner who authored an authentic version of the 1962 war in NEFA "When Generals Failed'. His first-hand experience is worth a read. While KKR Kumar, our favourite from the 20th course faded into oblivion in service, Ravinder Awasthi was with us at the DSSC and Ashok Mago, the great debater prematurely resigned from the Indian Navy. SS Kapoor, who later joined the Signals, resides in the same complex with us and has been our dear friend for the last 15 years. Hari Uniyal, the Services cricketer and a versatile sportsman who served with us later at DSSC Wellington, is settled nearby. LM Sassoon, 22nd Course I mentioned earlier is remembered to this day, as a very fine gentleman we served with at Agra. JPS Sandhu, also from the same course, with a wiry and athletic personality, encouraged me to run cross country with him. His toughness got me to 11th position in the Academy, in my third term. He had later served in the same Brigade in Mizoram as CO Bihar when I was BM.

Coming to the coursemates who made an impact on our lives during the service career. Suri Capoor of Alpha Squadron (the first to do the Staff Course in 1972) is a great friend who also served with me in Mizoram. Montu Choudhry (first Vice Chief) and I were first together at Arty Centre when I just joined the Air OP, later colleagues at DSSC. If I recall, there was a Ceylonese cadet Jebarajah, an ace swimmer, whose diving was both admirable and worth seeing. Can never forget the ever-smiling, spirited and gutsy persona in Kippy Kipgen, the ace Naga footballer, wounded in the 1965 war, who lived life full size and later passed. Our Gusty Sihota of Bravo Squadron (first to get Aviation wings and first to be Army Commander) NK Hegde, SN Guptan, Narayan Chatterjee were the first to qualify as parachutists along with Jaggu Mahalwar and me. The latter foursome served in the same regiment for the first six years, literally growing up together. Shekhar Sridharan, an early bird in the Indian Navy along with Om Kaushal before joining NDA, was our first submariner. We had good friends in Fox Squadron in the same Battalion, Mohan Burman, Ravinder Nath and Nikku Gill. Nikku Gill of the Xaviers' Jaipur fame, is still as lively and chirpy as ever an aristocrat to the core, he joined the Brigade of the Guards. Old habits die hard, Nikku will not forget his mimicry of Admiral Samson, which left us all in peals of laughter. Ravi, the tall Stephanian of the course, made his mark in academics and joined the Navy. Mohan Burman, a no-nonsense type and the squadron right marker like me, joined the Madras Regiment. From our battalion, Arun Bhargava, Minoo Panthaki and Om Kaushal joined me in the Gunners. Kinny Khanna, BM Kapur, Arun Nehra, Chaks, Kuku Randhawa and

Kamal Davar joined the prestigious Risalas. We also had a tall, handsome and unassuming Amrindar Singh from the Patiala royalty, a polo blue, who joined the Sikh Regiment. From our course at NDA, PP Kapahi, Kamal Davar and PMS Bayas excelled and played cricket for the Academy. Blues for hockey were awarded to Harcharan Kahlon, NP Singh and Kamal Davar, RPS Raghuvanshi, NS Koak, Kirti Gulati and RS Nagra for football and Kinny Khanna and SR Sethi for tennis. Our DSSC 1976 Staff Course also had a number of our batchmates Montu Choudhry, SN Guptan NK Hegde, Madhav Arren, CD Puri, Sudhir Chopra, KJ Singh, Amal Sanyal, Prem Kumar and Gurnam Gujral from the Army and Ravi Nath & Bibhu Mohanti from the Navy and VV Nair from the Air Force. Among our great sportsmen who blossomed and excelled in Sailing, VP Singh represented India in the 1972 Olympics in Munich. Our great fighter pilot, Ravish Malhotra, underwent training as a cosmonaut in the USSR in 1984, but narrowly missed the trip on Soyuz 11. RS Bedi, one of our leading lights from Scinde Horse was the first to be decorated in 1965 with a VrC, later opted for R&AW and was the DG till his superannuation. Today RS Bedi is the worthy President of the prestigious Delhi Golf Club and is doing yeoman's service in maintaining standards there. Richard Clarke, our own Mr NDA for many terms till we passed out, was an ace Naval aviator during his service, who was decorated with an NM during 1971 operations.

The Inter Squadron competitions added zest to life in the Academy, with a lot of josh & healthy competition in all games and sports, boxing, athletics and our camps. The desire to do well and be counted was paramount in each cadet. Squadron spirit inculcated kept you going and was a good indicator of our morale. In my first term, our

Squadron was the last, was the leftmost on the drill square and the last to march before the saluting dais. This position was based on our overall performance in inter squadron competitions and it did improve with the 19th course but fell back again to twelfth, the last squadron of our fifth term. In my sixth term, our Twenty-thirders brought the squadron as Champions for the first time, now leading the parade. With Richard Clarke as the SCC and self as the CSM and the whole senior course backing us up, there was no looking back. I don't even know why our Squaddie, Lt. Cdr. RV Arte reposed confidence and trust in me, there were better people around. Despite having put my heart and soul in weapon training, firing and fieldcraft, I did not make a mark with our *ustads*. Though I had done well at academic subjects, passed all mandatory tests I had not done so in Army subjects as our JCO/NCO instructors were very much impressed by more flamboyant and impassioned buddies (who also did a bit of apple polishing!). Both Clarke and I kept our boys in a high state of morale and kept encouraging them everywhere in our avowed goal to pass out as the rightmost squadron of the parade in Dec 62. In most games, activities and camps we were on top. In the drill competition, my personal drill mattered and I did not falter. We (Echo) won the Drill competition hands down. The last mandatory requirement to pass out was the 10m jump in the Swimming pool introduced by Admiral Samson and Brig. Hoshiar Singh. Not one of our gutsy guys from this great course faltered. So, there we were, leading the parade in smartly attired blue patrols and side caps passing through the quarter deck. There was a flypast overhead by the IAF fighters beautifully timed with the band playing Auld Lang Syne, just as we were on the last few steps of the quarter-deck, manned by the first termers on the ropeway. During our passing out, the salute was taken by our Commandant, Rear Admiral

BA Samson, who had been given this singular honour. Later, I had the privilege of spending some good time with the Admiral while he had settled in Ooty. He was the chief organizer of Spic Macay functions of his daughter, the celebrated Bharat Natyam artiste, Leela Samson, at the DSSC every year. In our course get-together, we invited him and he gracefully accepted being an Honorary Member of the 23rd course, which he loved so much. My children always looked forward to his visits to our home and the choicest of chocolates and cookies he gifted to them, whenever he came.

None of us from the 23rd course can forget our end of term concert in our final term. This prestigious function is a regular feature of every course and the favourite one of the Commandant's wife, who spent a lot of time arranging and even directing the play, where most cadets and officers and even some ladies participated. At the beginning of the function, the Adjutant, Maj. Bhim Singh, noticed a very sparse attendance, meaning that a large number of cadets had skipped. He left the assembly hall accompanied by a few officers and raided the squadrons. They found some cadets loitering around when we should have been present for the play. They included two of our coursemates from Alpha Squadron, who were charge-sheeted for absence from the parade. When the duo was marched up to the Commandant Admiral Samson, they admitted their mistake and were summarily relegated on disciplinary grounds. Subsequently, during the interaction with the passing out course, during the cricket match, Commandant's XI versus Passing Out Course XI, and the end of term feature. The Commander met one of them who had clean bowled him, in the match. During the casual conversation, he politely informed him that his parents have already left Allahabad to be at this passing out parade the day later. The same day the duo was recalled and marched up to the Commandant. The Admiral had this to say, "I don't want to punish your parents for your mistake". He allowed both of them to pass out with the course. That speaks volumes of the greatness of this man, Chippy Samson.

We were in a strange predicament. After undergoing training at NDA for three years, we were without even an Intermediate certificate to our name. A certificate was made available on my request later, which allowed me to take my BA Examination. It is obvious that we didn't need brilliant academicians. Our physical fitness was at its peak, our self-confidence and leadership qualities moulded us into strong personalities and provided us with a basic foundation for everything and anything one chose to take up. There was something more intrinsic which we had acquired in NDA. This was the right mix of academic subjects (like science, mathematics, social studies, proficiency in foreign languages, writing dissertations and humanities) with professional subjects punctuated with outdoor training. Nobody hankered for an academic degree those days. You could pursue a higher technical or an academic career, based on your interest by taking study leave. Though I did not avail myself of any study leave in my entire career of 37 years plus, I was able to complete my graduation privately in 1978 from North Eastern Hill University based on the foundation provided by NDA subjects. I was encouraged to submit another dissertation on China later in my Higher Command course in War College. My dissertation for M.Sc. Defence Studies from Madras University in 1986 on *Insurgency in the North East with Special Reference to Mizoram* is based 'on the job' experience. My articles on China have been published in various journals and have been well received. Today, I owe this entirely to my NDA training, which provided me with a solid foundation and enabled me to achieve academically, what my father had ordained for me but did not live to see.

Now, the cynosure of all eyes – The one and only Twenty Third

My course knows that I am not the guy to give in to peer pressure and protocol for accepting to write for the course. What I can say with my conviction, is, the sense of belonging came in automatically, without any pretences or prodding from anyone. The undying legacy of brotherhood, camaraderie and unity nurtured in those three years at NDA Khadakvasla is not easy to forget. We meet regularly, revive old memories, exchange banter (sometimes ending up in a quarrel) and jokes, regale incidents and events that took place during our time. This is what keeps us young. I have some reminiscences of what makes this course so unique when compared to others.

- The only course to have the opening and closing address by the same Commandant, Rear Admiral BA Samson, also honoured with the honorary membership of our course, which he gratefully accepted. We were the proverbial guinea pigs for the Deputy Commandant, Brig. Hoshiar Singh who experimented with his newfound ideas on training at NDA, to churn out tough, resolute and confident young men with steel nerves and strong moral fibre. Not one refusal on a 10m jump for confidence & guts, is proof enough.

- The only course in the Indian Army's history, necessitated by the Sino Indian conflict of 1962, which had 15 officers commissioned at 19 years plus, six officers commissioned at 18 years plus, all performed admirably in the conflicts that followed. It is also noteworthy that barring Infantry and Armoured Corps cadets who remained in IMA for commissioning, all others proceeded to their respective training establishments for pre-commission training. We all passed out from our respective training establishments on the same date, i.e., 30 June 1963. Despite our truncated training for no-fault. of ours, we also hold the record of the maximum number of officers to achieve higher ranks, in all three services. (12 three stars, 13 two stars and 35 one stars) Do not forget one Secretary, one Addl. Secretary and several Military Attaches abroad.

- Of the many large-hearted personalities of our course, once electronics engineer from the EME, Col. Rattan Gaba CEO Veteran Defence Forces Group, a rock-solid coursemate, provided financial backing from 1986 onwards till date. Thanks to his dedication and commitment to our course activities, he has been able to provide liberal financial solutions to our course with excellent investment opportunities, yoga *shivirs* and financial assistance during all our get-togethers.

- The unambiguous clarion call of the course made famous by the universal KG School brotherhood resonates in every get together of the course. "*Ola, Mola, Chadha, Sundd, Maha Singh, Kahlon, Chillar Ale*" and (I have quietly added our only invaluable gem, Natarajan (KG Bangalore) and the star performer Gahlot (KG Nowgong). There are a few more in hiding (maybe MM Kapoor and Sati Cheema). They all have undoubtedly done a commendable job in the three services.

Our contribution to the nation in the realms of politics, first. We have the leading light of the course in the warm-hearted Capt. Amarinder Singh, from Delta Squadron, a former MP and twice elected Chief Minister of Punjab. His dynamic leadership, unsurpassed devotion and fine political acumen has brought Punjab back to its glorious past and is doing yeoman service to the country. Amarinder is the pride of our course and was also an outstanding polo player, with spurs/polo blue from the NDA.

We were fortunate to become battle-hardened in the first eight years of service. We have participated in 65 and 71 wars, where some of us were recognized for conspicuous bravery on the battlefield, Our Gautam Mubayi (India Squadron) of 9 Dogra was awarded the Maha Vir Chakra posthumously in Sialkot Sector in 1965. In 1971, Capt. Gusty (with s and t not interchangeable) Sihota, Billy Bedi, SS Jamwal and the gutsy AS Mamik won their Vir Chakras for gallantry. Arun Nehra, Cheema and Koak won Sena Medals for gallantry. Our very dear VV Tambay (Charlie Squadron) was another brave fighter pilot who was declared missing in action in 1971 and is one of the 54 prisoners last reported to be in Pakistan jails. So much for many of our decorated coursemates, is just not enough. In brief, our contribution during the wars has been nothing short of exceptional. I also wish to pay tributes to my coursemates who have departed in the line of duty or after fulfilling their normal tenure in this world. It's a privilege to have been together at this great institution as your coursemate. Two of our decorated coursemates and one not so decorated stand out for their recognized conspicuous bravery which I felt, deserve approbation.

SS Cheema, 3 Grenadiers

Sati, the gallant company commander in the battle of Jarpal, attacked across the Basantar River in Sialkot Sector on 8 Dec 1971, was awarded the Sena Medal. His saga of heroism and valour was a part of the attack in which 2 PVCs (one posthumously), a couple of MVCs and other awards were won. Ironically, in an area of 700 square yards, the enemy too had awarded two of their highest awards which goes to indicate how fierce the battle was.

Satwinder is from Bravo Squadron.

Narain Singh Koak, 2 Sikh

Narain displayed conspicuous gallantry while leading his company in the attack on an enemy strongpoint at Pul Kanjri in Western Sector on 5 December 1971. Showing great presence of mind, he brought down effective artillery fire and repulsed the strong enemy counterattack which followed immediately thereafter. Though wounded, he kept motivating his men and refused to be evacuated till the reinforcements arrived. He was awarded the Sena Medal.

Narain is an Academy football blue from Delta Squadron.

Kamal Davar, 7 Cavalry

Kamal, as a young subaltern, on 17 September 1965 led his troop in the attack against Chattanwala post in the Khemkaran Sector. Displaying raw courage and guts he moved forward rapidly and neutralized the post with accurate tank and machine gunfire. Heavy retaliation by enemy artillery and mortar fire did not deter him from capturing the post till he was wounded and had to be evacuated. Though he did not receive the gallantry award for which he was recommended, he has the great satisfaction of participating in his Regiment's moments of glory in the sector. Later, in December 1971, he served with distinction again with his regiment in Shakargarh Sector. Kamal was our first Chief of Defence Intelligence Agency as a Lt. Gen.

Kamal Is an Academy hockey blue from Delta Squadron.

Our brothers in arms in squadron teams, on our passing out parade on 8 December 1962 at NDA Khadakvasla, as they passed the quarterdeck, is given below.

No 1. Battalion

Alpha Squadron	Bravo Squadron	Charlie Squadron	Delta Squadron
SS Bains	SK Banerji	SS Singh	Amarinder Singh
AK Nehra	JS Grewal	Ashutosh Mathur	NS Koak
Naresh Chand	Ramesh Shanmugham	JS Mahalwar	AIS Dhillon
Nirmal Shah	SC Mehta	MS Parmar	JS Bath
Shantonu Choudhry	Devinder Singh	SC Goel	SC Chopra
RS Gaba	KK Lamba	VP Mohan	MM Goel
SS Ahluwalia	SK Mediratta	TP Chopra	Joginder Singh
PK Aggrawal	Shekogin Kipgen	Praveen Badhwar	UD Thorat
SN Capoor	GS Sihota	Suresh Gupta	HS Puri
Alvinder Chand	SS Cheema	MI Siddiqui	Prakash Suri
PS Theyunni	Pradeep Mehrotra	SR Chakraborty	Kamal Davar

TM Asthana JS Sisodia SM Sareen	JP Chhetry NP Aul Vinish Mathur	VV Tambay DPS Mangat Gurdial Singh	S Kanjilal MS Bains SPS Mann RK Khanna Jitendra Singh

No 2. Battalion

Echo Squadron	Foxtrot Squadron	Golf Squadron	Hotel Squadron
HS Sangha	KN Wazir	HS Kahlon	Shakti Malhotra
MR Dar	SK Gulati	KJ Singh	MM Kapoor
Dinesh Mathur	RK Arora	BS Bedi	SS Jamwal
BK Kohli	NP Singh	JS Sethi	VKS Karnik
RS Bedi	MS Gill	Lalit Roy	Madhav Arren
HL Banerji	MN Panthaki	Naresh Sharma	Maha Singh
Romesh Chugh	MM Burman	VP Singh	NK Mukherji
BM Kapur	RK Saldhi	Prem Kumar	GS Palta
VK Sodhi	BK Singh	AK Bhargava	KC Gupte
RS Nagra	MS Venkatraman	NK Hegde	KS Singh
RM Pherwani	PP Kapahi	MV Karnik	KC Debrass
SS Mone	SC Chopra	SK Sangar	Karun Khanna
SVS Gahlot	RO Ban	SP Singh	VV Nair
FR Clarke	GS Bal	Azeez ur Rehman	GS Mann
Ravish Malhotra	UR Dabir	JB Ale	SC Mohla
	Ravinder Nath		KS Rana

No 3. Battalion

India Squadron	Juliet Squadron	Kilo Squadron	Lima Squadron	Kilo Squadron
HS Hundal	SK Sharma	Samarji Mitra	Surjit Singh	SC Rikhye
KS Rajan	HA Khare	Ravi Chaudhri	LC Idnani	VM Pradhan
GS Chahal	AR Kumar	Vijay Verma	VK Kapoor	SN Guptan
NK Sehgal	RK Mehta	KS Chillar	PD Singh	JS Sawhney

GS Chhatwal	GR Sajjanhar	SR Sethi	Partha Sen	Narayan Chatterji
RN Wadhawan	DN Pandit	RPS Raghuvanshi	VM Kapoor	VA Joshi
KK Gulati	SK Bhatia	KC Chawla	AS Mamik	BB Ghai
AN Mishra	Prosenjit Barua	RD Salwan	SL Chadha	BK Mohanti
Gautam Mubayi	A Natrajan	Pramod Pareekh	PK Singh	SK Shikarpuri
CD Puri	US Ahluwalia	CN Kaul	UBS Kohli	RK Sundd
YK Sharma	OD Kaushal	GS Randhawa	DK Sen	RK Bansal
MC Sachdev	SK Sapra	Shekhar Sridharan	SS Jawandha	JS Malik
AR Deans		VK Chaudhry		PK Chakraborty
BJ Collins		JS Brar		GS Gujral
SV Purohit				HR Byrne
				AK Sanyal
				AK Awasthi
				NA Thivy

Behind every great Twenty Thirder is a wonderful lady

For me, success in spouse selection lies in the ability to spot someone you think is right for you to spend a lifetime with. All my coursemates are Wills Made for Each Other couples, even today. Right now, write-ups about my buddies and their spouses have been recorded accurately in this magnum opus, without exaggeration or underplay. Mental fatigue has not set in so far, which would call my honest views, befuddled, confused or disoriented. If you take offence to any of my quips or even the lack of them, my full apologies are all that's on offer.

First things first, two of our stalwarts DN Pandit and Amarinder were first to tie the knot on 9th August and 31 October 1964 respectively. Pondy married Asha at Bombay and Amrinder to Praneet at Patiala. Another couple, Mohan & Sushma Burman share their anniversary with us, on 20 October 1969. The great Burmans and us were together at Wellington for almost two years and had a wonderful time with them and their lovely daughters. Sushma, an astoundingly gorgeous and sophisticated lady with an athletic build, has represented the country in bowling. Montu and Preeta are known to us since my Air OP days when they were posted at the Artillery Centre. Very quiet and affectionate, Preeta had endeared herself to all of us in Centre and later in Wellington as well. Arun Bhargava and I once called at their residence to ask for directions to Montu's office. She said, "Dabbu, just follow the perfume and you will reach". Montu was commanding the training battery of mules & horses then. We were sorry to lose her recently after her prolonged illness. Raghu, also one of the early birds, married Vijay at Lucknow. They were always our unsuspecting hosts for impromptu dinners many times over, during our Air OP tenure at Nasik Road. He was also the first person to pick me up after my Krishak forced landing, due to engine power loss, near Gangapur Dam in Feb 1970.

Beginning now with Sis and his demure Sandhya, they have been the ideal sober couple and a copybook of correctness. Suri Capoor, though he has never attended a single get-together, was quite close to us when he married Sudha from my clan and anointed himself as the undisputed "Jamai Raja" of Mathurs. Medhi and Kiran were always on Arun Bhargava's (and mine) radar for dinner raids in 48 OG Lines Deolali, while we were on the Air OP course in 1969. Our greatest sapper, the evergreen and multi-faceted stalwart, Prakash and Kamlesh Suri once played hosts to us in CME Kirkee, when we were on a Scientific Orientation course in 1975. His sterling contribution in the course affairs continues. We were fortunate to have joined up with another dearest sapper, Chand Dev Puri and the vivacious Veena, on two courses, Staff College and SC at Mhow. Sudhir now sporting his goatee beard with the ever-smiling Nandini, the newlyweds on the Staff Course at Wellington. The great Sir John Kapahi and another Veena, the paragon of dedication & devotion, have been a source of great inspiration for all of us. We have some friends in common and keep meeting now and then. The die-hard Infantrymen, Romesh Chugh, of the Sawai Man, our evergreen marshal and his charming wife Rekha, are always present for our get-togethers. The great wrist-spinner Bayas and his sophisticated Sulbha, whom we had met at NDA, after a long time in 1999, are now very active, in all course get-togethers. I had the good fortune of meeting Billy Bedi and his lovely wife Dilraj when they were posted at the IMA in 1968 before they left for Nigeria. Our dear Hira Banerji and the nightingale of our course, Krishna were once our neighbours in Pratap Chowk in 1988-89 when I was serving in Ladakh. Very sad, Hira departed like a flash of lightning, so suddenly without any illness. Mohan and Mohina Dar, a lovely couple have been in and out of our get-togethers. Satish Gulati, our brave Grinder, and his pretty wife Reeta make a very affectionate couple, who have always been close to all of us In our great entrepreneur Pramod and the happy go lucky Nisha Aggarwal, we have found a delightful couple. We also found a like-minded couple in Ravi and Sadhna Chaudhri at Jhansi in 1980, when we were both commanding. We were together both at Chandigarh and Calcutta, get together and had a great time exchanging anecdotes.

It was great to learn that one of my schoolmates of the fifties, an army kid, Uma had married one of our finest coursemates, the handsome ADC to the President, Alvinder Chand. Uma and Al make a very charming and spirited couple. We had met them for the first time together in 2016 when they were holidaying here in Delhi. Incidentally, Uma's older sister Asha, also married another smart ADC, Bharat Talwar of 26 NDA who did the Staff Course with us. We had Jojo Nair and his very spirited Nalini along with our one and only Stephanian, the very mature sea dog, Ravi Nath and the vivacious wife Madhu on the same course. Shivjyot, another army kid from Sanawar, married to the evergreen Gusty Sihota, is an excellent hostess, the paragon of sophistication and elegance in all our get-togethers. Damyanti Subedar Tambay, an outstanding national badminton player married Vijay Vasant Tambay, who failed to return after his last sortie over Karachi raid in 1971. We are full of admiration for this very brave and spirited lady for her perseverance, courage and devotion. She has gone through great tribulation & privations which she endured bravely. Two very sophisticated ladies, Ferzana married Inam Siddiqui and the other, the very charming and the versatile Gunmala married Brij Kapur, our dashing cavalier. Dr Gunmala's immense contribution to the environment and social life in Bhopal is worthy of mention. Gullu Chatwal, our finest aviator and the Nasik squadron commander and his very sporting wife Mala, played hosts to us. when coursemates from the Military Special from Wellington, turned up at all odd hours. Our RK and the very reserved Dolly Mehta were the new members of our group at Wellington during 1985-88 and we spent a good time together. Our military attaché Madhav and his elegant wife, Anita were the life of all our parties in Tac Wing Deolali when we were posted together. Deepak Sen and his wife were their worthy successors. Sadly, he is no more with us. We had the pleasure of receiving the young bride Chanchal with Joginder, a fellow aviator during my LGSC course in 1973, We also attended the same Staff Course later at DSSC Wellington in 1976. The naughty smile on the great persona of Nat continues. He and his lovely wife Usha tied the matrimonial knot sometime in early 1969 and are going strong towards their Diamond Jubilee, looking younger by the day. The baby of our course, Ranjit Nagra married a very accomplished and charming lady in Dr Rabi. We had the unique pleasure of dining with them at their residence, the last time she was here. We are saddened to learn about her demise after a protracted illness in the USA. Our very colourful personality, Nikku and his very spirited and multi-talented wife Indu, the official chronicler of the course, always smiling (karmic philosophy notwithstanding) despite all the mishaps at their lovely home in Sainik Farms. They are the life of all our course get-togethers.

Finally, our 17 Para lot. Our very vivacious and shy, the all-time great Shyli married Neeru Hegde when we were at Deolali/Nasik together. We carry fond memories of them coming over to our place in Centre after movies at Topchi, and later at Talbahat, where we spent good times together as COs in the same brigade. Our ever so charming Janaki and Sushil, the great *mallu manush* from Shivaji Park, were with us and Hegdes at Wellington and later at Deolali. Unfortunately, we met our very dear Chandrima, much later after my retirement. Chandrima has married our Rimcollian master gunner and greatest walking talking encyclopedia of all times, the brilliant Narayan Chatterjee from the same Regiment. Chandrima too is an exceptional personality in her own right, with her sterling contributions to the hospitality industry and lending glitter to all our get-togethers.

The undying spirit called Twenty Third Course is very much alive and kicking. My course buddies do make promises, some make it a point to keep in regular touch with each other not only at get-togethers but even otherwise too. All of us, without exception, have learnt to live life to the full. Keep it that way and may God bless us all. I am now tempted to write something, which may invite brickbats:

"Not every Twenty-thirder has a sense of humour, you know,
And crossing a thin line can turn many a friend into a foe.
So, I try to be careful what I say, in this magnum opus,
But I really have ensured that all isn't hocus pocus".
Amen.

Training at the IMA

Having said au revoir to NDA in December 62, we were on the term break which extended to the first week of January 1963. All kinds of rumours, regarding our commissioning in the wake of the recent war with China. When we learnt that both the third and the fourth termers in IMA had passed out, there were even more conflicting reports about our future. Even though the Chinese had declared a unilateral ceasefire, there was a national emergency in force. There were good chances for the operations to recommence any time to regain lost ground and most importantly, the prestige. Battle reports about the bravery and valour of our junior officers, including the ones we knew kept pouring in. Our course was itching to be a part of the operations but we were still to cross the hurdle called IMA. We waited patiently for IMA to re-open after the vacation. Our 23rd coursemates Shantonu Choudhry, Gautam Mubayi, NK Hegde, Lalit Roy, Naresh Sharma, MS Gill, CN Kaul were the few who were together as Gentleman Cadets, in Kohima Company. We also made good friends with MK Singh, who later joined 3 Para with us at Agra, and was my colleague later at Deolali as well. There was another break. Some of us, the local guys, reported directly at the IMA Premnagar and found ourselves in Kohima Company. There was another wing of the IMA at Clement Town where some of our coursemates went. We were accommodated in Premnagar in the popularly known Dhobi Ghats. No two ex NDA were allowed in one room, so we ended up sharing a room with some unknown direct entry cadet. IMA was clearly in turmoil because all of a sudden, some 1000 cadets had reported for training and more were expected. All 138 of us from the 23rd Course had reported, looking very sharp and confident, as if combat with the Chinese, was about to commence now. Our coursemates of 32 Direct Entry and 17 NCC, by their being in IMA before us, were given all the cadet appointments, for all practical purposes were made to look senior to us. It was officially announced that IMA would function in the emergency, as an officers training school and all courses would pass out in the truncated duration of six months. Nobody knew what lay in store for us. Two OTSs had also opened at Poona and Madras, for the training of more officers, during the emergency.

Personally, I had nurtured great hopes and aspirations in IMA. Its reputation as a premier institution and also the finest institution in the Commonwealth was never in doubt. Its outstanding and battle-tested instructors were known to give us a flying start. My visions of coming home on liberty, meeting old friends and sometimes paying a visit to my school in IMA mufti, were all there for me. The passing out parade, slow marching through the portals through its portals and the pipping ceremony in the Chetwode Hall, all lay shattered as we were put through the emergency course. There were strict instructions on going out even on Sundays. Our uniforms, weapons and an OG bicycle to commute were issued. The .303 rifle was deposited in the armoury (*kote*). Gradually, the NDA lot got our bearings right and accepted the fait-accompli of truncated training and the prospects of being posted straight to the battlefront. Initially, a fair amount of time was spent with the newcomers, re-learning the same weapon training and fieldcraft that we had already learnt at the NDA. Except for the few driving lessons in the good old 1 ton, there was nothing new to learn. PT laid more emphasis on log exercises, less on apparatus work and we found unarmed combat something new. It was only after some time; we were introduced to platoon weapons. We learnt how the firing mechanism worked, learnt handling and firing of rifle pistols and sten on the ranges. Sten firing was the most interesting part with several targets (3) placed at regular intervals depicting the Chinese, to be shot at speed. After our stint on the bayonet fighting course was brief. We also practised grenade throwing at another small range, near Premnagar. Besides this, the regular feature was the rifle drill in front of the Chetwode Hall. We had regular night training, in which we were taught stalking, patrolling, laying of ambushes and counter-ambush drills. Games periods were converted into some lecture demos, which we all hated. Three months went by in a jiffy.

It was quite some time before I was permitted to go home. Since every term now was of three months, we were nearing the completion of the first term. Then came the bombshell. We were allotted our arms and services based on the proforma, which I must have submitted some time back, along with many other forms we used to submit. I was allotted Infantry and asked to continue in IMA for another term of three months. When I represented to the company commander, Maj. AW I stated that Shahane, I had always aspired and hence opted for Artillery as my first choice. He said, "As a very physically fit youngster from NDA, it's a shame you are avoiding infantry. You want an easy life". I then told him that it was my lifelong desire to wear an air OP flying badge, he dismissed my request as unreasonable and asked me to reconcile to a good infantry regiment life, for which he was prepared to help. Both my company mate CD Puri were allotted infantry. CD called his battalion commander at NDA from his residence, which was attended to by the wife. When CD explained everything, she promised to convey the same to her husband, which she did. Two days later CD got his change of arm to Engineers. The new term was about to start and I had still not got my change of arm. I represented to my Company Commander again for the change of arm and this time he relented to recommend my name for a change.

My orders for a change of arm arrived, after a week or so. After taking all the clearances, I returned all my issued kit and the rifle, collected my movement order and the railway warrant and made a rather ignominious exit from the IMA. I had always looked at this institution as a youngster. Whenever I visit Dehradun, I still make it a point to visit this temple of learning, like a pilgrimage to Char Dham. The imposing heritage buildings, well-manicured and trimmed lawns, the spick n span drill square and well-maintained PT/polo grounds, are etched in my memory.

Now, the most iconic Chetwode Hall, the centrepiece with the adjuncts above, has historic significance and an aura of sanctity. Its resplendent looks and with the addition of the massive auditorium and stadium, it is the mainstay of our military leadership. My deepest regret in life is the truncated training at the IMA due to panic created by the Chinese aggression of 1962 and the "one-off decision" of the higher-ups to shunt us out, for commissioning from Deolali. It is my sincere prayer that this must never happen again in the annals of the great Indian Army. What I missed at IMA will always remain my greatest loss in life which no one should miss out on. Finally, the immortal words of Field Marshal Chetwode still shining as our immortal credo, in the main hall reads:

The safety, honour and welfare of your country, come first always and every time,

The honour welfare and comfort of the men you command come next,

Your own ease comfort and safety come last, always and every time.

Training at The School of Artillery, the Alma Mater

I arrived in Deolali two weeks later, the so-called Cadets Course had been combined with the young officer's basic course, before commissioning. Nobody knew how, when and where we would be commissioned. There was another speculation that we might go back to the IMA, for the passing out parade. Located at the shadow of Sahyadri ranges, this small picturesque town of Deolali, with its sylvan surroundings is the gunners' *mecca*. Along with the Artillery Centre, located 8 km away at Nasik Road, it formed a massive military complex with the Air OP flight located at the fringe of the Centre. The legendary Brig. FSB Mehta, was the Commandant, a centurion today, the last of our founding fathers of the Air OP. He had been credited with having cleverly flown his Auster Mk V from Lahore to Amritsar, just before 15 August 1947 to ensure that it didn't go to Pakistan after partition. The School functioned normally with Field, CB & AD Wings after the Coast Wing was disbanded. The School Adjutant was Capt. DP Bahl, a silver gunner of the 6th JSW Course, an outstanding and a very smart AD gunner, whose contribution to AD Corps is noteworthy. He was commissioned in 2 Field Regiment (SP) where he stayed for six years before his conversion to AD.

The School of Artillery was designed to train about 75 young officers freshly commissioned from the IMA, at best, and now 400 odd cadets were running around in this small town. Most people did not comprehend the status of cadets. Slowly and gradually, it started dawning on them that this lot was a different kettle of fish. We were not allowed in the Temple Hill Institute and the Officers Mess. Cathay and Adelphi cinema halls had reserved seats for officers, which were to be left by cadets. Bharat Cold Drinks and other eateries had a field day, as the evenings were spent in town, whiling away our time. Two messes functioned for cadets in Hamden and Wellman Lines. We looked all around and found all full Colonels with red bands on their peak caps but sporting three stars. How was that? We then realized later that Instructor Gunnery of any rank is entitled to wear the red band.

The School of Artillery had hurriedly raised a Cadets Wing under Lt. Col. BB Bhatnagar with three batteries, P, Q and R batteries commanded by Maj PR Saranjame, VK Nair and BJ Gardner. I reported my late arrival in D Troop to my Instructor Gunnery, Capt. YK Kapoor, of 6 JSW and was told to change into dungarees and join the gun drill with others. So, in place of foot and rifle drill, it was a gun drill, wearing leather knee pads. For a few days we were lost and just didn't know what was happening. Here I met my coursemates from the NDA,

Neeru Hegde, Nat, Jogi, Gullu Chatwal, Vinay Mohan, Om Kaushal Sukhi Jawandha, Ranjit Nagra, Gurbaksh Sihota, Naresh Chand, Sapra, Kirti Gulati, Chat, Essen Guptan, Raghuvanshi, Arun Bhargava and Minoo Panthaki, to name a few. Others had also joined from the IMA and the two OTSs. I latched on to Neeru who kept guiding me in all aspects of gunnery taught so far. The JCO/NCO instructors like Subedar Shinde and his team were also very helpful and gave me extra coaching during afternoons, of course under instructions from the IG. The first test was a fire discipline quiz in which thanks to Hegde, I scored the second highest. I slogged my heart out to catch up with the course and was very happy after the IG in the class openly castigated others and told them how a chap arriving two weeks late was doing far better than most of the class.

Being the last to arrive for the course, I was allotted a room in the T-10 barrack of Hamden Lines along the main road to the Wings. Our remaining pocket money was transferred to the School and there was no way we could get anything extra. We had our batch mates from OTS, who had served in the corporate world who had opted for an emergency commission to serve the nation, out of patriotism. Their approach was way different from ours, the seasoned 'mercenaries' from the NDA. Though not all of them were imbued with toughness & professionalism, one realized they would wilt under pressure, when the call came. Some of them were always flush with cash and readily treated us in town. We always looked forward to the day when we would enjoy comparable status. Few reliable shops like M/s Selections, located inside the camp, were there to provide us with all clothing and uniform including the khaki service dress, then in vogue.

Our training was rigorous, but interesting all the same. We were trained on a basic gun, the 25 pounder and getting the gun into action by a detachment of us six youngsters, especially getting it on the platform was a daily ritual. Then followed a series of technical orders from the command post, which were acted upon by the gun crew, which changed duties and positions on orders from the Ack IG, the *ustad* for us. This was to give everyone a chance to be the gun crew and other technical duties in the command post. We were under the watchful eyes of the IG throughout. Next, we were taken out for reconnaissance of gun positions in the Deolali ranges, put through umpteen number of miniature range practices, to train as the observation post officers. We had live firings immediately after the gun drill practices, which hardened us more as gun position and OP officers. We interchanged duties and learnt to observe artillery fire for the first time with the IG giving us tips on how to correct the fire using our binocs.

We had regular course shootings on the ranges, which finished quite late. One day, towards the end of the course, after coming back late in the evening, I discovered to my horror, my room with the doors wide open, my clothes in the box and the cupboard ransacked. The orderly was summoned, who expressed his total ignorance of what had happened. There was a theft of my belongings and all my best clothes including suits and blazers were missing. My report of theft to police meant lock up for the orderlies in the block and all my coursemates pleaded with me not to do so. Therefore, I made no report at all. The worst part was that the police got my details from the burglar. He had been nabbed and had led them to my room when the police tried to re-enact the crime. I was summoned by the court several times to identify my clothes, to finalize the conviction of the accused. The court only wasted my precious time as none of my clothing was returned and I could not understand anything, as all proceedings were in Marathi. To this day I regret how the cadets course went for me; I arrived two weeks late, tried very hard to catch up with the rest of the course and again had to attend court at Nasik for one full week, for a theft I didn't even report. The good part was that I slogged even more, proved my worth and very nearly upset my classmates. We all noticed the empathy and concern of our IG, who we all looked up for guidance. From the very beginning, I had no doubts who my role model was, a big brother who put you on course to work hard and prove your worth. His maroon beret inspired us no end and I gave my first choice as Para, along with almost all my ex-NDA coursemates.

We got our postings to 17 Para Field Regiment by sheer good luck, because of the existing vacancies leaving all our friends bewildered. We still have our IG's words resonating in our mind, "You may think that having got your choice of Regiment, you may think the world is in your pocket. You've got to work hard and prove yourself to be retained there. If you are lucky to be retained, aspire to be four barreled (with Para, Air OP, LSGC and Staff College) like Maj. Ben Gonsalves, our Chief Instructor. I'll wait and watch to see who gets there". Traditionally, there is an unshakable bond between all IGs and their students, which exists for a lifetime.

We had a course break up party in the Wellman Lines attended by the complete faculty. We had thought we would be pipped then by our IGs, but nothing of the sort happened. There was no Chetwode Hall environment here at the School of Artillery during the emergency we were in that time. On a hot and humid Friday morning on 29 June

1963, a day before the official date of commission, we had our course Silver Gun ceremony opposite the old Sarvatra Hall & Library. We were told to come in uniform, wearing a single star of a Second Lieutenant, a Sam Browne belt with peak cap issued by M/s Selections. This put paid to my dreams of being pipped by my parents in the Chetwode Hall at IMA Dehradun. In our course, Gurbaksh Sihota and Ranjit Nagra, deservedly, were the top contenders for the Silver Gun. Gurbaksh was awarded after a close contest.

Life in the Regiment of Artillery

The Fledgling Years Including Operations

We were no strangers to the truth that our Army had suffered a humiliating defeat in 1962 in NEFA. I had been commissioned into 17 Parachute Field Regiment, which had participated in the war in the two sub-sectors in NEFA, viz Tsangdhar and Walong with one battery plus personnel. We suffered three officers and five jawan casualties with two officers and some 50 jawans taken prisoner. The posting to a para unit is always on probation of one month, which is extendable. The CO para unit is empowered to select officers from para duties and reject those not found fit. Nobody can challenge the CO's decision. We were granted 14 days annual leave and had to report on probation commencing 15 July 1963 at Agra Cantt. Having informed the regiment about our travel plans, in a hurriedly written DO to the commanding officer, we were received by our senior subaltern, Lt. MS Mehandru, on the Punjab Mail. My luggage was taken by some jawan helpers in the jeep's trailer and I sat behind in the rear seat of the jeep.

As a 2/Lt. with 17 Para Field Regiment

It is also a well-known fact that the initial grooming you receive in the very first unit shapes your career for a lifetime. All of us coming from varied backgrounds, from different parts of the country with different religions, cultures and languages joined the cohesive team, functioning like clockwork, despite the setback in NEFA. On arrival at 29 Prithviraj Road Officers Mess, two of us were led to the end of the barrack where our luggage was unloaded. A small wash up was required but we continued in the uniforms that we wore throughout the journey from Delhi to Agra Cantt. We waited for other officers to arrive and then moved in for lunch. The other three who arrived afterwards were also accommodated in the room adjoining mine. All of us were expected to share rooms, which we did. In any case, being on probation one couldn't be sure of being retained. Living in officers' messes was very spartan those days. MES provided the most antique furniture of all, rickety *niwar* beds sometimes infested with bed bugs, steel mosquito net frames, a small side table, one easy chair and a study table with another chair. We settled in two adjoining rooms, two to a room, and noticed that the Indian style WC in toilets were in a row behind, again to be shared by the four of us. Yes, we did have two ceiling fans in the room which moved at five miles per hour and made so much noise, we were better off without them. Summers can be really hot at Agra and we were in the thick of it. The rooms and the furniture in all messes were the same, yet nobody ever cribbed and accepted it very gracefully. There were more fastidious one like Capt. VK Choudhri, who had hired furniture from M/s Shive Furniture Mart in Sadar Bazar.

The next day, the senior subaltern ushered us into the Adjutant's office. Capt. NK Chadha, a Rimcollian, was in the chair and he gave his customary pep talk and the probation program. We were in charge of the senior subaltern, who had already briefed us on our conduct and behaviour as newly posted young officers in the regiment. Our commanding officer was Lt. Col. Arjinder Singh, a short fatherly figure who had been the veteran of World War II and had been the young officer of the same unit. The Army after 1962 drubbing by the Chinese was in turmoil, coming to grips with the important aspects of what went wrong. One of the reasons was physical fitness which was the regular whipping boy of our seniors. Everyone knew about our truncated training period at IMA and School of Artillery, where most passed their mandatory PT tests held at Artillery Centre Nasik Road, without having to exert much. On our first Sunday around lunchtime, the CO expressed his desire to see a gun manhandling competition between the newly posted officers and the old officers in the mess lawns. Off we went on our bikes to the gun park, took out a 75 mm Pack howitzer with all its stores. With guidance from a gunner jawan from the battery, we sprang into action. The six of us lugged the portable gun on its two wheels to the mess lawns and did a tactical deployment. So did the other old team who looked better than us. Deployment drills of both were observed by the CO and we, the new youngsters lost hands down to the oldies. We again packed the gun back to its gun park immediately.

All tests conducted for us in the Regiment were much more stringent because it was felt that we guys had no worthwhile opportunity at IMA for physical fitness. I could make efforts to complete our truncated training at IMA, even now. Apart from qualifying on regular PT tests, with mat, beam horse, and rope as in NDA the 'ill-trained YOs' that we were called those days, we now had to qualify in battle order with a sten gun, once again for the monkey crawl, wall and the ditch. Then came the route marches of 2, 5, 10 and 25 km, which you were to qualify for in the strict timings laid down by the regiment. The last one was also in the form of a post drop action combined with map reading and initiative test somewhere around Fatehpur Sikri. We were expected to find our way back to the regiment. Amazingly, all four of us from the 23rd course, arrived together at the finish, leaving everyone bewildered how that was possible. The toughest test I thought was the two miles which we were to complete with battle order and sten gun in the regimental standard of 16 minutes which we all did. Now came the interview of the senior subaltern and his team, who recommended only the five of us to be retained for para duties, and it was accepted by the new CO, Lt. Col. RC Butalia. That's how we adorned the maroon beret and became a part of this great regiment. As soon as we got our wings, Gun Fitter Fateh Singh was given the five new names for making our brass lettered nameplate, which each one of us proudly displayed at the entrance of his room. I remember, it cost us some thirty bucks each made of polished teakwood.

Three of us, Narayan, Bunny and I joined 49 Battery. Our BC was Maj. Peter Mendonca and the famous mountaineer Capt. Jagjit Singh, his second in command. Later, Peter went to 51 Battery and we trained under Maj. Jagjit Singh, our newly promoted BC. Jagga was a hard taskmaster, who slogged us hard, held night training four times every week. During the day we were religiously doing gun drills under Chinappa and carrying out maintenance in the gun park, after that. We came immediately after lunch in dungarees to supervise maintenance again, before joining the jawans for games like football or hockey. We were asked to open notebooks/diaries which were checked regularly by Jagga personally. In that, the personal and professional details, including pay of every jawan of your troop was jotted down. We also had taken bikes on hire from Binodi Lal Tara Chand, our unit bania on a charge of Rs. 30 per month and joined the regimental team of cyclists. Everyone from senior dining members, Maj. GD downwards used to cycle daily to the regiment. Only CO had a car and a Vespa scooter, 2IC, Maj. Bhardwaj a scooter, Jagga a Lambretta and Peter Mendonca a motorcycle.

Akbar Barracks in the Cantt area, where our regiment was located, was a cluster of four gigantic colonial barracks, several smaller barracks and stand-alone buildings designed to accommodate a British Indian Army battalion. These heritage buildings, constructed sometime in 1914, were on the main road running to the Brigade HQ. They were single storey, high ceiling roofs with red sand sandstone flooring, now patched up by cement at places. There were huge verandahs on both sides, cubicles existed for barber and dhobi shops, some battery stores and for NCOs. Two thick steel wires used to run from one end to the other, for tying mosquito nets at night. There were gaping holes on the sidewalls for another set of ropes, which was designed for hand-pulled *pankhas* (fans), probably to keep the tommies cool in summers. These contraptions were still there when we joined the regiment. The battery offices were at the entrance of the subunit, followed by the gun park and then the jawans living (on both sides in one line) by troops, interspersed with various stores like Q and MT towards the end of the barrack. The family quarters of each subunit, of slightly newer vintage, were after these barracks. Each subunit had its small little kitchen garden connected to the wastewater outlet coming from the community toilets.

The stand-alone buildings opposite the main road were the four jawan's messes and cookhouses and JCOs Mess in one line, In the centre, stood the RP post, the nerve centre of the regiment, which again led to the unit quarter guard and then on to the PT ground. Opposite the RP post stood the imposing regimental headquarters, the fountainhead of all power. Other stand-alone buildings were the map depot which probably came up later, the LAD and Signal section. The regimental mandir under Pandit Mishraji and gurudwara under Gyani Jit Singh Bhor and the wet canteen of Binodi Lal Tarachand were part of the RHQ building.

Our mess was once the emergency ward building during the Second World War, which used to have a road running from the gate, straight to the portico of what is now an imposing mess building. The corner room of our living barrack on the opposite end, closest to the road, was the mortuary, from where dead bodies were placed for removal. There were 8-10 rooms of varying size, occupied by bachelors. There were two lawns on either side of the road. The left one facing the building was the Diwan-i-Aam and the right one was the Diwan-i-Khas. The famous four barreled brass gun was installed on the right lawn. Generally, we used to frequent Diwan-i-Aam, where our dinner was laid out by the mess staff during the peak summer months. Except for three days of the week, Mondays, Tuesdays and Fridays which were the dinner night days inside, this being the accepted diktat of the 2IC. Our senior dining member was Maj. GD Sharma, with others being Capt. NK Chadha, Capt. VK Chaudhri, Capt. Shanti Prakash with senior subaltern Mehandru and five other

2/Lts. formed quite a team with another lot of new five. 2/Lt. Amarjit Behl and Capt. HS Talwar were still on leave after their repatriation to India. In the regimental headquarters, we had the new 2IC Maj. HK Bhardwaj, the veteran from NEFA who had overseen the operations of 52 Para Field Battery, Capt. RC Masur the QM and Capt. B Chaddah the OC LAD. This senior lot of 2/Lt. colleagues were Amarjit Behl, Bittoo Gill, Vijay Batra, Ashok Cariappa and KS Rao.

I must not forget that our mess staff those days were all outstanding and dedicated to a set of jawans led by a legendary figure, Havildar Sua Ram. He kept the mess in a very tidy condition at all times, whether we were dining inside in the main building or the lawns opposite. Food members used to give the menu for lunch and dinner regularly for a week. He used to take it down in his notebook. Messing was pegged at Rs 1.75 per day as per diktat from the 2IC and he took pains to ensure this was kept in mind always. The whole of Agra supplied Jumna water which was *khara* and tasteless. Mess used to draw sweet water from the well in a church located in the vicinity. Sua Ram arranged this on a very nominal payment to the padre. Cold coffee was served black and you could add milk if you wanted. Bittoo was fond of his *kachchi lassi*, which became popular soon. Purchase of butter paper for packed meals was also on the charter of Mess Havildar. His biggest crib was that ever since these five new officers have come, the extra messing has gone up because of excessive consumption of butter, bread slices and cold coffee. During dinner nights, Sua Ram in his white mess dress with a red sash, maintained a discreet distance, sometimes remaining behind the curtains noting down who had what. It was difficult to keep a tab on your wine and sherry consumption, while the decanter was being passed around.

There was a guest room caretaker, a pensioner Pheru Singh, our last link with the Rajput Regiment days, who was kept more for ceremonial reasons, than anything else, of looking after the Ladies Room and billiards table.

We used to have a billiards table those days which was located where the present Ladies Room is. I remember it was fully functional for a year or two and fell into disuse and was disposed of. I can say with a lot of pride that I learnt to play pool as early as 1963 on this table and was sad to see its state when the regiment went in and out of Agra for operations. In the kitchen Cook Special Kailash, Cook Balak Ram with Bairu Johre as the masalchi, Lallu and Parmanand as the mess waiters, Abdars (wine waiters) Krishna More, Krishna Nand and Sultan Singh later, were the part of the four mess dets a Para field regiment was entitled to. The mess grand old man was the *safaiwala*, Bhure Lal and the *dhobi* Kaloot. Both were civilians from Lalkurti, very fond of their tipple and accompanied the mess on camps as well. If my memory serves me right, in a battery we used to have 8 officers, 5 JCOs, 238 ORs and 14 NCsE. The regiment strength was 28 officers, some 32 JCOs and 792 ORs and 56 NCsE which included LAD of 70 odd all ranks.

By July end, the weather had improved somewhat, though it was still hot and humid. We all slept on our cots with mosquito nets, which were in one straight line opposite our respective rooms, laid out by our *sahayaks*. There was a huge *peepal* tree in the lawn whose huge branches extended over the cots, and up to our barrack. This tree was the nesting place of vultures, crows and many types of birds, even bats. We got used to the noise early mornings and late evenings. It used to be fun lying on our beds and chatting among ourselves about inter battery competitions, discussing the gunnery problems of an eight gun battery vis a vis six-gun batteries. We were forbidden to talk shop in the mess, particularly the mention of ladies' names in conversations on dinner nights. There was a good amount of camaraderie between the five of us, which continues even now. The "sirring" we were used to, from NDA days continued but there always was an air of informality. We always looked forward to interactions with the greatest entertainer of our times, Peter Mendonca. A regimental officer par excellence with a ready wit and a great sense of humour. As a battery commander, he was a paragon of knowledge, full of bawdy songs and limericks. He with his wife Julie and two sons Michael and Tony were regular visitors to the mess.

One of our immediate seniors, a 2/Lt, used to be mortally scared of sleeping under the *peepal* tree. Whenever his cot came under its huge branches, he used to drag it away to the open space to the right. One night he claimed to have seen a nurse dressed in white, wheeling a dead body to the mortuary, the last room, which happened to be occupied by his coursemates now. His two other coursemates seemed unimpressed and unfazed, yet a word went around that there were evil spirits around in the mess. Someone suggested periodic *havans* by the regiment Panditji under the tree, but nothing serious happened. Our CO was very dismissive and told him not to be superstitious. In the meantime, our senior again swore, he saw the same nurse at the same place at night doing the same job. During my last stay at the mess with my grandchildren in 2016, the *peepal* tree brought back memories of our stay as bachelors in 1963. When my grandson asked me what I thought about this incident. Was it true? I said I am unable to explain. I suspect that his subconscious mind was at work expressing, reproducing and manifesting according to his habitual thinking. The psychic impression so created could be attributed to excessive thinking and weird imagination.

Our 49 Battery was a good Thambi cum Maratha outfit. We had senior JCO like Subedar BR Dhake, Subedar MM Chinappa, and Naib Subedars Namdev Khade Mapare (famous as Gen. McArthur's driver during Korean Ops) and BHM Malaya Swamy. The last one was doing the NCOs course in School when we were on our course and we were impressed by his 6-foot four frame, a live wire on the gun park with his *joshila* gun drill. Troop HM like Kadir Velu and Kalgude, TA Hav Sathyam, NK Sidharthan, L/Nk Gangadharan, ORAs Subramani and Ramachandran, and Drivers Ali Kutty and Syed Ali Rahman were my team members who accompanied me to the Rann of Kutch and later to Lahore Sector. Just as the "ill-trained" lot like us arrived, Kadir Velu once confided in me, very tactfully that this new draft of jawans had little or no training, like you new 2/Lts. What the Centre taught them nobody knows. He was illiterate and whenever you passed some orders, he made it a point to note down very diligently in his notebook. He came back once to me, to enquire what was the second last point I had given him that day. He showed me what he had written. I saw plain letters written serially numbered like 1G, 2J, 3L, 4A, 5F it looked codified. He forgot what serial 4A meant. I told him it was airborne training course detailment of two jawans and not arms maintenance that day at 4 o'clock. He was confused by his method of taking orders.

We all did our Para Basic in Oct 63 along with our coursemate Jaggu Mahalwar of 2 Para. We thought this would be a really good break for us, we were in for a rude shock. Jagga continued to play merry hell with our evenings. There was no respite from training and maintenance, even after coming from the Para Training School at Kheria. I must confess that we were so perfect in the gun stripping and assembly as well as the maintenance schedule, that even the so-called limber gunners were mortally scared of us. This was our bread and butter, which a gun position officer was expected to know. Mobilization drills were practised and all stores were marked accordingly by us in various groups. Fire discipline and duties at the gun followed next and Jagga was determined to make us tough professionals, as he was. Both Chat and I got good doses whenever we made any mistakes in the command post exercises with guns. Sometimes a summary punishment was given in front of the men. That was his style but he had no malice in his heart.

We were put through a Brigade TEWT sometime in Sept 63 and this was the first time we saw our brigade commander Brig. Sagat Singh and his very competent staff comprising Majs Ranjit Dayal - the BM and Sampat Salunke - the DAA & QMG, Bhawani Singh (ex 3 Cavalry and the PBG) recently transferred to the Parachute Regiment, as the GSO 2 (Air). Other officers in the Headquarters were our own Capt. HS Talwar, affectionately known as Tally, the GSO3 (Air), Capt. RP Limaye GSO3 (Int) and Capt. RP Singh as the Staff Captain. Deputy Commander, Col. Sri Ram joined later.in early 1964. During the TEWT we were out in the Barauli area of Rajasthan for quite some time. During discussions, we were the captive audience and generally kept on listening watch. CO had once said in the mess, "2/Lts are meant to be seen and not heard". In one of the overnight stays where the brigade established themselves, I remember Brig. Sagat Singh going around visiting every unit mess by turns and speaking to all of us, the newcomers. Five of us strictly followed the COs diktat Then, what followed, was an acrimonious discussion between Brig. Sagat with our Jagga and Maj. KS Pannu of 2 Para, criticizing him for his orders forbidding bachelors calling on separated families. We youngsters just faded into the background, we heard some charges being traded, not worth mentioning. What was remarkable was that the next day, when the Commander was conducting the discussion, he appeared perfectly normal, harboured no ill feelings against the duo and gave respect to their opinions. Like a good soldier, Sagat forgave both of them and had not kept anything to his heart. No wonder Sagat was one of the greatest military commanders produced by this Army for his role in 1971 operations as a Corps Commander and earlier at Nathu La against the Chinese in 1967.

A few days before the Adjutant, Capt. Naresh Chadha and Capt. Shanti Prakash were to proceed on leave, to invoke the bonds of matrimony, the remaining bachelor crowd, some fifteen of us, decided that their send-off from the mess be celebrated in a befitting manner. The broad consensus was to celebrate it outside the mess and certainly, not in a hotel. The venue selected was the forest rest house at Kitham Lake, located some 25 km from Agra. A late-night weekend party was privately organized by Capts VK Chaudhri and Saxena from COD Agra, in a very hush-hush manner, with strict instructions that the information must not percolate outside the bachelor crowd. At around seven in the evening, our senior dining member, Maj. GD Sharma, who had planned everything to the minutest detail. The bachelor crowd left with the mess staff in a 1-ton and assembled at Kitham Lake. I remember that day, GD kept looking for some memorabilia of his trip but found the place vandalized. We learnt from GD about his trip to Port Blair from Madras in 1959, as a senior

Captain in a small yacht belonging to the Para Brigade. We still retain the expedition's white round ring buoy with ropes around it, adorning the portico of our main mess building in Agra Cantt. In the meanwhile, the bar became functional, yours truly the barman. The mess staff after establishing the bar, food and snacks, were quietly packed off back to the regiment. We had a good evening together singing and merry-making. That evening, VK Chou and Saxy (Saxena) arranged the special item number; an attractive professional singer cum dancer, who sang and danced without any breaks for almost three hours at a stretch. There was a code of conduct observed that evening and her performance was only confined to singing our favourite ghazals and filmi songs. Tiger Behl and Bunny Khanna were amongst our lead singers, who could lend their voices to good effect. We got back late at night carrying great memories of the lovely party. I remember very fondly that such fabulous get-togethers organized with a lot of effort contributed much to the camaraderie and strengthened the bonds of friendship amongst Team Seventeen forever.

Along with the sendoff from bachelors, we had made grandiose plans for the welcome of the newlyweds after their wedding. I went to Lal Kurti, which was right behind our mess and made inquiries. There was an assorted marriage band of sorts available. It had two drummers, one trumpet, two huge brass cymbals and one *shenai* and players who could try and play at the Agra Cantt Railway station. They weren't new but they hadn't progressed much and could play some filmi music for villagers, the EWS colony of the Lal Kurti residents, on special occasions. They were highly recommended, costing us Rs 25/- per hour. I bargained for Rs. 20, saying only half an hour of music required with rickshaw charges paid, as advised by our senior subaltern. This band was fixed for the Chadha couple first, However, this highly seasoned Rimcollian, true to his base instinct, got wind of it. He arrived unannounced late at night by Pathankot Express and succeeded in dodging us. We now waited for the Shanti Prakash couple and learnt about their arrival by Taj Express in the morning. The reception was well organized by Mehandru and all of us. They got a royal reception on arrival at Platform No 1, much to the amusement of the onlookers, I went forward and presented a cauliflower to the new bride. She was flabbergasted at the weird things happening around her. I think she never forgave me for my indiscretion. The couple gracefully accepted what was laid out, after that all the tomfoolery was called off and we drove off to the mess.

We went for our first live firing course shooting sometime in November and were tested by almost everyone you name it. We were two old GPOs Cariappa and Rao and the other four were Chat, Essen, Neeru and myself. A regimental survey was done by Mehandru and it was found to be accurate. CO also allowed us to come to the OP where Maj. HK Bhardwaj was the conducting officer. When I got my first shot as an OP officer, he commented, "*Andhe ke hath mein lag gaya bater*". That was when the first round landed on the target, which I had great difficulty in checking back. He was a very likeable and competent officer, an excellent instructor, who had done his LGSC in India and Staff College at Camberly.

Jagga, as our battery commander, took us for battery camp at Dholpur. Besides being a good sportsman and a mountaineer, he was a keen shikari, as well. We always had some partridges for snacks, in the battery mess. Whenever he went out with battery on exercise, his double-barreled gun was by his side in his jeep. Being a serious no-

nonsense type, he spared no one. In one of the conferences, he made a funny remark in Hindi, that the soap placed in the dish must not convey the impression that it is being used for the first time, just before the inspection. Narayan and I looked at each other but Narayan could not hide his smile and a bit of a suppressed giggle. Jagga only said, "What's so funny, Chatterjee" and packed him off on a run around the barracks, much to the amusement of the officers and JCOs present. We also had public speaking sessions with troops during the roll calls and later. In one session after the assassination of President Kennedy, on 23 Nov 1963. Narayan, the sophisticated anglophile from the RIMC, drew a great deal of laughter even from the Thambis on his remark that, "*Kissi ne President Kennedy Sahib ko goli kar diya*". Chat always had the benefit of being mentored on the professional plane, by another star performer with his booming & anglicized voice, Vijay Batra the CPO, also from RIMC. Both had taught me useful lessons of life, the instinct of self-preservation and PR, which I carry always. I also learnt the subtle art of variable social behaviour and management of seniors from these two which helped me later, during the command of my regiment and the brigade.

We again got busy with technical training for our annual Practice Camp at Babina Ranges, in Feb 1964. A special mention needs to be made, the first one, after our return from NEFA. Practice Camps are considered a true test of technical gunnery of the unit, the IG team from the School of Artillery, tests you on gunnery and is, therefore, given an exalted status. I saw the CO and his battery commanders very confident, seemingly unaware of this team. Drama or otherwise, I can't say. We had several exercises involving moving with guns on various roads in and around Agra regularly, till we came to know every inch of ground. Jagga had trained us very hard and we had developed the confidence he always talked about in his younger days. We were fully well versed with duties at the GPOs command post, I quickly realized that our immediate boss was the CPO, 2/Lt. VB Batra, who had to be satisfied professionally and socially as well. I did that to the best of my ability as was evident from the Practice Camp and other activities. We have rated the best battery with bogey timings. I remember the umpire Bittoo Gill announcing that Alpha Troop had the best round to round timing in the Regiment. Maj. Bhardwaj, who conducted our battery test exercise was thoroughly impressed when Kadir Velu correctly stopped him from spreading rumours. Kadir Velu became the talk of the regiment for his loyalty and bold action. There was also one incident in which I had made a wrong decision to go to Delhi by train on a weekend without permission and arrived late for PT, the following Monday. As luck would have it, the train got delayed enroute. Neither the Adjutant nor the 2IC wanted to be a party to any official action but were forced by CO. Despite admitting my error of judgment, the CO insisted on a summary of evidence, ostensibly to scare me, till the Brigade Commander cautioned him not to do so, saying youngsters will make mistakes, by all means, correct them, do not kill them. I was also deprived of my annual leave during the year 1964 in retribution for the offence committed by me. When I look back, this incident has shaped my life. When I commanded a regiment in 1980 at Talbehat, I was faced with a similar situation. One of my youngsters left the unit without informing anyone and proceeded home. I took the call and immediately dispatched a JCO to his home to bring him back. On his return from absence, I analysed his problems and the matter was resolved at my level only without resorting to an overkill action. One needs to use both his head and heart, adopting a more humane approach and yet maintain unit discipline.

Immediately after the Practice Camp in March 1964, Majs GD Sharma & Peter Mendonca left for Wellington in April. Maj. HK Bhardwaj, who had been closely watching my overall performance in the unit just before his departure to take over a new raising, had these words of encouragement. "Trouble is, Dabbu, you are too honest and simple. CO is unhappy with you because of what happened earlier. You need to forget about it and move along in life". Jagga, my hard-core supporter, had left on posting to the NDA and Maj. Prem Chandra took over as our BC. In addition, Capt. Shakti Singh who was an aide to COAS, Gen.PP Kumaramangalam, had returned to the unit and was the new Adjutant. Immediately thereafter in April 1964, we were stand-by for deployment in Thimpu, Bhutan as part of the Para Brigade. It was during the crises created by the assassination of Bhutanese PM. The uncertainty continued for about a month in readiness, when we were asked to stand down.

We had now got into the grind in the regimental and battery activities. Regimental *sainik sammelans* were held regularly and our men continued to display great josh and high morale. As duty officers on the regimental rosters, we were to check guards at various timings given by the Adjutant, checked the guard at Agra Fort and tasted food in all subunit cook houses. Your performance and you for what you are, whether you are a thorough professional officer who would stand by his men, always or not. We were in admiration and awe of one towering personality of "the most officer like JCO", Subedar (AIG) Ishwar Singh VrC of 51 Battery, who sometimes trained us during the regiment command post exercises and took our gunnery lectures. He sometimes pulled his bachelor BC's leg on his prolonged bachelorhood, in chaste Haryanvi, "Saab, when milk is cheap, why buy a cow?"

The Regiment kept slogging us to the hilt. I think all of us rose to the occasion and never gave anyone a chance to check us. We went through our Retention Test arranged by the senior subaltern and passed all subjects in one go. I had committed to my father that come what may, I will make all-out efforts to be the best in the regiment and work to perfection in all duties assigned to me, regardless of what anyone thinks of me. I admit I was always under the sword of Damocles hanging over my head for being pushed out at the first available opportunity to any mountain composite regiment. My BC trusted me implicitly and had faith in me but he lacked the courage to take a stand with the CO for anyone, least of all myself.

There was a para drop at Gauchar in Garhwal in an airborne exercise with 22 Establishment, in which one troop was dropped along with the gun detachments, the GPO and his party. Our CO exercising his prerogative selected Bunny Khanna in my place for this task. When I brought this to the notice of my BC, he just post officed me to meet the CO in his office, who fired me up and told me, "You are a barrack-room lawyer. Just tell me which mountain composite regiment you want to go to?" I think I needled the CO unnecessarily but at the same time, I expected a more mature and balanced response to my request. During this time, I was detailed on D&M course at Faizabad and did very well on the course. Prem Chandra made me in charge of the battery boxing team. Our boxers regularly sparred with me and sometimes left me to see stars, pulling off some really good punches on me. It was unbelievable when we beat 52 Battery for the overall championship.

Now, three more officers, Ravi Kant, Melville de Souza and VS Patil joined the regiment in July 1964. We found there was a great emphasis on brigade sports. Ravi, Melville, Mehandru and Bhatara had already won the brigade football trophy beating 3 Para in finals, there was a repeat performance in hockey where Ravi and Melville excelled to beat 2 Para Workshop and again Vithoo Patil and Karupaih were our star performers in basketball. In boxing, I had trained the team hard and the boys did remarkably well. The regiment proceeded on Practice camp in Dec 1964 with Maj. SS Sant, the new 2IC Capt. Shakti Singh as the Adjutant. I was again adjudged the best GPO with the best round to round timing by the IG team from outside (12 secs). It was the first time that my BC Maj. Prem Chandra gave me some credit, but I was still not sure if the CO did. It didn't matter as I had learnt to stand on my own feet and worked hard to achieve what I did. We were joined by two more youngsters in December 64, Ashish Dube and Harbhajan, who had come as a last-minute change for Chinu Mahanti, who was then posted to 1 Field (SP).

We had barely settled down after Babina, when our battery received orders to move with 2 Para Bn group by train to the Rann of Kutch on 09/10 Apr 1965. Mehandru joined the Battery and we mobilized quickly. We boarded the metre gauge train at Agra Idgah and moved on white-hot priority up to Ahmedabad (Sabarmati) sometime on the night of 12 April. We again continued the journey and arrived at Gandhidham, the next day. The battery convoy left by road and reached Khavda by evening 14 Apr 65. Khavda was then a small village amid numerous sweet water wells and groves of palm trees.

We settled in for the night in the tents pitched up by our advance party in the camp established. In addition to Mehandru, Capt. OP Khanna had joined from the School of Artillery. The Infantry Brigade at Vigokot had already taken over from Sardar Post eastwards to a new inter-formation boundary with 50 Para Brigade, which was under move to Khavda. Kilo Sector was formed under Maj. Gen. PO Dunn.

The Rann starts about 10 km north of Khavda. Chhad Bet lies about 56 km from Khavda, where 4 Para moved in. As soon as we entered the Rann, the entire surface was covered for miles with a thick shining crust of fine mixture of salts, sometimes more than a foot thick. This continued till we reached Mori Bet, on 16 April 1965. Bet, I learnt, is a slightly raised piece of ground, a kind of island in the Rann (the sea) with low vegetation and scrub, where we hid the guns under camouflage nets. Our 2IC Maj. SS Sant took out my troop of guns from the hide and moved me forward, much ahead of the troops deployed at a place known as Biar Bet post, where a company 2 Para had just moved it. Point 84 post further east was occupied by company 3 Para under Maj. PP Singh with Bittoo Gill as the OP officer. A foot track from Biar Bet and another one from Point 84 converged at a place called Arjun Tree. Para guns with their inherent problems of limited range have sometimes to deploy from roving positions ahead of infantry units. This was one of them to reach a Pakistani ranger post called Vingoor which was just across the sand dunes ahead of Arjun Tree. 2IC & Mahendru were in the jeep ahead. We had no one-inch maps and we had to make do with the quarter-inch maps. Yet my TAs did not disappoint and we engaged the Pakistan post with 80-90 rounds of HE mixed with airburst to cause maximum casualties. From intercepts, the colossal damage caused was an ammunition dump cum weapons *kote*, some tents on fire, and at least 8-10 casualties. As soon as the task was completed, we retreated and deployed ahead in a temporary position at Dharamshala, with both troops operating independently in support of 2 Para in Biar Bet. The remaining battery headquarters under Vijay Batra, our boss remained with the regiment.

We were deployed for 4-5 nights in temporary positions, fully camouflaged and dug in. Dadhwal was GPO Bravo Troop when Chatterjee moved out on his selection as the Regiment's Survey Officer. Radhey Sham Dhingra & Ravi Kant had just joined and were troop leaders with Dadhwal. Registration of targets and engagement took place continuously. Sometimes the air OP called for fire and we responded immediately. Our post at Biar Bet was attacked early morning, around 6.45 of 26 April 1965. I saw dust kicked up which looked like tanks. The companies from 2 Para (Dhaliwal) and 3 Para (PP Singh) and their OP officers also withdrew together just before the Pakistan attackers could reach. I distinctly remember Bittoo Gill with PP Singh of 3 Para withdrawing through my gun position from Point 84. Bittoo with a transistor slung on his shoulder went past telling me that tanks were ahead. I could see that and was prepared for such an eventuality. Next to go past my gun position was 2/Lt. Bunny Khanna who also told me to see the dust kicked up by tanks in front and suggested I should withdraw immediately. I told him I was yet to receive my orders from the BC and would do so only when I am ordered to. In the meanwhile, air OP, presumably my cousin, Maj. Shilu Mathur dropped a message bag with a scribbled note "Tanks ahead of you". I then enquired from my BC Prem Chandra, for permission to withdraw. He told me to cease fire and withdraw. I ensured that no equipment was left behind, my LPs were called back, all weapons and guns were intact. Vehicles were summoned from their hides and we withdrew with the Pattons hot on my trail, after finding the post ahead abandoned.

We headed hell for leather for Dharamshala and then on to the Regiment gun position in Mori Bet. In the normal course, all troops ahead of 3 Para positions should have been warned by the CO/BC who had given me the orders to withdraw. This probably did not happen and I came under fire from anti-tank guns of 3 Para. My command post vehicle was hit and damaged beyond repair. One of the best TA Naiks of the regiment, Nk. Sidharthan who was with me at that time got a direct hit by an RCL spotter round which must have missed me by a few inches. He was bleeding profusely on the right side of his head. I helped him into a jeep and evacuated him to the ADS. In the meanwhile, one Maj. Bhattu Bhargava of 3 Para came forward to identify us. We reached the regimental gun position after an hour after seeing Sidharthan evacuated in a helicopter. Around the same time, Echo Troop of 52 Battery with Essen Guptan as the GPO also withdrew under pressure from the enemy Pattons which overran Point 84. Essen gave Tank Alert to his guns and engaged them, scoring at least one direct hit, forcing them to abandon their foray towards the gun position.

At this moment, both of us GPOs at different locations did not expect to get accolades from the CO for our successful withdrawal in the face of the enemy. Poor Essen got no credit and instead, was ordered to recover the trailers his troop left behind, the same night. There was no talk of 3 Para RCL firing on my troop mistakenly. In fact, I was told to accept such friendly fire casualties and Sidharthan was no exception. My loyalty lay in ensuring that he was attended immediately at the ADS by a very smart and agile doctor from 60 Para who I still admire for his professional work. I followed Sidharthan's treatment at MH Pune later when I learnt that he had been boarded out with a full disability pension.

Rann of Kutch can be extremely hot during the day and very pleasant during the evening. Our time was spent in the limited shade provided by the cam nets. After some time, we noticed flies galore in the mess and the living bunkers and it became impossible to survive without a fly swatter. Hygiene and sanitation were ensured by all of us but somehow the menace continued, We used to rest in afternoons in mosquito nets. Fine sand blowing most of the day used to hurt in the eyes because of the salt content. Sunrise was early and the visibility was fantastic. I was assigned for OP duties and joined 2 Para along with Prem and OPK. Lt. Col. Ram Singh Yadav, CO 2 Para and I were eyewitnesses to the accident where Maj. SS Sawhney of 411 Para Field Company lost his foot in a mine blast and had to be evacuated.

We used to come back to Mori Bet, to attend wherever there was a get together at the regiment mess or even outside if such an occasion arose. During the Captain's promotion party hosted by Bittoo Gill at the regimental mess, there was a cloud burst and heavy rainfall followed next. OPK and I tried to reach 2 Para locations only to find our tents floating/fully submerged in the deluge. The whole night was spent looking for our vehicles/trailers which had our belongings. All vehicles were nicely camouflaged and parked in depressions which were now huge fish ponds with only tarpaulins visible from the top. This was around 30 June 1965, as the next day was the Part A exam presided over by Lt. Col. K Sunderji, CO 2 MAHAR, which I had to miss out on. I was nominated for the dirty job of recovering vehicles of the regiment to Mori Bet which were lying submerged. Having worked day and night to get our vehicles out, unshaven and shoddily dressed, my OP party stood on the bonnets of our jeeps to get the compo ration packs dropped on us. The Brigade Commander, Brig. Nambiar was in the chopper supervising the drop. I reached Mori Bet two days later and accidentally bumped into the CO. "Why aren't you properly dressed, why are you unshaved?" These were the few words with which he welcomed me back. I quietly shaved and dressed properly before entering the mess. I guess he was right and I learnt another lesson of my life: never to be improperly dressed, the sanctity of a place such as the officers' mess must be maintained, even during the war. Not very many will understand the values which were being inculcated in us by the CO.

After a brief interregnum at Bhuj, the regiment moved back by train from Gandhidham to Agra around 15 Jul 65. The Survey board was held at Agra which took almost two weeks to complete. Some of us tried to get back to social life in the peace station and tried Agra Club and its *teetar paratha* in the evenings. Ceasefire in the Rann of Kutch, notwithstanding, Pakistan had no intention of putting an end to the hostilities. We kept getting reports that Pakistan's much-vaunted Operation Gibraltar had already commenced in J&K. One of our officers from 1 Para, Arvinder Baicher, had already arrived, all shot up in his legs at MH Agra awaiting further evacuation. Lt. Col. ML Chadha Commandant HAWS at Gulmarg was shot dead by infiltrators who had been creating havoc with our forces. As the war clouds loomed large on the horizon, some postings and detailments on courses like GTOs courses also took place. We had not been able to implement the leave program during the Kutch operations, so we did so, on arrival at Agra.

The moment we sent jawans on leave, the balloon went up on 1 September 1965 when hostilities began in Chamb Sector.

General recall from leave meant another week for the jawans to return. When our convoys moved by road on 8 Sept to join the the Infantry Division in Amritsar, we were short of drivers. Whosoever had a valid driving licence and could drive was entrusted with a vehicle. We had our first halt. in the convoy ground in Delhi Cantt. We got a lot of help from Maj. MC Dogra, BM AD Brigade, an ex Seventeener and very spirited officer. One of the jeeps had its engine seized, and was replaced overnight on his orders so that it could join the convoy later in the day. We halted several places alongside the GT Road, whenever enemy Sabres flew past, an odd LMG mounted in AA role did open up. We explained to the gunner that the chances of getting an aircraft are far-fetched. Long halts delayed our move to the night of 9 Sept and we were touched by the gesture of villagers carrying *dal pateelas* and *roti* on their bicycles, to feed the troops. We continued to drive till we crossed Amritsar, in the early hours of 10 Sept when we reached an orchard in Khasa, our final halt. 17 Para was taken off Para Brigade and allotted to the Infantry Brigade north of GT Road on Axis Ranian Kakkar to clear the enemy, 49 Battery was in direct support of a DOGRA *paltan* and BC and OPs married up with them. I was with one Maj. Thapa as the FOO. We man packed and followed the track from Ranian to the first village across the border which was our first bound, Village Chak Allah Baksh is located on the *dhussi bandh*, a flood control measure made by villagers. As is the normal drill we secured the bound by late evening. Thapa and I found the complete village abandoned by the residents. My operator Ramachandran and Syed Ali Rehman, driver operator of my Romeo Alpha, noticed some

Urdu graffiti, written on the wall with charcoal. The villager who owned this house had conveyed that he and the family had to flee this house in a panic, much against their wishes. He had placed all his family jewellery and valuables which he could not carry, inside a steel sandook, which was placed along with the Quran Sharif at height in a small gap in the wall (called *alla*). He said he would come back to claim his valuables. While tea was being served to Thapa and myself by my OP party. At this time, out of sheer inexperience or call it a false sense of righteousness I ordered my party not to touch the *sandook* I wasn't sure when the war would end and whether our CO would like me to touch this war booty. My driver Rehman, a deeply religious Hyderabadi Muslim, too said that I should not take possession as it could invite curses from the owner. This jewellery box kept lying in the house and on a tip by Thapa, the 2IC, one Maj. Thomas took the *sandook*, in his possession the same night. Though I don't believe in superstitions, I learnt much later that the 2IC, Maj. Thomas, died in enemy shelling the next day. The *sandook* became a hot topic of discussion in the mess. It became famous as Dabbu's *sandook* and everyone in my Regiment laughed at me for lacking the guts to pick up a war booty for the regiment. This went on for days!!!

This was my first experience as a forward observation officer of the artillery, also my first taste of working with infantry. Our vehicles remain with infantry vehicles and we manpack with our complete equipment, weapon and communications. It used to be a funny sight with an operator carrying a huge wireless set 62 from where rubber leads emerged connecting it to the lead-acid battery carried by another operator on his back. We used to call it a husband-and-wife team. Though the infantry commander was invariably moving along with you,

you had to keep another wireless set 31 with you. Luckily this was lighter, had its inbuilt dry battery, which your technical assistant carried on his back. We used to have another operator carry a heavier 75 AH battery tagging along behind you. So, my immediate OP party consisted of Muniswami technical assistant. Ramachandran manpack station operator 1, Subramani the operator 2, and myself. Others were Ramakrishnan, operator 3 carrying spare batteries, and Rehman, the driver who also operated the vehicle station wireless, basically to bring up the vehicle, when required. Our packed meals for the day came only once at midnight. If you failed to collect from the infantry food carrying vehicle, you were without food the whole day. OP party. Luckily, my party had great cooks like Ramachandran and Muniswami. Equally adept in living off the land, their hawk-like eyes scouted for livestock, poultry and vegetables growing nearby. One stove and utensils, with onions, potatoes and masalas, cleverly hidden in a depression, out of everyone's view, they got going and cooked you a lovely meal. We foot slogged two to three more days to the bound, surprisingly we got no enemy opposition enroute. I never deviated from accurate and honest reporting. We also heard Maj. Saran Parshad's voice frantically asking for div Arty fire during the Punjab *paltan* attack for which he got a mention in dispatch. He had just joined us during the operations as BC 52 Battery but I only met him after the cease-fire.

On 15 Sept after four days, we were asked to rejoin the Para Brigade for its attack on Village Bhasin, which kept getting postponed for various reasons. At this time, the Infantry Division had already established itself on the GT Road axis and northwards up to Dera Baba Nanak bridge. The Infantry Brigade covered the area along GT

Road from the Railway Bridge at Jallo to the road bridge and another brigade to its north. The third brigade was covering the DBN axis including the bridge. Advances made on the first day were so fast that it went out of artillery & replenishment range. Sabres also knocked out the F echelon transport vehicles and no replenishment of ammunition and supplies was possible thereafter. Consequently, the brigade fell back to their firm bases. It was then that the Para Brigade was moved up. I had the opportunity to visit our Regimental command post where the newly posted in 2IC Maj. BK Kaul was seated inside a school building and Lt. Chatterjee, the new Adjutant briefing him. Both looked very sombre, had their helmets on. I got ticked off very rightly by the 2IC who said at our first meeting, "Where's your helmet?" I was wearing the jungle hat and had to rush back to fetch it from the vehicle. From Chatterjee's briefing, I learnt that Pakistan had constructed a major tank obstacle in the form of Ichhogil Canal which runs East-West approximately 12-15 km from the border. Khairagarh Canal, which was dry at the moment, comes out perpendicular to it. 2 Para, which was tasked to capture the marked areas on the Ichhogil Canal, had already been staged forward close to the Khairagarh Canal, some 3 km short of the Foot Bridge, from where I had just come for the briefing on the fire plan.

While the GT Road axis was being taken care of by the 54 Brigade, the 50 Para Brigade was then assigned a fresh task of capturing area Railway Bridge on the Ichhogil Canal, near a place called Jallo. I attended CO 2 Para's orders. In Phase 1, 2 Para was tasked to capture the east bank of the Ichhogil Canal with A & C Company by 2300 hours and dominate the west bank. In Phase 2, 3 Para had to pass through and capture the Railway bridge at Jallo by first light 17 Sept 65. H hour was 2115 hours. 3 Para in a preliminary operation was to provide a firm base by 2000 hours. 6 Para was the Brigade reserve, to be located at the Foot Bridge. As a subaltern, that's all I could mentally make a note of, then. My reproducing the attack plan of the Corps/Division now has no meaning.

In the morning of 16 Sep, 1965 both Bunny Khanna and I proceeded on a recce and registration of objectives along the Khairagarh Canal beyond the forward defended localities of the Infantry Brigade at a vantage point, where we could recognize the objectives with our company commanders. Our task was to recognize and register our objectives which we did with great difficulty in the face of fire by enemy MMGs. Billy Bedi of Scindia Horse, then a troop leader in the vicinity, cautioned me that they would invite more fire if I went any further, for my observation task. Nobody carries a written fire /attack plan in his pocket for the attack. At the most, you marked your map with a chinagraph pencil, in the small map case you carried. We returned after the successful registration of targets and made preparations for the night attack. We moved at last light with A & C companies of 2 Para and did not find 3 Para in the area firm base. The net result was C Coy 2 Para under Lt. Parab, had to secure its firm base and mark its FUP. We moved forward after a delay of about one hour, at 2230 hours. The tactical move from bound to bound towards the objective, with the battle cry, *"Chatrapati Shivaji Maharaj ki Jai"*, made us feel braver. There was MMG tracers fire from the pillboxes located on the Ichhogil Canal and artillery fire intermittently. My OP party kept moving forward in the company HQ with Lt. Parab, making periodic reports. Bunny's wireless set stopped functioning and he crossed over to my side of the Khairagarh Canal, for intimating his progress to our BC. The fire plan was eventually fired at 2230 hours. We advanced along the dry canal coming across abandoned RCL jeeps, filled ammunition boxes and stores. There were trenches on the sides of the Khairagarh where some dead bodies were lying. Some automatic and tracers were firing very high and we closed in. On reaching the junction of both canals we found the place unoccupied and abandoned by the enemy, just before we reached. There was intermittent tracer fire from the far bank and regular shelling. We crawled into the enemy's trenches and took cover. No mines were encountered, I reported to my BC. The effectiveness of our divisional artillery fire forced the enemy to withdraw to his home bank. During the heavy shelling that followed now, Lt. Parab got a direct hit by an airburst shell on his head and died instantaneously. I got a splinter on the right side of my waistline, where my compass was attached to the web belt. There was a very effective MMG fire coming from a high ground ahead which appeared to be the far bank. I gave a correction of Add 400. Our CPO Vijay Batra kept asking to check OT my compass had been hit by a splinter but I had the sense to give the approximate OT 270 degrees (due west). This compass was returned to my Battery and a replacement was provided the next day. I missed the golden opportunity of retaining a souvenir because it was already backloaded to ordnance when I returned to the regiment.

On the death of Lt. Parab, CO 2 Para asked me on wireless, to summon Subedar Janardhan, a VrC from Jhangar operations. I never saw this man from the time we left the FUP and I reported that to my BC. My party had not left Parab till his death. His operator was in too much of a shock and unable to handle the set. I must mention that the *josh* of the Maratha jawans was not affected and they kept egging me on to cross the Ichhogil Canal to avenge their *sahib's* killing. There was a young Maratha CHM and some jawans who wanted to go and occupy the far bank after wading through the 2-3 feet of water. I could hear frantic calls from their CO for Janardhan on my 31 set but there was no reply. Luckily my 62 set was through to BC who conveyed the message to me, I should fall back to Tilly's location, which meant Village Bhatha. Those orders were from the CO 2 Para, Lt. Col. Ram Singh Yadav. I never understood why it was done but learnt later that it was orders from the Brigade commander who wanted to avoid heavy casualties caused by the enemy sitting on the higher west bank, dominating the east bank. C Company and my party got back to Bhatha in the early hours not before I thought I had lost my operator Ramakrishnan, a brand new jawan, who was carrying the spare battery. I found him hiding in a trench on our return. He hadn't even moved when the last enemy shell landed and looked petrified. I gave him a piece of my mind and brought him along to 2 Para. I met our BC, Prem Chandra, who with a pat on my back, now asked me to proceed to B Company, whose company commander was Amarjit Grewal. Our location was heavily shelled by the enemy for the next two days. Our regiment was busy firing elsewhere the whole night, on a target nicknamed Meena Kumari. Both Bunny and I were first debriefed by the BC and then our CO under the camouflage net, where his jeep was parked in the Brigade Headquarters. I hadn't slept for three nights and looked like an absolute wreck. CO kept heckling me for unnecessary details, just to corroborate what I stated. I made it a point to speak the truth, what led to Parab's death. When Bunny tried to chip in to help me, he brushed him aside. I learnt later that I was being recommended for a gallantry award, VrC, which I came to know from the unit war diary. For the first time, I received a word of praise from my CO, which I thought was very unusual. Ceasefire with Pakistan came into effect on 19 Sept 65 at 0330 hours, probably the last salvo they fired claimed the lives of two LAD jawans, in the wagon lines.

Deployed as OP after the ceasefire

After the ceasefire, I was asked to go with 2 Para and retrieve the dead body of Lt. Parab. after the cease-fire. A flag meeting was arranged with the Pakistan troops in contact. I remember that the Pakistan JCO kept making excuses that his officer was unable to meet us for some unknown reason. I did find how very tactful and effective their JCOs were. It was amazing to see how we had walked through the same minefields the night before, now marked with small red triangular markers with white tapes by the Pakis to guide us through unmined areas. Whether it was our good luck that nothing happened when we went past or they were plain duds and didn't explode, I can't say. I guess we were just lucky nothing happened. After 2 Para attacks on the Ichhogil Canal, the previous night, 3 Para was tasked to capture the area lying between the 3 JAT and the Para Brigade. This area was south of the GT Road on the Ichhogil Canal and was on the inter brigade boundary between the 54 Infantry Brigade and the Para Brigade. It consisted of a built-up area of a village Jhuggian Mohd Baksh (JMB) and some pucca houses on its periphery. It was held possibly by Pakistan infantry company beefed up by elements of recce and support battalion. CO 3 Para, Lt. Col. Bakshish Singh, a seasoned campaigner, was being forced to attack the very next night and took his time for the deliberate attack. He also asked for a tac R and photographs of the area showed his company commanders their objectives. The firm base was provided by 2 Para and was within close proximity of B Company 2 Para, where I was located. I remember Mehandru, the FOO with his party passing through my location to the FUP for the attack on JMB on 19 Sept 1965. It was around 9 pm which probably was the time when our fire plan started. As soon as the enemy saw the attack coming, they withdrew to their side of the canal and heavy shelling followed. There were perimeter minefields laid in front. Maj. Gurbir Man Singh of 411 Para Field Company and Lt. Alagh arrived with their breaching party. Around 3 am, the sappers created a safe lane and by first light, 3 Para fired their success signal. When the support echelons moved, Mehandru's jeep and the remaining party were sent up by me personally.

Proceeding on leave from Lahore sector

After a spot of leave after the cease-fire, I returned to Lahore Sector and resumed my duties as an OP officer in support of 2 Para. Regimental life was fun in Punjab, but our 2IC kept us on a tight leash with regular dinner nights, even when we were deployed. Our annual confidential reports were required to be initiated by the CO. Like the last two years, I knew what to expect and signed when my turn came. This time again, I was called in my turn. I sat down as I was ordered by the CO and the report was placed before me. I signed blindly without even reading the pen picture, written in the manuscript so painstakingly by him. How could it be different from what he thinks of me? He angrily retorted, "Read the report first. One day, you will sign your own death warrant". I did that and was stunned on reading what he had written. Here was a man I thought was not at all fond of me, paying me the greatest compliment of my life, "I will take this officer with me to battle anywhere, anytime". I have written what you deserve. Those days reports were in flowery English and recommendations and no numerical assessment like today. Para Brigade has not fared well, as per the Infantry Division. For some reason, he couldn't get me a gallantry award for my performance in the 2 Para attack. Maybe this time around, CO's best efforts to push it through, failed! His words of appreciation were good enough for me and I wanted nothing more.

The Para Brigade proceeded to Ferozepur as a part of Ferozpur Fazilka Force which was located in Ferozepur Cantt. Maj. BK Kaul was then in top form as our 2IC, and rightly so. We had a rigorous schedule from morning PT, training with troops in the open fields where we were deployed and ending up with evening games like volleyball, softball and football. RHQ and 49 officers were in tents in one colony we called the Canal colony and 51 & 52 were staying in the Railway Colony. There were around 28 officers at that time and it was very convenient for the 2IC to send anyone asking for leave to go on annual leave for two months. 2IC's grand idea to break the monotony by calling the families from Agra for two nights to visit us resulted in a sand model exercise in which ladies were to conduct the sand model, along with the officers invited. I remember overnight gardens coming up in our desolate camp area. Mrs Saran Parshad began by introducing the sand model and did a near-perfect job of it. Other ladies too, contributed and added to the fun and frolic. There could not have been a better replacement for Peter Mendonca in Maj. BK Kaul. A hard taskmaster with a great sense of humour. Dinner nights as usual on Mondays, Tuesdays and Fridays (MTF) again kept us busy and we had some officer classes in the afternoons, as well. A beginning was made in book reviews by officers after dinner, which was seriously put into effect, on our return to Agra.

Both the CO and Maj. Kaul were determined to improve the quality of mess life of the bachelors. CO introduced a *chota hazri* set for the officer. Our *sahayaks* used to carry our tea from the cookhouse to our rooms in a thermos to be poured out in the room in our mugs. Looking at it now, it was done to lend dignity to officers' service. Four bachelor rooms were constructed away from the mess in what is now the Nursing Officers Mess. He directed that four of us coursemates will occupy these rooms. Our rooms were inspected one day by CO and 2IC, glaring weaknesses pointed out. I had to replace the old curtain which my mother had given me sometimes back from the home. As a final act for the unit, CO drew grandiose plans for the new Officers Mess layout. The road separating the two lawns was to be removed and the Diwan-e-Aam and Diwan-e-Khas merged to give a circular/oval appearance by planting a new hedgerow. CO got the Garden Member, Bittoo Gill to mark the new road alignment from the main gate in a left-handed circuit going to the portico and coming right around it like a garland. Inside this circular lawn with three corners covered by flower beds and a new bar constructed in the fourth corner, with a kidney-shaped dance floor in front. A new garden plan for the winter season was drawn, the gardener kept cribbing but he worked for a change. Now the flower beds outside along the hedgerow were allotted to each bachelor by name. We thought we were lucky as our rooms were on the other end of the bachelor's den. We were in for a shock when we found nameplates embedded and displayed very prominently. Now Bittoo began a crash program, which flower was what. We learnt from him phlox, verbena, salvia, dianthus, nasturtium, calendula and poppy etc. We dreaded the prospects of failing to differentiate one from the other or any plant dying due to our failure to water the beds regularly. All lapses were to be brought to the notice of the CO.

Comrades-in-arms

My posting as Captain Instructor at ASMT Faizabad was received before I completed three years' service. Everyone thought that it was good for me. I was very unhappy and requested by BC to ask the regiment to take up my case for cancellation. Since the reporting date was within two weeks of the issue of the posting in March 66 the CO gave me a patient hearing but refused to entertain my cancellation request. Career-wise it was good for me and there were no valid reasons for me to ask for it. For ten days nothing happened, there was someone who needed the posting more than I did. I had reconciled to my posting and was packed, ready to move. The regiment also dined me out formally and I was in the process of getting my bookings done with the RTO. First, the order came that the posting was held in abeyance, followed by the cancellation, a few days later. Maj. BK Kaul then ruled that I would have to foot the bill for the dining out held in my honour. I was very happy to stay back in the regiment.

As we got busy, writing off the losses in the field for the second time in one year, through the route of Survey Boards, our new QM, Capt. VP Sigh reported and was a very useful member of the team. The innings of Lt. Col. RC Butalia, our CO for almost three years came to a close, when he was tasked to train brand new air OP pilots at 660 Air OP Squadron Patiala, using Pushpaks of the Flying Club. Lt. Col. KK Hazari, one of our leading lights, a PSC from Camberly was to join us in July 66. In the meanwhile, Maj. BK Kaul left for JSSC at Latimer and Maj. Saran Parshad took over as our 2IC. Our BCs were Prem Chandra, Harjit Talwar and Amarjit Behl. Massive inter-postings of officers took place and I found myself in the 52 Battery. This churning was an attempt to curb prolonged exposure in one battery, the healthy rivalries and the petty loyalties emanating out of it. Amarjit Behl left for the NDA and I was officiating for almost four months till the arrival of Maj. DP Sahoonja. We were now on motorcycles and scooters, instead of the cycle on hire from Binodi Lal, the unit *bania*.

There was a total change in the atmosphere in the regiment with the coming of Lt. Col. KK Hazari. Though 'apple polishing' had reduced, some of our old stalwarts had still not changed. First to leave on promotion was Maj. Saran Parshad, who on his dining out was not very happy that the CO had to proceed on temporary duty at short notice and only the junior lot under his best friend, Prem were there to see him off. Prem, a bachelor still, also left a month later, on posting as MA to COAS at New Delhi. In the meantime, he sent me on a secret mission to make enquiries in Dehradun about a certain lady with whom his matrimonial correspondence was in progress. I gave him a thumbs down after meeting the lady in person. Prem was very grateful and settled for someone in Delhi. We were all invited to his wedding to Miss Urmil (who, sadly is no more) in Greater Kailash Delhi. Our battery officers Vijay Batra, Bunny Khanna and self were the toast of the evening, eyeing pretty young girls and getting the right royal treatment. I can never forget that we barged into his room in Kotah House Mess, stayed without even asking him earlier. To make matters worse, we got hold of his orderly, Gunner Babu Rao from 49 Battery, to find out where his scotch was lying. We helped ourselves to his liquor, made ourselves comfortable, showered, perfumed and powdered and arrived for the function nicely attired in blue patrols, well in time. We saw our BC in his groom's attire and he asked us where we guys were staying. My immediate reply was, "Sir, your room in Kotah House". He appeared shell shocked initially, then recovered and queried from inside the mandap, "Where did you get the keys from?" Gunner Babu Rao was there to look after us". Prem, always a good sport, appreciated this gutsy gatecrashing. He never asked who the mastermind was, he knew his officers too well. (If Dabbu was there, he must've organized it). We extracted his invitation eventually as we had no choice, but to allow him the use of his room.

On orders from the CO, Lt. Col. KK Hazari I was to take 52 Battery on a four days battery camp to our usual haunt at Dholpur, sometime in November 1966. He insisted that no senior Capt. be inter-posted and I be given a chance to train & handle the battery, despite my inexperience. We were full strength in 52 Battery with Capt. KK Bhargava, Ashish Dube & TN Raman and 2/ Lts Rajendra Kumar and Manmohan Bhardwaj. We had to shift to a six-gun battery first and we did that without any problems before this camp. 52 Battery had clerks like Ram Gyan Mishra, the permanent compere for *barakhanas* and Chattar Singh Panchchi who were not fully clued up and gave you anxious moments during COs inspection. MT NCO Govind Singh told me, "Sahib, you seem dissatisfied with my performance. You will soon be having Mukhtiar BA as your MT Havildar in my place and there will not be any more problems in MT documents". When he arrived, I then realized then he was *angootha chhap* & illiterate. Troops sense of humour must be appreciated when they called him BA. We prepared for one full week before battery camp and I was personally briefed by Maj. OP Khanna, BC 51 Battery. We had a concentrated dose of command post exercises with guns, loading as per the composition of various parties/battle groups in a new six-gun battery and dummy fire and move exercises. Our battery test exercise set by Maj. OP Khanna, was attended by the CO himself and he praised the all-around efforts at both gun and OP end. Though I made a lot of mistakes, this exposure proved invaluable when I commanded a battery later as a Maj. in the 9 Para Field Regiment.

17 Para Field Regiment in 1966

In mid-October 1966, we celebrated the Silver Jubilee of the Para Brigade. As usual, we were assigned duties, far above what the battalions and the brigade units had got. We established a Reception Centre in the mess and had to accommodate a large number of guests both outsiders and gunners. 25 Field Regiment Royal Artillery from the UK sent Lt. Campbell and two other ranks who travelled in a Land Rover to join us in the festivities. They also had another task to perform, to study the Battle of Maharajpur, near Gwalior. The other ranks were accommodated in the JCOs Mess and the officer with us. During one of the formal dinners, I saw Campbell wearing his maroon regimental tie which had the elephant's backside and 1843 depicted all over. I suggested that this may cause some embarrassment to us hosts, because Rani of Jhansi, is revered and considered a legend and is shown in poor light. She did put up a stubborn fight and did not run away as depicted. Straightaway, Campbell took the hint and removed his tie and asked me for a replacement. I got one immediately from the canteen and I still retain his tie, which he 'presented' to me as a souvenir. The Silver Jubilee dinner held in Cecil Mansion was attended by a lot of British officers like Gen. Pike, CIGS British Army, ex CO 9 Para Field Regiment and the serving lot like Gen. Kumaramangalam and many more. I remember our ladies led by Mrs Meera Hazari and Mrs Sajjani Nayyar (BM's wife) practising the *giddha*, on our recently renovated mess kidney floor.

Next to follow, were the brigade boxing finals in the 3 Para Garden, we were running neck to neck with 3 Para. Our regimental boxing team was being trained by Dube and myself. We had done very well so far and in one bout, our Balaji Kadam almost knocked out the Oriya boy of 7 Para. Inder Gill, our Commander, got so cheesed off that he left in between, for the bar to fetch a drink. Som Sharma of 7 Para was also at the bar. Inder Gill let Som have it when he said "Look at you. The gunners are making minced meat out of you guys". He then splashed his drink on Som. Som also retaliated and splashed his drink on the Commander. This everyone thought was a serious situation and we tried to keep away. The next thing we saw was the Commander embracing Som and making up at the end of the function when 3 Para beat us by just one point. A great occasion to celebrate their victory and also forgive and forget. I have never seen such a big-hearted individual like Inder Gill, another outstanding field commander.

Lighthearted banter at the Mess

Regt took part in Exercise Betwa in MP. It was quite an interesting exercise in plains, where the Corps under Lt. Gen. KT Satarawala, was pitted against the exercise enemy Infantry Division with Para Brigade as a part of it and our division commander was Maj. Gen. SS Padda. We were out for almost two months and were busy recceing delaying positions for the div against the Corps offensive. During the exercise I had the good fortune to meet the CASC, Lt. Col. UN Mathur, my second cousin, from Jubilee Villa Dehradun, who was a batchmate of our CO. During his exclusive talk with me, he asked me if all was well now, with the change in command. I confirmed but he gave me a bit of his mind. "You have KK as your CO. You must hitch on to his bandwagon. That's the way successful officers work. Go out of your way to look after his wife and children. Otherwise, Dinesh, I can assure you, you won't go far". I nodded but maintained my views. I had bought my first motorcycle after the exercise and palmed off the Lambretta to my brother. Our BC Maj. DP Sahoonja returned from the course and left on posting to take over 6 Field as CO.

A month later, our Regiment received move orders to the Sugar Sector as part of the 51 Para Brigade, which was already located at Kasauli. Sure enough, being the senior Capt, I was made in charge of the advance party. Our regimental advance party, of which I was a part, under our new 2IC, the great Services wicketkeeper-batsman, Maj. Atma Singh left Agra and made a night halt at Transit Camp Kalka. The next day we were at Jhakri and finally entered the Sugar Sector with a night halt at Pauri, the regimental headquarters. All was not smooth sailing as there were a lot of hold-ups due to roadblocks enroute in the rainy season. After a few days, we proceeded to join the Sikh garrison at Kaurik, a nice long drive, along the River Parachu, bypassing Pooh enroute. I remember Sherry Kalha and I reached late in the evening and reported the arrival to the Adjutant Sikh, the outgoing battalion. The next morning, I was briefed and shown around my battery area, to settle down first before the operational recces were to commence. Maj. SS Ratra, a decorated flyer from the air OP was to join us as our BC, later in Oct 1967. Sherry and I took over the op location, studied the defensive plans against the Chinese including the defensive fire tasks, location of the infantry company's and also defence stores, The outgoing battery of 54 Mountain Regiment also introduced me to the AT Company and the mule loads for the move of battery on mules if required. I was very happy to receive my old IG Maj. YK Kapoor, as the new BM with the Commander, Brig. Bhumi Chand Chahaun in the Sugar Sector in late October 1967. This was expected for a long time after he completed the Staff Course in March

1967. He had to leave for the USSR on a gunnery course at short notice.

Amazingly, our Himachal border with China (Tibet) came to be known as Sugar Sector because of the Shugar Ridge overlooking the last outpost at Kaurik in Lahaul Spiti. Another guess maybe after the famous Shipki La pass in Kinnaur District. The beautiful lush green hills around Simla on the Hindustan Tibet Road are a traveller's delight. I was posted to a comparatively dormant sector in 1967 and again in 1973. The typical Himachali landscape beyond Karcham is terraced fields with houses built. on slopes one above the other. There are heavily forested mountains with pine forest scenery all-around. The eternal snow peaks in the far background are picturesque and inviting for mountaineers. The scenic beauty all around and the eternal snow view are picturesque. The charming Kalpa Valley, the district HQ Kinnaur is another pretty place. For a moment, imagine the greenery here and then its transformation into the desolate and barren landscape when you reach Kaurik, which is more akin to the Ladakh region. Pinecone fruit called *chilgosa*, and all dry fruits, apples especially the inside blood red variety and apricots are galore at lower heights. The summer season was called the ABC season because of the abundance of apples, *badam* and *chilgoza* in summers when families were permitted. The local population is very patriotic and the youngsters are willingly prepared to act as guides and porters for the army.

This indeed was the finest border to serve in. We had about 30 odd jawans in the advance party and we settled down in the brand-new Nissan huts, some still incomplete but handed over all the same. There was a MES team still completing the work. The allotted location was on the banks of the Parachu River, maybe on the old course of the river, as it was full of huge boulders. The problem was the huts were sited within these boulders. There was no way that my thirty men could clear this area for training and assembly. The first day Sherry and I were so demoralized that we kept looking for avenues to find a solution. Not to be cowed down, we sat down with our jawans and asked for ideas. I was more worried that this work had to finish within this month before the arrival of the main party. No JCBs were available for miles. Human ingenuity has no limits and I knew there has to be a way out of this. Our recently promoted MT Havildar Govind Singh suggested we use tow chains of gun tractors along with ropes with two vehicles on either side, to move boulders to the sides of the river. That would also serve the purpose of an anti-flood measure and give us the required space for the gun park, MT Park, gun drill area cum softball ground and a volleyball court. Believe me, working day and night we manually removed all boulders and cleared the area of stones. Our battery area got an additional area for gun cum MT park and someplace for our quarter guard. My exclusive contribution was the construction of the battery quarter guard building made of CGI sheets painted in a disruptive camouflage pattern, which was the talk of the garrison. This was completed well before the CO's Inspection, later in the year. Sherry and I kept planning on the drawing board like architects and helped to make the place as presentable as possible with the scarce manpower we had. We paired up in Nissan huts and welcomed our BC and the remaining battery, in fully completed Nissan huts. The bigger H3 hut was used for our battery officers' mess, which was furnished with gifts by officers. Each time you returned from leave, you brought something as per BC's orders.

52 Battery in Sugar Sector

The 52 Battery Quarter Guard in Sugar Sector

ADS located next door had an excellent doctor in Capt. VS Joglekar, who got along very well with us. Another officer Capt. RS Kane joined the team of myself, Ashish Dube, Rajinder Kumar, TN

Raman and Manmohan Bhardwaj. BC also made sure that we had our battery competitions, individual trade training as well as daily PT and games. He also put me through some pre-course training, spared me for studies as I was unable to find time while I was taking over. 16 SIKH ensured that both of us had a familiarization stay in Kaurik at Pong Maidan and OP Hill, where the Arty OPs were to be located, in the event of a war. I learnt of my nomination to attend the Regimental Officers Course at the School of Arty Deolali on Oct 67. During the course, I met Tally at the Tac Wing where he was the instructor. He was under posting to the regiment and I was happy to help him wind up at Deolali. He took over 51 Battery at Namgiya Dogri with 7 Para. The course was extremely educational for me and it was a good stepping stone for me for courses like Air OP and the Long Gunnery. Jagga, my first BC, had rejoined 49 Battery and was co-located with the headquarters at Pauri. The course went very well for me. During the course, I visited Khadakvasla Pune and stayed with Tiger Behl, still a bachelor, who went out of his way to make my stay as comfortable as possible. After a spot of leave in Delhi, I returned to spend the winter in Kaurik with our team of 52 Battery under our fine gentleman Maj. Ratra.

We all had a very good time in the battery under Kuky Ratra, as he was known. After some time, I learnt that Mrs Ratra (aka Shireen Talibuddin) was my schoolie in St Thomas, though she was much senior to me. We used to train outside even when it was snowing, to ensure that the weather did not get the better of us. Afternoons were spent playing softball and believe me, there was so much healthy rivalry that it invariably ended up in a fight, our BCs decision was final. Later in the evening, everything was a closed matter, nobody ever thought of raising any issues concerning baseball and the discussions on that were forbidden. Nothing like the team having a drink together, served by good old Sultan Singh, the *abdar* from our share of the mess staff, which were allotted by the Regiment. We were visited by the Bollywood team of actors and singers and they stayed in our mess. Everyone was out to impress Daisy and Honey Irani, the stars of yesteryears. Our BC had also arranged welcome *mashals*, on the hill opposite, for them lighted up exactly at the time they arrived. Both girls grew very fond of Brando and Birdie, during their short stay. I, too, was enjoying my stay under Kuky Ratra, a wonderful man who could take cudgels on your behalf, fight for his officers and his battery. One felt reassured, he wasn't the guy who let anyone down. I would have liked to continue in the same team and was enjoying my stay. I now learnt officially that I had been selected for the AOP course at EFS Bidar to commence on 05 Aug 1968. There was a garrison dining out in which then lt Col. MS Panwar spoke on my role in bringing up the most difficult location and bade me farewell. I thought it was a great gesture for him to attend the function in the battery mess. Ratra, who was an air OP pilot himself, gave me his blessings to become a double winger and later qualify with LGSC and staff college qualification. My stay with the 17 Para Field Regiment and the wonderful team since remains a happy part of my memories. It only affirms one's faith in one's self and to do one's duty without asking for anything in return. Yet the result comes in one form or the other. I said au revoir to the Regiment the following day at Pauri when I was dined out by another of our wonderful COs, Lt. Col. MC Dogra.

Learning to Fly and Operations

The first problem was to locate Bidar in the Railway Time table as there was no station like Bidar in Karnataka. It was Mohammadabad Bidar and with that, my railway warrant and movement order were issued. Ten of us, army officers were selected out of the list of 24 gunner officers found medically fit. We arrived at Bidar and were transported to our barrack located alongside the cadet's barracks. It was a makeshift arrangement as at Pilots Training Establishment at Allahabad, had just shifted lock stock and barrel to Bidar and ours was the second course along with the cadets. The only saving grace was that we used to drive down to the Officers Mess, which was about 3 km away. We had a few more officers training with us. From the Navy, Lt. PP Sharma and Sub Lt. Faggy Mehta (later the Navy Chief). There was a Flying Officer from the Royal Malaysian Air Force Hatta bin Ibrahim and two more Iraqi officers, whose name slips my memory (one was Kasim). Being the first exposure to the Air Force, it was fun dining with our bachelor instructors. Since Bidar town had nothing to offer, most officers and families gravitated to the mess. Officers and ladies were very informal and we got to know almost everyone by their first name. We also t met our squadron mates from NDA, doing their degree course at MCEME Secundrabad. We exchanged very pleasant memories of our stay at the NDA.

We started training on HT-2 trainers in earnest. First, we were asked to master Pilots Notes which I crammed till it became second nature. We had a good dose of ground subject lectures which formed part of the trainee pilots training. My roommate Arun Bhargava and I got along very well, except for his perpetual problem, that he could never be on time for any parade. I used to push him out of his bed at 4.30 every morning after the alarm went off and it took one full hour for him to get dressed in flying overalls and flying boots. As the course senior again, I had to report to the AF Instructor at 5:30 sharp for Met briefing. Flying commenced after we cleared tests on Pilots Notes. My first instructor was Sqn Ldr AS Bansi, a Sardarji, with a trimmed beard whose reputation travelled far and wide as an Army officer hater, God alone knows why. Jogi, my coursemate from the previous course warned me, "Dabbu, God help you if you get Bansi as your instructor" and lo and behold, Bansi was waiting for me. The first few sorties were good and he always asked, "Feels like driving a car, doesn't it?" By about 5 hours, around the sixth or seventh sortie, Bansi lost his top when I mishandled controls that he had given to me mid-flight. He straight away got the controls back from me and went into a steep dive, pulled up over the airfield and kept gaining height up to about 10k and commenced his aerobatics. First a loop, a barrel roll and then steep turns and kept on trying manoeuvres I couldn't decipher. We got back after the sortie and the debriefing commenced. It seems I had annoyed him. I had unlearned whatever was taught in the past two weeks. I was too stiff on the controls and appeared to be doing foot drills instead of flying. He also stated that was the trouble with all you army officers. He advised me not to wear flying boots and from now on, wear canvas shoes for flying.

Unfortunately, around this time, my great friend Bully Sangha with me on the pillion met with a minor accident in the market. It was an oversized bull, quite enraged by some shopkeeper, came charging wildly and somehow, we were on his radar. The net result was we were overthrown from the scooter. Bully, tough as he is, just had minor scratches on his chin but I landed on my right elbow. There was a gash, which got me six stitches and was off flying for three weeks. It was now the end of September and six of our coursemates had already cleared solo. Two were suspended from flying and sent back as unfit for pilot duties. Both Sangha and I were dreading the prospects of being sent back. Sangha was a Regiment of Arty team polo player and he used to say, "Either I go solo or I play polo. 'We also knew the Air Force game well. When there are interruptions in flying, it's ideal to keep giving progress checks before throwing the officer out.

Flying an HT-2 in Bidar

Luckily, I resumed flying under another instructor, Flt. Lt. Peter Boosey, a happy go lucky Anglo Indian, whom every Army officer liked. He had a soft corner for the eight of us. He gave me three or four sorties and I still was unsure of going solo, because of the break-in flying. The next day the Flight Commander Bansi was on leave and

Boosey was officiating. He comes to the crew room and says, "Captain, come on. Let's go". When I flew with him, I did not realize it was a solo check. After about 30 mins we returned to the dispersal and he asked me on the radio, "Hey Capt., can you go solo?". When I said "Yes Sir," he got out of the aircraft and gave me a thumbs up and off I went again to the runaway. I did all the checks taught, opened full power and got airborne, did a left-handed circuit called downwind banked left again. Called finals on the radio and landed safely. This was around 10 October 1968, when I had almost given up. Boosey, a great believer in the maxim, "What goes up, must come down". When he debriefed me, he deliberately didn't inform me of the solo check. Had he done so, he said I would have become tense. That was my best sortie ever. My solo was also good, which he had watched from the ATC. Next week, were three more solo checks and there was no looking back. I had such a concentrated dose of flying that everything else was secondary. Arun, my roommate and Sangha were pillars of strength and kept encouraging me. Had it not been for them I may not have passed. Bad luck had always dogged me earlier but Arun told me that it was my good luck really that Bansi was away on leave that day. I completed 75 hours on HT-2 with 60 hours coming in the last month.

With instructor Flt. Lt. Peter Boosey

Around December first week Arun with me on the pillion moved from Bidar to our new destination Deolali. Paramjit, Sangha, Karve, Sawhney, Madan Pal and MG Singh left by train and agreed to carry our steel boxes and bedrolls. We moved via Hyderabad Solapur Pune together with PP Sharma and Faggy Mehta, later the Naval Chief and PP Sharma on their Jawa bike. The countryside was very drab and there were very few eating places enroute. Driving also was not fun because of the poor road conditions. Our Naval friends peeled off at Pune and drove to Bombay. We covered the Pune-Deolali route around 900-1000 Kms, in two days with one night halt enroute. At Pune, we drove into CME where our 23rd Coursemates were doing their Degree Course. They laid on a fabulous dinner in their Officers Institute for us. Our great sapper friends, Prakash Suri, Kohli, CD Puri, BK Singh, Lalit Idnani, Narinder Aul, Bhatia, Pramod Agarwal Awasthi, and Madhav Arren organized a very good get together, full of light-hearted banter, merriment and laughter. It was a very enjoyable all bachelor evening, we cannot forget. Our NDA course spirit was still intact!!!

Getting back to Deolali once again was quite exhilarating with many coursemates and friends around. Our course of eight officers was allotted P7 and P9 Single officers block facing M/s Selections. For a change, we had a room to ourselves along with some of our coursemates in the permanent staff. A 1-Ton vehicle was used to take us to Nasik Road where our Air OP training flight was located. No 5 Air OP flight was the training flight for the conversion from HT-2s to Krishaks. Air OP was still an air force unit, officered by the Army with two components, viz. Army component of artillery operators, drivers and few gunners, around 35 all ranks and an Air Force component of two officers and 50 airmen and 10 civilians un-enrolled. The flying instructors were qualified flying instructors trained by the IAF at Tambaram. Maj. CM Bhalla was the Chief Flying Instructor with the other two, Majs Sukhdev Singh and RS Mann.

Budding pilots at Nasik Road

These three were also instructors for ground subjects. Most of the ground subjects pertained to air OP tactics, airmanship, artillery shoots, communication and aircraft flight checks Course took off well and the weather was excellent for flying. Sukhdev was my instructor who continued till the first solo. He hardly ever spoke on the radio and believed in sign language. He left for Staff College and Maj. Virendar Singh replaced him. Flying a Krishak a high wing aircraft was different from HT-2. Having got that well we were all put through a solo check at the 10-hour stage. Bhalla checked me and cleared me, after a repeat sortie. Actually, they deliberately did not clear you the first time so that you did not get overconfident. During our training, Air Chief Arjan Singh came on a farewell visit and met the officers and airmen. We had other officers in the flight like Capts Sukhwinder Bhangu, MS Reen, RC Gupta and Raje Jain in 5 Air OP and Capts Suresh Kripalani, Pat & Nat in No 1 Air OP. There were 15 pilots on the two flights at Nasik Road those days. Though we continued to stay at Deolali, being the responsibility of the School of Artillery, we used to commute to Nasik Road, six days a week.

We had a healthy respect for our very experienced flying instructors, more mature than the Air Force instructors, with infinite patience and treated you with respect. The greatest advantage was that they were from the Regiment of Artillery and had a lot of regimental spirit. By about April 1969, we had completed 140 hours of total flying which enabled you to qualify as a full-fledged air OP pilot. It was a dream come true for me. I remembered my days in Dehra Dun when I first saw my cousin Capt. Sushil, proudly displaying the embroidered blue wings with the artillery grenade in the centre, He had said, "You've got to slog for it". How true he was. We got our wings pinned on our chests by the Commandant School of Artillery, Brig. KD Vashisht on 31 May 1969 in a wing presentation parade in front of the quarter guard of the Mountain Regiment (their PT ground). After joining our flights in Nasik Road, we settled down in the Artillery Centre Mess. Madan Pal and I were in adjacent rooms while Sangha and Paramjit stayed on the airfield. Maddy & I were invariably together for all functions whether at the Centre or the THI as I was without a conveyance for some time. Father retired as Principal on 30 Jun 69 the day I had completed six years of service. He got an assignment in Meerut University for five years as Pro-Vice-Chancellor cum Director and was busy plying between Meerut and Dehradun

Wing Ceremony in Deolali

Air OP pilots ready to take off

On receiving my wings, I immediately dashed off a letter to my cousin Maj. Sushil who was then doing his BM's tenure in J&K for his blessings. Hoping to emulate his example. I had joined 5 Independent Air OP Flight now commanded by Maj. BS Ahluwalia. Maj. CM Bhalla was the Chief Flying Instructor, the Adjutant Capt. Sukhwinder Bhangu with other Capts MS Reen, RC Gupta, & Raje Jain. We had an Engineering Officer Flying Officer RD Deshpande from the Air Force. I was without conveyance for the last one year and bought a Vespa scooter in Dehradun and brought it along Nasik Road by train. Flying was pretty well organized every day. We used to come before the first light for briefing in the crew room and were given regular flying early morning. After flying we went home for breakfast. I had joined a wonderful team with both majors from the same course but absolutely no friction between them. The flight had a very healthy environment between airmen and jawans, who were well integrated, hardworking and well-disciplined.

I applied formally to my CO, for permission to get married two months before 25 years. A special dispensation was made and the permission granted. The wedding was fixed for 20 October 1969 and I left for Dehradun around 10 Oct. Since I had incurred heavy expenditure on my brother, Indresh's trip to Canada, I had to borrow about Rs 1500 from the flight *bania*. Manju and I had made plans for a two weeks honeymoon in Srinagar. Around the 19th, friends Sangha, Paramjit and Arun Bhargava arrived to join us for the wedding. Other friends who attended the wedding were Capts from my 17 Para, Naresh Bhatara, RP Rai and Ravi Kant. All the festivities went off well with a lot of fanfare. Between the *pheras*, I noticed that all my friends were nowhere to be seen. Normally on the day of the wedding drinking is a strict taboo, a bit of drinking in the quiet was for only my friends and close relatives. I did not know this, till Ravi Kant brought some water for me to drink, in a stainless-steel glass containing neat scotch. The dinner which followed was under good old Kwalitys' which I think was well laid out, the excellent cuisine I don't remember now. Bida followed the next day and the allied functions after the reception at Doon Flora.

As planned, the newlyweds left for Saharanpur by road on 24 Oct 69. Mother had cautioned both of us, earlier, about the jewellery and advised that a steel box was safer than a huge suitcase. We then caught a train for Pathankot, which was the terminus. As was the form, we took the officer bus to go to the transit camp at Pathankot. After breakfast, we called for a taxi to drop us at Jammu airport. We were to board the Indian Airlines flight to Srinagar which used to cost Rs 40 after 50% army concession. My luggage comprised one steel box, bedroll and one attaché case. The driver placed the bedroll on top of the luggage carrier and strapped it casually, saying it was very safe. The steel box went in the boot of the taxi. Somehow the bedroll flew off without our noticing it and we reached the airport minus one item. Suddenly we found a local cyclist with the bedroll perched on top of his bicycle heading for the entrance to the airport. This local simpleton handed over the bedroll to me. We were mighty relieved and tipped him handsomely for his honesty and sincerity.

We had got the reservations confirmed through Manju's uncle Shri Kripal Chand, the Director of Finance Indian Airlines. The station manager was pacing up and down waiting to meet us. We had already delayed the flight by not showing up. After seeing us come in, he said, "Capt. Mathur, would you please allow the Indian Airlines to take off?" We had already caused a delay of 25 minutes, the baggage just rolled in and we were checked in. With embarrassment written on our faces, we boarded the flight. Everyone noticed a black steel box and a huge bedroll, which was an eyesore to everyone. On arrival at Srinagar, the carriage of the box and bedroll in kandis also posed problems for the coolies. We reached the Hotel Lala Rukh near Lal Chowk, in the city where we spent almost two weeks. This was Manju's second visit and she took pains to be my guide. Those days there was peace and tranquillity in Kashmir. The lush green pastures, the mountain peaks all around, and the valley teeming with tourists provided the idyllic setting for our romance, it seems. We visited during the autumn and nature was getting ready for the harsh winter. We went sightseeing to all the places, you name it. Dal Lake, and shikara ride to Char chinar and back, Shalimar, Chashme Shahi and Nishat Gardens, Shankaracharya Temple besides a day trip to Gulmarg. As soon as the money ran out, we returned to Dehradun. We spent a few days up to Diwali with our parents before moving to Delhi.

We returned from leave around 08 Nov 69. As I got down at the Railway station Nasik Road in uniform, we were received by a whole lot of our officers and ladies. They ordered me to change into civvies which I had, we were taken in jeeps to the entrance of the Air OP near Gandhi Nagar, Nasik. At this point, we were to disembark and board a new conveyance. A 1 Ton trailer with two chairs placed inside driven by two mules. My great pal Madan Pal, seated on a third chair trailer, was the driver with a whip. Two buglers were leading the trailer. As soon as the bugle was sounded, mules took off on a gallop, with the two of us clinging to our chairs and scaring Manju to no end. We were then heralded through the Air OP officers colony and the airmen's billets and driven to the airfield. Amazingly, my colleagues on my flight, all five of them in formation, gave us a flypast by dipping their wings in turns. We were then driven to our Flight Commanders house in the Air OP Colony for breakfast. What a wonderful way to welcome us into the fold of the Air OP family, something to remember for life. The best part was a tent pitched in Air OP Colony with bare minimum furniture – one cot- one dressing table, two chairs and one table was shown to us where we found our luggage placed nicely on tables. Manju threw a fit on seeing this collection and said "I thought you had arranged proper married accommodation". This joke was played as I had yet to attain the age of 25 years which was necessary to be entitled to a married accommodation. After the joke was over, I moved into temporary accommodation of one of my flight pilots, who had proceeded on leave for two months, followed by four more till my turn came for temporary accommodation. I had five shifts in all and thanks to my dear friends in the Air OP. The leave program was so well organized by the Adjutant Sukhi and the flight commander, which ensured that I always had a place to stay.

What followed next were the lunches and dinners at every air OP officer residence as the entire lot had called us for the first This was the best time of our lives for the two of us, enjoying life together, getting to know each other and the warm company of our friends both at Deolali and Nasik Road. We were so engrossed with our social commitments that we forgot to attend a dinner in our honour hosted by Maj. KLK Singh and his affectionate wife, Yash. Of course, I got a rocket from Majors KM Seth, PN Jaywant and all Seventeers. To make up we hosted a party in the Centre Ladies Room for all Seventeeners. My in-laws joined us for about a fortnight's stay in the temporary accommodation, made from used CGI sheets, located inside the mess complex. This accommodation was constructed with troop labour and was known as the honeymoon quarters. They had outlived their life which kept getting extended, due to an acute shortage of married accommodation in the station. While terming the temporary sheds as "really temporary" with dry sanitation, Dad too felt that the housing in the Army had still a long way to go. We did up the house as best as we could and also entertained guests in their honour. We hosted a thanksgiving party for all Centre and Air OP officers at the Gazebo, which was a grand affair. The Centre was really good for socialising. We saw English movies regularly every Saturday at Topchi followed by dinner in the Mess. Sometimes the air OP bachelors used to raid us, which was welcome as they invariably called for their food from the Mess to be served by mess waiters.

Life was great with the bachelor friends Sangha, Paramjit & Madan Pal paying regular calls and seeing us almost daily. We had also intermingled with the Centre crowd very well. Montu Choudhary, Raghuvanshi, Agarwals, Rupi Brar and Keshav Bhargava, Karpu Datta also joined in. Suresh Kripalani, Rupi Brar, RP Singh, Sittoo Bhargava and Karpu Datta got married around the same time. The last to join the newlyweds were P Madhavan, a good friend and his wife Lata. The Centre Commandant, Col. BP Bhalla and his wife a very pleasant and sociable couple, added colour and charm to the social life in the Centre. The Artillery Reunion was held during this time and a very well laid out set of events followed. There were lots of top Army brass which comprised the Colonel Commandants, Gens Kumaramangalam and KP Candeth, JFR Jacob and many other Brigadiers attending the guest lunch to which we both were invited. I was the first to find out that my ex-CO RC Butalia, now a Brigadier at Bareilly, is one of the invitees. Very hesitantly, I ventured across with Manju, introduced her to him. He is very warm and effusive towards both of us. I was absolutely stunned when he told her, "Manju, you have got married to one of my best officers". Speechless, I remained mum while he made discreet enquiries about her father, an ex-Ordnance officer, who had just retired as Director Stores & Purchase ONGC Dehradun. I told her he hated my guts and don't you believe a word of what he said. All said and done, Butch had won me and my wife over and I admire him for his magnanimity and change of heart. There were few other officers we were very fond of, Maj. Anil Heble, and his wife Nina, Lt. Col. SME Adams (popularly known as *Baba Adam*) of Arty Association, Maj. DT Prabhakar & Maj. Jel Bitto, in whose houses we had stayed till a temporary accommodation was allotted to me. Anil and Nina are our good friends, even today and remember our good times staying together.

Things were moving very well till the flying mishap took place. On 4th Feb 1970, Krishak aircraft BN 1019 flown by me developed engine power loss while I was practising force landing in a nearby cultivated area close to Gangapur Dam. As I was practising an emergency landing, the jawans in the training camp located nearby were very surprised that I landed near their camp. Normally the aircraft with an engine running on low power comes down to 50-100 feet and once the pilot opens full power, it climbs to complete the manoeuvre. In my case, the aircraft refused to climb and I had no choice but to save myself and land there itself. I came back and immediately reported the matter to the flight commander, Maj. BS Ahluwalia, who gave me a patient hearing, In the court of inquiry that followed, my boss supported and commended me for my alertness. After getting finally cleared by a court of inquiry, I resumed flying in about 15 days. I express my deep gratitude to the Almighty God for saving my life and to Maj. BS Ahluwalia for supporting me to the hilt. The undying spirit of Air OP, not letting each other down, took care of my career.

During my flying stint, I made frequent trips to Pune and Bombay by Krishak either for official work with No 2 Wing for official duties or cross-country training. Sometimes it was combined with private work at CDA(Officers) or some purchases in Pune. There was also the first Krishak ferry to Sulur in which Manjeet Reen was my senior pilot. Subsequently, I did several ferries, all by myself, till it was my turn to train Bhim and other juniors. Flying had become a passion and I liked the spirit, camaraderie and brotherhood between the air OP family. The additional allowances of Rs 400 per month made everyone jealous of you and most of us had the disposable income to go in for a car, in addition to a scooter. Two more pilots Raj Gogna and Bhardwaj joined us in 5 Flight with the exit of Reen and RC Gupta. Some more changes took place when Sukhwinder was posted out to 659 Air OP Squadron. He was the life of the Air OP with his daredevil flying and physical exploits as a goalkeeper for the Air OP hockey team. After his move to Kumbhigram, while on a detachment in Turial Mizoram, he had a fatal accident in mid-1970. We felt sorry for his distraught wife, Suman and her two boys.

Manju had adjusted very well with social life in Nasik Deolali. She also joined the ladies Club at Mrs Bhalla's invitation and was quite popular with all ladies. She sang ghazals and bhajans and classical music at all functions and get-togethers. As advised by my flight commander I appeared for my promotion exam Part D which was a written exam of six subjects and I passed all subjects in one go. We then decided on starting a family and Manju went to Meerut for her confinement sometime in March 1971. On 29 April 1971, our daughter Priya was born in MH Meerut. Finally, after a wait of almost nine months, we were allotted a new house with two servant quarters. The servants were permanent but the occupants of the quarter weren't. We had a full-time *ayah* for Priya and another one who helped in the kitchen. My mother who had accompanied us to help settle Manju with the newborn was of great help. On one of my trips to Pune, on official duty, we learnt that some money was being surrendered by the station being unutilised for car loans. We asked the officer concerned if AOP could be allotted some of it. Both Bhim Khemani and I were allotted Rs 12 k each for the car. A car was arranged for me at Lucknow by my brother-in-law, Anand, then the local Fiat boss there. I collected the same and drove up to Nasik Road with a driver who was then sent back. My flight commander, BS Ahluwalia, who had taken so much pain to make me fully ops was replaced by Maj. KB Deiswal. Another very helpful officer was our CFI, Maj. CM Bhalla, a great flyer and wonderful man to serve with, was replaced by Maj. SC Mathur. I had got over the flying glitches and was all set. I had two or three ferries to Bangalore and spent almost 250 hours on Krishaks during this period, which was good going.

While this took place, I received my posting orders for a new raising, No 12 (I) Air OP flight in the same station. This flight was raised under 25 ED Deolali. My great friends, Sangha and Bhim Khemani were the next to follow. The flight was to be fully raised by March 1971. Till Maj. Atma reported, I was the first officiating OC and then KP Shastri. We were allotted new aircraft from HAL Bangalore which we collected in a matter of three weeks between Sangha and myself, being the only two fully ops pilots then. During our tenure at Deolali, we had the pleasure to welcome another old colleague Charlie Maitra and his new bride Veena to the station. Sangha, Bhim and I had made massive preparations for their welcome in the traditional air OP style at Deolali Railway Station. Charlie and Veena got the wind of our preparations and made changes to their plans. Veena, who was posted as the Cantt Executive Officer at Deolali, decided to stay back after the wedding for a few days attachment at New Delhi. Therefore, they travelled on two separate days and joined up here at Deolali, much to our disappointment. However, we kept raiding their bungalow at all odd hours at night, as our retribution. Soon thereafter, I was also given the job of proceeding to Jodhpur for op familiarization of the

Infantry Division Sector in May 1971. I remember being briefed in front of the map in the Division ops room as follows :

"Consequent to the happenings in East Pakistan and the heavy exodus of refugees into India, there is every likelihood of a war with Pakistan shortly. If that were to happen, we must be prepared to put our operational plans into effect. What those plans are, will not be disclosed at your level, but suffice to say that your flight being an integral part of this division would be mobilized to move to this sector when we feel that you need to move. You will familiarize yourself with terrain in the divisional sector and look for likely landing grounds from where you may be asked to operate when required. We plan to hold an op alert when you would be asked to participate with all aircraft. Tentative dates are 01 - 25 October 1971. It is added here that HQ Southern Command will also be moving to Jodhpur in the event of the war. For any queries, please refer to the GSO2 Ops who would be taking you on the familiarization sorties of the sector "

Maj. RK Verma, the GSO2 Ops also an ex veteran CO from 5 Air OP Flight flew with me to Jaisalmer, Pokhran Ramgarh, Kishangarh, Ghotaru, Sadhewala, and Longewala and Tanot. We completed the op recce in two days with an overnight stay at Jaisalmer with a Rajasthan Armed Constabulary battalion. I got back via Ahmedabad and met Lt. Col. MC Dogra, our spirited CO who had taken over from Col. KK Hazari, then serving in NCC. Nothing had changed, this wonderful and warm-hearted personality had brought packed lunch for me. How very thoughtful!!! On my return to Nasik Road, I tried to brief the flight commander Atma Singh but he just wasn't receptive. Probably he never expected that one day we would be flying there in the same area for operations.

As the war clouds emerged on the horizon sometime in October 1971, the field regiment was the first to move to Jodhpur/Jaisalmer by train, I had barely settled in the new house with Manju, my mother and Priya, barely six months old. Orders for the move of 12 Flt. were received on the morning of 17 October 1971. We were told that rolling stock would be in position by evening. Atma just didn't discuss who would be the OC Train and straight away ruled that it would be me. Aircraft were to follow after three days. We had to load in our transport and move to Deolali railway siding in the evening. Loading was to be complete that night as the train was to move out the next morning. As there was a paucity of lights at the station, I used a few jeep headlights to illuminate the area. After completing the loading in the Cs and Fs. I decided to go back home for my dinner, while the drivers were busy lashing the vehicles. At about 9.30 pm, I took a driverless jeep and drove it myself to the Centre. Unfortunately, it was one of the jeeps used for illuminating the siding and the battery had drained off. The lights dimmed near the causeway Waldi River, as it goes down. I was planning to stop at the other end of the causeway when they failed. I didn't stop in the middle of the causeway. With no lights and trying to reach the other end, I had rammed into an animal cart in front. The jeep was slightly damaged but the animal died. I paid Rs 300 to the animal cart owner on the spot and later for the jeep repairs, as per my flight commanders orders. I admit my mistake to have taken a driverless jeep, though under wartime conditions. The next morning the jeep was loaded in the train and covered by tarpaulin to not attract attention. The train had been combined with the Division Loc Battery and we moved on white lot priority to Jodhpur. After off-loading at Jodhpur, the whole night, we transshipped to a metre gauge train to Barmer. From Barmer, we moved by road to Jaisalmer, which we reached late at night on 20 October. I suddenly realized my second anniversary was still around its dying hours and our Flt. Lt. CP Naidu and I called for a bottle of rum from the officers' mess. I also asked the airmen and jawans to have a drink on me. We were allotted tent plinths by the AF Station under Wg Cdr MS Bawa, the next day. All four aircraft arrived the next day flown by Atma, Sangha, Bhim Khemani, KP Shastri. I think the fifth aircraft arrived later flown in by Bhim. We stayed at Jaisalmer for a month or so and did regular familiarisation sorties of the landing grounds (ALGs) and the border. We also did some training with the Air Force. The mess was functioning with our nucleus staff in the base ops, the underground shelter for both the Air Force and Army.

The month of November at Jaisalmer was spent in preparations and mobilization for the impending operations. I was flying to Sulur with one aircraft due for major servicing and collecting one new aircraft allotted to my flight. I took the shortest route via Ahmedabad – Nasik Bidar- Bangalore and then on to Sulur. The new aircraft N 970 was ready for the customer flight. Being the last aircraft in the hangar at HAL one engineer also requested that he wanted to accompany me for checking the instruments. I then requested for the engineer and took off towards the local flying area for the flight test. While flying over Ulsoor Lake I suddenly discovered, the elevator did not respond when I moved the joystick. The flight engineer seated on the co-pilot's seat was unable to explain. This emergency was immediately reported by me in a 'mayday' call to Bangalore air traffic control. Disconnection of the elevator from the joystick is something very rare but serious enough. I flew the aircraft from the local flying area back to the airfield with the help of an elevator trimmer. Everything was going on fine and

I was confident of making a safe landing. While making my final approach, I rounded off slightly high but landed safely. I was medically examined and found fit. A court of enquiry under AF Training Command Bangalore found me not to blame, as the cause of the accident was a bell crank pulley that had fallen off in flight, which may be due to faulty maintenance. HAL quickly covered up the small damages and allotted another aircraft to me to ferry to my unit. After a flying check, I resumed my journey back to my flight at Ranau. All kinds of stories were afloat at HAL Bangalore. There was a metal piece found in the aircraft which read "Long Live Mao" etched with something sharp. Since the enquiry was closed by HAL at its level, there was no scope to report anywhere. Whatever was said in favour of my taking appropriate action or pilot to be commended for his alertness and flying skills, remained unknown to everyone. Anyway, for me, that was the third mishap in the year of which two were air accidents and one jeep accident. So much for my karma!

In the meanwhile, after my return, apprehending danger to Krishak engines due to suction of sand air cleaners and its ingestion in engines, Atma received orders for conversion to Pushpaks at Jaipur Flying Club. The first to go was Bhim Khemani and then myself. This was around 3 Dec 1971 afternoon. when I was having a cup of tea with a relative in Jaipur city. There was a blackout out and then we heard the news. I learnt that our airfields had been bombed by Pakistan and the war had just been declared. All flights and trains to Jodhpur had been suspended. Now how do I reach my unit? I requested the flying club instructor Navin Chandra to finish off my Pushpak flying training and allow me to go back to my unit. After the mandatory three hours dual flying on Pushpak, I got my solo on

Pushpak on 4 Dec 1971. Since moves by day were prohibited and by night only side lights were allowed. I also fixed up my move the same night in an Ordnance Depot 1 Ton proceeding with stores to Jodhpur. I reached Jodhpur in the early hours of 5 Dec and had to wait for the next night to move to Jaisalmer. As soon as we moved out of the Jodhpur Ordnance unit, with sidelights, the driver did not notice the Indian Oil tanker coming from the opposite direction and rammed into it. I now had to get out of this mess without getting involved. I slipped out quietly with my attaché case and looked for some other means of conveyance. Luckily, there was a Home Guards jeep going up to Phalodi, which offered me a lift. I reached Phalodi late at night. Next door was the police station, whose sub-inspector was going to Jaisalmer. I requested him to help as I had to get to my unit at Jaisalmer as early as possible. I reached Jaisalmer airfield on the night 6/7 Dec, I was dressed in my flying overalls, carrying my Id card, a suitcase and no weapon. Some airmen had never even heard of an Army Captain flying overalls. It took some time for them to understand who I was. Total panic had set in amongst the security guards. After a lot of cross-questioning, I was allowed to speak to the base commander who allowed me entry at 4 am. I was picked up by a flight vehicle, reached my tent and found that the flight hand already moved for Ranau ALG. The flight engineer, Warrant Officer Brahma Nand briefed me that as per instructions, I was to fly out to Ranau in the last aircraft which was left behind. This aircraft had some technical problems, a day prior, and has also to be air tested before the move. After resting for about two hours, I got ready to fly N 959 for the air test. The ATC refused the airtest and told me to get airborne and fly to Ranau instead. I lined up at the beginning of the runaway, opened full power and was mighty relieved when the aircraft got airborne,

Maintaining the concealed approach and height of 50 ft, I followed the road to the forward landing ground at Ranau. After crossing Ramgarh and Ghantyali ka Mandir, identified our ALG at Ranau landed carefully around 8.30 am or so and was welcomed by our colleagues. Both the boss and Sangha played very crucial roles in the battle. I was nominated for the next sortie around 9.45 am and headed straight to Longewala area and way ahead towards boundary pillar 638. I had a rear observer seated behind, saw some tanks and vehicles still burning, knocked out by our Hunters. Some equipment and guns and trailers were left by the fleeing enemy. I was flying well ahead of my post at Longewala and had a grandstand view of the enemy's tanks withdrawal which kicked up a lot of dust. The battle of Longewala was already over the afternoon of 3 Dec. It was the engagement of the fleeing elements, which I was observing and engaging with the Arty guns, at their maximum range. I did see one of the AD guns and its crew getting a direct hit, and some retreating heavy vehicles also being hit by our shells which I reported from time to time.

As in Mahabharata, for Air OP pilots it is a gentleman's war. We fly round the clock from first to last light, when the war is over for us. One aircraft flies and is replaced by another till the daylight hours are over. Reporting of information formed a vital part for the next few days. There was no movement after the Pakistan armour spearhead had been halted at Longewala on 4 Dec. We spent evenings in a shared 180 pounder tent by rotation where the mess staff served us drinks and snacks followed by early dinner. Those days, Pakistan low flying bombers were regularly attacking Jaisalmer and the satellite airfields. Unmindful of all this, Sangha, Charlie Maitra, Bhim Khemani, CP Naidu, KP Shastri and self-drank our Old Monk regularly. We were confident that no bomber aircraft would come for this small landing ground and we ignored all warnings. What came to be known as 'dynamite' was the fried *sabut masoor* dal with red chillies sprinkled, which the mess had been bought well before the war commenced Light-hearted banter and some entertainment followed every evening, sometimes even *teen patti* became popular till one day it came to Atma's notice. He immediately put a stop to this and warned us to desist from the same.

DG Arty Maj. Gen. KD Vashisht in Rajasthan Sector

After the war, I received an award of Mention in Despatches for my performance during the operations. The Pushpaks were now flown in from Jaipur to replace the unserviceable Krishaks. Having qualified on Pushpaks, both Bhim and I ferried five aircraft from Jaipur. When applications were asked for after the war for the LGSC course beginning in July 1972, I decided to apply. Few batchmates like Natarajan had already completed this course, just before the war and was doing a tenure as IG before getting back to the air OP. I was unlucky in the air OP with two forced landings and when the time came for proving myself, I was away on temporary duty. I could just make it to the unit after one more road accident, the thought now looked ominous. I wasn't chickening out of flying but I thought of greener pastures outside. I was posted on staff to the School of Artillery and I came in March 1972 when Manju was down with jaundice. Most of the time was spent looking after Manju and Priya before I could think of coming back to gunnery at the grassroots level.

Our Course commenced on 05 July 1972 and the all-important basic leg did not go off well for me for various reasons. Course IG SM Chand seemed quite cut up as I was busy with my MH trips to see my wife who was admitted there. Other members of the IG team were not favourably inclined to me because they felt that a student officer has been given permanent accommodation, in exchange for houses with Natarajan on Depot Battery Road with one in the Artillery Centre. My mother had left by then for Meerut and there was no one to look after my one-year-old daughter. My sister Anjana and her daughters Jyotsna and Harshi came over to stay with us for a few days. They did their best but were unable to help me out with my studies which were neglected from the very beginning. I never realised that I could go down so much in Maths, Ballistics, Electronics, Equipment and other legs like Survey. Most equipment tests are assessed by JCO/NCOs where apple polishing does matter and I was averse to it. Even though I fared well in shooting in Battery & Regimental Gunnery, which were my strength, I had lost out on this important basic leg initially and could never make up. I thought I had fared the best in Tactics leg so that I could improve my grading to BY, but that did not work as I was placed somewhere after 20th on the course by our Tactical Wing IG Kulbir, whereas I expected to be in the first three. I felt I was deliberately done down in Equipment & Battery Gunnery assessments by JCO/ NCOs as I could have been given a higher grade, had our Course IGs been more considerate. They always got the impression that air OP pilots can never do well on LGSC, you are doing well enough for CY, the only course where I did not fare well despite my best efforts.

Our stay at Depot Battery Road Deolali was otherwise excellent. We had a lot of friends on the course who were frequent visitors to our home. Jogi from my course, PK Sharma VrC, MG Singh from Air OP course and three from 17 Para besides me were on this course, viz, Dube, Brando and Birdie. We had created a record of sorts but being from the same battery, 52. A large number of officers have forced bachelors for the Basic leg and another lot got married after it. As a result, we had a lot of young brides, all at once. I remember Jogi & Chanchal were the first to be received at Deolali Station sometimes around 12 December 1972 when they arrived by Pathankot Express late at night, Our LGSC crowd comprising Brando, SPS Gill, Pappu Bains, Birdie, Sandhu, Shivi Sidhu, Keen Jetley and self were there to welcome them and eight outriders escorting them to THI guest room. Naresh Katyal and Munna were the next to arrive and stayed with us at our Depot Battery house for a while. Priya got used to staying with the full-time *ayah* in the quarters and would see me only after I got back from classes. Manju was admitted for almost one month when the course commenced. My deepest regret is that I didn't decide to drop the family at Delhi before the course commenced.

After the course got over, I was posted to 9 Para Field Regt under Lt. Col. SS Ratra under whom I had served earlier in 52 Battery. I moved to command 23 Battery of 9 Para in the Sugar Sector. The rest of the regiment was located in Dagshai. Manju and Priya moved to Doon Flora, Dehradun to be with my parents. My luggage and car moved to Dagshai in Aug 73 and remained in Q Stores. Car was kept in COs garage as there was no other place available. Nimi Mahajan was the 2IC and other BCs were SC Kuthiala and KC Satapathy. The Sub Maj. was Ghisa Ram also ex-17 Para Field Regiment.

To Himachal Pradesh and Back to Agra

My tenure in Sugar Sector with 23 Para field Battery commenced in Aug 73 and it was at Pooh, where the Sector HQ, with good old 2 Para was located. The weather was quite good at this time of the year and I was really happy to be back to regimental life after five years. The Sugar Sector was not new to me, the battery location was. This was the old location of 8 Para converted into a battery location now. I replaced my old friend Karpu Datta as BC. My team comprised Bansal, Tandon, Rosemeyer, later Daler Singh and Gurulal Singh Toor. Subedar Tara Chand was the Senior JCO with Innasi Muthu and Yeshkaran Singh, the other JCOs. I was not particularly fond of 9 Para Field Regiment as they were the ones who pushed us out from Agra in 1967, but when I saw the Regiment at close quarters now, it is indeed a very fine, well-knit and spirited *Thambi* unit, now on the way to becoming a mixed class unit. The josh and spirit were as just as good as the 17 Para Field Regiment, if not better.

Coming back from air OP to regimental life was a cultural shock for me but I got over it fast. We still had our morning PT, some gun drill to follow and other trade training in this high-altitude area. As the weather became colder the training was carried out indoors. PT continued in the open, though with all of us being well clad in our winter clothing. It was essential to keep fit by daily exercise and games. Night training was carried out twice every week so that once could keep trained for night operations. We also carried out battery deployment exercises outdoors with all guns and equipment to keep ourselves in trim. Coming to our operational role, it was a Sector HQ which was created out of the 51 Para Brigade which was located at Kasauli. As per intelligence assessment, the Central Sector comprising HP and UP were the less threatened sectors with few pockets like Kaurik and Shipki La Pass on the India-Tibet border being claimed by the Chinese form part of Kinnaur District. Rivers Sutlej enters India (from Tibet) near Shipki La pass and Para Chu enters India near Kaurik. Ngari Prefecture in Tibet is bang opposite us The pass is one of India's border posts for trade with Tibet along with Sikkim and Barahoti in Uttarakhand. The pass is close to the town of Khab. We recced our old location at Kaurik and the 52 Battery location to refresh my very pleasant memories with Maj. Ratra and then proceeded to Khab on the new motorable road. Having familiarized myself and my OP officers we concentrated on the defences at Kaurik and Pooh. Gun positions were also recced and DF plans were updated. I also had to make loading plans for move on mules which the AT Company provided for us.

I had been briefed on our strained relations with 2 Para, by the 2IC, Maj. NC Mahajan. The two COs KS Pannu, the Sugar Sector Commander and SS Ratra were not on good terms. Despite the differences, I tried my best to avoid the unpleasantness and formally called on the Sector Commander in his office and assured him of my wholehearted cooperation and support. Problems started when our

CO visited the Battery soon after I took over. Pannu questioned me about how the CO visited the Battery without his permission. I said that I was in no position to reply and it would be better that he asked him directly. Pannu kept needling me but I resisted. I also got letters of warning and written explanations sought for a lot of imaginary lapses. I maintained my cool and kept CO informed and consulted him before any action. Nothing happened thereafter because I always looked Pannu straight in the eye. Being our Sector Commander, my battery gave him a very grand farewell, which he was entitled to. He was again overwhelmed when we gave him a very spirited send off from our battery mess, we parted as good friends.

Lt. Col. HS Talwar, an old Seventeener, a highly professional and competent officer took over as our next CO after Lt. Col. Ratra. Tally as he was popularly known had acquitted himself commendably while at Namka Chu with 7 Brigade and was taken prisoner in 1962 along with Brig. JP Dalvi. In his book, 'The Himalayan Blunder' has described Capt. HS Talwar, "A tall strapping Sikh Para gunner with a great sense of humour, kept everyone in high spirits in captivity," Tally had done a BM's tenure before his promotion. In the meantime, Pannu also left, so there was peace and there was no confrontation with CO 2 Para, Lt. Col. BS Dagar, again.

Tally created a very tension-free environment in the Regiment. All three of his battery commanders were staff college aspirants. My battery in the Sugar Sector was the first one he visited. He stayed for almost four days and inspected my battery threadbare, looking at all aspects very minutely. He also assigned me some tasks, first, pertaining to the op readiness at all times, down to very minute details, adopting a tougher stand against disciplinary cases and dispatching my sportsmen to Dagshahi, which I had already done. He had words of appreciation for the manner I had organized the operational readiness, training for war and the interior economy. He made no bones about it and followed up with his DO letter of approbation. He specifically asked that I should help out the Regiment in the procurement of liquor which was cheaper for troops deployed in the field, which I always did. We had excellent relations with the CO and the first lady. Manju decided to make it to Dagshahi from Dehradun for the Raising Day on 01 Apr 74. In my regimental life, I don't think I ever felt so happy and reassured to have a CO like him, a soldier to the core who would support you if he was convinced that you have a point. Mrs Amrit Talwar, a perfect first lady who treated everyone with great love and affection. She confined her interests to family welfare measures and never interfered with the unit affairs. Manju and I always saw her as an example to emulate later in life, if and when I became a CO.

We had put in a lot of hard work and were Champions in all regimental competitions despite being in the Sugar sector. I watched the performance of my Senior JCO, Sub Tara Chand, who had also applied for a commission in the PT Corps since he was eligible. My recommendation to my CO was that you cannot find a JCO so keen, loyal and straightforward as him. He had served as a PT Havildar in the 17 Para Field Regiment and was a national level gymnast. His keenness to learn gunnery prompted the then CO to take up his case for conversion to Artillery. He did very well to be recommended for LGSC (JCO/ NCOs). He qualified as an AIG and was posted to the 9 Para Field Regiment, where he did well. Being relatively young, he tried several times for the SL commission but did not succeed. This opening for Master at Arms was his last chance. Luckily, we realized in the nick of time that the last date for the application was within a day or so at Command HQ.

A helicopter on a cross country sortie landed at Pooh around the time, when I was planning to leave by road, on receiving news of my father's illness at Dehradun. I came home to Dehradun in Feb 74 under very strange circumstances. As I was carrying Sub Tara Chand's application for Simla from Chandigarh, I received a message from Brig. Adm Western Command, my cousin Brig. Satish Kumar, of Deccan Horse, that my father was now admitted in MH after a heart attack. It was a shock for me as I could never imagine that a physically fit person, like my father, could ever have a heart attack. After delivering the application at Simla, I went back to Chandigarh to take the night bus to Dehradun. On arrival, I made it to MH, Dehradun and met my father while he was in the officer's ward. He looked alright to me and I thought a few days in hospital would do him good. He had been admitted four days back and had become quite well known and popular with the staff. I slept in the same room and remember carrying my JC notes for company. He was recovering very slowly but repeated attacks ultimately resulted in heart failure on 3 Feb 1974 at the age of 66 years. His sudden passing was a great shock to the family as many things were on his mind. A day before his passing, Shri HN Bahugana, Chief Minister UP had committed in my presence the post of the Vice Chancellorship of Garhwal University, that time. He also wanted a revision of the MSc/BSc chemistry books he had authored, which was a full-time job. He had visions of the establishment of a residential public school in Dehradun with Manju, all remaining unfulfilled. An illustrious academic career emulated only by my brother Indresh, a fountainhead of knowledge, always a source of inspiration, his self-discipline and an abstemious, almost austere lifestyle with strong views on politics left us a rich harvest of memories to cherish, honour and emulate.

I was asked to proceed to the next JC course at Mhow. After a few days at Dagshai, Tally personally briefed me on the finer aspects of the JC course and his few words of encouragement did help. I was disappointed with my performance on LGSC, for reasons beyond my control. I had very little preparation for the course because you don't get the time in the field. I left for the JC Course at Mhow around 15 Apr 74. I was fully charged up and determined to do well. There were other paratroopers on the Course, Shivinder and Harbhajan and a lot of Para commandos also. In the very first exercise, I was nominated as the patrol leader. My roommate, Raju Rawat, also my schoolie, made my full briefing which made a lot of impact on the Commandant, Lt. Gen. Eric Vaz. I was also lucky to make full use of the amplification notes given to me by Maj. Avtar Cheema, the Everest hero of 2 Para. Subsequently, I topped the written final examination also and was awarded A (I) for standing first on the course of 310 officers. At Mhow, I received orders to rejoin the advance party at Agra instead of rejoining my battery at Sugar Sector. In my absence on JC Course Maj. RP Rai was sent to command my battery. I joined Maj. NC Mahajan our 2IC, at Agra and took over from him when his posting came to MS Branch.

On arrival at Agra Cantt in June at the peak of summer, it was tough. Manju and Priya joined me and stayed in the mess for a few days till I was allotted a house on Station Road within the cantonment. I was also to appear for the DSSC entrance exam on Jan 75. I saw the massive preparations of Hegde, KC Satapathy, Sudhir Chopra when they had regular meetings in the mess for combined studies. None of these gentlemen were keen that I join them, because I had not even started the preparations. They were on their last chance and I was making my first attempt. This point was clarified by them and to me and I did not mind that at all. Therefore, I studied all by myself with no one to guide except Tally, who had placed a lot of hopes in me and predicted that I would make it in one attempt.

Till Sep 73, there was no question of serious studies for DSSC and was detailed for Pre-Staff course at Amritsar by Western Command, which came in extremely useful. Others had already finished attending Central Command Pre-staff in July/Aug held somewhere, maybe Lucknow, Dehradun or Meerut. I was already late because of the JC Course terminating in June 1974. CO received DG Arty's DO of appreciation to say that I stood first amongst 64 gunner officers. CO replied and corrected him that there were 310 officers on the course where I had stood first. I was also congratulated by Brig. MS Panwar personally in his office. Having missed Central Command Pre Staff Tally was determined to help me and asked Brig. KK Hazari, Chief Instructor Western Command Pre Staff if he could allot me a vacancy at Amritsar. Around this time Sub Tara Chand was officially cleared for commission in the PT Corps. I can say he truly deserved his promotion, though luck played a good part also.

Having got the confirmation from Command, I drove down by car to Amritsar and was accommodated in 81 Armed Regt in New Cantt Amritsar (jawans accommodation) near their Officers Mess. We had two very committed instructors who cannot be easily forgotten, Maj. CK Kapur and Maj. Vijay Oberoi. They grilled us every day till we got our basics right in Tac A & B and Adm. We could manage Current Affairs, Military History and Military Law on our own. I returned in October 74 and stopped by Shahbad Markanda when I met my first cousin (even older to father by six years), Dr Ghansham Swarup, just before his demise. This was my last meeting with him as he passed away some days later and I also got back to attend his 13th day as the family representative.

Life at Agra during winter was hard. In our house at Station Road, we had to heat it with two blowers. One in the drawing-room and one in the study where I was preparing for the DSSC Entrance. I cannot say that my preparation was top class but I did study with a vengeance to make up for the LGSC dip in my performance. My little daughter, Priya generally came and sat on my lap promising that she would not disturb me. Manju kept herself busy with her welfare activities in the unit as and when Mrs Talwar asked her to come. Peacetime activities like welfare meet, ladies clubs and mess parties were in full swing and it was a pleasure to get back.

Amid my regimental duties, I had a brush with the occult also. One of the JCOs of my Battery Subedar Yeshkaran Singh, who had also served with me in 17 Para earlier, came to me with his problem. His young, college-going daughter had suddenly disappeared from the JCOs quarters. They had searched all over including their local relatives in Mathura and Hodal, thinking that she may have gone there without the parents' knowledge. Now that two days had elapsed, it was something quite serious and he needed my help. I expressed my concern as well and asked him what he wished to do next. He told me that his daughter is a very principled girl and he has full faith in her. She has probably been abducted/kidnapped by a gang that operates in Bhind Morena ravines. He told me that he has already visited a Baba in village Kagarol, near our para dropping zone in Agra who is known to possess mystic powers. He has pinpointed the exact place where the girl is held captive and also the name of the person who has abducted her. When I asked what he proposed to do next, he requested permission to take a jeep from the unit with two armed jawans to that place in Morena to rescue his daughter. He also tried to play on my emotions that he had placed a lot of hopes in me from my 52 Battery days and I will not disappoint. Being caught between the devil and the deep blue sea, I gave the matter deep thought.

Speaking to CO for permission to use a jeep with armed jawans was out of the question. Another JCO was sent to Kagarol to verify what the mystic said and he confirmed. In the meantime, Sub Innasi Muthu, the quiet Senior JCO, brought a leave register of all the guys who left on leave for the last week. There was one jawan, Mahabir from Jammu who took 10 days casual leave and was also Yeshkaran's *sahayak*. I sent another jawan on temporary duty to Jammu to the home of Mahabir, who brought back the news that the girl had got married to Mahabir in Jammu and was quite happy there. Yeshkaran, in the meanwhile, was all set to go to the ravines in Bhind Morena. He was thoroughly disappointed with me that I did not help him. When I broke the news to him that he should now distribute sweets instead of sulking, he broke down and wept in my office. That's how the problem stood resolved on its own. Goes to prove how gullible our jawans are to all these occult practices and arts. Their abiding faith in the *babas*, Godmen, mystics, and faith healers sometimes can be quite a challenge.

One of the first officers' mess functions organised by us was the farewell lunch for Lt. Gen. DK Chandorkar, the Corps Commander. I remember that the soup was so hot that the General nearly burnt his tongue. Of course, he did not complain otherwise the Mess Secretary would have bought it. Other activities such as Athletics and Boxing finals for the brigade were organised, which went off very well. My team of Bansal, Tandon, Rosemeyer, Daler and Toor were top class spirited youngsters, who made me proud. Besides the officers, 23 Battery was a good subunit to command. I thought the JCOs and jawans too, were very hardworking and sincere. 22 Battery initially commanded by KC Satapathy and 24 Battery by NK Hegde. Maj. Mahajan had left on posting and Kali Satapathy officiated and Daljit was then promoted to BC 22. All three of BCs were approaching the DSSC entrance at the same time. As the date of the DSSC entrance drew near, 10-15 January 75, I was yet to do my first revision. CO had excused me PT and allowed me to study in the office. I was granted leave in two spells 33 days plus 12 days. CO could not give leave 60 days because of the other two being away. He had to split my leave so that there were two Majors in the regiment at all times.

A board of officers was ordered by the brigade to select a field firing range in general area Sirmuttra sometime in September 1975. I had just returned from Western Command Pre-Staff College Course under Brig. Hazari by September end. Since Tally was the Presiding Officer, he decided to take on the task personally with either Hegde or me as members. I was finally detailed to accompany Tally to Barauli PWD Rest House, where a JCO from my battery had established camp a day prior. We were given the areas North and North West of Sirmuttra towards villages Chandpurs and Konessa. For four days, we were driving around on the available axes crisscrossing the cultivated areas where fire and move exercises could be carried out. Tally changed the proposed range boundaries, checked all gun positions and target areas for safety and the restricted impact areas in great detail. There was one corner for the infantry mortars and the grenade firing also since Dawki ranges were being decommissioned soon. We were surprised to receive an invite for dinner at one Sardar Satjit Singh of Barauli, who had secured the complete decorative/building red stone quarrying rights for exports abroad from that area. If you want to see affluence, you have to see their massive bungalow, modelled after Jaipur palaces, with every conceivable gadget central heating cum air conditioning, gold-laced drapes, pure silver decorations and cutlery. Of course, there were three good looking *firangs*, married to his three strapping sons, educated abroad. They were in touch with the Regiment at Agra and we repaid their hospitality later. My battery had the privilege of carrying out the first-course shooting, to be ever carried out followed by battle inoculation for the brigade. These ranges are now patronized by the Para Brigade, based on Lt. Col. HS Talwar's great contribution.

We completed the entire Sirmuttra ranges project, before my DSSC Entrance examination on 12 Jan 75. With Priya seated on my lap and the blower functioning down below. I remember, with Priya around, I was only able to put in some 4-5 hours of study every day. She did promise not to disturb me but I invariably ended up playing cards with her in the drawing-room. Though I had attended my JC very late, I will not say that I had not been quietly preparing for DSSC Entrance earlier. I stayed with my brother at Green Park Delhi, my examination centre was Raj Rif Centre. In the bitterly cold verandah, the exam was held and we braved the weather for six days. After the exams were over, we proceeded to Sirmuttra Ranges for our practice camp for one month's duration. The regiment was assessed above average and Tally was very happy. We also organised the Regimental Raising Day on 01 Apr 75, our first official function in the station. I had invited our family friends Shri MG Mathur CGO from COD and GB Mathur, DEO Agra for the function, as our guests. With the Raising Day over, other activities such as intersubunit competitions, games and sports and social functions, continued. We also celebrated Priya's fourth birthday with all the regimental children and her uncles Daler and Toor.

Priya had just started her schooling in July 1975, at Junior School St Claire's Convent, just next to our mess, where Jeff Rosemeyer's mother was her first teacher. Her schooling was interrupted by my course at Pune. We left for Pune for eight weeks, for the Scientific Orientation course at the IAT, and stayed at Ramesh Apte's house in Deccan Gymkhana. I had to commute daily by bus to Girinagar for the course. Pune weather had incessant rain and we stayed home most of the time except for a few outings to CME. We saw the picture "Sholay" in one of the theatres first-day first show, on its release. Priya was scared and kept crying throughout the movie. On our return from Pune, Mummy and Daddy joined us for Dussehra/Diwali celebrations at Agra with the rest of the family. Manju's brother, Ashok who was at IIM Ahmedabad also decided to join us. I remember extricating him out of the window, of sardines like a packed II class bogie, as he travelled without reservation. Prema Jiji and Jijaji along with Sandhya and toddler Rahul also joined and we had a full house. On Diwali, while we were bursting crackers, Priya with a *phool jari*, got a spark into her maxi, and sustained a small burn near her right armpit. The burn was attended to immediately but the poor child cried more about her maxi than the pain she had to endure.

On 25 June 75, the PM, Mrs Indira Gandhi, after the landmark judgment of the Allahabad High Court, had declared an emergency. We saw the efficient manner in which municipal tasks were executed at Agra, from Cantt railway station to Cantt and then onwards to the City. First of all, all encroachments on government lanes were removed, illegal shops/vendors moved out, creating a place for the pedestrians. Sadar Bazar area was generally beautified and Transport Nagar was established for buses and heavy trucks outside the city. I am personally not aware of the other drives by Sanjay Gandhi such as *Nasbandi*, being on the Staff course at Wellington there was nothing much to see, the prestigious Ooty Racecourse was closed by the DMK Government, which came to power recently. It was pathetic to see the once-prized horses abandoned by their owners, starving in the paddocks.

The Flood Gates to Nilgiris

Towards the end of the year, we started packing for Wellington Sadly, the Regiment also received orders for its de-para and was slated to move to Gwalior, after we left on course. Three of us shared a VPU wagon for the cars and luggage. We gave our names for the DSSC special train which took us to Mettupalayam after a three days journey. All arrangements on the train were beautifully tied up and we had a comfortable journey. We could also have taken the toy train from Mettupalayam to Wellington but it takes ages to reach. We were picked up in a shared jeep station wagon two couples to a vehicle, for the journey to Wellington. We were received with great fanfare, taken directly to the mess for a lovely Chinese dinner, which we all enjoyed. And my, surprises of surprises! I remember meeting my schoolmate, Asha Milton, married to Maj. Talwar of the Assam Regiment. She was her normal chirpy self and was the life of our parties in our homes later. We hit off very well, her husband Bharat and I were in the same Division. We were also very happy to learn that Asha's younger sister had married one of our leading lights of the 23rd Course, Alvinder Chand.

At DSSC Wellington

Outside the mess, the administration had arranged for the maid/staff to be present. We were taken to our flat in Wellington Hall, half a duplex each to two officers. This meant that the ground floor with one bedroom and drawing dining was one unit and the first floor with two bedrooms, with an improvised kitchen was the second unit for another family. We got the ground floor and Bunny Khanna, the first floor of the same flat. We had Pramod Chopra and Jaisheel Oberoi as our immediate neighbours. We studied the geography of the Nilgiris Hills where Wellington is situated, it is between 76th and 77th degrees East longitude and between 11th and 12th degree north latitude. The average height is 5,500 ft and we have the highest peak Dodabeta 8700ft in its vicinity. This also had the most accurate telescope located at the observatory there. The temperature in areas around Wellington remains 23 degrees Celsius for nine months a year. It rains between April to June but its salubrious climate made it very popular. Little wonder, that our founding father Gen. Shiv Verma, selected this place, in preference to all others. There are four major towns worth mentioning, Wellington, Ooty, Kotagiri, Coonor and Upper Coonor. Along with the blue gum trees, there were some tea plantations which abut the golf course. Bang next to the golf course was the biggest ground in Wellington which had multipurpose use, as golf fairway, Gymkhana Club races, helipad and you name it. Gymkhana Club of 1885 was our favourite haunt for weekends as you hardly got time, during the currency of the course.

The course went off very well for me, I think. The first tutorial particularly was full of studies in a small table located, in the other half of the drawing-room, alongside the dining table. I had made arrangements for a late-night study. Priya attended Class I in Holy Innocents High School with Miss Almeida, as her teacher. She did well at studies after a lot of coaching by Manju. She made up for the KG, which she missed at Agra while we were at Pune. Timings at school coincided with DSSC working hours, so there was no problem dropping and picking her up after her school. My first tutorial kept me quite busy so there was no question of socializing. We also met one of our relatives, Lt. Col. VB Mathur who was posted as the Anesthetist at MH Wellington. We spent some time with him and the family over meals, whenever they invited us over.

Priya's full-time maid was Vasantha the wife of the tennis marker at the Gymkhana Club. She became very attached and remembered her when I returned to Staff College as a DS. Vasantha was a very good cook and took complete charge of the kitchen. Manju and I could go around socializing, she kept Priya with her. The ladies in Wellington Hall had their morning coffee together and whenever there was a written assignment, left their husbands to themselves. I remember ex Ullushola which was a written appreciation against time. We went to the ground, discussed plans and wrote later individually. As a race against time, I was able to complete it, in the locker room itself. I was assessed highly by my then DS, Col. R K Anand, later Lt. Gen. Other exercises too went off very well. We also made good friends in Narindar Bal, Bunny Khanna, Chuski Verma, Harry Dua and Sqn Ldr. Soni who we met in Chandigarh. We celebrated Priya's birthday on 29 Apr 76 and got ready for the midterm break in June.

We chalked out a necklace tour during the midterm break, with our dear friends Narinder and Manoj Bal, and their newborn child, in my Fiat UPD 3278. First, we visited Madurai and traversed the entire east coast of Tamil Nadu, stopping at Kanyakumari for an overnight stay. Next, we stopped at Mandappam, visited the famous Ramanathaswamy Temple in Rameshwaram, one of the Char Dham divine sites and its 22 wells or water bodies inside the Temple. No time for a holy bath, we returned to Mandappam. The next day we were at a convent in Nagercoil buying their lovely lace embroidered linen. After an overnight stay at the Kovalam beach, we left for Palghat, before returning to Wellington. We also left for the Industrial Demonstration tour sometime in August 1976 for a month and visited all the establishments while on the train. At Bangalore, the College arranged to have the families join us for three-four days, for an extended jaunt. Overall, the tour was very educational and meticulously planned. At Secunderabad, I remember, during the visit to Indian Express publishing press, the senior editor had the guts to openly admit that we were not speaking to a free press, which possibly hinted at the government-imposed curbs during the emergency. I admired her guts!!!

After a hectic first tutorial, we got a bit of respite during the break. My neighbour Bunny Khanna and I lived in a shared duplex house in Wellington Hall. I had half the house with drawing cum dining and study on the ground floor and Bunny had the two bedrooms on the first floor. The funniest part of our shared house was when Bunny used to give me a shout to put the geyser on because the switch was in the study of my part of the house. We rejuvenated our old times with regular get-togethers as both the families had become very good friends. Meera and her one-year-old daughter got along well with Manju and Priya. Bunny was the first person who threw a challenge at me when he made fun of me and said, "Dabbu, not everyone can play golf. Not only expensive, but you've also got to be temperamentally suited for golf". Bunny said he would be surprised if he ever found me in the golf course and he thought I would rather get immersed in your books than play golf. That was the veritable trigger and I went with him during the break to brush up on the basics that I had learnt from Mr Jarolov at NDA. I took lessons from Robert for golf and played with the Club set since I did not own a golf set. Those days a lot of us students took to golf because of the added attraction of seeing the Japanese officer Col.Matsumara's pretty wife, also trying to learn. With dedication and commitment along with words of encouragement from friends like Bunny, Shanker Prasad, and Jagdish Chander, I reached a reasonable standard at the end of the course.

The pro, Robert, took us to the training driving range where he coached/supervised four or five of us simultaneously. I took a package of 20 lessons over two/three months and practised very hard to get my body into a rhythm and getting to know the nuances of this fascinating game. Bunny used to check my game once in a while and encouraged me whenever I felt I had a setback. In our backyard, sometimes he used some perforated balls to show me chipping and wedge shots. In a month I had picked up a lot and could execute good drives. I had still not reached a stage to go around the course with Bunny and Shankar Prasad, who were seasoned campaigners. Course commitments did not allow golf to be the regularity one wished. By about midterm Robert proved to be a good coach and had cleared me to go around with him and two more novices like me. The more I played, I got addicted to the game. Somewhere in the fifth tutorial, the course had an inter-division competition where I took part with a handicap of 24. I had such an excellent round that Shankar, who was my partner, was very impressed. That I was temperamentally not suited for golf was given a go by and I kept going for golf on borrowed shoes and golf sets. Towards the end of the course, I bought shoes with spikes and some items of kit presented by friends. Golf remained suspended till the end of Mizoram tenure. I did play regularly at the famous FRIMA after reaching Dehradun for two months.

Our course terminated around 28 Nov 76 and I had done very well as per the Commandants final interview. He specifically mentioned that I was among the first ten and could expect to be back as an instructor. Our postings were brought by the MS, Gen. Kundan Singh. There were a lot of changes manipulated after their receipt in Wellington around last week of December 76, we took the flight from Coimbatore to Delhi via Hyderabad to spend a few days with our cousin, Lt. Col. Suresh Endley. We reached Delhi in the first week of Dec 76 and proceeded to attend my nephew Deepak's wedding at Moradabad by my car on 28 Dec 1976. I received the sad news that my brother in law Girish Jijaji, who was ailing with brain cancer, had been admitted to hospital in Meerut. Both Yogesh Bhaisaheb and I, left the wedding party in my car moved to Meerut instead. It was a very sad period for my sister Meenakshi and her children on his passing on 01 Jan 77. After settling her LIC claims etc., I moved to Dehradun and stayed put for a month before proceeding to the North East for the first time, and that too by train on orders from my brigade.

Back to Gwalior

I joined the 9 Field Regiment sometimes after availing my joining time. I had kept my annual leave in reserve for the time being. So, after a short trip to Dehradun, I moved with my bare minimum baggage to Gwalior. The complete baggage was lying in Garhi Cantt, as it was in packed condition except for a few boxes which were opened by Manju during her stay at Rajpur Road with her parents. Our CO, Lt. Col. OP Khanna and I had served together in 17 Para Field Regiment and I was very happy to take over 24 Battery this time. Maj. AL Gogna was 2IC, SB Singh, Hadrianus. Gullu Puri and Sivinder were the other

Majors. A lot of water had flown down the Ganges when I saw my Regiment after two years on staff. The de para tenure had played havoc with this fine outfit. There was a lot of emphasis on peacetime activities, the regimental farm and the Navrattan Cinema at the cost of professional soldiering. The officers too were not from the select lot of paratroopers, quite a few were on compassionate postings, some passed over and the remainder, the deadwood of the Artillery. We also received a full draft of elderly jawans from the Pioneer Corps, on its disbandment. I had to stay in the mess for about a month or so, till I was allotted permanent accommodation in Morar, based on my field seniority.

I was granted leave to enable Manju and children to join me when a house was allotted. I reached Dehradun with two jawans to help me out with the baggage lying in Dehradun Cantt. Having dispatched the luggage by truck, I decided to move by car UPD 3278 to Gwalior. We spent a day in Delhi with my brother. We decided to start the next day for Agra to spend some time with Karpu Dattas, have lunch with them and depart thereafter for Gwalior. Some more delays took place on the pontoon bridge enroute. After about an hour or so, around the last light, I found that the lights of the car had dimmed when the battery stopped charging. We were somewhere near Bhind Morena. Driving with little or no lights, and pitch darkness around, I didn't want to stop and pressed on. We did not notice what was lying ahead. The car went over a carcass of a dead animal and I made a screeching halt. As it became darker, we were so scared that we continued going. After crossing Morena. Manju took off her jewellery and hid it inside the car. Suddenly a good samaritan on a scooter came to our rescue. He drove in front of our car and provided us with lights up to Morar Cantt. On reaching the mess, we heaved a sigh of relief. We requested him to our room in the mess, and I made the mistake of offering him some money for petrol, which he flatly refused to accept. What he said, I can never forget, "*Sahib Bhagwan ki daya bahut kuch hai, paise ki zarurat nahin hai, maine insaniyat ke taur se apki madad kari hai*". I could see he was a well to do farmer in a khaddar kurta pyjama. What is more important, there is still no dearth of very good people on planet earth. We considered this as divine help, he was probably the harbinger from our Benefactor. There was no way we could show our gratitude, except to thank him profusely.

We were very happy to be back in the same Regiment. We had struck good friendships with other officers and families in Gwalior. My classmate from the 1958 Senior Cambridge batch, Sudha Hoon and her husband Maj. SP Das, the multi-faceted personality of 14 Dogra, were very good friends till I got posted out. We also caught up with Dharamvir Piplani and Ashok Saidha from the Air OP. Dharamvir Piplani was from my old school, Ashok and I had served together in Seventeen earlier. We renewed our friendship, from where we last parted. Our Niners jawans were still very good, they wanted to tell you something but somehow felt constrained. In the meanwhile, we got ready for the Raising Day on 01 Apr 79, which was an exceedingly well-organized function in the station.

9 Para Raising Day celebrations in Gwalior

It also coincided with the retirement of Brig. GD Sharma, our Commander and chief guest. He was just not happy with the Regiment that he had commanded earlier and called me separately to the MES IB the next day for a dressing down. He chose to thank me first for the great send-off, then informed me that Tanny Bhalla would take over soon and I should get my shoulder to the wheel and get the unit out of the morass that they were in. After another befitting farewell to Lt. Col. OP Khanna, Tanny Bhalla and his wife arrived at the station. Tanny's wife Meena had told me on Army Day At Home on 15th January 1979, that they would bring their team to Seventeen and I did not form part of it. I then requested for Nine hoping that would be alright. I was now quite apprehensive about my status in the unit, now that they had turned up here instead. I went up to Tanny and asked if I could be posted out since his team was expected. He categorically told me he had no such plans. He had no problems working with me and asked if

I had any. When I said I had none whatsoever, he just told me not to worry and continue the way I was working. We had a lot to do to get the Regiment back on track to its old days as the finest unit in the Para Brigade under Tally. Tanny, the CO had just fallen sick with a back injury. I had to crack the whip, most of the time, the Niners came out of their slumber. We had numerous command post exercises with guns in the sweltering heat in May June 1979, before moving to Babina for our Practice Camp. There was no doubt in my mind, Nine didn't require to be prodded. It would come back on its own, given the right directions. The practice camp report was outstanding which was a great improvement from the previous year. Nine, the fine unit, responded very well to Tanny's call.

Here I must mention, Sivinder was appearing for his last chance at DSSC and I tried my best to help him out. All this was done at specified timings and Tanny seemed unhappy with me for helping him out, sometimes during office hours. I stopped that but, in the evenings, I had to be harsh to get him on track for the preparations. I did all his corrections and did my best to guide him. One evening, I got so annoyed with him that I told him off that you had the temerity to sleep, while I was giving out some tips. My harshness must have bugged him as I saw Tripta in tears also. We also played golf regularly at the ragtag course at Gwalior. I must add here that Sivinder was also the best colleague to serve with. He had also selected a gem, Gunner Hari Singh for duties as my orderly from his battery for which I will always be grateful to Sivinder. One cannot find a more loyal soldier than Hari Singh. He continued with me till he retired from service, rings up now and then to enquire about us and the children. Children too, remember him even now with lots of affection and respect. Very recently, I was informed about his suspected heart attack by his son and I rushed to Sonepat and was relieved to see him in the hospital. it was a false alarm, but Hari Singh had tears in his eyes that I had come to see him. Our ties are very strong and we will continue our relationship for many more years.

I left for Mhow for a Senior Command course sometime on August 79. We were very fortunate to have my mentor and CO Lt. Col. HS Talwar and Suresh Endley hosting us for a few days. Manju and children had joined me temporarily in Shangrila, honeymoon quarters, for the course officers. What Priya still remembers is one of my coursemates from Sri Lanka, Lt. Col. Jaywardhene who told her, "I am Ravana from Sri Lanka and I have come to take your Sita away". This scared the wits out of Priya and I had a helluva time trying to convince her that it was all in good humour. They went back after about 2-3 weeks and I got into the grind for the course. I did very well with a possible BI which I was told at the end of the course by the SC Wing Commander, Brig. Amarjit Singh. Those days SC Wing, in keeping with the transparency norms, has just opened up to inform the grades to students when transparency was advocated. This gradation did not last long as they discontinued these grades and went on to Q and QI now.

My approval for the next rank came when we were at Gwalior with Nine. As was customary, a get together was arranged that evening, at our residence which went up to the wee hours, in the morning. The CO rightly did not cancel the next morning's PT, which was a disappointment. As I was away on temporary duty most of the time, on various study groups, précis writing and pre staff college courses, the CO, very rightly asked me to hand over accounts to Maj.

Hadrianus. During this period, all kinds of messages from our Directorate came to me, such as a posting to Tactical Wing School of Artillery on promotion which I declined. I then wrote to DG Artillery Lt. Gen. Kr Surendra Singh that this delay was very mysterious, as many of my juniors had already been promoted. He replied in a private letter to me that "the need for a high-profile CO was foremost in my mind while selecting you personally for a new raising". Having no godfather to inform me what was going on, I kept waiting for my posting. The only words of encouragement and comfort came in a one-line DO from Brig. HK Bhardwaj saying that I am being adjusted in the same brigade. When I was away on temporary duty, my orders finally came to take over 141 Field Regiment on 25 June 1980. I pleaded with the Chief Instructor Brig. MS Kandal and with great difficulty, managed to get out of the pre staff commitment, on the pretext of Corps Commanders visit and returned to Gwalior to finally wind up. I moved from Gwalior to Talbehat by road on 21 Jun 80 and proceeded directly to the Mess for lunch hosted in our honour.

The Unforgettable Years at Helm

My tenure in 141 Field Regiment has been full of challenges, toil and hard work. I was determined to make it a success. Having seen several COs by now, I prayed to God that I must avoid traits like vindictiveness, biases, unprincipled conduct, unprofessional ethics and playing favourites within your team. As for the style of command, I always kept my old CO, Lt. Col. HS Talwar's command as a model to emulate. His clarity of thought, professional knowledge, ideas on regimentation and astute man-management stood foremost in my mind. Tally had just moved as GSO1 of an Infantry Division before taking over an Infantry Brigade. Not surprisingly, I received a DO letter of congratulations from Brig. HK Bhardwaj, Dy MS (C) who also said that I should have Harjit Talwar in front of me and I should try to emulate his example. He said he had placed a lot of hopes in me, I would excel in my command, like him.

This Regiment was raised at Talbehat on 1 July 1979 under 36 Artillery Brigade, a mixed class unit equipped with 105 IFGs. Raising commenced immediately thereafter and all officers and men reported arrival by October 79. Equipment and guns with all stores arrived in good time and new CO, Lt. Col. Vinay Shankar arrived by the end of August from the 16 Field Regiment. As per the new policy that only those who had done more than a year in command, would be posted as COs. I was also empanelled with this unit but was deliberately kept out at Gwalior because my batchmate was already posted there. When the board results came, he did not make it the first time. Vacant barracks at Talbehat were utilized to accommodate the unit and all vehicles, equipment, stores and guns were received. Course shootings were carried out and after a visit by the Brigade Commander, Brig. UC Chaturvedi to the unit, as per accepted norms the Regiment was declared fit for war. Unit celebrated its completion of raising in March '79 after nine months. Everyone had taken it for granted that now it is almost like any old unit, with the team of best officers in the brigade. I took over the unit after CO, Lt. Col. Vinay Shankar returned from two months annual cum sick leave before his move to Mhow on Higher Command Course. After a few days, one COs house fell vacant and I moved in.

As CO 141 Field Regiment in Talbehat

What struck me was that the officers, JCOs and men of this unit were a happy lot full of fighting spirit and willing workers. I took my time to draw my conclusions and also took care not to blame anyone when I went around. I followed Tally's dictum; mudslinging is no substitute for positive action. There were glaring inconsistencies in storekeeping and local purchases which can happen in any new outfit for reasons of inexperience and urgency. I was prepared to overlook that. I also noticed that over a while the 2IC had assumed such extraordinary powers, in anticipation of his taking over, that he had usurped it from the outgoing CO. A competent officer from the ranks with loads of gunnery experience had hit the bottle very hard in the unit. Officers tended to be his informers and also display sycophantic tendencies. Whenever any tasks were assigned to them directly by me, they consulted him first. The 2IC wanted me to run the Regiment the way he had desired and had planted his favourites in key appointments in the unit, eg, Adjutant and Mess Secretary. His reply to everything was that your predecessor never did this or that. My leadership was put to a severe test immediately after a few days when I received the orders that the Corps Commander, Lt. Gen. TS Oberoi would be visiting you the next day. My Commander Arty from Dhana, already on his way, sent the message that they both would be staying in the VIP guest rooms, which required to be well done up.

There were cocktails planned in Station Artillery Mess in the evening, followed by a quiet dinner. When the Corps Commander arrived by road, the guard positioned in front of the guest room, turned out by mistake. The great man that he is, Tirath Oberoi, never said a word, turned out the guard and moved into the guest room, without even a murmur. He told my Commander not to bother to pick him up for the cocktails and asked me, instead to do so. When I went to pick him up, he told me, "Dabbu, this cooler makes so much noise, I developed a headache". He then asked who all were coming. I told him all Gunner COs in Talbehat, all paratroopers, the GE and all their ladies. He asked me if I had invited the local Station Commander. I just said that I had slipped up. He seemed annoyed and told me that you now call him and apologise. Brig. & Mrs UC Chaturvedi arrived in good time despite my last-minute request. After an uneventful evening, the General goes up to all ladies and says how do you all spend your time here? When he was quite satisfied that all ladies were usefully employed, he seemed quite happy. There were absolutely no doubts that the station kept everyone employed. I think that must have relieved him a lot. In the meanwhile, I sent someone to replace the cooler.

Immediately after the cocktails, I had asked for a readiness report for a command post exercise with guns and OP deployed on the parade ground. Tally had always propagated this when he was our CO because maximum activity could be seen by the visiting officer. When I gave the orders to 2IC that I wanted to see the Regiment ready by 9.30 pm that evening, it did not happen. Some excuse was made and I readily said, "Ok one hour later". None of my officers had taken a drink that evening, because we were on parade after the cocktails. When I went around, nothing was right and I spent almost four to five hours correcting things, till well past midnight. The next morning, all officers and JCOs were lined up, first for C Arty. When I drew close there was an unmistakable whiff of alcohol around the officers. Toothpaste and brush did make some difference. When the. Corps Commander was being introduced, there was no whiff, and thankfully, things went off okay. He gave a parting shot to the two passed over officers, to be useful team members and not create problems for the CO. After the introduction was over, the Corps Commander was briefed in my office, his first question about this very officer. "Has he got a past? Is he behaving well? "I replied that he certainly has a record of drinking to excess. However, it does not affect his performance in the unit". I had to cover up but how could I conclude without giving him a chance? The Corps Commander spoke very little. I was convinced that I had it for all of last evening's fiasco. I had been specifically briefed by my Commander not to invite the Station Commander; it may send a wrong signal to him. He only said, "Continue your good work, Dabbu". I was relieved and I am glad that I adopted a wait and watch for all officers and men in the unit, before jumping to conclusions that could wreck the team. Problems of passed over officers are not insurmountable. Both required tactful handling, firmness and understanding. There was no need to display my superior credentials, which were known to everyone. I first called that particular officer and asked him why he had drunk to excess before the visit when not one officer had a drink during the cocktails. All his alcohol and boisterousness disappeared when I asked him to proceed on annual leave immediately. He said that the first-ever Practice Camp was foremost in his mind and an IG team to assess the unit was coming from the School. Then there was the CEME and AIA Inspection to follow. After that was the Adm Inspection by the Commander. Besides, there were still many things to be completed like the unit SOPs. and standing orders. I told him that I appreciated all his concerns for the unit. I would like him to just complete the SOPs and standing orders and push off on annual leave, on their completion.

Other officers from the grouped units of the Regiment of Artillery were not those carefully selected. I wasn't looking for above-average officers like para units. I only wanted officers with potential in a reasonable career profile, whose loyalty and integrity was never in doubt. These are the ones on whom you could rely through thick and thin and who when asked for their opinion were fearless, not yes men. Some sportsmen were also on my bucket list but I could hang fire for the time being. I had brought a whole lot of Niner sportsmen like Muthappa, Pillai, Narain Kutty and a few more who had wanted to move with me. The next person to be changed was the Adjutant, my choice was senior most Capt. Sushil Kumar, who was not liked by everyone because of being straightforward and being too strict. What followed now was a major reshuffle of officers, quite a few went back to their parent/empanelled units, either for earning their reports or being due for staff. In the early years of the empanelled unit's policy, there were teething problems.

I must mention here that my RMO Capt. Chandra Kant Raheja was a pillar of strength to the unit. He had an exposure which any gunner officer would envy. Sometimes as my Adjutant, OC RHQ or LRW even officiated as BC once and of course the most sought-after appointment of a canteen officer. He did a long unbroken tenure of six years with the unit. When he wanted to go on release, I succeeded in persuading him to stay. I spoke to DDMS Command (from Wellington, where I was posted then) and got him nominated for specialization in Anaesthesia. We later served in Ladakh together. He is doing very well as a private practitioner and we continue to be very good friends in Delhi. Another great asset was our OC LRW, Capt. SK Panda who served the unit exceptionally well. An excellent sportsman, he had come to us after his red ink entry from EME School Baroda. He had got into trouble with some local hoodlums there, soundly thrashed an MLA's son for eve-teasing a colleague's wife. He felt very safe and reassured when he was welcomed into the One For One family. Some postings out and in took place and I am happy to state that our first YO, 2/Lt. Neeraj Verma, groomed by my team, retired from DSSC Wellington as MG Admin in 2018. I was able to manage another youngster with a potential who bagged the silver gun on YOs Course and is our hope for DG Artillery in the next few years, Maj. Gen. RK Singh ex MG IC Adm Central Command, now a Commander Sub Area.

Both Raheja and Panda got married during their tenures with the unit. Our team One for One and ladies welcomed the new brides to the Talbahat Station with great pomp and show. All officers were at the railway station to receive them. In continuation of the air OP welcome we received; a nice welcome was arranged in their honour. There were gaily caparisoned bullock carts with two buglars in front leading their way to the mess. As expected with the sounding of the bugle, the bulls bolted and the couple stuck to their seats, frightened like hell. They still remember what reception the youngsters arranged for the newlyweds. A good tradition borrowed from Air OP still lives and is now an SOP in the unit.

During the next week, two things figured on my agenda. First, the liquidation of the black fund existing in the unit, which over a while had reached a handsome amount and was the virtual entertainment fund to be spent exclusively on the VIP visits. Orders were given to merge it with the Regimental Fund and made white. With no scope left for irregular and malpractices, I was the first CO to present a mess bill to the Commander, which he appreciated. The smaller funds like the piggery & soda water factory which was selling rum soda were banned and only soft drinks were sold henceforth to the station. Some accounting irregularities were noticed and the guys responsible were booked straightaway. Bradma machine was introduced and all transactions were electronically done, to obviate fudging of accounts. I had learnt this from my commander, Brig. Surinder Nath who had introduced this in Raj Rif Centre to obviate the risk of fraud. My QM, Maj. Manohar Lal, ex Gunner from my EC-1 course had devised foolproof accounting procedures and inventory control which today are accepted by ordnance also. We had good links at COD Cheoki (Commandant Brig. Ronnie Bose ex Para OFP) and COD Jabalpur (Brig. Harivansh Kumar ex COD Agra) who helped us with metal scrap. Brass scrap was melted for making the metal plates and quarter guard brass boards. Next was our Dharam Sthal under the Religious Teacher, who was very intrigued when asked to celebrate all religious festivals from Eid to Xmas and give a discourse on each function. Overruling his objections then, I knew he had no choice. Even today, this is being followed. in the Regiment. The next problem that needed attention, the number of overstayers of leave and absence without leave, was a live problem in my regiment. They were never reported and subunits were adjusting the days from next year's quota. I thought this was not the right approach to discipline, the covering up made it even worse. A jawan went on leave and got back a month late, going scot-free by giving some cock and bull story, as reasons for overstay. Few guys left the unit without permission and got their absence regularized later in subunits. Seeing all this, left no doubts that this was malpractice that had to be nipped in the bud. My orders, from henceforth, no subunit commander would sanction advance of annual leave to anyone. All ranks without exception will pledge the Prathna Sthal in front of the deities and the Panditji take a vow that he will not overstay, leave and return in time. This worked well, but there was still one case of overstay. Very sadly, I did the first and the last court-martial of my career, of a jawan for overstaying of leave and this nonsense came to a complete stop for years to come.

The regiment had no officers' mess, till now. There was plenty of teakwood available for auction at Saugor at a throwaway price because nobody made a bid for it except my representative. We picked it up officially in our transport and got the mess furniture made by the excellent unit carpenters. The Commander also saw the workmanship of the pooled carpenters and approved. While at Bangalore on leave, I learnt that Bartons & Co were selling their silver trophies at bargain prices. With my contribution of Rs 3000 and officers' contributions, we purchased pure silver trophies and mess cutlery worth Rs 20,000. Big sum then and with proper sanctions from the commander and the correct use of canteen profits two Featherlite sofa sets were also bought. I thought it impossible to bring my regiment at par with 9/17 but I could lay the foundation for my successors and not wait for things to happen on their own.

After some time, GOC of the Infantry Division, Maj. Gen. Ram Krishan visited the unit accompanied by my Brigade Commander. They were very happy with the Regiment and the Practice Camp report, "Outstanding", we had achieved on the Babina Ranges. GOC after seeing my unit layout, accounting procedures and the SOPs ordered full mobilization on the last day. We got ready to move out well in time and were told to stand down. I remember GOC and Col. GS discussing that all unit COs in the division must see my Regiment's neat layout and excellent administration. Each CO of the infantry battalions and other arms/services visiting my unit asked me the same question, on what I fed the GOC and the Corps Commander with? Nothing was my reply but no one believed me. This was the greatest compliment paid to me. I would like to also admit that our Brigade Commander also played a very big part in this. Our relations with the Brigade HQ located at Dhana were very good. I also maintained good relations with the local Brigade Commander at Talbahat, Brig. RC Chaturvedi. On taking over, Capt. Ashok Pant of my Regiment got married to his daughter, Poonam and I had the pleasure of leading the baraat to the Flagstaff House from my residence, where a small function was arranged. He was now kind of related to us, like a '*samdhi*' and we kept the sensitivity of this relationship in mind, in all my social interactions. This relationship continued till the changeover took place with the Brigade at Dhana.

Raising Day party in Talbehat

A spate of postings out brought the regiment down to its normal strength of around 18-20 officers. The 2IC returned from leave and was again sanctioned a month's leave this time, on his request to go to Vaishno Devi and Amritsar. He was also approved for promotion in his last look. I took him to all mandirs and gurudwaras around us to pledge that he will not drink alcohol anymore. He did that and left on posting to 99 Mountain Regiment. I was happy that I could help my coursemate to mend his ways and get him his rank, even when he felt there were little hopes of his making it. Sheru Thapliyal attending Staff Course was posted as one of the BCs. The next from my course, Maj. Tarsem Singh wanted a posting closer home and he too left. Maj. Panicker now the 2IC did well to execute my policies. The regiment did well in all games and other activities. In the meanwhile, the Brigade HQ shifted from Dhana to Talbahat. Change in command and control from to another Corps and adjustments brought the Medium Regiment back to the brigade. Other units were a Field Regiment at Dehradun under a very distinguished winger Gurbaksh Sihota, a Field Regiment was still at Dhana under Harjit Brar and a Light Regiment, under another very spirited winger, Akhilesh Sharma. We all had a good time together; a ready-made bridge foursome with the Commander, Jawandha, Akhilesh and myself. Ladies were extremely talented and were important cogs in the wheel especially in the local KG School run by the station. Akhilesh and his wife Rita, with their two bubbly girls, were the most popular couple in the station. Our new Deputy Commander RP Murgai also joined but was no match for his predecessor, the dashing and ever-smiling Col.Nandu Srivastava.

I was attached to HQ Infantry Division at Bhopal for the writing of Exercise Ram Rekha sometime in March 1981. I kept away from the Regiment and was in Bhopal for almost 1½ - 2 months. In the meanwhile, one medium regiment was replaced by another under coursemate Lt. Col. Sukhbir Jawandha. The first reporting year went off very well as Commander Brig. Jagbir Singh appreciated the unit's performance both in the practice Camp and the Adm Inspection. When I was away on leave, there were two or three anonymous/ pseudonymous letters against me at the brigade and the Division. My Canteen account was inspected in my absence to see whether I had made an exorbitant profit in the sale of rum. Sometimes back, Brig. PS Warrier, located at Kamptee in Maharastra and his affiliated Infantry Brigade were in Babina Ranges for battle inoculations. They left behind almost 500 bottles for my Regiment. before returning to

Kamptee. I had told the new 2IC, Maj. Panicker to take the entire lot on charge and fixed the price at our UP rates, which were very high as compared to what we had bought from the Infantry units. I had verbally verified from the Excise Deptt who told me earlier, that since the sale took place in UP (Babina) the question of excise duty payment by us did not arise. The author of the anonymous letter did not realize that I had not violated any UP excise laws and had just made cooked up & baseless allegations. Everyone thought I was at fault but when both Maj. Panicker and the Canteen Officer, Maj. Amar Kapil did a great job in obtaining an Excise Deptt waiver. Much to my relief, the case was closed even before I returned from leave.

It was smooth sailing for us as the Regiment did not undergo very many changes. On the professional front, the Regiment participated in a Corps exercise Shiv Shakti in the general area Aligarh - Etawah. Administration under QM Manohar Lal was well buttoned up and we never had to look back. Maj. Panicker was doing the duties of 2IC exceedingly well and engaged in course shootings and artillery staff duties which gave me some respite. All four of my coursemates in the Brigade, viz Gurbaksh Sihota, Sukhi Jawandha, Akhilesh Sharma and NK Hegde did well in all activities and the Commander Brig. Jagbir Singh was very proud of us. He found it difficult to rate any of the units anything other than above average/outstanding. My gurus taught me that my professional and social conduct must be above board and getting a good report was the least of my concerns. My posting came to Tac Wing, School of Artillery exactly in a year and 10 months. I requested that I be allowed to remain up to our Raising Day from 01 July to 10 July 82. My report arrived by post and I got what Commander felt I deserved. It is possible that the GOC Maj. Gen. Ram

Krishan had probably moderated the reports well. Hegde and I were selected for Higher Command at College of Combat Mhow. Gurbaksh Sihota, too, was detailed for a foreign course on NBC warfare in the USA (meant for NCOs, by some mistake at the MS Branch). Jawandha too left for Iraq on an instructional assignment with their Arty School. I had promised a pure silver trophy costing Rs 3,500 as a token of my gratitude and affection for the unit which provided me with an opportunity to further my personal advancement.

Mrs Jagbir Singh with Army School teachers in Talbehat

It would be worthwhile to mention here that both my children Priya and Rohit did their schooling in Talbahat. Rohit commenced school in the school where Manju was appointed the Headmistress by Brig. RC Chaturvedi based on her experience and also being a MA BEd. The children's school was located inside the Regiment area and three of our ladies, the indefatigable and involved Kalyani Panicker, the vibrant

Poonam Kapil and the very reserved Rita Sharma did a fabulous job teaching our kids there. Our welfare and ladies club meets were the talk of the station with their excellent organisation. Our Central School was definitely below par and required a revamp. Despite best efforts, this was not possible as the locals who made up the teaching staff had no experience/exposure to a good school. As a result, Priya's studies suffered like all the kids of her age group at Talbahat.

Few points are worthy of mention in my tenure. As the second Commanding Officer, I had a young fledgling unit that had less than a year of existence. In modern times, no unit can claim readiness for war with all equipment, stores and guns delivered and a battery course shooting on its belt, as the qualification, It requires years of hard work and toil, punctuated with many ups and downs, I had only tried to lay the foundation of a robust organisation with updated standing orders and SOPs, meticulously planned training to maintain op readiness, excellent standards of maintenance that at the call of the bugle, my regiment can enter the battlefield and defend our country. All our Regimental Institutions functioned very honestly and with effectiveness. For this, the entire credit must go to the 2IC, Maj. Panicker who slogged endless hours to put everything in place. From 1988 to 1999, the unit went from J&K to the North East coming back to the Siachen Glacier after volunteering for service there. One of our officers on the Siachen Glacier, Capt. Pritam Kumar died before he could be evacuated. Capt. PV Vikram, the highly motivated son of my 2IC, Maj. Panicker volunteered to take his place and remained there till the regiment received orders to move to Kargil where they were truly battle-tested in the Infantry Brigade Group Sector. It is with immense pride, that the guns of my Regiment provided an efficient ad hoc FDC of 8 fire units which proved very crucial fire support to infantry in their attacks in the Kaksar and Batalik sectors. Capt. PV Vikram, after returning from a very eventful tenure on the Siachen Glacier, continued his good work as an OP officer with 14 Jak Rif and brought down effective fire on the enemy causing mayhem and heavy casualties. He was hit by heavy enemy retaliatory fire and made the supreme sacrifice on 2 June 1999. Our unit suffered two officers and three jawans casualties, during the Kargil operations Team Kargil Victors, as they prefer to be known today, received a COAS Commendation in addition to the Honour Title KARGIL. Capt. PV Vikram was awarded the Sena Medal (Gallantry) posthumously.

An extract from 141 Medium Regiment (Kargil) records is reproduced below:

"141 Field Regiment was in direct support of 121 Independent Infantry Brigade Group deployed over a frontage of 125 km along the LoC from July 97 to Nov 99. The unit acquitted itself with distinction, both while providing fire support to the infantry deployed along the LoC and during Operation Vijay, where the unit was committed right from the initial stages in Dras, Kaksar and Batalik sub-sectors. The unit continued to support the containment and eviction stage with accurate and devastating fire. In addition, the unit established an ad hoc fire direction centre at Ledge with 6-7 fire units under command.

Guns of 141 Field Regiment provided crucial fire support to the infantry during all the attacks in Kaksar and Batalik sub-sectors. Capt. PV Vikram, while directing fire on Bajrang Post in Kaksar sub-sector, in support of an attack by 14 Jak Rif, made the supreme sacrifice on 2 Jun 99. He was awarded Sena Medal (Posthumous) for this act of bravery. On 6 Jul 99, Gunner Jugal Ramesh Kumar Vikram Bhai while assisting the gun detachment in preparation and loading of ammunition, in utter disregard to his personal safety, was hit by innumerable splinters from an enemy shell and attained martyrdom.

The guns of the unit fired 44,000 rounds during Operation Vijay. In addition to the number of individual awards for valour and the indomitable resolve displayed by its troops during Operation Vijay, the unit was conferred with COAS Unit Citation and bestowed with Honour Title "KARGIL".

Since then, the Regiment has performed commendably in various peace and field stations to earn great recognition as KARGIL VICTORS. Today 141 Medium Regiment (KARGIL) is one of the seasoned and battle-ready outfits of the Indian Army and is now fully deployed against the Chinese in the forefront of Ladakh Sector "

What more can I ask from the child I nurtured for over two years?

Back to Alma Mater Once Again

I reported at Deolali around last week of July 82 lock stock and barrel. My luggage and car fetched up almost immediately thereafter. We were accommodated in P1 Single Officers accommodation where families were permitted. Straight from command, this was a great come down, as all officers with at least two children had a very uncomfortable stay. The waiting period for permanent accommodation was at most one year and there was no choice. With so many of us in Field & Tactical Wings staying together there was never a dull moment and socializing was at its peak. Instructional tenure in Tactical Wing was considered a prestigious posting those days, tenable only by selected double-barreled PSC LGSC qualified officers.

Our Commander, Brig. Kuldip S Aujla had declined command of an Infantry Brigade and chose to stay within his arm. He had a reputation of a hard taskmaster and a very professional gunner. We were conducting the last JC Arty course based on the syllabus of JC Infantry at Mhow. This course was introduced in the tenure of the then Chief Instructor, Col. YK Kapoor with a select band of all arms DS and the School came into the limelight for its outstanding professional content and fair play. More and more officers from other arms were opting for the JC Arty Course but for some reason, it was discontinued. We also had our share of sand models and war games which were of a very high standard. Senior command course run here was for officers, who had missed senior command at Mhow and were otherwise good enough to command Regiments. Another course was run for the staff officers of Arty Brigades like BM and DQs. This was a condensed course which was a prerequisite for Arty Brigade staff appointments.

The atmosphere in the Tactical Wing was excellent. We had as our colleagues, BS Thakur from the Armour, Naresh Chandra from Engineers, RR Chari from Signals. Gunner officers were PS Bhandari, Kewal Puri, Akshey Kapila, K Vishwanathan, RS Datta, BP Singh, Arun Mehandru, Naresh Chand. We were sharing offices two or three to a room. Tac Wing also looked after B Mess and the Golf Course. Staff Officer Tac Wing initially was KC Satapathy, followed by Jagmit Singh and then VP Sharma. We shared our duties very well and a very professional atmosphere prevailed in the wing. On the social plane, all birthdays and wedding anniversaries were celebrated as a wing. Get together and a spirit of camaraderie prevailed. Brig. SK Mathur, MVC joined as Deputy Commandant after NDC and Brig. DP Bahl was AD

Wing Commander. Brig. SS Ratra was Trials Wing Commander with Maj. Gen. SK Talwar as our Commandant Field Wing. Commander was first Brig. YK Yadav and later Maj. Gen. JS Herr. We had regular get-togethers with my cousin Brig. Sushil and his charming wife, Dolly. Sometimes CO Adm Regiment, DS Hada, from our golf foursome arranged picnics outside at Darna Sports Club and Nasik.

My cousin and role model Brig. Sushil Mathur MVC (later Maj. Gen)

We got our permanent accommodation after about 8-10 months and were happy to be allotted a ground floor house, in our turn. Manju had a few asthmatic attacks and required frequent medication. Priya joined KV Deolali with other children in the hope that it was doing better than Barnes School. Rohit was admitted to Barnes School Class II which he liked immensely. Both used to ply by bus and there were no problems whatsoever. Priya had learnt to cycle with a lot of help from Hari Singh who had moved with me from the Regiment. She had a minor accident and there was an injury that had to be attended to at the MH. We stayed in the officer's accommodation known as Connaught Camp behind the main road of Deolali. I remember fencing the guava garden around the house with barbed wire, two strands of which were pilfered quietly at night by the *sahayaks*, from GE Deolali's fence.

Golf was a passion with me those days especially when you are entrusted with the course maintenance as Golf Secretary THI Deolali. I used to rush off every afternoon to play at the course and spent long hours planning with Brig. Aujla, the conversion of browns and greens. The grass was ordered from Taj Nursery, Agra kind courtesy 17 Para. First, the plucked grassroots were watered and kept in trays to bring it back to life. We selected a portion of three greens where the process of grass plantation was done by working parties from units under the supervision of THI *malis*. During our visit to Ahmednagar, we got to know what they had done to accelerate the process of greening. We ordered tan from the tanneries around Nasik, which is their by-product. Tan was mixed with soil and tea lives to give the right mix. Within two months or so our efforts bore fruit. We also got the pipelines laid to all greens which was not a problem as the main water supply pipelines passed through the golf course after co-opting the GE as a playing member. Deolali has perpetual water supply problems. DC Nasik was co-opted as a playing member of the course who ensured uninterrupted water supply for us. We opened the membership of the Golf Club to civilians of status, which ensured all our teething problems were resolved. Robert from Wellington now sent his cousin Swami, with a request to get him a job on the course. Since we had DC Nasik's backing, we got Swami enrolled as the Range Lascar on the payroll of Station Headquarters Deolali and ensured he was present at the course for duties as the Caddie Master. I can say with great satisfaction that the Commandant, Maj. Gen. Talwar and Brig. SK Mathur had no opportunity to point out anything as all nine greens, then, were doing very well after we had laid the foundation, before my departure for Mhow.

With Amarjit at THI Deolali

After about six months, the old lot of PS Bhandari, Kewal Puri and Naresh Chandra had left, taking with them all their experience of running one of the best JC Arty courses. With the arrival of some new faces like Kalha, BG Duggal, BM Verma, Sunil Bahree, Tiger Behl and Natarajan, our crowd once again became a very conspicuous lot on social functions at THI, mess functions and the golf/tennis courts. The concept of "think tanks" with a proper Faculty of Studies was also put into practice, for a short time. Though Brig. Aujla did have the right mix of social and professional conduct in mind, we found that it was somewhat hectic for a few of us, at times. There were no compulsions and the two/three of us like BP, Vishwa, Rangachari and myself kept ourselves busy with the courses and attended the mandatory mess/THI functions only.

Around March April 1984, we kept abreast of the unfortunate events in Punjab, which was hurtling towards chaos as a result of the inept handling by politicians. We used to avoid discussions on the brutal killings taking place in Punjab for the fears of offending our Sikh colleagues and student officers. Things were headed for a confrontation when DIG Atwal was shot dead in front of Harmandir inside the Golden Temple Amritsar Complex on 23 April 1984 by the armed Sikh followers of Bhindrawale. Not a day passed without some outrageous killing and retaliation by the police. Punjab, known for its industries as well as agriculture suffered a severe setback on the threats to non-Sikhs from the terrorists holed up inside the Golden Temple. None of us thought that the situation would escalate to the level of armed intervention by the Army. We were stunned when someone coming back from Amritsar gave the news that the police cordon had been strengthened by the Army and the situation was poised for an intervention by the Army. When the inevitable happened on 6 June 1984, we were all horrified to hear about the killings that took place of both the Sikh followers and the devotees as well as the army casualties. In the operation, the failure of intelligence, and the underestimation of the extremist Sikhs will to fight was evident. It is a tribute to this great institution that we all stood united like rocks and never allowed the discussion with student officers on this topic. We had the fine example of 175 Field Regiment, a pure Sikh cooperating unit in which the CO and his officers were in full control, the JCOs and jawans steadfast with unimpeachable loyalty. Hats off to the School of Artillery for maintaining complete peace, unity and harmony during troubled times.

By about April May 1984, the HC list was out and along with Gurjit Randhawa (new Armour DS) and BM Verma, I was also nominated to attend Higher Command. Once again, our baggage left for Mhow in a truck, Hari Singh and Singha were of great help in the packing. Saying goodbye to Deolali has never been easy. My old CO Brig. SS Ratra who was very fond of all of us felt that I was keeping away from him for some unknown reasons. Our friend, philosopher and guide Brig. DP Bahl was also unhappy with us that we had not even called on them. My cousin Sushil, the Deputy and his wife Dolly had laid on a great meal in our honour, according to their parents' desire. His parents were also our neighbours from Dehradun and we had excellent family ties. We did try to make amends in the last week of our stay and gave our friends no cause for complaint before we left.

The Amritsar Sojourn and Alma Mater Once Again

When I moved to Ladakh in 1988, I was first allotted G-8 Mayapuri, which was not at all convenient for my daughter, Priya, who had to change three buses to get to her college. I then requested my coursemate, Col. BM Kapur, then MA to COAS to help me out. Thanks to BM I was allotted a separate accommodation in Pratap Chowk. Manju took up a job in Delhi Area Primary school. My son, Rohit, was doing well at Army Public School, though I had to arrange for a Maths tutor for him. They continued to stay in Delhi Cantt for almost two years when I received my posting on promotion to Amritsar. At this time,

Priya was still in II year Honours and Rohit had still two months left for the academic session to finish. Our uncle, Mr Kripal Chand, ex-Director Finance Indian Airlines, came to our rescue by offering to accommodate Priya in his residence in Oberoi Apartments, Delhi. She stayed with them for a year which enabled her to complete the Honours course. Manju and Rohit were slated to move when the academic sessions were over in their respective schools.

I had to proceed immediately to ranges on 28 Feb 90 for a week's stay to witness the course shooting of my brigade units. On my return, I called on the GOC, Infantry Division, Maj. Gen. BKN Chhibber, and was very impressed by his views on command in the disturbed state of Punjab. He held very straightforward and forthright views and appeared to be very dynamic and thoroughly professional. I had settled in the mess initially, as I arrived single. This also allowed the family of Brig. GS Khara, my predecessor to continue their stay till we wound up in Delhi. Rohit cleared Class VIII at APS New Delhi, Manju completed her teaching assignment at DAPS and the luggage got dispatched in a 3 Ton to Amritsar.

Amritsar tenure started with a bang. Punjab was amid insurgency second phase in the early nineties instigated from across the border. One of the units had its vehicle hit by the terrorists, being mistaken for a police van. The involved terrorists were hunted down and killed later by the unit. No Army vehicle was hit by terrorists thereafter and the terrorists sent in an apology. First of all, the GOC ordered the tightening of security in the Old and New Cantt. I was directed to write the SOP on security along with two other junior officers. We completed the task in good time and the red book on the security of Amritsar Cantt exists even now. This SOP had been borrowed by almost all

Cantts in Western Command and was considered an authority. This was primarily thanks to the guidance by the GOC and his staff, who gave me full credit for a job well done by my team. We continued to follow the SOP for the rest of our stay in Amritsar.

Immediately after the incident with the terrorists, there was a sudden spurt in terrorism in Punjab leading to tightening of security measures. It was evident that Pakistan was openly aiding the Sikh extremists, who were based in Pakistan from safe sanctuaries across the border. Law and order situation had worsened and the rural areas were being gradually affected. Our GOC had carried out a review of the situation and was able to put it across to the PM, Mr VP Singh and his entourage who had come sometime in March 1990 on a tour. I remember the PM (also the RM) accompanied by the Cabinet Secretary Mr Deshmukh IAS, the Army & Corps Commander along with DG Police KPS Gill and his staff seated in the Panther Mess for a meeting. Earlier, the Corps Commander has arrived with his orders group, We, the Brigade Commanders were seated in the last row and were privy to the current plans under discussion. At the end of the meeting, I remember Gen. Chhibber telling KPS Gill something that I can never forget, "*Gill Sahib, Tussi apne kale kachhe walon nuh kabu kar lo, ussi insurgency nuh khatam kar denge*". There was pin-drop silence and there were nods of agreement with the GOC's assessment. It was amply clear that the Punjab insurgency was not a mass movement but a creation of Pakistan, to fish in the troubled political waters. This was the closest we went to war with Pakistan, which was narrowly averted.

Per division orders, all artillery units were made to move forward to the DCB and occupy defences in infantry roles to plug gaps in the border fencing near dhussi bunds, places near streams that were identified as Infiltration routes of terrorists from across the order. The normal reaction for any Arty unit was, this is not our job and who would look after our guns and technical equipment. Our battalions were also on peace tenure and this job had to be shared equally. I accepted the job as a challenge because it was not the first time that the Arty units were being used in an infantry role. GOC's plan had made an impact on me and I thought it was an opportunity for my brigade to prove its worth. When the GOC asked me to discuss my plan of execution, I explained the concept that I had in mind was based on the occupation of a 10 km sector by each regiment on the DCB with no gaps between the batteries. Three quick reaction teams based on two jongas LMG mounted with communications were positioned in each battery, two batteries worth of guns would be mothballed and kept in the rear along with the equipment in their stores. Unit administration would move forwards leaving minimum jawans at the rear. After two months there would be a rotation of units so that we do not disturb the COs training directives. For training purposes, we deployed two guns per battery, in the forward area. When not on infantry duties, gunners could carry out their gun drills. I got this approved by the GOC and this probably was done for the first time in recent years. I can be blamed for accepting this task without any hesitation. There was no complaint/representation from any unit that their training had referred to. In our infantry role, we achieved great success at par with infantry Brigades. We patrolled our area of responsibility and fulfilled our new role well. We also had some apprehensions and capture of weapons and ammunition. Our doctors, who manned the primary health centres, also did a commendable job in treating locals of that area.

Manju arrived after the Holi celebration, though Rohit had joined me earlier. Two of us stayed in the Gun House till Manju's arrival, Rohit was admitted to Springdale's School on Fatehgarh Churian road run by one Mrs Sandhu. The school was spoken of well and within easy reach of the Gun House. Rohit commuted every day in a jeep to school and back for security reasons with an escort at all times. We found this arrangement good and carried on for almost two years. Manju then got about getting the house in good shape and organizing welfare activities within the brigade. She got our gardener, Desh Raj to remodel the garden for the coming year's flowers show and generally beautify Gun House. We also had a two-acre plot adjacent to the house which was being cultivated by the brigade for two crops in a year, one of rice followed by a late variety of wheat. Brigade farm in the New Cantt under the "grow more food campaign" was given to all units of the brigade to cultivate the vacant plots so that no encroachment takes place there. All this area would eventually be occupied by the Armoured Brigade but was lying vacant temporarily. The farm produce was property accounted for as per existing orders then in force, 25% revenue is deposited in the treasury, as per existing practice. We had an experienced hand, a re-employed officer looking after the farm and for every season a proper board of officers accounted for the farm produce. The Division had instituted safeguards on the farm accounts and we ensured no mistakes.

Assuming command of an Arty Brigade at Amritsar

At the time of taking over, I had made up my decision that would work according to the dictates of my conscience with utmost honesty, integrity and loyalty to the organisation. Now with 27 years of service and being only 45 plus years old, I thought I should continue my professional conduct, look after the welfare of my officers and men, upholding the same in the highest traditions of this fine Army. We both led very simple, austere lives, ensured camaraderie, good professional climate and ensured no rat race between units. I saw to it that professional standards were improved upon further and did not accept existing standards. This bore fruit, as all five field regiments and two medium regiments secured outstanding reports during the annual camps and had excellent maintenance reports from EME and Ordnance. Other units like a Light Regt and a SATA Battery also performed very well. I made several visits to the units to monitor their training and gave full laxity to COs to train them without my interference.

Command of an Arty Brigade is a tremendous experience, diverse weapon systems each with their varied characteristics networks, huge transport fleet and a sound administrative backup. I endeavoured to see that 100% serviceability was maintained at all times. Mobilisation drills were practised every alternate month by everyone including Brigade HQ. Physical fitness was one aspect that needed attention, and participation by officers in all troop games and athletes was keenly monitored by me. It is with immense pride that we bagged almost all sports competitions except wrestling where we stood second. Officers' participation in all teams ensured sure shot success. In the athletics final, the most prestigious officers relay event 4 x 400 m was always won by the Arty Brigade.

The Artillery Brigade had no dearth of funds but I endeavoured to regulate all expenditure judiciously. We spent a substantial amount on the training of our sportsmen, athletes, welfare activities of families and some amount on improvement in jawans and officers' messes as well. There were services and national level athletes and boxers from the brigade whom we sent on our costs to NIS Patiala for coaching. As per Senior Colonel Commandants directions, we decided to raise regimental messes and returned some staff to units to run their messes. It was also my desire to let COs run their messes in peace stations so that when the unit moves out to field, it is not faced with a situation where it spends all its funds acquiring mess property all at once. Besides, the camaraderie and the esprit de corps developed in regimental messes is what I learnt from my tenures in the Para Brigade.

With Corps Commander Lt. Gen. BKN Chibber at Amritsar

As I was beginning to enjoy my command, the GOC Gen. Chhibber moved to Jalandhar Corps as its commander on promotion. We had established a very good rapport with the strict GOC and he appreciated my good work as Commander Arty Brigade. I also received my appraisal for the years which was well beyond my expectations. I maintained very good relations with my colleagues Brigs RP Singh, JBS Yadav, SP Kapoor, KL Bakshi and of course, Gurbaksh Sihota commanding the the Mechanised Brigade.

In the same reporting year, the Corps Commander tasked me to write the Corps wargame under him at Jalandhar during the winter of 1990. I headed a team of officers who wrote the war game under him at Jalandhar, during the winter of 1990. My team had visited every nook and corner of the Corps sector and studied the terrain thoroughly just before I submitted the written war game to the GOC for his final approval. All Brigades were asked to establish their operations rooms in their caravans in the Corps parade ground in Jalandhar. We then established the lower control under one Armoured CO (Lt. Col. Sansar Chand), GSO-1, SVP Singh, three other Majors who performed their duties as CO and subunit commanders very well. In the initial stages, I accompanied the corps commander for briefings at various Brigade HQ and learnt a lot from the briefings by the various infantry commanders. These visits were unannounced and all at odd hours of the night. In the conducting stage, the actual operational plans were put into practice through war games. This wargame proved very useful for own general and professional improvement. In summing up, the Corps Commander personally congratulated my team for their excellent effort in making the wargame a success.

We had very good relations with the Dy GOCs, next-door neighbour initially it was Brig. Ashok Dewan from the Gurkhas followed by Brig. PR Bose from the Gunners. I made it a point to invite him for all functions in the brigade being Gunner senior to me. They were a very spirited couple and very supportive and appreciative of our efforts to promote esprit de corps. Our other neighbour was my colleague Brig. KL Bakshi who was commander of the Infantry Brigade. His daughter Piya and Priya became good friends and enjoyed a good rapport. Bakshis were good card players and kept the new GOC Maj. Gen. HK Bajaj in good humour.

Maj. Gen. HK Bajaj from the Corps of Signals took over sometime towards the end of 1990 around the time I was picked to conduct the war game again. I had met him briefly at Wellington before he left on posting in 1985. He was also BM of an Infantry Brigade during the 1971 war, in Bangladesh under Brig. Mishra. Though a serious professional and without any sense of humour, he enjoyed his card game. I had made up my mind that I would not be found lacking in my performance and exhorted my units to put their best fast forward during the visit by the GOC. In all our Gunners Day and other mess functions, we laid it on thick and looked after our guests well. There were restrictions like only cocktails on Gunners Day which we scrupulously observed. We played regular golf at Panther Golf Club together with GOC and two other officers. We also organised regular functions at Panther Cub which were appreciated by everyone in the station. We also made some civilian friends like Manohar Lal Saggar who had a shop in Hall Bazar, Anil Sagar a rice merchant living on the periphery of the Cantt and Mr Himanshu Mathur, Manager of Grindlays Amritsar. Besides this, there were local dignitaries like DC Shri Kashmir Singh and DIG Shri MS Bhullar. We also found Brig. JB Singh (Retired), Vice President OCM and his wife excellent company. Playing cards, except bridge, has never been our forte and we kept away from this great activity. Gen. Bajaj was a keen bridge player also and we occasionally formed part of the foursome. Golf again after a lapse of 18 months in Amritsar was excellent. We played three to four days a week unless there was some official commitment. Gen. Bajaj, Krishan Bakshi and Anil Sagar were our fixed foursome.

We had regular visits by dignitaries from Army HQ, relatives and our friends/colleagues who were visitors to the Golden Temple, as well. DG Arty Gen. Ashok Manglik paid a visit and was briefed and taken around by me. We invited him for a meal at our residence, followed by a mess night at the Arty Mess. I was particularly impressed when he asked for his bill for the blazer cloth he purchased from OCM. The Army Commander asked for some confiscated items from the custom-house which were purchased and sent with bills. When COAS Gen. Rodrigues staff requested some cut glass, we again presented the bill, which was cleared later. Even when Ranjana Malik, wife of the Maj. Gen. VP Malik requested for a Bukhara carpet to be purchased, I sent the bill along with the carpet. In my mind, I had never an iota of doubt that this expenditure could ever have been footed by my brigade.

Our stay in Amritsar was one of the most enjoyable ones in my career. Rohit had settled down well in his school and was doing well. Priya finished her final year at St Stephen's and moved from Delhi to the newly opened AWWA hostel for girls. She had now joined Alliance Française for learning French, working part-time and also used to visit us, whenever she was free. In one of the major station events, the garden competition where the Gun House was adjudged the best, she decided to join all of us here. My mother was with us for more than a month and enjoyed herself when we were 'at home' to all our brigade officers who had come to admire the garden. A day later, Corps Commander Gen. Chhibber and his wife also paid us a very hurried call early in the evening and congratulated Manju personally. They did not stay on for a meal and had a cup of tea instead, in the lawns. Besides these visitors, we also had Maj. Gen. VM Patel, GOC of an Infantry Division and Maj. Gen. Vinay Shankar and DG Arty visiting the brigade and being hosted a meal at the Gun House. We also hosted the Higher Command course, especially all Gunners and my schoolmate Vijay Raheja, who were on a study tour. In the meantime, my brother-in-law, Ashok Swarup also got his transfer to Delhi from

Calcutta to join Jagatjit Industries, and Priya finally moved in with them.

With Manju at the Panther Institute

I was at Jalandhar for the Corps War Game 1991 and was staying with our great seventeener Brig. Narayan Chatterjee, the CC Arty. He was also in the running for NDC after outstanding reports in from his previous postings. I had missed out and was disappointed. I had performed my duties to the satisfaction of my superiors. Despite best efforts to have my posting orders as Deputy Commander Field Wing, School of Artillery rescinded, I could not manage it. It appears that from those left out of the NDC, the Commandant School of Artillery designate approved my name. I understand Lt. Gen. Harish Kapoor did try to get me as Brig. Adm of his Corps, but failed in his efforts. The prospects of another tenure in the School of Artillery rattled me. Apart from this, Rohit's 10th board was in March 1992 and the organisation was determined to move me out in 22 months, before the conclusion of the academic session. Till now I did not even know that Maj. Gen. PS Bevli was the Field Wing commander. After all, efforts to stall the posting failed, I left for Deolali in Jan 1992. Manju had to vacate the Gun House and moved with Rohit to a single room in the Panther Institute. Our luggage moved to Deolali by truck and as usual Hari Singh and Singha came to my rescue. I took all this in my stride as I thought maybe it's for my good and God Almighty had willed it.

Before our move from Amritsar, we were called for the evening at Corps Commander's residence at Jalandhar, along with others who were posted out. It was quite a big gathering of Brigadiers and above. We drove down from Amritsar and reached slightly late. Gen. & Mrs Chhibber went around the guests making polite conversation with the ladies. I did not fail to notice that a gift package was lying on the centre table, from the time we had arrived. We saw some officers arriving with gifts, in full view of everyone present. Mrs Chhibber acted tactfully and defused the situation by calling one of the jawan helpers to take them all back to be deposited in their respective staff cars, adding softly, "Surely you know we don't accept gifts". One of our dear friends and his wife persisted and tried to present a silver salver as a token of their love and affection. This too was not accepted by the lady and promptly returned. Most of the guests had left and we were a handful of Brigadiers left with our spouses, possibly Brig. Bakshi, Sati Cheema, Kohli the Chief Engineer and myself. There was pin-drop silence all around and it was then, that the Corps Commander remarked that a new culture had crept in where some officers carry gifts for senior officers, in violation of professional ethics. He added that he was sure those who carried gifts, now heading for the NDC course, must have felt rebuffed by the return. As we had no gifts for the General, I felt there was no need for me to express my opinion.

Having reconciled to a posting to Deolali, I arrived there around mid-Jan 1992 leaving the family in the care of Col. SC Vohra, CO of one othe Field Regiments. Manju stayed in the Panther Institute guest room for two months, to enable Rohit to finish his board exams. On arrival at Deolali, Bevli promptly pushed me out to the ranges that very day. We were allotted three rooms in P7 Block in B Mess. Luggage was kept in the QM Store awaiting allotment of the permanent accommodation. School Commandant was Lt. Gen. Romesh Khosla who was in the process of handing over to Lt. Gen. Kulbir Singh, Maj. Gen. Rocky Talwar was his Deputy Commandant and the famous gunner mountaineer Brigs Darshan Khullar the BGS and SK Mohindra the Brig. Adm. Tactical Wing Commander was Maj. Gen. NC Mahajan with Brig. BS Gill as his Deputy. I was asked to select a Col's accommodation for myself which would be properly renovated for me. I was shown the OC Supply Depots residence, vacated by one Lt. Col. Khorana at that time which I gladly accepted. After renovation, we moved in and made ourselves quite comfortable. It was nowhere near what everyone aspires for, the prized bungalows alongside Alpha Mess on the Generals Road, bang opposite the THI. The damage done by the upgrades was evident!!

Life in Field Wing was generally good with Maj. Gen. Bevli as the Commander, under the benign atmosphere existing in School of

Artillery. I watched Gen. Bevli closely and thought that we had struck a good equation. This meant the acceptance of his simple style of functioning which precludes any delegation of powers to anyone except himself. One fine day, to my great surprise, he informed me that I should look after YOs and Junior Leaders Division. The very next day he changed his orders. Some good highlights of Field Wing were the morning prayers on Saturdays which laid down the work program for the next week. He used this forum to debrief junior IGs for their acts of commission and omission, which was the right thing to do. I also noticed that he sometimes flogged the complete wing, yet not a murmur from anyone. He had a few handpicked IGs for the gunnery jobs like Gurmeet Kanwal, HR Sharma, Gulati and Popli on whom he relied very heavily for comments or study reports when asked for, by the School HQ. After settling down, I decided to have a heart-to-heart talk with Bevli. I suggested that golf was possible every afternoon if we left the office daily by 2:30 PM. To my surprise, he agreed and we both played golf every afternoon. We also fixed up four times with Col. Pandey and one of the Tac Wing instructors. Junior IGs from Field Wing were encouraged to play troop games with their respective course, like six a side hockey, basketball and volleyball.

Social life in Deolali was quite hectic, especially at the THI. Being the Chairman, I generally had to oversee its functioning, the Commandant invariably turned up for most club functions, which was a good thing. In one of the meetings of Commandant with the Commander Field Wing, I was invited to give a THI presentation, as a part of the Field Wing responsibility. After a casual look at the accounts, it was no rocket science to conclude that the state of the finances was far from healthy. After careful analysis and an internal audit for almost two weeks, the Secretary and I were able to analyse the main reasons for this state of affairs. Firstly, the expenditure on salaries of employees on the rolls of THI was far in excess and a cap on this account was required. Next, the Institute incurred losses on daily local purchases made for permanent staff, and the last one was miscellaneous losses that could not be accounted for. When I made a formal presentation, the Commandant seemed annoyed at the excessive expenditure on salaries. He was surprised to know that a cook and *masalchi* were still serving a retired and a serving senior officer. He then ordered them to be withdrawn immediately. When a formal DO letter recalling staff from retired senior officers was being addressed, he declined and directed me to do so. I did this unpleasant task and requested the concerned officers to return the staff by a particular date. The practice adopted for catering to the permanent staff for their daily requirements was discontinued leading to some murmurs amongst the staff, which were ignored. In about three months, the results began to show and the famous THI was able to come out of the red. Bold decisions always yield results.

My afternoons, when free from golf, were spent with Secretary Lt. Col. BU Kumar to set all systems in place in THI so that it becomes younger officer friendly it is freely patronized by the members. The first thing that we noticed was the décor which needed a lot of doing up. Both Manju and I spent hours trying to get the bar and anterooms with decent colour schemes, taking the upholstering, curtains and floor tiles into account. The dance floor outside was also required to be done up. As the Monsoon Ball was approaching fast, seeing the poor MES response, I requested Commandant BEG Kirkee, a fellow DS from Wellington, Brig. AV Sathe for help from some masons. Six sappers helped do up the tiles of the dance floor. They also completely renovated the two clay courts to make them cemented. As the Chairman THI, I took it upon myself to write a letter of thanks to the BEG Commandant. The Monsoon Ball 1992, was a roaring success. Our biggest clientele were the young officers attending the course who now patronized the THI in large numbers. We had taken upon ourselves that we would not curb their little exuberance in the cheering during the function, provided there were no catcalls, and the required decorum was maintained. Youngsters behaved well throughout, without their IGs being placed alongside them. I was overjoyed to see these two cemented courts in extensive use by youngsters, immediately after they were ready.

Field Wing, being the largest wing with maximum commitments, had its own set of rules which sometimes ran contrary to that of the Headquarters. It was not possible to accede to everyone's request and let our course commitments suffer. I noticed a simmering discontent in the Wing which I had to nip in the bud almost daily. Enjoying the confidence of junior IGs, I did my best to defuse all crises, calling the youngster to my office and allowing him to let off his steam. With better management, it was possible to adjust everyone's requirements as neither was there an emergency that existed nor was there any shortage of instructors. I remember one junior instructor being sanctioned three days leave to go to Hyderabad to drop his ailing wife, who was asthmatic. He was sanctioned three days leave to proceed to Hyderabad. His brother-in-law was to pick up his wife and the officer was ordered to take the next train from the platform opposite and return by late night, and get on to his class the next morning. When I interviewed the officer, he had tears in his eyes and told me what had been instructed. I sanctioned seven days leave instead of three and then spoke to Gen. Bevli personally and got his ex post facto sanction. He first enquired who would fill the gap during the additional four days. I gave him the name of the substitute and assured him that everything would be taken care of. He professed ignorance of the officer's wife's problem and expressed gratitude for my timely intervention. Sometimes, the staff do not project the requirement properly leading to this situation. I wanted to play my role as a buffer between the officers and the Commander, which I think I did well, in my tenure.

I was also assigned the task of preparing a statement of the case for grant of MSc Weapons and Armaments to LGSC qualified officers by Pune University. I contacted Brig. AM Warty, a retired gunner who helped us. Taking a cue from DSSC Wellington from their case for grant of an MSc Defence Studies by the Madras University, I prepared a watertight case for approval by the Pune University. This involved several trips/interactions with Pune University officials. The statement of the case prepared by me was accepted by Pune University a year later after I departed from Deolali. Of the many projects assigned to me, one was the renovation of the newly constructed building in the KLP, for the LGSC Course graduation ceremony. Starting with acoustics, seating, carpeting and the stage everything had to be planned/created with the MES by minor/major works. I was given free hand and this project met the deadline of the first LGSC Graduation Ceremony in October 1992. We were also responsible for opening a new tea room for students in Field Wing in the old AD Wing sheds. I felt very happy and satisfied that I had contributed to the alma mater in my humble way.

Sometime in Aug 92, I was detailed to carry out an inquiry at Artillery Centre Nasik Road, on orders of our Commandant. This inquiry pertained to the misappropriation of a 12 Bore shotgun of Centre Shikar Club by an officer and a clever substitution of another gun, in its place. The COAS had also paid a visit during this time and we all saw the same officer had pleaded for COAS's indulgence. The two members detailed with me were two other Colonels. I had noticed that both these officer members were the interested parties, who wanted to see the officer go scot-free. I pointed this out to the Commandant who overruled my objection, I understood later that the Commandant too, had served earlier, with the concerned officer. In the initial investigations done by the Centre Commandant, a prima facie case was already established. Therefore, after I examined witnesses, I did not exonerate the officer from the attempted misappropriation. While I was in the process of completing the inquiry, Commandant called me one evening at his residence on the plea of ascertaining the progress of the inquiry. When I intimated my draft finding and opinion, the Commandant expressed unhappiness over my draft opinion. The next morning, I was summoned by the Commandant in his office. As an officer loyal to the organisation, I stated that the findings and opinions were the same as given by me. He could at least tell me where I have gone wrong. He angrily retorted and asked me to submit the court of inquiry, as I deemed fit. Subsequently, the completed inquiry was with Commandant for one full week. If there had been some glaring errors made by me, he could well have asked me to rectify before forwarding the same to HQ Southern Command. Once having forwarded the same, it meant that he had approved the inquiry too. After my posting out from Deolali in December 92, I learnt that the court of inquiry had not been approved by the Army Commander. The Commandant's opinion exonerating the officer for this act was contrary to mine. The Commandant's opinion had to change, later to agree with what, I as Presiding Officer had opined. I think the Commandant carried a burden of guilt for quite some time. He tried to meet me many times in Delhi on Gunner meets but I deliberately avoided him. I finally met him at the DG Arty Golf Tournament in 1997 and he admitted that he was wrong about his opinion of the officer and my inquiry was right. I thought it was very magnanimous on his part to admit, though it was too late now.

Outside Regiment of Artillery

The Alluring Jungles of Mizoram

Mizoram was earlier known as the Lushai Hills District and was once a part and parcel of the undivided Assam State, at the time of independence. This district was renamed Mizo Hills District in the 1960s. This district shot into the limelight in 1959, when a massive famine was reported. Locals believe that a "*mautam*" comes every 100 years when the bamboo starts to flower. Nature then allows the rat population to proliferate. Most of the grains produced in their *jhooms* (cultivated areas) are consumed by the rodents, creating scarcity, which leads to famine-like conditions. The Assam Government ignored these warnings and local movement led to the creation of self-help groups like the MNF, which converted into an armed insurgency for almost two decades. First a UT in 1977, with an area of approximately 21k square km and a population of 4 lakhs, was sometimes compared to Karol Bagh Delhi for population and NCR for the area.

Amazingly, the Mizos believe that they were once the lost tribe of Judaism who found their way here after the persecution in their native land. The accepted ancestry, however, is to SE Asian tribes which migrated to these hills, called Lushai Hills, in the 18th century. There are 18 identified tribes, mostly Lushai. Pawi, Lakher and Kuki with a sprinkling of Tuntunias, Hmars. Reangs, Paite and Chakmas. They are close to Burmese in their mongoloid features and have close ties with the tribes across the border in Arakans the These tribes came under Christian missionary influence and 87% are either devout Presbyterian or Baptists. As a result, the literacy level also is second only to Kerala, a whopping 92%. If one goes around the churches, you could see, they doubled up as a school by day and a church by night. As far as Mizo culture is concerned, they are way ahead of the rest of the country in matters of permissiveness in society. The parents allow their girls to mix freely with the boys for a "*nula rim*" a kind of date on all days of the week. Love for western music and various soft community dances, including the bamboo dance at the community centre are regular features. Traditionally, the community arranges accommodation for a month's stay and live-in for boys and girls, on reaching puberty. I once asked the 90-year-old Scottish padre married to a local woman at a parish church near Lunglei, why were the girls dressed so provocatively at church meetings. He replied, "Not all of them are. It is usually the young ones. How else do you find a suitor? They do need to display their wares first". Likewise, when I had been around in the Southern Mizoram with one of the patrols from Bungtlang to Chawngte, we came across the half-clad Tuntunia women, and I was reminded of the padre's reply. Incidentally, these are now the relics of the past, they must have realized the undue attention by outsiders, becoming unworthy of their exhibition.

Briefly some more interesting facts about Mizoram and the alluring jungles. After two months leave from DSSC Wellington up to the end of January 1977, I left for the North East for the first time, being posted to a Mountain Brigade in Mizoram, as a BM to Brig. AG Minwalla. The brigade had moved from Agartala in early 1975 to South Mizoram after the IG Police was shot dead in his office by Mizo insurgents. Luckily, I had the opportunity to study the entire Mizo insurgency in DSSC, where ample literature was available. The causes of the insurgency, operations conducted during 1966-67, results achieved and the ongoing talks with Laldenga. Generally, everyone takes the flight up to Kumbhigram (Silchar) with a change at Calcutta. As a soldier, I chose to travel by train from Delhi to Allahabad then on to New Bongaigaon, up to Gauhati. Then took the Barrak Valley Express via Lumding to Silchar. We then drove down from Silchar to Masimpur by road and stopped over at the division's rear HQ. Mizoram starts from Vairengte, the drive-through picturesque hills interspersed with thick pristine forests, dwelling all along the road. The villages were grouped in 1966, as a part of a grouping of villages under Op Accomplishment One, then introduced by the Army. Some villages that were allowed to break away from the grouping are located on the way off hills, next to river sources but away from civilization. It took me a full day's drive to Aizawl, the beautiful state capital, where the main Division HQ was located and we settled for the night in the local brigade guest room. Youngsters called Aizawl the "Paris of the East", as you could see the latest trends in fashionable, chic and well-dressed college girls cavorting around their boyfriends, loud music blaring away from their two in one Sony cassette recorders, which had just entered the market. Shops and bars were in plenty, nightlife severely curtailed by the curfew. which had come into effect a year back. Youngsters on reaching Aizawl were fascinated and tended to keep extending their stay. Aizawl gives you a feeling of the Nilgiris hills of Tamil Nadu, surrounded by hills and is nicely perched on habitation areas on ridges of steep hills. These are overlooked by the sylvan valley between two rivers. The old river bed of Turial in the south had an airstrip from where my old air OP flight mate, Sukhwinder took off with his friend, the medical officer. The Krishak piloted by him had gone into the exotic landscape of the verdant hills around them, never to return. Besides remembering Sukhwinder, all I could think at that time was what would the new environment be like for the next two years.

Mizoram is a beautiful place to visit for a short trip but not on posting as a non-family station. Yet, an amazing land of rolling hills, valleys, rivers and lakes numerous ridgelines and plains scattered all over. When I mentioned the Nilgiris hills earlier, I failed to notice that there is a peak Phawngpui, also known as the Blue Mountain, situated in the south-eastern part of the state in my brigade sector. Essentially, Mizo life revolves around agriculture. They own land in the forests where they carry out a wasteful practice of shifting cultivation called jhooming. They clear a patta of the allotted land, burn it, cultivate the same for some rice corn, cotton and vegetables. After cultivating it, abandon this jhoom after two or three crops, before shifting to another jhoom. Those days, there was just one, the single main artery going through the entire length of Mizoram Silchar- Aizawl- Lunglei terminating at Lawngtalai. To admire the Blue Mountains, you had to proceed beyond Lunglei to the paltan at Lawngtalai, then proceed on a jeepable track to the base of the hill and trek thereafter.

I reached Pukpui near Lunglei, where my Brigade HQ was located by evening, after five hours back-breaking drive from Aizawl. I relieved a gentleman by the name of Maj. SS Brar, a sapper who was anxiously waiting for me. We lived in a colony of bashas made from bamboo which was nicely fastened to the cemented plinths with proper lighting and good cane furniture. Though we all had fairly decent rooms with an attached toilet, op works had ensured good sanitary fittings and electrical fittings and fixtures. My basha had a bamboo partition with that of the DQ and had an additional waiting room and a verandah in front. Beyond the verandah, you got a lovely view of the sunset in the hills. I always felt mesmerized by the beauty of the surroundings amid jungles. Sunset at about 4.30 every evening, after which you only heard mosquitos or the strumming of guitars. Sunrise was early morning at 4.45 giving you a gorgeous view of the valley once again.

Within three months, the new commander Brig. Surendra Nath of Raj Rif arrived and a new GSO 3 (Int) Capt. Jagtar Grewal joined in his place. Capt. Ravi Gupta was the Staff Capt. who fitted well in the team and was my student at DSSC later. The DQ, Maj. HK Jha and I became very good friends and he introduced me to yoga asanas which I have continued thereafter. Our paltans, Kumaonis were commanded by Lt. Col. RN Bakshi and later by Lt. Col. JK Chadha, Jats were commanded by Lt. Col. SK Singh later replaced by Bihar under Lt. Col. JPS Sandhu and Jak Rif commanded by Lt. Col. AB Patil. There were two more para-military forces like Assam Rifles commanded by Lt. Col. VK Gupta and a BSF battalion commanded by Commandant HL Sachdeva which formed part of operations. Overall, we had a very good mix of troops, who were a seasoned lot, having seen a lot of operations very recently. ADS under Maj. Yadav functioned near our Brigade HQ at Pukpui and there was a compo platoon commanded by Capt. Bant Singh, also in the location. Our Sparrow, Maj. Shashi Sawant is still in touch with me from Kolhapur, where he is leading a quiet retired life. We had company-sized 30 air-maintained posts, which were along both the borders with Bangladesh and Burma. DC Lunglei was Shri Baleshwa Rai, IAS and the SP was Shri Virendra Rai. Both these gentlemen were from the AGMU cadre, whom I met later just before my retirement. We were tasked to plug routes of infiltration and exfiltration across these borders. The cost of maintaining posts by air is at least ten times that of normal maintenance by road and our boss would play havoc with the staff if there were any foul-ups. There were times when the airdrop had to be aborted, due to clouds over a particular post, that gave the pilot the latitude to jettison/drop the load at any post in the vicinity, rather than take it back to Masimpur. Problems arose if 100 kg potatoes were dropped in excess, the troops then complained. They were eating potatoes for breakfast, lunch and dinner till the stock finished. If there were surplus rations at posts nearing their expiry, we had to send extra troops from nearby posts to consume them. The problem of turnover of rations was the poor DQ's nightmare. We could, otherwise, be faced with a surfeit of rations whose life had expired, causing a massive loss to the exchequer.

We got used to the daily ritual which existed from the days the brigade moved in here. The morning prayers commenced with an intelligence briefing, a summary of previous days operations and the difficulties faced by our troops, covered by my intelligence officer. Then was the admin briefing which included the air maintenance monsoon stock levels peculiar to this region. Then was my turn to apprise all present of the impending operations for the next day if any and the actions taken on previous directions of the Commander. In addition, BM was expected to report progress on various op /project works undertaken as a part of controlled fraternization in the brigade sector. We took our job seriously, all these actions were so well coordinated and taken in good faith. They were executed with absolute integrity, honesty and loyalty to the organisation which restored normalcy in Mizoram. We were busy with our daily routine, kept our youngsters on a tight leash so that they did not get involved with the local women. We had a few instances of our personnel fraternizing with the local population more than necessary and that practice was nipped in the bud. Our liquor from the canteen was very popular with locals, especially women who loved our beer and were forever requesting it.

When I joined my brigade, there were a lot of jungle operations in progress in Mizoram. The insurgency was resurgent, ever since the new Gen. Ershad regime took over in Bangladesh, following Mujib's assassination. Till then, the insurgency lay dormant for a few years. It then got a fresh lease of life, then established links with the Nagas & Tripura National Volunteers, at China's behest. Training had begun in the camps established in the Chinese Province of Yunnan. A Mizo trained gang was intercepted in late 1976 on their return, carrying about 150 weapons, somewhere near Imphal. This gang was promised safe passage through Manipur and Mizoram by SIB, under the present NSA, who were then the chief peace negotiators. This gang slipped through my brigade and we came to know about them when they were on the verge of crossing over to Bangladesh, at a place called Ruma in the Chittagong Hill Tract. In an early morning heliborne raid, we were able to apprehend 18 hostiles and a large number of arms and ammunition inside our territory. The bulk of the gang had already crossed and was now under the protection of BD Rifles. We were under strict instructions not to touch the gang, yet we did hit the elements of their rear party and managed to recover weapons and ammunition. Thanks to the excellent planning by our bold GSO1, Lt. Col. SPM Tripathi, timely response by the helicopter unit and a very daring company commander Maj. Pushkar Chand from Raj Rif, we achieved success, way beyond our expectations.

Talks with hostiles remained suspended because of the raid, we knew that they were trying very hard to obtain maximum concessions from the government. They retained their weapons for the continuation of the insurgency, based on what the Chinese had briefed them. The government is showing its sincerity, announced elections in Mizoram giving just 45 day's notice. In the meanwhile, the Eastern Army Commander commended the brigade for the successful conduct of the raid. He further ordered those operations to remain suspended during the election period and no apprehensions of hostiles without arms.

During this period, sometime in March 1977, some 'reportedly armed' hostiles, in the process of tax collection, clashed with our patrol near Lawngtalai and in the crossfire a pregnant woman was killed while the hostiles made good their escape. We asked the patrol not to break contact and continue to search the area and recover the weapons which the hostiles had thrown into the ravines. The weapons were never found. This used to be a problem that the hostiles while escaping, dumped weapons into ravines and joined the local population as if nothing had happened. The next morning, Commander dispatched me to Lawngtalai to do a bit of fact-finding, investigate the shooting incident. In an insurgency ridden area as in the NE, there are less than 1% of population insurgents, 3-4% are sympathizers and the balance 95% are fence-sitters. There were massive protests at the place of the shooting and my jonga was gheraoed. Our Superintendent Police South, Mizoram AK Singh, an army officer's son extricated and accompanied me to the house, where the shooting had taken place. There were conflicting stories about the clash and it seems that there were hostiles present but were unarmed. The SP had cleverly placed some live POF ammunition inside the house for us and gave me the lead, to justify our opening fire. We got such bad press for days and were mute spectators to the locals boycotting election canvassing. Brig. T Sailo (Retired) of the Peoples Conference after his release supported us in all meetings, telling Mizos to forget the incident and resurrected the election process. Though we got away with the incident, the Army Commander came on a visit immediately thereafter, summoned the Brigade Commander & the CO at the helipad. Before my op briefing could commence, I was asked to leave. He then listened patiently to the CO's explanation. Both the CO and the battalion were moved out forthwith As a gentleman, the Army Commander respect for the institution of a CO and neither thought it proper to disgrace him publicly for the failure of command nor did he want to know more details of the officer's conduct. Thereafter, the Army Commander drove down to Lunglei High School grounds to speak to the staff, students and the citizens who had also gathered there. We had arranged some toffees and sweets for distribution to the children. Music runs in Mizo blood and it was normal for the school band with all the instrument pieces proudly displayed, in front of the gathering. Our Army Commander spoke just two sentences in English to convey his happiness to visit the school and nothing more. He then walked across to the school band and asked them to play the Mizo National song called "Lentaipui "which all the children sang beautifully, along with him assuming the role of the conductor. I am sure he knew all the notes and his hands and body movements showed how well he could communicate with the kids, and also the boys who formed an ensemble of musicians. He left us all speechless as he had given his healing touch to the Mizos. This was his art of command, in its finest hour and he left no doubts in anyone's mind. Retribution in the armed forces is immediate and exemplary and there is no inquiry/inquisition and witch hunt to follow.

During the elections in Mizoram in 1977, we provided at least 30 columns of a section each for protection of the ballot boxes and the electoral officers. Elections in South Mizoram went off peacefully and the new government of Brig. T Sailo was sworn in at Aizawl. The problem now arose, the hardliners in MNF walking out of the negotiations, while the moderates under Laldenga were subdued for the moment. We were told to suspend the counter-insurgency operations with the MNF hostiles, except those operating from new bases in the CHT called Parva. Low key preventive operations of limited cordon and search, mobile QRTs active patrolling hot spots, surveillance of the main town, was still being carried out. In addition, we were to ensure that there were no cases of tax collection by hostiles, extortion and looting of treasuries, banks and of course, the carriage of weapons by hostiles. This was always a possibility of the cash boxes belonging to civil administration and border roads under local police escort, getting waylaid while proceeding for pay distribution. The insurgency levels came down after the elections but the atmosphere of counter-insurgency operations remained. The biggest problem now was to distinguish a hardliner from the hostiles and whether he was carrying a weapon or not.

We did have a few jungle operations close to the trijunction between Burma India and Bangladesh, at a place called Parva, where the main hostile camp was located. The border with Burma is porous, there is freedom of movement permitted by local authorities up to 40 km. Things were not the same with Bangladesh, the border delineation again is not clear cut, with erstwhile East Pakistan. There are pockets/enclaves along the almost dry water channel, Thega Khal and there was no free movement. During the flag meetings between BD

Rifles and our BSF, their standard accusation was, the Buddhist Chakma rebels were being armed by us and were enjoying safe sanctuaries in Mizoram. This was not correct as we were officially forbidden to do so. I remember we once raided one hostile camp on our side of the border at a place called Rangkachia, as reported by BSF. Based on real-time information two companies affected the cordon at night. The next morning, we found the village was half inside Bangladesh, the BD Rifles post inside it. There was another village Rangkhachia inside Bangladesh, whose map reference was given by my staff by mistake, clearly admitting a border violation. We recovered a huge cache of weapons, ammunition and Indian currency looted recently from one of our treasuries along with five hostiles including one self-styled Captain. That was good going for our Kumaonis but there was a border violation protest by the Bangladesh government which became a starred question in the Parliament later. Thanks to our GOC and Army Commander, we were supported to the hilt and the clear map reading error condoned. Brings me to the eleventh principle of war, "Work not checked is seldom correct". I had learnt a good lesson and should have checked the map references myself.

My Commander, a die-hard infantryman, was very keen that all brigade staff accompany important patrols sometimes for familiarization. Accordingly, I was the first to go as my new GSO3 Gary had just returned after his darshan. With my pack 08 and one set of spare uniforms, items of toiletries and my pistol with one filled magazine, we started from Lawngtalai by road. Then the trek started up to Diltlang, located only 13 km away but we had to cross three ridgelines and two streams, one of which was a raging torrent. Our troops were very happy to see their BM footslogging with them. When we reached the post, we were treated to a feast of mostly vegetarian preparations, lots of milk preparations including the famous *churma*. We had a whole evening of *raginis* from the boys and all our tiredness and the leech we tackled enroute, were forgotten. Our next post to visit was Bungtlang which was generally along the ridgelines and about 20 km which we did quite well to reach by early evening. We had a hot bath in the post commander's hut, relaxed for a while before a repeat of the previous days' function took place. The boys went a bit bold by asking the local boys and girls to strum on their guitars and sing Mizo as well as the latest English hit songs. We drank the local brew called "zu" which was fermented rice beer, with varying levels of intoxication. They had also arranged a barbeque of a baux sa, a roast pigling in my honour, having heard from the people that I wasn't enthused by the Jat vegetarian fare. We had a great campfire type atmosphere, I was wondering why these simple, God-fearing folks were undergoing such privations for no fault of theirs. I could see that they loved their Zoram (their Mizoram) and knew nothing about India. They said they heard of Indira Gandhi but only knew the Indian Army well. Some civil servants came now and then, but never saw the DC. They claimed to have met some school/college teachers from Lunglei College recently. Our last leg was a visit across the inter battalion boundary with Kumaonis at Chawngte. They had sent another patrol of three to intercept us enroute, to carry my pack from thereon, to their post. I naturally declined because of my ego but I kept regretting every step forward I took towards Chawngte. Here we were received by their best post commander Maj. Negi, who had bagged the maximum captured weapons by the brigade. A quiet, unassuming officer I met later when the *paltan* was at Delhi Cantt in 1988. We were quite exhausted and requested an early meal with no fanfare and merrymaking which Negi agreed. The next morning was another 8 km trek to the road head coming from Demagiri, where my jonga was waiting for us. This trek was nothing as compared to what other officers kept doing regularly, during their tenure. The places we visited were full of leech, dim dam flies and other insects. The water we drank from the local streams despite the water sterilization kit issued to us was contaminated and gave me two severe attacks of hepatitis there necessitating a H pylori bacteria treatment, much later in 2008 after retirement.

My stay at Pukpui was very eventful and rewarding. We had kept surveillance over civil medical stores and the general stores in Lunglei. Having an intelligence detachment working for you is an experience by itself. Whenever the hardliners were in town our sources promptly alerted us. Immediate disappearance of medicines such as paludrines, antibiotics and stomach ailment, meant it had gone to hostiles through someone in town. In their heart of hearts, Mizos were now fed up with insurgency and wanted to end this madness. I made good friends with a Dr Lawlama of Serkawn Mission Hospital who had once confided in me that few hostiles wanted him to treat their comrades in their hideout. We immediately placed a cordon around the hospital, provided discreet protection to him and succeeded in obtaining the surrender of a large number of hostiles. On Brig. Minwalla's farewell, I loved the cuisine made by Dr's wife and remarked that the baux sa (pork) was excellent. When the Commander pointed out that he thought I didn't eat bawm sa (beef) he then told me that all the dishes had beef which I had walloped by mistake. I learnt yet another lesson that in the NE, one needs to inform the host that you don't eat beef, otherwise you may be served just that.

The knowledge of counter-insurgency operations at the grassroots level was very fulfilling and rewarding. I had a working knowledge of the Mizo language based on English script because all of us had no choice. A week at the world-famous CIJW School Vairengte, along with one of our incoming battalions later, provided me with the inputs which only is seen to be believed. We saw the troops on gruelling and tough training at close quarters including the jungle lane shooting, at which I also tried my hand. The intelligence collection plan, organisation of the intelligence set-up, the conduct of patrolling, the psywar and winning the hearts and minds of people are things in writing. Putting them in practice requires the right frame of mind to execute. Troops led well will always produce results. Loyalty to them, listening to their problems, keeping them in a high state of motivation by attending to their welfare and administration needs no elaboration. We had such good field commanders like Gen. Ramachandran and his very competent GSO1, recently joined gunner, Lt. Col. PS Kapoor, Brigs Minwalla and Surinder Nath who returned our loyalty in equal measure and gave very clear-cut orders. This experience in the insurgency ridden area came in very handy later when I was posted in Punjab during the troubled days of terrorism. In the meantime, thanks to some professors in Government College Lunglei, my papers for BA Pass Course were accepted and two other officers appeared for the written final examination of North Eastern Hill University Shillong. Though I could not manage all the reading material with subjects like English, English Literature, Public Administration and Education, I cleared without any difficulty in 1978. There was a cash award of Rs 10k given by the University, I donated that to the college, which allowed me to appear.

With Manju at the Army Day 1979 At Home at COAS residence

Towards the end of my staff tenure, Dy Commanders post was sanctioned and Col.PS Warrier arrived. I was happy to be relieved of duties of OC Troops, which took your afternoons exclusively for the same. I received my posting order to 96 Field Regiment initially. They had earmarked me as OC Advance Party to move again to field in Chhamb Jaurian (Field). On 15 January 1979, I was attending the At Home with my wife Manju, at Army Chief's residence on Army Day 1979, when I met our old DSSC Commandant, Lt. Gen. AM Sethna, now the QMG. When I apprised him that I have again been posted to the field after my staff tenure, he was naturally concerned. I did not know the General personally except the fact that he had been our Commandant DSSC. Right in front of him was an officer from MS Branch Lt. Col. Raghavan. He called him in my presence and asked him if I could be posted back to my Regiment in peace now. 9 Para Field Regiment had been "de paraed" and moved to Gwalior in 1977. I was happy to get back to my regiment based on a freak chance meeting with Lt. Gen. Sethna. Not one line of representation was submitted by me, the General lived up to his words. Happily, Nine's status as parachute field regiment has been restored.

The First Post at Mhow

Mhow, as a cantonment has always held a great fascination for all of us, in the olive greens. My First Post and the Last Post at Mhow shows how attached we were to Mhow as a peace station. People hold differing perceptions on how it got its name. Some aver Mahu got its name from the local *mawua* tree. Others say it's after the Mahu village near the Mhow Cantt or may be taken from the age-old acronym, military headquarters of war. The juice of the *mahwa* tree is intoxicant for the locals. Right from early times even during the first war of independence, the British troops were stationed here. Later, in the first and second world wars, its role was again very significant. The famous Chindits of Burma were trained here. Located 23 kilometres south-west of Indore city on Bombay Agra Road, there were two military institutions like the Infantry School and the Signals Engineering College (MCTE), which came up together. Later College of Combat also came up in a brand-new campus, now War College. The best legacy left by the British is the sprawling bungalows, a well-organized

Institute with a verdant golf course, inside a beautiful cantonment bustling with activity. There is a good marketplace next door, like the Lalkurti or the Sadar Bazar in most of our cantts. You'd be amazed, the tailors and drapers are one of the best in the country, the handmade shoes and the ladies smoking dresses and linen are just exceptional. In our younger days, we all got our blue patrols, dinner jackets and service dress stitched by Mhow Tailors, on a very comfortable instalment plan for two years, purely on an honour code basis. Every Indian Army CO would ensure the timely payments of instalments, just on the sincerity of this firm. I also read a very fascinating book called "Last Post at Mhow" by Arthur Hawkey, sometime in 1973 during my stint in the Sugar Sector, which inspired me to visit the grave of the British Staff Sergeant Crawley, in the cemetery opposite the War College, when I was doing my JC course. It is an enthralling narration of the British Army pride, its arrogance and prejudices of the army life, full public view, in preventing this poor Sergeant from taking the boat to England on priority. Events kept building up, leading to a hunger strike, his subsequent court-martial and eventual death, despite the forced feeding that was done. Dear Old Blighty at its best!

The next time the stay in Mhow for the HC course meant, they say, a "year of irresponsibility", when you are forever questioning the army concepts, to think out of the box. We drove down from Deolali to Mhow via Dhulia. It was a straight drive on the National highway, after a brief halt enroute for lunch, we reached our destination late in the evening. Our luggage arrived with us almost together. We got an independent house as opposed to other HC Course officers, who stayed inside the campus. Our house was located at the rear gate of the College of Combat, about a 5 min walk to the college. Hari Singh and Singha accompanied the truck carrying the car and the baggage. We also found a dilapidated servants' room without a toilet which was occupied by the *sahayaks*, after improvements by the MES. We allowed them the use of one of our toilets, next to my study.

The course had three or four tours of forward areas in the Northern Western and Eastern frontiers, along with commitments, such as regular war games after each tour and kept us quite busy. HC course had DS Brigs Jameel Mahmood, VP Duggal from Raj Rif, NK Oberoi from Dogras. Our commander was Maj. Gen. Kripal Randhawa, the course was run by the Commandant, Lt. Gen. Ashok Handoo, who took it upon himself to train us. He used our DS as errand boys and ran our course like the only Directing Staff of the course. His tactical and strategic concepts had a lot for us to learn and most of us benefited immensely. Being not very fond of gunners, Gen. Handoo was the repository of strategy, operational art and tactical concepts, which were at his fingertips. A guardsman to the core, he set impossible standards for us during the wargames and presentations in the HC Wing.

Higher Command course at the War College in Mhow

During a talk by Field Marshal SHFJ Manekshaw on 'Planning and Preparation for 1971 Operations' against Pakistan. As the FM and Handoo exchanged light-hearted banter, it was great to see their camaraderie of the 1971 operations in the Sialkot Sector. The meeting of FM Manekshaw with Gen. Tikka Khan of the Pakistan Army during the Sutchetgarh came into focus and very pleasant anecdotes were exchanged between the two. This was followed by another round of drinks and anecdotes in the anteroom, followed by a sit-down lunch. We were generally making polite conversation and I was seated well away from the main table which had the FM, Gen. Handoo, Kripal Randhawa and the three DS seated along with the senior lot of our course. After the main course was served, there was a slight commotion, as I saw that the Commandant was in distress and had to be helped out by the waiters immediately. FM, the fine gentleman that he was, remained calm, as if nothing had happened, allowed others to take care of the Commandant and continued to speak to another officer on his right. Remaining cool and unruffled in times of adversity is a tremendous attribute.

A few months later on 31 Oct 84, we were busy with the team from CDM Secunderabad under Gp Capt. Vinod Patney. Around 10.30 am I saw some DS and students had their ears glued to a transistor set which gave the news that the PM had been shot at by her security guards and had been evacuated to AIIMS. We were all genuinely concerned but with the CDM presentation in progress, we waited for it to finish at 1.30 pm. Nobody gave much attention to the news received earlier, hoping nothing would happen. I left to play golf around 2.30 pm. At around 2.45 pm we saw the newspaper boys waving with the local paper, announcing loudly that the PM had died. All of us finished the game there and then only. Our Commandant's four-ball was ahead of us. I saw him throw the golf club away, on reading the paper. We finished the game there itself and returned home. This happened at the end of the first half near Hole No 9. This was after Mrs Gandhi's assassination, we could gauge the mood prevailing at that time, which justifiably so was a matter of concern. Immediately after news of Mrs Gandhi's assassination became public, there were incidents of manhandling of Sikh soldiers in Mhow town. We also heard the news of the killings in Delhi and also where. All of us sat glued to the old Philips TV given to us by my sister, Anjana. If I recall correctly, we were in no mood for dinner. A pall of gloom had descended on our house as well. Just then, Hari Singh brought the news that our neighbour Col. Iqbal Singh decorated his house with divas to celebrate the assassination of Mrs Gandhi. I did believe this initially but learnt later that one of the Sikhs Guruparb also fell on that day. I think better sense should have prevailed in the full view of the public. I made it a point to correct Hari Singh's erroneous impression, it is their Guruparb also.

The AG, Lt. Gen. K Balaram addressed all officers in the open-air theatre and warned Sikh officers in Mhow to stop their anti-national activities. There was pin-drop silence as he said this with all seriousness. We all expected there would be some local curbs on Sikh officers but luckily nothing happened. When we met our closest Sikh friends, the discussion invariably led to the assassination and its sad aftermath, the Delhi massacre in the aftermath. Our very dear friend Lt. Col. Labh Singh Sitara, who stayed at the Swarg Mandir area, was very apprehensive about what would happen next. There was nothing to suggest what AG had said was true and I didn't believe a word of it. The news of a young officer from 150 Fd. Regt, Capt. Toor being killed was received with sadness and grief by everyone. Immediately after this, as a part of our Western tour, we visited the Golden Temple, post Op Bluestar. Sometimes in the first week of Nov 84, we found massive destruction with debris lying all around with total disarray everywhere. There was news that Akal Takht is being rebuilt with Kar Sewa but all indications were, we were in for a long haul. In our course later too, there were some heated discussions, we avoided hurting others feelings, especially after seeing the death and carnage at the Golden Temple.

I also received the letter of allotment of a flat in Noida by AWHO. The amount to be remitted was Rs 2.60 lakhs. I did not have more than a few thousand in the bank. The options were taking a loan from HDFC @ 16% and selling my car. I sought help from everyone including my brothers, father-in-law and close friends. I only received one response from my friend, Maj. Ramesh Apte, who at that time was on SC course. He gave me a cheque for Rs 10,000 which I had to return after I surrendered the house. I consulted a lot of people who told me that the bridges planned for Arun Vihar were still not through and it would take quite some time for Noida colonies to become inhabitable. Contemplating a posting to Wellington, I decided not to go for the AWHO flat and asked for a refund of my money. Here again, I think my decision proved correct as I gave priority to the quality of life, over the acquisition of property.

The Nilgiris Invitation

We had liked Mhow as we made new friends and also renewed a lot of friendships. We enjoyed the 'year of irresponsibility', loved its climate and the facilities. The way the cantonment was organized was spectacular and something to be admired. Everything was priced reasonably and the cost of living was well within one's reach. However, my next halt was Wellington, as per orders received from the Army HQ, which was considered good. Manju purchased a lot of linen and the smocking work nighties in preparation for Wellington. I got cracking for my clothes stitching and the wardrobe. We had paired up with my colleague, Col. DK Khanna and family and we travelled together. It was around June 85 when we reached Wellington, in the middle of the 41 Staff Course. All of us were roped in immediately on the course and got busy with the daily preparations for the tutorials, sand model exercises, corrections and other associated course work. As there was hardly any time, I had to forget golf for the first tutorial at least. We got our temporary accommodation at Kinara on Kotagiri Road. Our neighbours were Pankaj Joshi, Binni Shergill, C J Appachu and GD Sharma. At Kinara we were on the second floor and Manju had several attacks of bronchial asthma. After several visits to MH Wellington, she stabilised with the homoeopathic treatment by Dr BA Kanikraj of Ooty. We stayed here for almost one year before Neelamber 4 was allotted to us. Our car UPD 3278 had arrived in Wellington thoroughly bashed up from both sides. Thanks to Car Check run by Trevor Mendis, we got it back in good shape after a while, when the insurance claim was passed. Mendis also became a good friend and a well-wisher.

Both Priya and Rohit got well settled in their schools once again Priya joined KV Anivankudu Class X and Rohit Holy Innocents High School Class IV. A lot of sports and other activities kept the children busy round the clock. We kept them insulated from the VCR culture which had just crept in. We allowed them to see the movies in the WGC once in a while. Priya also took part in extracurricular activities in school and won several prizes in singing both group and solo efforts. For Rohit, the school activities were confined and few. The college had organized some games and hikes to nearby places. Rohit joined me at Riding Club and we rode together for the hack rides on weekends.

Hari Singh and Singha, both not very fond of each other, finally settled down with us. Their college mess was quite some distance away and they took turns fetching each other's meals. Our fresh rations were delivered right at our location, which was a boon. We had the right mix of professional and social commitments, thanks to the very well laid out curriculum for the course. Most of the household work including cooking were done by the full-time domestic help, who happened to be the sister of our previous maid, Vasantha. Both Singha and Hari Singh supervised and helped out on add jobs and outside work, There was a fair amount of entertaining to be done and we were indeed very fortunate to have them on board. Wellington and lower Conoor were very reasonable and cheap those days, especially chicken, meat and fish. We also purchased a Solidaire colour TV from Coimbatore, on a good rebate, thanks to our gunner friend, Col. Manjit Chaudhry. This kept both of them occupied when we were away for social functions, which were quite a few. In the meanwhile, Ashok Swarup with his wife Nalini left for the UK on a holiday. His four-year-old son, Arjun arrived with a chaperone and was personally received by me at Coimbatore. The boy only knew no one else but me and we looked after him for three weeks before. Nalini arrived, for two weeks stay with us

During the first year at DSSC, we kept busy with the course both professionally and socially. We are required to sponsor a foreign student along with his wife and children. After the current course session terminated in December 1985, it was decided to run a short staff course of three months, in the interim period. We met a whole lot of Lt. Cols/Majors and their equivalents in the other two services who could not qualify for DSSC entrance but were considered good otherwise, to hold staff appointments. Maj. Nati Chand, who was with us in 17 Para Fd Regiment, was now serving in 141 Field Regiment, which I had commanded. I had met him with the regiment at Pattan, very recently. Both Nati and his wife Aarti fully enjoyed being on the course. We developed good bonds with Nati and his wife, Aarti, during the course and are in regular touch with them. Since there were no gradings on the course it was a lot easier and no rat race ensued amongst the students. Short staff course finished in June 86 and for about a month, we were on leave up north. After earning my PSC dagger, just after the short staff course, I graduated to my next course 42 Staff Course, slated to commence in June 86

The first course with July – May session commenced formally on 5 July, though the orientation course commenced mid-June 1986. My sponsored student was Lt. Col. Mohd Ismail and his wife Samia with two children 4-6 years old. We were compensated nearly Rs 300 three times for their entertainment/meals which were very reasonable, in those days. We tried our best to make them feel at home within the constraints. Samia had to be examined by Dr Kanikaraj at Ooty as she was also an asthmatic. She recovered and had no further problems for the entire duration of the course. As a couple, we found them to be very simple and humble, very gullible and could be taken for a ride by other students on the course, on the slightest pretext. I had to defend him many times when others tried their best to fool him. We did not hear from him after he left India. There was news later that the whole family perished in the civil war in South Sudan, which followed.

Golf was on top priority at Wellington. As a DS I did avoid playing in my first tutorial because a fair amount of preparation was required daily. You cannot fool everyone all the time, your students are no exception and would notice your lack of preparation. We had to ensure that your preparations were complete before commencing regular golf on the weekends. Wellington course had become more challenging and was always fully subscribed every day with both DS and students and some planters/civilians. We used to play six days a week except for Tuesdays which was a closed day for maintenance. The Captain of the Course was Brig. RK Gulati and Col. Shami Mehta was the Secretary. A large number of tournaments were organized and a proper Golf Calendar was prepared for the year. We had reciprocal visits to High Range Golf Club Munnar, Ooty Gymkhana Club and the Coimbatore Club, where we went on the weekends to play and enjoy their hospitality. I think my golfing career peaked in Wellington when I had reached the finals of the DSSC Open by beating students and DS alike. In the semifinals, I played Kailash Dhingra, a 10 handicapper who played very well and so did I that day. He had to give me 8 strokes and he kept cribbing, that I was a hustler and needed to revise my handicap.

We were running neck to neck and were tied, after the eighteenth. As per rules, we were required to play a sudden death after that and we started with the first hole again. Dhingra's two long drives and a pitch shot landed just at the base of the mound on which the first green is laid out. I was way behind Dhingra with my lucky fourth shot reaching the edge of the green, more than 15 feet away from the pin. When Dhingra took his fourth shot from below the mound, (without asking me to mark my ball) his ball hit my ball squarely and got deflected out of the green. My ball was replaced at the same place, as per rules and I putted soundly to make a par. Being my stroke hole again, Dhingra had to sink a birdie, a long putt from outside which he failed to do so. The game was now mine. Dhingra cursed himself for the chipper he used from the base of the mound. Three days later I played Dilip Gole in the finals. As the new Golf Captain, he got my handicap revised to 14 and posted it on the notice board just before the match. I kept questioning his actions and lost 8 and 4 on the 14th. I kept on arguing throughout the game, pointing out his cheekiness, but the game was lost. Later, Ashish Dube and I participated in the Ibex Cup which we had won fair and square. Unfortunately, Hari Uniyal had seen my ball go into a dung heap and I had no choice but to change my ball. We were disqualified on a complaint made by Uniyal, which we thought was bordering on squealing, but we accepted the verdict.

Socially Wellington was very hectic. We made some good friends in a planter from the local Kundah Tea Estate, a Baddaga tribal, Ramalingham. We had met them at the Ooty Gymkhana Club through our common friend, Justice Obal Reddy, also known to Ashok Swarup, my brother-in-law. We, accompanied by the Dhingra family, went to Kundah by car to spend a weekend at their tea estate in the Kundah countryside. We were in the most pristine environment of rural Tamil Nadu and its scenic beauty, which we enjoyed very much.

With Bibhu Mohanti and Mohan Burman at Wellington

My Senior Instructor was Brig. SK Behl, also a gunner, who during 41st Staff Course left for NDC. Brig. JS Dhillon from the Marathas took over and we generally had a very good time with him. He gave me a lot of respect and of course a lot of work such as the assessment exercise and sand models. Our Commandant was Gen. FN Bilimoria and the Chief Instructor was Maj. Gen. KS (Bulbul) Brar, who had just joined. We had one dinner at 4 Neelamber where we called Lt. Gen. & Mrs Bilimoria, Maj. Gen. & Mrs KS Brar, our SI and his wife, the staff officers and their wives besides some DS. My colleagues were Cols Melville De Souza, Shantanu Choudhary, GD Sharma, DK Khanna Shergill brothers, Sarabjot Saighal and PS Miglani besides Shammi Mehta and MR. Sharma. We also had our NDA 23rd course lot comprising Cols Shantonu Choudhry, Inam Siddiqui, BM Kapur, RK Mehta and Mohan Burman from the Madras Regimental Centre. We had get-togethers by rotation, every month and this kept the course spirits going very well. Mohan Burman being the Deputy Commandant MRC invited us to all his station functions. Another record of sorts in DS, was the para gunner lot, seven of us. This comprised Cols NC Mahajan, Vijay Batra and Bunny Khanna for a short while. Thereafter, Cols Melville de Souza and Rajendra Kumar, followed by VG Patankar and Ashish Dube later.

17 Para picnic at Wellington in 1986

When I was halfway through the 42 Staff Course, around the time of the Industrial Demonstration tour, I was moved up in the Col. GS chair, based on my performance as a DS, probably on the recommendations of the Offg CI, Brig. Birendra Singh Nalwa. I had enjoyed his trust and was delighted to assume this prestigious appointment. Nalwa was posted out on promotion as GOC of an Infantry Division and had come to our house late at night with a bottle of scotch, which he opened for us to celebrate his appointment as GOC Division. His representation was upheld and being very close to us, he did us the honour. My in-laws were also staying with us at that time. They were very impressed with Nalwa's sincerity and honesty and wished him all success in the command of the Division.

Of the gunners who attended the Staff Courses, when I was the DS were Majors AS Lamba, Mohan Kunnath, GLS Toor, Devinder Singh (Delta), Gurmeet Kanwat, VS Toley, SG Chatterjee and Ravi

Gupta (from 6 Sikh) who was the Staff Capt. in 311 Mtn Brigade. All our Adjutants of 311 Mountain Brigade, where I was the BM, Sandeep Sen (5 Kumaon) Rameshwar Roy (7 Jak Rif) and JS Bajwa (5 Kumaon), all attended during my DS tenure. I need to mention here that VS Toley was placed in my syndicate by SI, Brig. SK Behl specifically, when he was falling short of his 'A' which he eventually got. The culture of adopting unfair means to help students just did not exist and I did no favours to anyone. We, therefore, kept within the law and did not invite these officers to our residence for a meal during the breaks so that we did not waste their time on social engagements. The college did not encourage the DS to socialise with students and we observed this directive scrupulously.

I must relate a few incidents while working as Colonel GS (Coord) to Gen. FN Bilimoria and Gen. Gurinder Singh. Both Generals were outstanding officers who later became Army Commanders. Serving as Col. GS with Gen. Bilimoria was a great privilege as he always looked after those who worked under him and trusted them implicitly. In one episode, one of my coursemates came on a Monday morning, relating an incident on the fishing trip near the Dam at Mettupalayam where he had got into an ugly argument with the General. At that time, the ACRs had already been initiated by the IO, they were lying with the General. He wanted me to oversee that all was okay. When the General received the same. I got to see the friend's ACR before it was dispatched. I was pleasantly surprised to see that the General had still rated him very high despite the escapade, he had over drinks. Just went to prove what a fine gentleman Bilimoria was. Another officer, on his way abroad as Military Attaché, was also apprehensive about an endorsement in his ACR given by another of our SIs, Brig. That too I found was without basis. I could vouch for the fact that over a while, our seniors had set high professional standards, stringent social conduct norms, implicit trust in subordinates and were very magnanimous in reporting.

Immediately on completion of two years at Wellington received my posting as Col. Adm, Infantry Division at Dinjan in the wake of the Sumdorong Chu/Wangdung incidents with the Chinese. The outgoing Commandant took up my case for cancellation, as the new Commandant was yet to report. This cancellation went against me and could be the turning point of my career, as one could see later. I enjoyed my enhanced stay at Wellington with stalwarts like Kultar who was a medical category and therefore could not move, and a brand-new set of DS like Sathe & R Subramanium from Engineers, Pat, and Dube (once again), with whom I had served before. There were Cols YS Teja, Agarwal and HS Attari. SCADS was rather active those days with the staging of two plays, one Hindi and one English besides musical evenings and variety shows. In the course earlier, Ayn Rand's "Night of January Sixteen", a powerful courtroom drama, was staged by students and was a great success. With the new Commandant Lt. Gen. Gurinder Singh, the DSSC raised its sights higher at joint manship between the three services, as ordered by the COS Committee which created a stupendous amount of work for me, in the syllabi restructuring. With all three DS Coords, we sat down to an agreed syllabus for the three wings for training in jointness. Ultimately, Chairman CORTOS, Admiral RG Nadkarni approved our hard work and it was to be executed with effect from the next course. The net result was, my own BM much later, appeared out of sorts as he was the "guinea pig" who had done the Naval Wing staff course. Whether the aim of this jointness was achieved or not I cannot say. I gather that the joint syllabi has undergone changes but the exchange of officers between wings has been discontinued.

As the Col. GS Coord, I was intimately concerned with every conceivable activity in the College starting from the professional course in the three Wings, the Production Section which was producing all the training material and the Pamphlets Issue Section and of course the University Division. Maj. Abinder Singh was the IC Production, Mr George Baby managing the Stationery & Pamphlets Issue Section and Maj. AC Soneja, the GSO2 of the University Division. I had an exceptional retinue of clerical staff who had done donkey's years in the College, trained by the multi-faceted CSO1, Shri PK Raghupathy. There were other individuals like Shri Ram Swarup, the Chief Draughtsman and Shri Kari who had been with the College, from the time it shifted from Quetta. The allotment of various grants like Training, Office Contingency and Education was most liberal and I still marvel at how that quiet, unassuming and efficient George Baby managed the entire show with no audit objections. The top-class standards of security of material, scrupulous honesty and integrity norms, set by the founding fathers ensured no misuse of funds, by anyone in the hierarchy. My biggest bugbear was the arrangements, which had to be tied up with various industrial/Cat A establishments in the Southern Command for the Industrial Demonstration Tour called Bharat Darshan. It meant continued liaison with Railways, Army HQ and establishments including sending of DS in advance to tie-up arrangements. Also connected was the Forward Area Tour for the Naval & Air Wings and foreign/civilian student officers which required so much coordination that it gave me sleepless nights. The calendar of Sports and Pastime activities including golf, tennis parasailing, hang gliding introduced, yachting & sailing at Pykara was something that required constant monitoring and attention. Riding and Polo under a very dynamic Col. AP Singh of the RVC functioned very well. We visited Munnar and Bangalore for sporting activities and also made arrangements for reciprocal visits by UPASI planters. This kept me on the tenterhooks, for fears of an unforeseen fiasco happening. One cannot imagine the magnitude of the damage to the good reputation of the College if it were to happen. The blame was to rest on the Col. GS.

There was a bombshell thrown by the Army HQ to organize the MSc (Defence Studies) degree written examination, for all officers before 1978 who had passed the course but were not eligible for the degree. We got hold of the list of the officers desirous of appearing for the examination and allowed them to select a subject for dissertation from the list of subjects provided by the College. We then had to allot our DS for assessing these dissertations. I also paid numerous visits to Madras University at Chennai and discussed the modalities with the Head of Department, Defence Studies. After their approval, we issued the General Instructions of the examination to be conducted at eight centres under the aegis of the MT Directorates. The Commandant had set the paper which was approved by the Madras University and the sealed copy was kept in my locker for safe custody. A month prior, this sealed copy was sent to MT Directorate for making additional copies to be issued to the centres by dates to be decided by them. Seeing the implicit faith placed in me, I ensured utmost security was maintained. It was also my great privilege to be the staff officer to our great Field Marshal SHFJ Manekshaw whenever he called me for instructions. I paid numerous visits to his residence "Stavka" in Upper Coonoor and also enjoyed their hospitality for drinks, one evening before leaving Wellington.

My posting after three years tenure in Wellington came for 28 Arty Brigade as Dy Cdr. I had expected a better posting and paid a visit to MS Branch who was very adamant about a change. The incoming BGS Brig. SBL Kapoor also advised me not to ask for any changes. Unfortunately, some misapprehensions crept into my mind, I wanted another outside the corps appointment, like my other coursemates. I had not realized how hostile the environment was outside the Corps. It is also possible that my DSSC tenure made me a bit complacent and overconfident.

The Ladakh Sojourn

I finally got posted to an Infantry Brigade at Ladakh as Dy Commander. Brig. GS Sirohi, an Armd Corps officer was the commander under posting for a good 4-6 months. I was ordered to move with the Tac HQ to a location close to Chushul at the height of 11,000 feet, where I stayed till January 90, Brig. Krishan Pal arrived at HQ and I had hoped for a better time now. I had stayed put at Chushul most of the time and was enjoying my stay near a Rajput, a Grenadiers, a Madras batallion and Ladakh Scouts. The Rajput battalion was commanded by a very dynamic CO Col. Sukhdeo Awasthi. The Madras battalion was commanded by Lt. Col. PV Mohanan, a decorated officer, who was another live wire. Col. P Mohanti from Grenadiers was an asset in this fine setup. During this time, I worked very hard and got to know the entire defensive layout by staying out with the units for 2-3 days each. There were two major events planned for the next two quarters. I was asked to prepare the papers for approval, for a Division TEWT at Chushul which was to be carried in that quarter & a Command level presentation on China four months later. In addition, a lot of comments/study group recommendations were prepared by me. As our DQ had been attached to N Area for a logistics base, I also supervised the work of the Staff Captain. I tried my best to guide him indirectly by giving the drafts of replies. Brig. Krishan Pal, who had arrived as the new Commander, had a lot of faith in me. When he was away on temporary duty to Army HQ, which was quite frequent, the command of the brigade rested with me. I moved back to Brigade HQ for the writing and the approval. The TEWT went off very well and was appreciated.

With Brig. Krishan Pal at a SFF Raising Day

We had made good friends with the locals and the troops located in the immediate vicinity like Ladakh Scouts, Madras and the SFF troops. My visits as a sector commander provided me invaluable inputs about their employment and envisaged role during operations. There was a RAP established at Chushul next to the helipad, manned by a very cool-headed Capt. Nambiar, the RMO of Ladakh Scouts. I had interacted with him several times and found him to be very professional and a very caring person. That particular morning, I had driven down to his post for a casual meeting. As I entered his *bukhari* heated cubicle, I heard him very agitatedly tell a Ladakhi Scout jawan patient, "Go to the lama, then". The moment I arrived; he came to greet me. After exchanging pleasantries, I inquired if all was well, as it was for the first time, I had heard him raise his voice. He apologized and then frustratingly complained that "I don't think I am required here. These Ladakhis prefer lama's medicine to mine. They never report being sick for minor or major ailments, they prefer to go to their Amchi (medicine lama) instead. No chopper required in their case as they hate evacuation by helicopters". I just laughed it off and a long winter month passed. I learnt there was a medicine man who had been attending to jawans' ailments, from a village Merak located some 35 miles from here. Weeks passed and I met another officer, Victor from Ladakh Scouts who said he was waiting to meet Doc Nambiar in connection with his chronic amoebiasis. Doc Nambiar attended to him first but Victor didn't seem impressed. Victor then narrated the story about his jawan Dorji, who took medical leave to visit the Amchi. Dorji was called at my behest and he claimed he was feeling much better, possibly cured of his stomach ailment by the Amchi. Victor, the company commander, had also been recommended this treatment by the same Amchi, at Dorji's behest, I suspect. Victor confided in me that he would be visiting the Amchi at Merak soon as Doc Nambiar's medicines are useless. Ladakh has its system based on Tibetan medical science and their medical practitioners are called Amchis.

Though Ladakhi landscape seems very barren and devoid of vegetation, it is very rich in herbal resources. Stomach disorders are very common in locals and our troops are no exception. Umpteen volumes of literature from Buddhists and Tibetan scholars, researchers and traditional practitioners exist, the locals have had great faith in their herbal medicines for centuries.

Accompanied by our guide cum interpreter Dorji, Victor and I arrived at Merak and were received by the head lama. We followed him to a dingy, very cold and badly lit hut from which a suffocating smell of yak butter emanated. There was a biggish black and white yak skin carpet specially laid out for us and we sat in one corner. The hut had an imposing terracotta golden Buddha statue, in front of the carpet. Prayers commenced amidst chanting of mantras by other lamas while the Amchi got going on the blacksmith's leather bellows. A red-hot iron rod emerged from the fire. Victor lay spread eagle and the Amchi knelt beside him looking into his eyes as if to mesmerize. He felt Victor's stomach with his fingers for a long time and stopped at one point. I saw the look on Amchi's face as he chanted some mantras. He made a surgical incision at the very spot that he had latched on to, and not a murmur from Victor. This incision in the stomach was enlarged when his fingers went searching for something. Some blood also oozed out but he held on to something he had pulled out. What appeared was a fishbone and a small decayed portion of the intestine removed. Stitching the intestines together and closing the wound was no problem. All was over in about 50 minutes, I noted. Poultice was applied to the incision and the bandage tightened. Amchi explained in his lingo that Sahib will be okay in three weeks, Dorji translated that. We drove back in our jonga and Victor wasn't to be seen for some time. Dorji was personally attending to Victor. In my mind, the fear of being taken to task kept coming back with amazing rapidity. Witnessing an unauthorized event was bad enough, taking no action to stop all this, was another court-martial offence. I prayed for Victor's recovery and after about three weeks he was hale and hearty and laughing away at my nervousness. When I asked Doc Nambiar for his medical opinion, all he could say was that the intestinal blockage removal was more important than amoebiasis. Tibetan medical science, too, is also well developed. During my leave period, I looked around in Nizamuddin Delhi and Dharamshala for qualified Tibetan medicine doctors who treated my wife Manju for asthma very effectively. There are too many restrictions on the diet and added precautions besides the manner of preparation of the herbal concoctions.

After conducting the TEWT, I again got busy and dug into my old presentation of 1984 of Higher Command Course, some old Rand Corporation papers, and even contacted our MA in Hanoi, Venky Patil for the latest intelligence reports on China. Two events that came into focus were the fact that China had taken a bloody nose after its conflict with Vietnam in 1979, the four modernizations ordered by Chairman Deng where armed forces were the lowest priority. Therefore, it possessed limited offensive capability in hot spots like Ladakh and Arunachal Pradesh, right now (1990). Their stress at that time was on raising of mechanized/airborne/heliborne forces for use as Rapid Deployment Forces from one military region to another, augmentation and raising of fire support resources and force multipliers and creation of logistics infrastructure. China then, as a regional power was only capable of providing a strong defensive posture with limited offensive capability At that time, China also had a large number of border disputes, and could not afford to go to war. That is the reason why Deng had advised his successors "to maintain our position, meet the challenges calmly, hide our capacities, and bide our time, remain free from ambition and never claim leadership". If that was the scenario, there would be no major war but a low-intensity conflict using the rapid deployment forces, the third dimension under the existing nuclear capability, was a possibility. We alluded to their proposed formation of autonomous regions/theatre commands, but we thought their financial resources inhibited that. The crisp presentation, a command event, had been summarized thus above shows how deep we had carried out the analysis of the threat. The event was well received and in the question hour, we were bombarded with many questions, there was a lot to learn for the study group also. A lot of effort had gone into the collection of material from all sources to make the presentation a success.

RM KC Pant visits the Monastery at Chushul

During the visit of the Army Commander, Krishan Pal openly praised me in front of everyone for the presentation and the reconstruction of the Station Officers Mess. In the meanwhile, my report for the year 1988-89 was initiated during the closed period, when I was away on leave. This was done by Brig. Krishan Pal and reviewed by the GOC. Having done my best, I had no reason to believe that I would not get my due. Everything seemed alright and I received my promotion orders around the same time. Before I proceeded to Amritsar to take over my brigade, I got a call from my old CO, Brig. RC Butalia who called us over for drinks at DSOI Dhaula Kuan along with Col. Patankar and Rashmi. Pat could not attend because he had some last-minute engagement. Butch and Mrs Butalia were so warm again in their hospitality as if I was his best officer from 17 Para. Manju knew I wasn't very fond of him but she commented that they are very affectionate. It was very clear that Butch as a CO may have had all his weaknesses and idiosyncrasies, but he was an excellent human being.

The Desert Safari

After a year at the alma mater, I reached a place called Lalgarh Jattan, sometime in Jan 92 for commanding a desert Infantry Brigade. In the first place, the name itself was nothing much to write home about. I heard it for the first time in Wellington when someone was posted as the Deputy Commander of a newly raised Armoured Brigade. We explained very nicely to friends, "Oh, it's some 12 km away from Ganganagar, the land of kinoos". This was once a large-sized village acquired by the Army in a rain-fed farming taluka that produces cotton, mustard, sorghum, sugar cane and maize. The

Bikaner Link Canal from the IGC has changed the entire landscape. The cultivated areas have come all around the military station which is on both sides of the road. We had learnt how the Haryanvi Jats came to possess vast land holdings in the early sixties. People were simple folks in a caste-ridden society, by and large peaceful and God-fearing. Women dressed from head to toe in jewellery, carrying brass utensils lined up for water at borewells and ponds. The menfolk, I thought, were very hard working with traditional methods of cultivation in the green *sarso* fields across our boundary fencing. The language spoken by people is mostly Rajasthani and Hindi with a Haryanvi accent. The villages around were full of rich farmers, who dispose of their produce in a local mandi, which were the order of the day under the APMC. One didn't fail to notice the difference. The military area had small little green patches called lawns, in front of unit officers' messes. The area around us was lush green with crops, irrigated from borewells and ponds. A lot of *kinu* had been planted in the Ganganagar Suratgarh area in the last three decades. Today, it is the leading *kinu* fruit basket in Rajasthan. Not to be left out, the first Station Commander, had also planted four kinoo and other fruit trees, which were lying unmaintained, in the Flagstaff House.

We were six gunner officers selected by the Army Commanders for general cadre per the existing policy. Gen. Rodrigues, the COAS, and our senior Colonel Commandant, in his wisdom, thought that clearing maximum gunner officers for the general cadre was a good opportunity for us. With Gen. BC Joshi as the new COAS now, there were three more Army Commanders from the Armoured Corps and two from the Artillery. This particular situation had not been taken kindly by the Infantry. A word was doing the rounds that no gunner transferred to the general cadre would be spared. A few like Ranjit Nagra, a future Army Commanders material from my course, declined the general cadre but I took it on as a challenge. Since I had tremendous faith in the organisation, of being fair and just, I decided to take the plunge. My strength lay in my professionalism and hard work which I thought would overcome in this hostile environment. I was probably wrong!

At Lalgarh Jattan, besides the Infantry Brigade, an Armoured Brigade was also co-located. The relations between the two Brigades were seldom cordial and there was a total divide in the station. The Armoured Brigade did not want to hand over the station to the incoming brigade, the Infantry Brigade and this dispute was on when I arrived. The previous occupant from the Armoured Brigade very reluctantly allowed me to enter the Flagstaff house after the corps commander had to intervene. In the past, the two warring Brigade Commander had snapped the electricity connections of each other's residences. Officers and ladies did not speak to each other. Two parallel ladies' clubs were running. Both Brigades boycotted each other at social gatherings deliberately.

We formed part of the Infantry Division at Ganganagar whereas the Armoured Brigade was under the higher HQ. I am sure this kind of bad blood existing at the station level cannot be tolerated anywhere. It is possible that the Corps Commander failed to notice this and very happily accepted the situation. Even at Ganganagar, there was no mention in my briefing. I was left to fend for myself on arrival at the new station. Therefore, my first task, in the order of priority, was to restore good working relations between the two Brigades and promote a healthy atmosphere in the station.

This allowed me to get down to professional soldiering in the Infantry environment in earnest in a peace station. First was the terrain familiarisation of the operational area, which took quite some time. Before I could finish, I was asked to attend an operational discussion at Meerut, being conducted by the Western Command. The Army Commander's presence there was to pick on the brains of those Arty Brigade commanders who had just taken over infantry Brigades in the western sector. During the discussion, several questions were directed at me, which was answered with ease as they had mostly to do with the then-current doctrines. I had also learnt about the fads of Army Commander on the employment of Ghatak platoons which I was asked to amplify. Throughout the discussion, the Corps Commander did keep a very good watch on us, sometimes making some notes.

On my return to Lalgarh, I recommenced the op area recce from where I left and was able to visit all forward locations within my area of responsibility. It was not difficult to relate the defensive concepts of desert terrain taught by us in Wellington/Mhow to the ground. I found it very interesting and had analysed the battle of the forward zone very minutely. The entire operational plan was on my fingertips in good times. The armour part was in fluid stage and kept changing from a full combat group to one combat team of one squadron armour and a company mechanized. We had discussions with the Armoured Brigade in each other's ops rooms for better integration and understanding. Brig. HS Narang who had just taken over the Armoured Brigade fully cooperated with me and had not harboured any old acrimony against the Infantry Brigade. We went on op recce together and had discussions on various operational issues, whenever they cropped up.

As a consequence of my concerted efforts to maintain peace and good relations in the station, I noticed a very perceptible change in the behaviour of officers and ladies in the station. This percolated down to the jawans and their families as well. On station matters, I did ensure, there was no deviation on orders pertaining to allotment of accommodation, the disparity in scale and quality of ration to all troops, and no favours granted to anyone. On one occasion, on a complaint by units, I had found the meat carcasses issued by the contractor to the station units, unfit for human consumption. I did not hesitate to penalize the contractor immediately. When the message went home to ASC higher-ups, they ensured that my station was always given the best consignment. In addition, I found that the Army School was not being run as per the laid down charter. There were complaints of favouritism in the selection of teachers which was perceived as another crib by the Armoured Brigade. This was corrected and the school had no problems thereafter. In addition, we renovated one shed behind the Inspection Bungalow created as our clubhouse for organised functions at station level. For all these actions, I had kept our GOC fully apprised and had taken his directions where required. The GOC attended one such function and complimented me on my efforts to improve the quality of life in the station as also the relations with the Armoured Brigade units.

At a Brigade officer's briefing

Per the GOCs directions, I liaised with my old unit, 17 Para Fd Regt at Agra Cantt and got a Parasailing team to train officers and men along with children in the sport which was becoming very popular then. This was appreciated by everyone and a total of over 60 personnel including children completed descents in the semi-desert terrain. We also organised boating in the water bodies located within the station. I also saw that our officers, men and families were going all the way to Ganganagar, to make telephone (STD) calls to their kith and kin in their home states. Some used their conveyance while some travelled by bus. Being apprised of the problem, I nominated the Signal Officer, Maj. Nautiyal to fix up my meeting with the Divisional Engineer Telephone, Ganganagar. We also succeeded in getting our statement of case approved by the Army for installation of an STD booth in Lalgarh Station. The STD booth was sanctioned within one month and started functioning immediately thereafter. This was such a great boon for all ranks. I received very positive feedback from both

Brigades and we made a good amount of money to recover our cost of installation, within a year.

In a pensive mood at Lalgarh Jattan

We were expecting the GOC to visit my Brigade HQ to listen to my op briefing as well as station briefing. This did not take place for a long time and instead, we got ready for the move for exercise Desert Fox. This exercise was meant for the Infantry Division in an offensive role in semi-desert terrain, commencing with the crossing of a canal about 150ft and break out thereafter. I attended the initial briefing of the GOC and discussed the conceptual aspects of the plan. Our GOC's plan envisaged the employment of my brigade with four Armoured squadrons, one mech battalion under command with the engineer task force, for leaning on operations up to the Indira Gandhi Canal. Operations were to commence by late afternoon of D Day and leaning on ops completed by around last light. Thereafter the mechanized battalion was to assault across the ploughed minefield, use BMPs to cross the canal obstacle, get across to the far bank and establish a shallow bridgehead. Subsequently, the engineers were to launch the bridges to allow the move of my brigade to break out from the bridgehead established earlier.

During this exercise, I was informed that the GOC-in-C, Western Command would like to listen to my leaning on operations briefing from a vantage point. As soon as we reached a prominently high sand dune, there was a jeep waiting there. I was asked to drive both the Army & Corps Commanders from the helipad in the vicinity, to the vantage point. As we drove up to the vantage point on the sand dune, the jeep nearly stalled and I had to apply 4x4 to move forward. We dismounted and I got my bearings for the briefing.

Having familiarized the Army Commander with the landmarks up to the Indira Gandhi canal the first question he asked me was "why is the Armoured Brigade Commander not in charge of leading on operations? Aren't my orders clear?" I looked at the Army Commander straight in his face and remained quiet hoping that the Corps Commander would give the reply since he had approved GOC Infantry Division's plans. The Army Commander's next comment after the studied silence was, "Obviously the Infantry Brigade Commander cannot be asked to do the job when there is an Armoured Brigade Commander present. Anyway, carry on". I then explained the tactical plan of advancing four Armoured squadrons up and contacting the minefield on a broad front with the engineer task force closely following and also the Mech battalion in BMP 2. He listened carefully, asked me a few questions which I answered. Subsequently, after the briefing, I drove the Army Commander back to the helipad.

After the last light, I moved forward to the canal and got in touch with the Mech battalion CO. I also took the 2IC of Raj Rif with me whose two coys were also waiting at the appointed RV. In one corner were the Army & Corps Commanders and MGGS Command discussing some matter. They left the site immediately thereafter. CO Mech informed me of the crisis, one BMP too had toppled over while getting inside the canal. Getting it turned on its back was a massive and impossible task. It seems no one wanted to be witnesses to an impending disaster, so they left the site immediately. I commended the daring and initiative of the CO who, with the help of the recovery vehicle, had succeeded in restoring the overturned BMP and saved valuable lives. After this, the induction of BMPs took place followed by trawling by the engineers. The bridgehead was established by the armour squadrons supported by Mech Infantry under my command. I then ordered the induction of my Infantry Brigade and by early hours, the breakout commenced, as scheduled.

On the termination of Ex Desert Fox, congratulatory messages kept pouring in especially from the Army Commander for excellent performance. Thinking that all went well, I got a shot in my arm and the encouragement, which a newly inducted Brigade Commander gets. Before this, the GOC proceeded on a spot of leave. This is when the Corps Commander chose to visit my brigade during the absence of the GOC and listen to my operational briefing. He was accompanied by the Offg GOC. After my briefing, the Corps Commander had several questions to ask which I replied to the best of my professional knowledge. One question pertained to the employment of armour combat group reserves which was still not approved by the Division/Corps. Immediately after the visit of the Corps Commander, I proceeded on my leave which was planned much earlier. During my leave, there was a DO from the Corps Commander to the GOC that during his visit to the Infantry Brigade he had noticed that some gaps in the tactical plans existed during my briefing. These were spelt out and the final sentence read "please take remedial action accordingly". My BM, Maj. Raymond Narohna informed me much later that the DO letter had been replied to based on a draft given by the Col. GS Infantry Division. When I asked why such a letter was replied to without my knowledge, he had no answer.

My GOC left on posting to Army HQ sometime in Sep 93. Before his departure, a war game was scheduled in which I was designated as the Nark Commander which meant a lot of knowledge of Pakistan Army tactics, its organisation opposite us and their deployment. I selected my team from the brigade officers and worked assiduously to formulate the strategic and tactical plans as well as the logistic support at the Corps level. All this required, total familiarization of terrain opposite the divisional sector, an intelligence appreciation and professional acumen for reading their tactical deployment in support of their offensive plans backed up by a sound logistic plan. I was required to set up an operations room. We got down to vetting our plans based on the aspects provided by the Higher Control.

I was fully prepared for my briefing as the enemy Corps Commander but nobody, including the new Army Commander, dropped in to see the amount of effort I had made. Sometime later in the afternoon, I was summoned to the operations room of the Infantry Division instead. I did not know whether I had to brief as enemy Commander or Commander of the Infantry Brigade. Having collected my wits, I presumed that my Deputy Commander, who was to brief, had been asked to make way for my briefing. I did a quick mental turnaround and completed it. The brigade briefing was over with continuous interruptions by the Army Commander which I knew was quite normal. Immediately thereafter, the Army Commander's visit to the station was announced. While flying over the station, he noticed shanty dwellings (must have been warned by the staff beforehand) inside the station which could be mistaken for an abandoned village inhabited by defence personnel. During my briefing, his first question to me was "As the Station Commander how have you allowed jawans to occupy the abandoned village inside the station and why no action has been taken to flatten the old houses in the villages?" I replied that this state has existed for years now because there was no written clearance from the higher HQ. "Do you have to wait for that?" he queried. "Now that you have given your verbal concurrence it will be removed, Sir, as early as possible", was my reply.

I gave a week's notice to all jawans and their families residing illegally in the village. There was a great uproar but I weathered the storm of protests from the local units which had connived to create this situation. My Adm Commandant himself on a bulldozer commenced the operations to flatten the village. We could recover a lot of timber and construction material such as doors and windows which came in very handy for the Health Club planned by me inside the station. I had just received my board results which came in after 14 months' reports in Apr/May 93 and was disappointed. Since I did not make it for the next rank, I worked with even greater zeal, honesty and singleness of purpose to see all my plans through. We got a nine-hole golf course laid out with the help of all units in the station. Our Gorkha *paltan* helped in the construction of an open-air squash court with each battalion chipping in a wall, constructed from the bricks recovered by us from the ruins of the village Additionally the Gorkhas took on the project of Health Club totally from the debris recovered from the village. We invited the new GOC Maj. Gen. CS Panag, my DSSC coursemate, to inaugurate both these places. He appreciated the hard work and the ingenuity in the creation of those facilities, and also warned me that he had to obey the diktat from the Corps Commander, to observe me. One of my biggest projects was conceived by CO Gorkhas, Lokindar Thakur. There was an acute water shortage in our area even when the link canal from the Indira Gandhi Canal was located some 3 km away. I deputed him to carry out a study of the link canal and got the blueprints ready for bringing the canal water to Lalgarh. The total distance involved was only 3 kms, and if each battalion contributed 1 km this task of digging a canal to connect the link canal to Lalgarh was not impossible as the terrain was almost like a tabletop. My conditions were that the entire digging should be completed at night time as a part of night training, to be completed in one month.

Inspecting the link canal

After the digging commenced, I kept the GOC in complete picture and got the engineers to install a pump at the link canal to pump water up to the newly constructed reservoir which was connected to the dug canal. Sometimes in Mar 94, at about 0400 hrs, Lokindar reported that the water had finally arrived and the canal was through. I conveyed the same good news to the GOC the next day. Today the canal is fully functional. In fact, during my visit to Lalgarh in 1998, as DDG DSC Army HQ, I was informed later by the next GOC of the Infantry Division, that proper engineer support had been provided and Lalgarh water supply is based on this canal. I also learnt that the GOC had been awarded a VSM purely for initiating the project of linking Lalgarh Jattan with canal water from an existing canal in the vicinity. The original spadework and the construction of the canal done by my battalions earlier was probably ignored. Based on this, the citation was forwarded for which my CO Gorkhas, Col. Lokindar, the mastermind of the project, should have been awarded. All three *paltans* were the pillars of strength for my brigade and I owed my success to them.

I commanded the Infantry Brigade for exactly 24 months to fulfil the criteria of a brigade command. The COAS Gen. Rodrigues had waived these criteria to 14 months with one full report and one interim report first. The MS Branch ensured that I did not move out for two years. If I was not to make it to the higher rank, where was the need for me to continue beyond 14 months. My subsequent period of command under the new GOC Maj. Gen. CS Panag was inconsequential. Immediately on his arrival, the GOC and I were detailed for a court-martial duty of a Brigade Commander at Kotah. Though the GOC had found nothing lacking in my command, he insisted that my report under him was sprinkled with 7s despite my request that it would prove very damaging for me during my review board.

The Corps HQ detailed me for carrying out a staff court of inquiry in connection with the igloo ammunition sheds which had developed cracks due to faulty construction norms. I took this opportunity to see the new Corps Commander to explain my supersession case as well. I found absolutely no empathy or support from him, even though he was also a paratrooper. He advised me to take my supersession in stride as such things happen in life. I assured the Corps Commander that I would complete the Court of Inquiry well before I vacate my appointment. There were a lot of problems, viz, obtaining the attendance of witnesses, the five members and the results of various lab/technical reports. I was particularly fortunate to have as a member, Lt. Col. Jitender Singh was DCWE in Bhatinda Zone who proved to be very competent in work procedures and helped me in finalizing the inquiry speedily. I used to commute daily from Lalgarh to Bhatinda for almost two to three months to complete the assigned task by that time. I retired to Lalgarh late every evening, there were other problems to attend to, in the Station. Therefore, I had to confine my Bathinda visits to alternate days after seeing the workload pile up.

In the inquiry, we issued non-bailable warrants to the witnesses (including one retired Lt. Gen) to secure their attendance. There were glaring lapses in the construction norms such as the use of bore well water for curing everywhere, resulting in saltwater cracks on the rooftops. We had to establish the fact that no arrangements were made for drawing fresh water from the canal. Samples of the debris fallen from rooftops also indicated the presence of salt in the concrete mixture. One very pertinent inference was drawn on the use of

Pazzolana cement used instead of the usual Portland cement. As Portland cement was in short supply (being diverted for the Asiad in 1981 in New Delhi) the Zonal Chief Engineer ordered the purchase of Pazzolana cement instead. This cement requires more time and water for curing which was not visualized by them. As such the expensive igloo ammunition sheds which were very expensive in construction developed cracks very prematurely in the late eighties.

The next problem was how to re-commission the sheds. We invited a lot of experts including my visit to CBRI Roorkee and got the views of one Professor VP Arya unofficially. He advised that we first open the cracks fully and then use epoxy resin to fill them up to the brim. We carried out one test case and recommissioned one shed. The Board had done a very detailed root cause analysis and had saved the exchequer some Rs 40 crores. When this was shown to the Corps Commander, who was very happy and commended me for a good job. By the time the case was expedited in the Command, I received my posting orders to College of Combat, Mhow. I was happy to learn that the repair work on the Igloo ammunition sheds commenced in earnest and finished in good time.

Before I departed from Lalgarh, I ensured that all other tasks which were undertaken by us were completed. The illegal village of shanty dwellings was completely uprooted and the OR families moved to the constructed quarters. Some officers were occupying surplus JCOs quarters. They were made to vacate and moved to temporary single accommodation of two rooms in their respective messes. My Brigade HQ had no guest room. They were allotted two guest rooms which were modified to function as such. We also created this guest room fit enough to be occupied by the incoming Cdr. This freed the

MES IB which was kept for outside VIPs. Next were the sterling silver trophies, which appear to be the ones taken as souvenirs from the Pakistan Army Mess in Bangladesh, in 1971, which was not on charge anywhere. How this silver was lying, who knows most of it may have already disappeared over the years. I instructed the Deputy to take these items on charge in the Brigade Officers Mess. These were polished before finding their rightful place in the Brigade Mess.

The Health Club was fully functional along with the squash court and the two tennis courts. A newly constructed canal, now christened Bela Lokinder Canal, brought in the much-needed water for the greening of the station. The golf course was made fully functional by the creation of two water bodies based on PBS rolls provided by the Chief Engineer Command. I was also tasked to write a Draft Training Note on Forward Zone Battle in Semi Desert terrain. This note after several additions/deletions formed the basis on which HQ Corps OP Planning note, on the same subject, has been issued. I had the satisfaction of leaving the station as a very happy man even though my board results were not in my favour. My continued hard work as Station Commander had rattled all officers and ladies in the station who wondered why this stupid man was still working at the same pace when he had already burnt his boats.

The Last Post at Mhow

I arrived in Mhow during the first week and was informed on my arrival, that my posting to SC Wing had now been changed to JC Wing. There had been a lot of interaction between the Commandant and the MS. I reported to Maj. Gen. RK Mittal, the Commander JC wing, (ex-Gunner) who also agreed with me on my apprehensions. He advised me that it was better serving under him as SI in JC than SC Wing. The proposal of posting Brigadiers as SIs in the JC wing had been accepted by the MS Branch. I took my job seriously, which meant overseeing the work of 6-8 DS Colonels and approximately 80-100 student officers of the rank Captain or Majors of all arms & services. The college had just shifted to the new KLP on Bercha Road and we also had a brand new DS posted and one PA between two SIs. I had arrived with my complete baggage from Lalgarh and was accommodated in single officers' accommodation of three rooms on the front lawn of the building. My baggage was kept in one of the rooms and I stayed in the other two.

Though the atmosphere was nowhere near DSSC Wellington, I found it good for imparting my professional knowledge to the young impressionable lot who looked up to you for guidance. Some sand models were taken by me deliberately so that I could set the best professional standards for others. I had a very good lot of DS body - AK Singh (Armoured Corps) Ravi Batra (Guards) AS Dhesi (Mech) CS Sandhu (Bihar) RS Suhag (Raj Rif) AS Alhawat (Arty) & Amit Sircar (Engrs). My colleague Sis, were Brigs GJ Mishra (Rajput), RM Sewal (Kumaon), Tubby Das (Armoured Corps) & Kambargimath who joined later when Sewal left on posting. We formed a very formidable professional "no-nonsense" team that believed in imparting the best practical knowledge to our students by sheer hard work and preparation. It was evident we were way ahead of other Brigs in HC/SC Wings. Most of my DS had been my students or had attended the Staff Course previously at Wellington and therefore had some idea how the instructional tenure had to be performed. Over some time, Ravi and Neelam Batra were our very good friends and we were irresistibly drawn by this charming couple and their children. Ravi enjoyed being the Mess Secretary and did a very fine job for the student body, with whom he was immensely popular. As the DS body comprised Colonels, who had completed their command tenures, still in the run for HC they had to be reassured that their career interests were safe, provided they delivered in their jobs. I felt happy to provide them with the catalyst in their profession by my example by relieving them of sand models or central discussions most of which I took on myself. Great fun interacting with youngsters and getting to know their views.

In the meanwhile, in response to a signal asking for Brigadier to volunteer for deputation to R & AW I applied to the Cabinet Secretariat. I was interviewed sometime in June 95 by the OIC Military Wing of PMO and Mr AS Dullat, the then Addl DG. There were not many differences of opinions when I expressed my views on "hot pursuit" in J&K. My answers on contemporary strategic analysis of the Sino Indian border dispute were articulated based on what I had imbibed so far, with my 32 years of experience, nothing unusual. Dullat seemed happy and told me that he would let me know a standard reply. I learnt later that MS Branch had not made me available for transfer to R & AW, on the plea that I had a good chance of making it to a Maj. Gen's rank. I consulted all my worthy seniors Lt. Gen. SN Endley, my first cousin, Lt. Gen. KM Seth the AG and many senior gunners. I sought an interview with the senior Colonel Commandant, Lt. Gen. Surendra Nath, and was very disappointed with his advice. "Dabbu, I have seen a lot of my highly qualified colleagues fall by the wayside. You must accept your supersession gracefully". Not a word of sympathy or support. Nobody was even prepared to say that they would try and help in my statutory complaint except Krish Seth. I was also told by the MS that I stood a very good chance in the review reports, as I had more than 10 months to go before I received any posting.

In the middle of 1995, Maj. Gen. RK Mittal proceeded on retirement and Maj. Gen. Arjun Ray of Mech Infantry replaced him. It took some time for the new Commander to get to know his team. I made it a point to do my duties as best as I could, with a lot of professionalism and zeal. I also ensured that we delivered the goods to our young and very impressionable student officers from all arms and services. There were a lot of coordination conferences, review of the syllabi, updating doctrines/ concepts, which the new Commander wanted to bring about. Being the senior-most SI, I tried my best to convey that I needed no motivation in my duties. Arjun Ray did recognize the fact, I had acquired tactical wisdom by learning, hard work and practice. We had long discussions on various tactical concepts and he respected my candid and forthright views. He commenced his discussions on operations in desert/semi-desert terrain such as Rajasthan, the obstacles ridden terrain in Punjab, the mountainous terrain of Ladakh and Arunachal, knowledge of counter-insurgency operations learnt in NE and Punjab. There can be no substitute for the experience gained during the physical handling of troops in various types of terrain on the subcontinent, which he thought I possessed in ample measure. This experience factored in new lessons which could be incorporated in the tutorial divisional discussions and sand models. Being a serious-minded professional Arjun Ray, also made very copious notes in preparation for his command of the Armoured division, which was to follow.

My very dispassionate and unbiased opinion of Arjun Ray was that he was a thoroughbred professional, trustworthy and reliable besides being a gentleman to the core. There were many stories about him which were afloat like being very ambitious his Staff College nomination for Camberly in his third attempt and that too based on *sifarsh* of the serving COAS. Arjun deserved what he got. If I was in the General's place, I wouldn't hesitate one bit. He had been groomed well and he fitted very well for higher command. He had performed the duties of BGS of a Corps under Lt. Gen. Padmanbhan. He worked very hard to complete his well-documented "Kashmir Diary".

With Maj. Gen. Arjun Ray and team at Mhow

Social life in Mhow during 95-96 was hectic as usual. Brig. Ghosal from the Artillery joined us as SI in the place of Brig. GJ Mishra who proceeded to CRPF as DIG on re-employment in 1996. There were a lot of changes in the syllabi and old exercises were revamped. After almost three decades, new exercises were approved by Maj. Gen. Arjun Ray which encouraged fresh thinking and an altogether 'out of the box' solution. Central discussions and new op-oriented wargames were introduced, which made the course more interesting and meaningful. When I compare the present JC with what I did in the seventies, the present one is a way ahead and provides a good foundation to our youngsters. In the Faculty of Studies Brig. Sudhir Johar fresh from Cairo as our Military Attache just joined. and could be counted for any help. There was another DS from HC Wing, Brig. RS Duggal from the Corps of Engineers. We found that the whole lot of us gelled very well, and we met socially every month or earlier if an opportunity presented itself. Arjun Ray an Englishman to the core, along with his very charming wife possessed socially conspicuous social graces and manners worthy of mention. It also reflected his self-discipline and austere lifestyle They kept the JC flock together through good social interactions, picnics and wing get-togethers. His tenure helped break the ice, built up an edifice of trust, faith and learning. It also brought back memories of the Soviets in JC Wing once again. The results were very evident for everyone to see, better prepared DS in tutorials, improvement in the conduct of sand models and divisional central discussions and overall improvement in student performance.

Students arrive at War College to learn from the battle seasoned Directing Staff, whose word they accept as gospel truth. Their motivation and confidence during briefings, sand models and wargames showed a quantum jump. They seemed reassured and quite happy. Families of student officers were also kept busy with ladies' meet and useful demos and get together. During the two years, I spent at Mhow I also had the privilege of attending the Rajput Regiment get together having served in 17 Para Field Regiment, the old 8th Battalion, the 7 Rajput. Though a great idea to connect with the past, surprisingly no CO 17 Para Field Regiment, for forty years, even thought of it. As our Commandant, Lt. Gen. NK Kapoor was the Colonel of The Rajput Regiment, I did not wish to convey a wrong message that I have very little in common with the Rajput Regiment, being a thoroughbred gunner.

Colonels of Regiments pay visits to Mhow regularly. I happened to be present at one such get together when our Commander tried to introduce me to the visiting Rajput Colonel of the Regiment, who just ignored me and went past me, I can only fathom that my complaint against supersession was not taken kindly by him. Later, both of us were unanimous in our views that it was a very immature act to avoid shaking hands and drawing distinctions between officers while being introduced. I had learnt that senior officers have to be very patient, tolerant and must have the unlimited capacity to suffer fools. Later, Arjun Ray was informed by the General that his son in law, a Maj., was coming on the September 96 course. Now the Eastern Army Commander had given directions, to have his son law placed under a particular Brigadier and not me. It seems Arjun Ray had a lot of faith in my judgment and fair play was very comfortable, to place him in my division, much against his professed desire. Everything moved in my division as usual and there was nothing to suggest that I took note of the General's son in law in my division, to settle scores. I did attend the tutorial discussion in all syndicates by rotation which was my daily routine and was given his due correctly.

The officer from the first tutorial onwards always came unprepared for classes, with the result that his DS graded him a low average. This was also confirmed by the written test at the end of each tutorial. In my mid-term interview, I had counselled him to improve his performance in the class and written work. I don't blame this young officer. The biggest problem with the young officers today is the abhorrence of anything written. In every battalion today, the CO sets the pace of what studies are needed by youngsters straight from IMA. Where the CO is someone, who thinks that professional soldiering only lies in small arms classification, route marches and drinking rum with your men, the youngsters remain inadequately groomed. This has a telling effect when our officers attend all arms courses like JC in which a fair number of studies of GS publications and manuals is involved. It was sad that this officer's performance remained low average throughout the course and I just agreed with the assessment by his three DS and I assessed him slightly higher, and not anything lower.

Towards the end of the course, Maj. Gen. Arjun Ray proceeded on posting and I was then the Officiating Wing Commander for some time. As it's normal practice I took the results to the Commandant for approval. When it came to the result of this Maj. the Commandant noticed that he had been assessed as C+. He then overwrote the grading and made it B. I then informed the Commandant that there were 19 officers above this officer who had been assessed C+ and it would be unfair for him to make this change until those 19 were also made into Bs. He told me that it was his prerogative as the Commandant and his decision was final. I did not press the issue further as I felt my point had been made.

A month back I had been posted as BGS at IMA Dehradun. Now to my horror, I found it changed to DDG DSC Army HQ New Delhi. I had sought an interview with MS to enquire why my last leg posting to home town Dehradun had been changed without assigning any reasons. The reply given by the MS was that some time back in 1994, I had requested for a posting to Delhi which had fructified now, after four years. Packing began in earnest and we got ready for the final posting of my career. A Maruti 10-wheeler truck was hired which took care of the complete baggage, car and scooter. Baggage was around well in time at the end of Feb 97 and was kept in Central Base Post Office stores on Rao Tula Marg, thanks to the help of my predecessor Brig. Satya Dev. My coursemate Maj. Gen. OS Lochchab, MG Adm & Coord who wanted me to take over as President RWA Shanker Vihar in the Mahipalpur area, to bring up the new colony. I was allotted a temporary two in one flat which was sufficient for a small family since it was half the normal entitlement. These flats were the brainchild of the COAS, who thought that the accommodation shortage would be overcome to some extent by temporary accommodation which could be later converted to permanent accommodation.

The Hanging Up of Boots & Uniform

MS had foreclosed the option of a home posting for me to Dehradun to accommodate someone else. My battle against supersession was continuing and there were a lot of developments on this score but there was enough time to accommodate both office job as well as my personal affairs. I endeavoured to put in my best as the DDG, and work tirelessly to justify my place on the appointments board from 1947 onwards, behind my chair. This is probably one of the very few appointments yet to be upgraded on account of its low profile. Though the force was 45,000 strong, all its manpower was dished out to the three services and DGQA. There were also 1200 all ranks hijacked which functioned directly under the Defence Secretary called the DHQ Troops. DSC Centre was located way South in North Kerala in Kannur (Cannanore). I have no intentions of casting aspersions on the performance of my predecessors, but it was amply clear to me that there was a lot required to be done to improve the standards of DSC as a Corps. Luckily, I got three years in the appointment with no liability of constructing my house, or children to settle and all my lifelong aspirations fulfilled. I resolved that I will accept everything as a challenge, and continue working at the same pace to improve matters. This was just the start. The task is so daunting that even after I have initiated the process, someone has to follow things up for a complete overhaul.

I was very impressed by the Kannur Cantonment. This Cantonment has changed hands as a military camp for Portuguese, Dutch and finally the British rulers. This was one of the oldest British cantonments in the 1880s where both civilian and military personnel resided. It is the Headquarters of Defence Security Corps now with the DSC Centre, DSC Record, DSC Pay Accounts located here. The Centre retains the heritage buildings constructed for an infantry battalion. Being located on the North Kerala coast it rains about 7-8 months a year. The British Commanding Officer constructed the pathway to all places which were to be inspected by him. The covered roof from one of his *paltan* to the other ensured that he never got a drop of water on his uniform. The most picturesque and one of the oldest golf courses, West Coast Golf Course, with cashew trees on either side of the fairway, the Arabian Sea on its west looked challenging but lay in shambles, unused. The seven-star sprawling glass guest house provides the view of the ships sailing past and the private beach is just out of this world and we were its frequent visitors.

It was an open offer to my coursemates, if they were looking for a holiday in North Kerala, this was the place. Kannur is famous for its cashew, spices and the pressed plywood sceneries and paintings.

Meeting the Officers and staff at the DSC Centre Kannur

My team found there was also plenty of time to devote to the professional standards, the battered image of DSC as a Corps to be improved and the betterment in jawans and families living conditions. DDGs over the years had contributed their services during their stint of two years and also prepared for their retirement, as was the normal practice. All the DSC troops were organized on a platoon basis each commanded by a Subedar Major/Subedar or a Naib Subedar. At places such as Ordnance Depots Factories, there was an officer posted in command of 5/7/9/11 platoons. All ranks were ex-servicemen from Regular Army or TA with an average age group of 40-55 years. It was not difficult to notice the various other shortcomings in the manner of functioning and the deplorable state of comradeship, poor administration morale and state of welfare in the DSC. The turnout and bearing spoke of it all. It was a pathetic sight to see potbellied soldiers man sensitive locations in South Bock and Sena Bhawan with a 303 rifle, which he could barely hold, acting in a manner that could surprise anyone. Their accommodation, scale of ration and other benefits were the same as applicable to the Army.

Within a week of taking over, I was faced with a problem of a recently widowed jawan's wife who with her escort, one Rajput Regiment retired JCO, was waiting outside my office, for airing their grievances. The lady stated that the husband from one of the DSC platoons located at AF Station Agra was hale and hearty three to four months back when he came on leave. A month back, she had received a telegram, after a delay of two/three days, that her husband had expired suddenly. By the time she and her escort, ex JCO brother in law, reached the unit at Agra, the last rites had already been performed. It appears that the jawan had got involved in a scuffle with his colleagues and had been manhandled after he had consumed a lot of drinks. As a result of the fight amongst the DSC jawans, he was the one who succumbed to his injuries. AF Station had carried out an enquiry in which some individuals were blamed for the fight, including the victim himself. The enquiry was yet to be approved by the Station Commander. When the jawan's wife accompanied by the same escort arrived, nobody was available to meet her except the platoon Commander JCO. He led her to a place in the cookhouse where the cremated remains, packed in a gunny sack, were found lying, in one corner of the room. This state of affairs highly infuriated the wife and her escort who asked for an interview with the Station Commander. An Administrative Officer interviewed the lady and her escort instead of the Station Commander who was out of the station at that time. When the lady and her escort approached me, a week or 10 days had already elapsed. When I approached the Air HQ, I was asked to meet the Air Officer IC Administration, AVM CK Krishnatri who had done Higher Command with me at Mhow in 1984-85. On his assurances, I paid a visit to AF Station Agra, after the inquiry had been finalized. There was no point in my trying to pick holes to cast aspersions on the management of the DSC platoon under the AF Station, which were poor standards, to say the least. I endeavoured to obtain the best benefit for the deceased's life and small children and then get cracking to improve their quality of life in India. A paltry sum of Rs 10,000 was given by the station from its welfare funds, I understood that DSC was not entitled to any Army Benevolent fund since there was no contribution by the DSC personnel towards the same. Another visit to Air HQ ensured that the Air Chief gave Rs 50,000 from the CAS Benevolent funds to the widow.

The coming week was spent in a visit to DSC Centre at Kannur. My wife and I arrived by air and were received by the Commandant Col. Som Vrat Joshi of the Kumaon Regiment. During the visit, I familiarized myself with the training, administrative and documentation procedures in the DSC. There were certain flaws in training that needed to be tightened up. While the army had kept pace with the latest concepts of modern weapons and training arms, nobody had taken pains to improve on the old stereotyped training in vogue in the DSC. My team's biggest worry was the response of DSC troops in border areas, counter-insurgency ridden areas like the J&K and NE, and the defence of vital installations. While it is understood that a higher age group commanded by even older JCO cannot achieve the same results as the regular army, the force at least should be able to carry out its basic task of protection of the installation. What it boils down to is to return the fire and provide a firm base for reinforcements of the regular army. With this in mind, I thought the jawans needed to be indoctrinated first on the possession of a high degree of alertness. The gleaning and gaining of information over some time can come later.

Inspecting the DSC Quarter Guard at Kannur

The question of proficiency in the use of personal weapons would arise if only they fire their weapons regularly. Some of them had never fired a weapon for years. The concept of forming part of a quick reaction team on airfield defence installation could also come later, once we introduce this in their training. Physical fitness assumed importance and we had issued orders making daily PT and/games compulsory. Obese individuals were placed on a watch for weight and served written warning for being discharged on the medical ground/physical fitness. First time in DSC history, BPET was conducted at all stations, in the presence of Jt Directors/Directors. I also visited DSC Records and found an outdated ethos of documentation, based purely on manual technique. They were promised four computers and were asked to depute 6-8 selected personnel for computer training locally, on expenses paid for by the Centre. These personnel formed the nucleus of our computerisation drive. We had also noticed the weakness in the communication training at the platoon level. We now considered training on the use of radio sets/ walkie talkies at DSC posts. Eight packages were lying in the stores all unopened. When I got them opened, these turned out to be PCs allotted to us by Army HQ sometimes back. Straightaway, they were allotted to DSC Centre Kannur for use.

Even the units which employ DSC accepted that a telephone line was enough, which resulted in a post-bound mentality. If you asked a DSC jawan if he had gone around his post on foot, he replied that it was not his duty. One had to get that mentality out of his mind, especially the *danda chowkidar* mentality. I knew it would take time, but this was just the beginning. Some of the DSC users were entirely civilian R&D organisations who were content with using DSC as domestic help or as office boys or as private car drivers. The Security Officers responsible for the DSC platoons paid scant regard for the employment and administration of DSC personnel as long as they were provided with a vehicle by the establishment. My visit to DSC units in the five existing commands in the tri-services opened my eyes. I could see a colossal underutilization of DSC manpower at almost all locations. At places, I found that there were almost 10-12 platoons at one establishment, each functioning under a platoon Commander, usually a Subedar Major or a Subedar, all at working cross purposes.

There was a security officer of the rank of a Maj. (TS) or a Lt. Col. who was either not interested in his job or was sold to the establishment. Duties to jawans were apportioned on the old duty roster which was in vogue for the last two decades. When queried about the same with DSC Directors in Command HQ, they could not give me a satisfactory reply. Each of the DSC Director Command also had some full-time job to perform, such as in change of Golf Courses, Mess/Officers Institutes Secretary/the Canteen Officer, in addition to their duties. It became essential for me to lay down the minimum number of days every month for the Directors to visit their areas of responsibility. In some cases, I found that the Director DSC of the command had an unwieldy span of control. There was a requirement of 8-10 additional officers of Joint Directors level (Lt. Col) at selected Areas/Sub Areas. My predecessor had done some spadework on this and I just followed it up with the MoD and was surprised that they approved an additional eight Jt Directors immediately

DSC Directorate is one of the oldest Directorates and comes under the control of COAS (T&C) Fortunately, I had served with Lt. Gen. MR. Sharma who was the new DOCAS (T&C) designate on my posting as DDG, DSC. As a new DS at DSSC Wellington, he had seen my performance there and was quite sympathetic to see me at this post. However, I was determined to do my best, whatever be the challenges, job profile and hurdles in the reorganisation/regrouping of the DSC. Being the Colonel Commandant DSC, we ensured that he received all the honour accorded equivalent to other Col. Commandants. This meant smartly turned-out stick orderlies for the office and residence, clerical staff and other accoutrements. We first arranged for the visit by Col. Commandant and his wife to DSC Centre

Kannur, where every single detail was tied up with great foresight and very minutely. I also arranged his visit to the Regimental institutions and brought him up to date with the problems faced by DSC troops. We found that Gen. Sharma was quite willing to listen if the presentation was based on logic and reasoning. DSC Centre had its share of problems with the Area Commander also jumping in the fray whenever any decision was taken to improve administrative conditions at DSC Centre. The first action that Gen. Sharma agreed to take was to order the cancellation of the demolition of DSC barracks which were heritage buildings built over 120 years back by the British Army when Cannanore was a staging post for troops returning home to Britain. The timber used in almost all buildings was in top condition (Burma teak) and could go on for another 50 years provided anti-termite and other treatments were done regularly. The buildings are doing fine even today.

During his visit to the canteen, the DCOAS remarked that the Canteen with assets of almost Rs 16 cores must be one of the richest canteens in the Army. I then broached the topic of share of canteen profits and apprised DCOAS that every Directorate is empowered to order the transfer of canteen profits, for the maintenance and upkeep and welfare of troops. Arty Directorate asks for 15% and other Directorates upwards of that. The transfer of 12.5% Canteen profit to the Directorate was approved. I had made a verbal commitment to the DCOAS that the money obtained would be sanctioned for enhancement of DSC image and welfare of troops to Directors and Joint Directors on a pro-rata basis, depending on the number of platoons under their jurisdiction. Our DSC Centre was extremely rich in Regimental funds but unfortunately, there were no clear directions to the Centre Commandant on how to spend. Since the emphasis was to improve the quality of life of DSC troops, we started with the Centre itself. First was the automation of the cook houses. Commandants were advised to spend anything for the fear of misuse of funds, that didn't deter us.

Gas *chullahs*, kitchen appliances, Central RO Plant, better furniture and crockery including a chapati maker had just come into the market. While modifying the kitchen chimney we introduced clean kitchen appliances purchased from Regimental funds, approved by us within my financial powers. Documentation such as three quotes and comparative statements were insisted upon. In one of my trips to the Centre, the existing golf course had to be closed down on orders of the Army Commander, Gen. Joshi, which I verified was correct. I agreed with the Commandant, that the Golf Club had become a den for heavy drinkers and gambling for retired officers, which led to its closure. I apprised the DCOAS of the same and took his permission to reactivate the Golf Course again. M/s Seagrams conducted a sponsored event during 1998, which was also reported in the local press. Thus, the golf course called the West Coast Golf Course established by the British got a fresh lease of life. Officers at the Centre, especially those retired living in close vicinity were warned to keep liquor out of the premises, otherwise, their membership would stand cancelled.

Inauguration of the Boys Hostel at DSC Centre Kannur

We also took a keen interest in the welfare of DSC families. Manju accompanied me at my cost, whenever I visited the DSC Centre. There was so much which could be done to make life very comfortable for the families. In our welfare meets now, jawans wives, particularly from the south, are well educated and very conscious of their rights. We ensured the participation was purely voluntary, and not forced. Ladies put their minds together and thought of better schemes such as computer education, vocational courses and working for profits, instead of the usual knitting and tailoring classes. With the nucleus of trained DSC personnel, we ran our computer classes for Jawans wives and children without any charges.

On my return from the DSC Centre at the Directorate, Col. TK Tikoo, my number two and self-prepared a statement of the case for DSC Jawans being eligible for Army Benevolent fund like all ranks of the regular army. We cannot fathom why this aspect had been ignored till now. DSC Jawans' families were at the mercy of their respective establishments at the time their husbands were serving, whereas the Indian Army AGs Branch washed its hands clean from DSC. We thought this was something we could try. Though we were warned that it is bound to fail. We thought at least, we would have the satisfaction of having tried. On contacting the AGs Branch with the statement of the case, I was surprised to learn that the matter is being dealt with by Secretary AWWA. This opening was most welcome, as Col. KK Bhargava of my 17 Para Field Regiment was the dealing person. We then requested a meeting with the President AWWA Dr Ranjana Malik, (my old classmate SC 58 Batch and Mrs Rekha Shankar in the President's office in South Block. The advice given to me was, "We appreciate your concern for the DSC family's welfare but it would not be correct to include DSC in the Army Benevolent Fund unless there is a contribution by all ranks DSC". I returned to the office and discussed the matter with the DCOAS, who authorised me to make a one-time contribution of Rs 5 Lakhs to the Army Benevolent Fund. We thus heralded the entry of DSC personnel in the Army Benevolent fund for the first time in 50 years. I felt extremely elated that my classmate Dr Ranjana Malik, President AWWA had honoured my request and convinced the Army brass that DSC personnel must also be included, as the beneficiaries to Army Benevolent Fund.

Discipline and turnout are the bedrock of any force. DSC personnel are drawn from all three services and the TA. This makes it a very heterogeneous mix and when the hapless jawan, who remains unemployed for a year or more, is forced to opt for the DSC. At this time, his domestic problems are at their peak. Many cases of indiscipline by DSC personnel about intoxication, insubordination and disobedience and overstay of leave are a direct result. From our analysis, we attributed these cases to frustration, and sometimes, to vagueness of orders and poor junior leadership. It was essential to see that we get down to setting over our own house in order before undertaking any exercise to improve matters. First, DSC Records was functioning in a very arbitrary manner. There was some clerical staff who had not moved out for as much as 8 years from Kannur and had been milking the jawans for money for the favour of choice postings. Since the OIC Records was due for a charge, we got a North Indian to personally function under Centre Commandant Col. SV Joshi who also felt the same way. Most of the key personnel, especially the South Indians gave way to the North Indians. The Centre Commandant also ensured that the North-South ratio was kept and wherever there was a South Indian in charge of a section he invariably had a North Indian number two. All cases of compassionate postings were personally approved by the Directorate. Written SOP fully revised and updated was issued and utmost transparency was ensured. The promotion policy was reviewed to include physical fitness and professional competence as the key matter. A lot of bickering was on out of turn promotions and we put a stop to all this, once and for all.

We had noticed that there was no pride, self-esteem and camaraderie amongst DSC troops. One could not help notice their turnout, faded uniforms, accoutrements and their state of weapons. I was aghast when I saw a large deficiency of weapons (5000) and the presence of obsolete weapons. 303 (1500) still in the inventory. We prepared another statement of the case for the phasing out of. 303 rifles. We also learnt that with the introduction of the INSAS rifle, the 7.62 mm SLR had been rendered surplus. After approval by DCOAS,

I called on the MGO Lt. Gen. JS Dhillon. He was my SI as a Brigadier at DSSC Wellington and gave me a patient hearing. Seeing my commitment, he ordered the release of SLR rifles to DSC and the backloading of all .303 rifles. I also sought his advice on the issue of a third pair uniform and combat dress to DSC personnel. We were able to push this through also after the DCOAS approval. All these steps required the review of weapons training at the Centre. We needed better and qualified instructors. We first selected young WTIs and sent them to Raj Rif Centre for pre-course training and then to Infantry School Mhow on Weapons Course. In about six months, the results started showing and the DSC Jawan was better trained now before he joined his unit for duties.

A careful study of the PE of a DSC platoon showed the authority of one motorcycle to each platoon for use by the SM in charge. We decided as a test case to ask for 10 motorcycles for platoons in the NCR region which were cleared by DCOAS. MGO was very kind in releasing these 10 MCs to the DSC. The problem now was to train the platoon commander who declined on account of advanced age. We selected drivers from our personnel, who were either ex ASC or Artillery and used them as dispatch riders for platoon administration. Further release of MCs to DSC platoons was ordered in bits and pieces during this period, I also managed to convince the MGO for release of Gypsy jeep to DSC Centre which would be used for the QRT duties in South Block, Sena and Vayu Bhawan in an emergency. This vehicle was located in the DHQ Troops location in the South Block hutments All shortages in clothing such as boots, short greatcoats, angola shirts etc. were made up. Slowly but surely, there was an improvement in the DSC image. We also took care to post a physically fit and younger lot to man our posts at Army HQ. A visit to DHQ Troops functioning under Col. Vipin Nautiyal, my student on the 41st Staff Course, made a lot of difference. We had excellent relations and all the differences between the DSC Directorate and DHQ troops were fortunately resolved in no time.

During one of my visits to the DSC Centre, I found the DSC band playing quite well on various functions. I promised them new sets of uniforms, musical instruments and better training procedures, by borrowing musicians from other centres to train our boys. I approached my friend Brig. Arun Mishra Director Ceremonials & Welfare AGs Branch of the Guards to consider our brass band's inclusion for the Republic Day Parade 1999. Selections by a board of three officers, generally commence around September and the bands arrive and train at Delhi for almost four months before Republic Day. Surprises of all surprises, took place when our band was selected to participate. It was a matter of great pride for me to see them playing along the Rajpath and salute our President. I couldn't have asked for more, Arun Mishra was very fair in his selection. This probably was the first and only time when a DSC band marched alongside the other regimental bands on Republic Day. They were also invited to Hotel Ashok to play at a private function. I was personally congratulated by the Colonel Commandant for this achievement.

At the DSC Directorate

During my tenure as DDG DSC, I had the privilege of interacting with several senior officers who were once my juniors in service and had a healthy respect for my professional integrity, competence and impeccable moral conduct. I was somewhat intrigued to hear from Maj. Gen. RL Magotra (ex Echo Squadron at NDA) who had known me from Para Brigade days, that the DSC Directorate had declined to collect the computers allotted by Army HQ to it. Being located in the same building as the DSC Directorate, we collected three computers immediately. We then collected 20 more and began a crash program for the computerization of the Directorate with his help.

First, in the guise of creating this capability in my office, we approached JS & CAO Mr Sharma, IAS for ACs for my office. After making me wait outside his office for about 45 minutes, he had the temerity to say that most offices with computers are functional without ACs. Moreover, Brigadiers and below are not authorised ACs in their offices and therefore a cooler has been provided for my office. When asked to show this order in writing, he said I could collect this authority later. Right now he had no time to produce authorities. Seeing his arrogant behaviour left me with doubt that I have to fend for myself. When I asked for permission to purchase two ACs from Regimental Funds, it was sanctioned by DCOAS. I then sanctioned 15 days leave to my SPA along with a cheque for Rs 10,000. to cover his expenses in a computer institute training. Two other volunteers selected were DSC personnel as I could see that the Directorate staff had civilians duplicated by uniformed personnel. The moment I took this action, our CSO Shri HN Bhatnagar suggested that it was more prudent to train civilians as they would provide continuity also.

Therefore, we decided to send at least two civilians and one combatant for computer training at local institutes at our expense (Regimental Funds). We also transferred, on voucher, six more computers in the first lot to DSC Centre and Records. Subsequently, when the second phase of army computerisation came in, we were prepared with our personnel fully trained to operate the systems within 18 months. There were computers on my desk, my Directors and 8 others in the Directorate and 12 each at DSC Centre and Records. We also went in for a massive revamp of the DSC Directorate after getting rid of the flimsy hessian partitions, antique typewriters, unwanted papers and files collected from 1947 onwards. New alucobond partitions and new furniture were provided by the CAO, after my second meeting, he appeared more cooperative. Amazing but true, I thought, it was time to order a destruction board per "Handling of Classified & Other Documents 1966". Maybe it was the fear that emanated that something might get destroyed which may invite action against the DDG. We took all actions in good faith and if there was something we did wrong inadvertently I was prepared to face the consequences.

All this was possible with my civilian team consisting of Mr Dua, the SPS, Mr HN Bhatnagar the CSO and Mr IS Singhmar ACSO and 12 members of clerical staff. My Army team comprised Col. Tej Tikoo of the Naga Regt for the first year who bore the brunt of my frustrations at work when things did not move. I was rather surprised to see such a competent officer being wasted in DSC and tried my best to redeem him, perhaps in the era of inflated ACRs, my excellent report on him was not good enough. I will always regret my decision not to give him an outstanding report as Director DSC. My number two Col. Tej Tikoo was relieved by Col. Jayant Thapa who had just taken over 2/3 GR when I departed from Lalgarh Jattan. We had a very healthy working relationship throughout and were instrumental in executing all the remaining schemes, in my full tenure of three years.

One of the greatest pluses of serving in the DSC as a DDG is that you have a pan India mandate to travel by air to visit your troops especially to far-flung border areas and places like Lakshadweep, Andaman & Nicobar and Wheeler Islands. I had the privilege of visiting DSC troops in the service of the Navy, Air Force and the DRDO. During my visit to DSC troops with the Navy, at Port Blair sometimes in late 1998, I was being taken around for sightseeing tour by our troops during the off forward parade hours by a very smart youngish looking Sikh jawan on a scooter leading my hired car as the outrider/guide. After the trip, I thanked this jawan and asked for particulars of his last unit and for how long he had served in Port Blair. He mentioned Sikh Regimental Centre as his last unit and he had served here for over six years in three tenures. I was naturally surprised to learn about this and made further enquiries. To my dismay, I learnt that there were about 34 odd Sikh jawans of Sikh Regimental Centre who were only to be posted to DSC platoons on these three islands. The same jawan had requested earlier on medical grounds of his wife which was refused. I also remembered meeting another Sikh jawan at Car Nicobar who was also in his seventh year there. When I got back, I made enquiries with the DSC Records who were giving me unsatisfactory replies such as, "Sir, it is a policy matter, some 15 years old that some ex jawans of the Sikh Regiment were, only to be posted only to these places". There was a list which was traced in the Directorate by the oldest serving CSO who explained that there was a directive from DCOAS (T&C) that some 34 recruits who were involved in the mutiny in the Sikh Regimental Centre at Ramgarh in Nov 1984 were transferred to DSC. There were specific instructions from the COAS Secretariat that they were never to be posted to DSC platoons in mainland India. When I asked for these instructions, there were none except a photocopy of an unsigned letter from the COAS Secretariat, which ordered their transfer to DSC as a directive of MoD. We took up a case with the DCOAS that while it was understandable to adjust these Sikh jawans in DSC, it was grossly unfair and discriminatory practice to keep them on the islands only. He agreed with me wholeheartedly and the matter ended there.

We also had the pleasure of my colleague Maj. Gen. GS Sihota (replaced by Maj. Gen. RS Nagra, ADG WE), Maj. Gen. CS Panag,

ADGTA, who was GOC of an Infantry Division when I was commanding the Infantry Brigade, Maj. Gen. Narayan Chaterjee/Natarajan, ADG Pawan Hans. These gentlemen along with ADG Engineers Ravi Chadha had served with me earlier. Seeing me, they must have been shocked to see that I was working at the same speed and efficiency as earlier. I am sure in their heart of hearts, my coursemates though they meant well, were quite happy to see that I was still fighting my case against supersession. I had also contacted Mr RK Anand, a Senior Advocate in South Extension Part II and paid an introductory fee of Rs 11,000 to examine my case against supersession. Visiting his office in civvies one day, I could see a nicely decked up secretary in a beautifully furnished chamber with a retinue of lawyers and liveried staff. After providing all the details and documents he called me later, after one week. In the presence of a legal team of experts he gave me the following brief:

- He would ensure that I get my rank as a Maj. Gen. just as he had got one serving Maj. Gen. his rank. My case was a fit one for filing in Delhi HC.

- MS Branch will always try to see that you superannuate before the court judgment is received. They would try to keep asking for fresh dates and delay as much as possible on some pretext or the other. Your date of birth, being an anathema for them would mean they have two years now to fight the case and four years if the extension of two years comes through.

- As far as the expenses are concerned his charges would be Rs 38,000 per hearing. There could be 8-10 hearings before your case is decided in your favour. A quick mental calculation meant Rs 4 lakhs for me. As Rohit was contemplating his MTech abroad also meant another Rs 3 lacs per annum. Hobson's choice before me was the promotion or his education abroad. I chose the latter.

As mentioned earlier, I also had the pleasure of meeting one of our all-time greatest paratroopers, the Adjutant General, Lt. Gen. KM Seth ex CO 17 Para Field Regiment, with whom I had the privilege to serve, albeit for a short time in 1963. His moral support and encouragement came in very handy. He thought it was too late for me now. Success lies in "hitching your bandwagon to a selected person" well in advance. Earlier the better. One of the finest pieces of advice I received from Gen. Seth was that he would try and see what he could do for me in MoD. "Dabbu, I will fire my Agniban to help you, let's see. You should prefer to send Rohit abroad for his Masters instead of wasting your hard-earned money on the legal case. No lawyer has ever got the rank for anyone. He can only request that the Board be held again as a review case. In your case, the Board would keep rejecting you again". The writing on the wall was clear for me and I agreed to abide by his wise counsel. It is only that my Dignity and Honour had been touched by some reporting officers, who in the open period of ACRs would never have dared to touch me, on professional conduct. There was no Armed Forces Tribunal those days, so I left it at that.

I once met one of our Army Commanders retired now, at the Army Golf Course, in Dec 1998, a year after his retirement. He asked me, "Dabbu Mathur, what happened to you? You were once a high flyer at DSSC". I replied point blank, "Sir, it was your reports as Army Commander when I commanded an Infantry Brigade, that did me in". He replied, "I had reported very well on you. Now that you have said what you did, I will check and come back to you". Twenty-two years have elapsed, I have been meeting him now and then, he has never come back on the same subject.

Ironically, on 1 Mar 2000 I completed three years as DDG DSC, an officer from MS Branch had a sneaky word with my wife Manju's Onco surgeon in the Army Hospital R&R and decided to post me out for my remaining 9 months to Calcutta as Dy GOC Bengal Area. Manju had to undergo chemotherapy over six more cycles which they said could be done at Kolkata. Despite representations by me, the orders were for me to move forthwith as if a warlike emergency was on. Luckily DG Artillery, Lt. Gen. Vinay Shankar who came to know my predicament and asked the MS personally to attach me to the Artillery Directorate, which was done. Not only was I denied my last leg posting to Dehradun, but I also was not even allowed to stay back in Delhi even on compassionate medical grounds. Though I had given up all hopes of getting any promotion after this, there was no reason why I should not work with utmost zeal and dedication, for the sake of my Dignity and Honour.

The next nine months in the Directorate were very eventful for me as DG Arty wanted me to conduct a special Pre-Staff course for Gunner Officers at Deolali and Secundrabad to prepare officers for the DSSC entrance exam. The course was for three weeks each and involved a lot of studies and correction work. At both stations, I spent the whole day lecturing on tactical concepts, various tips on examination technique and the corrections of every student, almost single-handedly. Officers were really happy after the course and the number of gunners who qualified for the entrance exam was at an all-time high. Not looking for laurels, I thought this would be an excellent contribution by me to the Regiment that I was in for the last 37 ½ years.

I appeared for an interview with USI, Lt. Gen. Satish Nambiar to join the Chief Instructor USI immediately after the sad demise of Brig. YP Dev in the USA. He told me to put in my papers, as I was selected for the job. I honestly declared to the Director that I had already booked my ticket to the USA to join my wife and children. This did not go off well with him and someone else was appointed in my place.

We returned to India around 15 Nov 2000 and I got busy with my pension documents which had come back duly sanctioned. This included my Pension Payment Order where my pension was fixed more than that of a Maj. Gen, on account of my two stagnation increments that I had served as a Brigadier for over 11 years, which was quite a record for the Army. Quite naturally, nearly all retiring Maj. Gens asked for a copy of my order to enable them to represent for higher remuneration than mine, which is permitted.

We then decided on a farewell visit to 141 Medium Regiment, in the first week of December 2000, in response to the request by CO and all ranks, that I visit them before I retired. We travelled to Secundrabad to attend our farewell to arms most befittingly carried out by them.

Farewell to arms at 141 Medium Regiment (KARGIL) at Secundrabad

I was pleasantly surprised to be invited by Col. Gashi Gill of the 17 Para Field Regiment, also a part of the same brigade. My first regiment had not forgotten me and also laid on a grand farewell lunch in their mess. I didn't have to prove that my first love is the Regiment I was commissioned in and next is the one I commanded.

On my return from Secundrabad, I took a few decisions, about the profession of arms, which I had served most faithfully, for almost thirty-eight years and loved so dearly. These are as follows:

- My uniforms, service dress and blue patrols shall be presented to the quarter guard of the Regiment I commanded, complete with my full medals, badges of ranks and other insignia, as I wore them last in the service.

- All my mementoes, gifts received from units and service institutions and professional books would be presented to the unit library of the same Regiment.

- I shall donate Rs 1 lakh as a corpus for creating a Meritorious Children Scholarship of JCOs/OR immediately. I propose to increase this amount at a suitable time. My children would maintain contact to supplement it further if the Regiment feels it necessary to increase this corpus, after my demise. This corpus shall not be combined with any other contributions to the Regiment.

After returning from Secundrabad, we were also dined out from the Directorate, thanks to Lt. Gen. Vinay Shankar. Though the usual fanfare was lacking, at least DG Arty had the good sense to include me also during his farewell. We retired on the same date 31 Dec 2000. I continued to stay at P-54, Shankar Vihar for the next three months, which I was allowed to retain, as per rules. Luckily, during my tenure with the DSC, I had become computer-friendly and had even bought one for the residence. With my son Rohit's coaxing and coaching, I was at least able to send emails, operate Skype and other features, like Excel. Having become computer literate, I did attempt to write a few articles, some of which were published in the Times of India and other papers. Someone like me with unknown credentials in the media will always feel the frustration of frequent pink slips from the editors. There were observations on articles being too long, please summarize. Some were returned because the quota on articles with the same theme had already been exceeded. I took it as sportingly as I continued writing. In the meanwhile, CLAWS offered me a full-time fellowship to submit a paper on Maoist insurgency in Chhatisgarh and published some articles which fetched me a good remuneration as well.

So far, I had written only military papers on subjects like Airland Battle, Battle of the Forward Zone and other purely Army doctrines and comments. During various operations where I participated as a Lt./Capt., I can only reproduce what I did. I have no desire to reproduce overall Army plans here, which I was not privy to and are available in all campaigns study books. I then thought I could offer the middle, 600 words to the Times of India captioned "The Birds Have Flown" written after a lot of encouragement by my wife, Manju who was beginning to see that I could be another Chetan Bhagat. Joys of Imperfection written by me during my stay at Albany USA, followed next, based on my own life now. First one first:

The Birds have Flown

Our house in Mhow Cantonment had remained unoccupied for almost two months before we moved in. Our baggage was laid out in neat stacks under the *peepal* tree in front of the garage, after unloading. Not much attention was paid to a lone cypress tree, standing like a *darban*, bang in front of the verandah, planted in the flower bed more by accident than by design.

One by one, the baggage was being moved close to the verandah. Suddenly, all hell broke loose. Two red vented *bulbuls*, sporting brown feathers with jaunty crests and bright red markings flew over my wife's head, warning that intrusion could be met with most ferocious pecks. Soon, the aggrieved *bulbuls* were joined by more sympathisers, also soberly dressed in browns, which gave them a perky well-groomed look. All efforts to locate their habitat were in vain because of the ruckus they created.

Finally, their habitat was located. Virtually at man height, carefully concealed between one of the branches of the cypress tree, but unobtrusive enough to pass as carelessly thrown cotton waste. Despite warnings, the *sahayak* insisted on inspecting the nest and found two blueish coloured eggs inside. Pandemonium prevailed as annoyed *bulbuls'* cacophony of dissent got louder. People say that jaunty temperament and cheerful musical calls make *bulbuls* popular cage birds. Far from it!! Only hasty withdrawal from the locale pacified them and the raids were called off.

Our morning tea in the verandah was right in front of habitat *bulbul*. Was tempted to look see the eggs; well, the previous afternoon's experience was enough. As I strolled casually towards the cypress tree, mama *bulbul* swooped threateningly from nowhere and occupied its nest. Beating a hasty retreat, I got back to my tea. Few days passed without an incident. We avoided the cypress tree.

My wife noticed it first. There was a muted chirping noise emanating from the tree. I think the eggs have hatched, she averred. Very careful not to annoy mama bulbul, I tiptoed up to the nest and found her with wings well spread out and staring me in my face. A few minutes later, she was off leaving the two scraggy chicks; beaks forever open and making screechy noises. Days passed. Look see at the nest was possible only when the mama bulbul was away on her daily foraging trips; mostly pecks at neighbour's ripened strawberries, insects and spiders near our garage. Gradually, the chicks got fine brown feathers, flapped their wings incessantly and their chirping got more raucous and louder.

That was a bright and sunny morning. A peep into the nest indicated no occupants. Probing further, I found the two chicks lying on their tummies in the flowerbed, struggling to get up. Chicks must have fallen and need help, I thought. Once again, alert mama emerged out of nowhere, to warn. One young chick braced itself and flew a few feet before collapsing. The second one followed, presumably on diktat from mama. The solo flights continued in tandem as they hid inside the hedge, following their mama. Now our worry! Cats and other predators were always prowling around and somehow, these chicks needed protection. So, the night was spent roaming around with a torch to keep predators at bay. But the chicks were nowhere to be seen.

Mama and her chicks were finally spotted the next day practising short takeoff and landings, level flying and other tricks to become fully operational. The following day they were gone. Suddenly a realisation dawned on me. A few days back, just as our two siblings had flown for their respective destinations abroad, these fledglings too, had come of age. A few days later, another mama bulbul was perched inside the same nest. Maybe, the accommodation has been allotted to another family. Life goes on!!

Joys of Imperfection

Once a strapping, bubbly and spirited youngster recently commissioned into a parachute field regiment, the only one East of

Suez, I glanced at the mirror and saw for myself now. I just couldn't believe it was me. A much-doted father, devoted husband and the much-admired highly qualified officer image was missing. Mirrors have inherent flaws of distorting images and I thought, this could be the result. of the fallout!!!

Children say that I am too loud and even brash. Sometimes, I go to the extent of being a source of embarrassment at their parties where they whisper into each other's ears. Am I supposed to lip read? Being a gunner and hard of hearing does not qualify me for concessions but my inability to lip read makes it even worse, thanks to my deteriorating eyesight. So, what do I do? I sometimes call a spade a spade but they accuse me of calling it a shovel which they say I picked up from mavericks of the uniformed fraternity. Wife too chips in to express her sympathies for my newly found freedom of speech after 30 years of nagging.

They talk of my atrocious table manners. Not only do I take large helpings, but I also keep spilling food on the very well laid out fineries and leave the table cloths in a mess for others to see. Children sometimes get tempted to say, "Dad, mind if I bring you a filled plate and seat you with your grandchildren on their table?" Just short of telling you if you require a bib.

I try my best to strike conversation after drinks to give the impression to the guests that the hosts are an enlightened and a happy lot but I invariably end up dropping bricks. The wife again comments that the number of times I dropped bricks were so many that we could have constructed our own house instead of selling these bricks to unsuspecting friends for their bungalows.

My toilet habits also come under fire. The first gripe is that I take too much time to get inside the loo. When I do get inside, I take too much time getting out. Look, I took care to select the toilet least frequented by anyone so that I could read newspapers Next complaint is that I spill water all over the place and leave the toilet in a mess. I don't know how to have a bath without spilling water all over my body under the contraption called a shower with plastic curtains all around it?

What takes the cake is my ignorance about such necessary modern embellishments such as mobile phones, iPods, DVD players, Blackberries and blue tooth technology. Why are you so backward, Dad? You still haven't started using the Blackberry we gifted you last year. Who is to tell them that it burns a sizeable hole in your pocket to activate the Blackberry? Besides, who is going to send me emails on the Blackberry when I have problems as it is reading the minute telephone numbers on the mobile, telephone directories and newspapers, leave alone operating the laptop".

Children think they are much younger than I was at their age and did a lot more household chores. Did you clean nappies and wake up at odd hours to feed the offspring as we do? It's a tough life raising children. I haven't told them when Mom raised the two of you, I was in field.

Dear children, my humble message to you. I learnt to shoot straight from my hips (read heart) in the Army. I have all the negative qualities which have surfaced over years of my sustained efforts to bring you up and give you a head start in life. Life at my age is not just survival but full of fun, frolic and enjoyment - the fruits of my labour. I have withstood the metamorphosis of sixty-four long summers and now I have a right to seek joys of imperfections in my life.

Post Retirement Experiences

Kutch Revisited at Bhuj

I retired in the afternoon of December 31 in the year circa 2000. That was the year when it was believed that the Y2K problem in the coding of computerized systems, would create havoc in all computers in the world and bring life to a standstill. It was a disaster that never was, as it became apparent that the likely incidence of failure of the computer systems had been grossly exaggerated, from the very beginning. I made my CV and with the newly acquired computer skills applied for UN assignments, UNDP, UNESCO and several NGOs. I was interviewed along with other candidates from the armed forces, some of them being ex DG Police, Retired Air Marshals and Lt. Generals. While they gave you full marks for your experience and qualifications, the corporate world has a different set of objectives and is a much flatter organisation with no pyramid of hierarchy. The realization dawned on me after getting a standard reply, we will get back to you and no one did. Two more requirements emerged. One was that my computer skills weren't good enough and secondly, you need to scale down your aspirations on the salary expected. I did go out of my way to prepare an Excel Sheet, MS Office and make PowerPoint presentations. My experience says that an organisation that has scant regard for your rank and service, can be made out in one meeting or a glance. Thereafter one must maintain his self-esteem and respect in the negotiations for salary by not making the first move. Ask the interviewer what the job content is and what's your offer. Just don't talk about perks, they come with a salary package, much later.

Considering that my pension was fixed at Rs 16k per month after 37 years and 6 months of service and I had terminal benefits of Rs 14 lakhs at the age of 56 years, I had to find a second career at my present age of 56 years. That second career cannot be found in places like Dehra Dun. I had invested about Rs 15 lakhs in a property in Dwarka during my service, at the behest of my niece Jyotsna and her husband Ravi Dayal. The final instalment was to be paid in March 2001 and I was quite prepared for a default. in payment. Fortunately, my son Rohit was given a part-time job with good remuneration, his Masters though, was still incomplete but my financial liability was almost over.

I shifted to a four-bedroom rented bungalow, in Sector 22 in Gurgaon primarily because I felt. my luggage was far too much for the flat that I had invested in Dwarka. I had already been advised by my older brother that it was not possible to accommodate my luggage in Doon Flora due to space constraints of space. Besides, old properties in Dehradun are infested with termites and I had already had the taste of it in 1973 when we lost some furniture. We shifted out on a due date, in an Artillery Brigade vehicle and my car followed close behind. Reaching Sector 22, bungalow No 446 with all help from the local Arty Brigade, I made numerous trips. I still remember meeting my next-door neighbour Capt. Pradeep Misra, ex Wing Commander, now an airline pilot, who saw me carrying a portable mizo cane bar from my car after all the luggage had moved in. He later told me that the Chivas Regal bottle carried in the portable bar was enough to confirm my acceptance in the neighbourhood. Later, we both enjoyed each other's company over drinks many times. He also reminded me that he attended 42nd Staff Course Wellington. When I asked him who the Col.

GS Coord was, he recognized me immediately. I then remembered that his wife, also a Manju, had won the May Queen contest at Wellington Gymkhana Club.

While my shift was in progress, I had wound up the desktop computer which opened after I had settled down. There was a message waiting for me to appear for an interview for the post of Project Director at Bhuj, for which I had applied sometimes back. Without getting involved in the unpacking, I went straight to the Head Office of CARE India at Hauz Khas, at the date and time fixed for the interview. After a long wait at reception, the four of us, one Lt. Gen. (retired much earlier), one DG Police and another Brigadier from the NSG recently retired like me, were ushered into the HR Section for initial screening. We had a series of interviews called very euphemistically "meetings" in the very crowded CARE office. Meetings continued the next day, with the Country Manager, Tom Alcedo and his No 2 Rick Hennings. Both met us individually and there was no indication whether you were in or out. After this, two of us were asked to proceed to meet Secretary FICCI, the well-known economist, Dr Amit Mitra. My meeting went off very well, the economist was only interested to know how I would establish camp and organize the relief and rehabilitation, about which he had little knowledge. I think my knowledge of disaster management learnt in the Army and the confident answers, including my stint in Rann of Kutch in 1965, clinched the issue for me. He then informed me that I had been shortlisted for the post in preference to other candidates. I was to meet Chairman Pepsi, Mr Sumant Sinha for the final round. Sinha was well known in the corporate world for his wonderful stint in Unilever, bringing it out of the red and was now leading Pepsi towards its rejuvenation. My first impression was that amidst all the fanfare and ceremonials, he was the self-anointed king who would not accept no for an answer. Like all high-flying CEOs, he had a highly inflated ego and people in Pepsi were more terrorized than being in awe of his towering 6 ft plus persona. There was no need for me to contradict his vision /expectations, the sense of commitment, ability to infuse transcending values in the new project. After Sumant Sinha's final nod I joined them on the salary of a consultant but in the post of Project Director FICCI CARE Gujarat Rehabilitation Project (FCGRP). At the time of the negotiations of the terms and conditions, I was told that I have to establish myself at Bhuj where the Project office would be located. I would be called to Delhi every month for briefings/debriefings, at the cost of the Project.

I assumed my duties as Project Director immediately after an appointment letter was issued by FICCI and CARE collectively. I then approached Army HQ for permission to take up the appointment which arrived in due course. Having completed all formalities in Delhi, studied all HR policies and operating procedures, I took a flight to Ahmedabad, and then left for Bhuj by road. The airport was in the process of being repaired after the quake. CARE staff had already established itself in a church compound and one retired Squadron Leader Satish Sinha, a relative of Sumant Sinha, was the Program Support Manager in the new set up, essentially to look after the administration. At that time in April 2001, the earth ravaged region of Kachch was experiencing aftershocks in regular frequency and some of them were as high as 4.9 on the Richter Scale. The drive up to Bhuj by road gave me a fair idea of how things were. We were only involved in three talukas of Anjar, Bhachau and Rapar which comprised mostly rural areas. There were 30 villages adopted by FICCI CARE, the project outlay was in the region of $32 million, equal to Rs 110 crores approximately then. Unlike other NGOs, CARE had no institutional presence in the state of Gujarat till now.

When we had barely settled down, our Country Manager Tom Alcedo and Sumant Sinha arrived for a meeting with the villagers at Anjar. I had taken personal pains to see that this reception was just to convey a message that we were working and not sitting on our haunches in the office. This is what we always did in the field while senior officers visited us. Villagers laid out some light refreshments and soft drinks with all sincerity, hoping that it would be appreciated. As soon as the soft drinks were opened, Sumant Sinha just walked away. We were all flabbergasted. We learnt that the objection was to the bottle of Coca Cola and Aquafina which the simple villagers had arranged for us. "As a soldier, you will never understand. The Pepsi boss later explained, if he had taken a sip of their product, Coca Cola would have drawn the greatest mileage out of it. I knew nothing about this and I could see him visibly annoyed. There was not a word of appreciation of the establishment of the offices and the tented camp functioning as the field mess, done within a month. In the corporate world, if you make the mistake of appreciating the good work done by giving the subordinate a pat on the back, it's blasphemy but a kick in the back, a vertebra away is considered far better. Contrary to all this, my Army background has taught me to create an organisational structure, draft a compelling vision and keep communication channels open. Next, build a well-knit team and delegate to my immediate juniors, after careful assessment of their capabilities. This would probably inspire the subordinates to their goals, without my need to push them around unnecessarily.

During April 2000, I got busy surveying the damage in the three talukas of Anjar, Bhachau and Rapar. A lot of information was available with the District Collector Bhuj and the agencies that had already established themselves like the UNDP, Sarv Shisksha Abhiyan, SEWA, Save The Children, International Commission of the Red Cross, ECHO and other NGOs both local and from outside. As the representative of CARE, the biggest NGO in the world, I was given the respect that I never expected. A visit by the CARE representatives on 27 April 2001 needs mention. We also had Mr Niranjan Hiranandani visiting us for the first time and giving us all the help and assistance. I learnt for the first time that I was also to report to another Project Director at Delhi, Dr Renu Suri. Another gentleman, Rick Henning, who was No 2 in the CARE hierarchy, was there to oversee her. Another HR Head Vasanti Vepa Ramiah was there to see the recruitment process. There was another Director External CARE Mr Harry Sethi, who was handling media and PR. This great congregation stayed in the only functional hotel but spent most of their time with me. There are a lot of angles that one must ensure while working for NGOs in a project, the strict adherence to documentation and the need to report every small event/incident accurately through email. This style of working is very similar to that in the defence forces where every job is monitored. I could add that PR and media handling are as important.

More than three months had elapsed since the devastating earthquake of 26th January 2001, intensity 6.9 on the Richter scale, which killed over 18,000 people and which had its epicentre in the taluka of Bhachau. The destruction, I could see, was massive and would take many years to rebuild. The destroyed houses, school buildings, panchayat ghars, health, community and *anganvadi* centres were a sight. NGOs and others worldwide had responded to the calls from the Government of Gujarat. Rescue and relief work had commenced from the day of the quake, pulling out people from the debris, providing food clothing, temporary shelters and medicines to save lives. The relief work which followed after the rescue was now over after the lives of the survivors had stabilized to a good degree. What followed now was the physical rehabilitation of the earthquake affected in terms of homes and shelters and economic rehabilitation through livelihood packages, implementation of which may continue for years. Though the epicentre was Bhachau, I realized that all the three talukas deserved the same priority. Village folks will always misunderstand if dissimilar treatment is meted out and undue favours are given. I had given strict instructions for maintaining parity in relief work. Even when the Army is deployed in a counterinsurgency region, we are careful not to play favourites based on religion, caste or colour.

I got to know the other members of my team. Accounts were looked after by Mrs Deepa Mukherji, an old CARE hand, later replaced by Tushar. There were others like Jayant Rathore who was looking after the important portfolio of Project Manager (Rehabilitation) CARE also took its former employees Chalapathi, Al Patel, Pawan Kumar and a few others on its rolls. My driver Qadri Bhai was also an old CARE hand. In the meanwhile, the process of hiring the local staff began. CARE has its HR policies and I was obliged to conform to the guidelines in the hiring of staff. I interviewed Hasmukh Thakkar for my PS job and straightaway appointed him. A very sincere youngster, he knew very little spoken English. I had to get him to speak after a lot of effort. I was already informed that one Shri KS Agarwal was selected as the Project Manager (Reconstruction) and he joined immediately. We appointed an IT Coordinator to set up the LAN network at three locations later Getting to know everyone in the organisation, communicate, listen to their problems and resolve them on the spot wasn't easy. Some mundane issues were resolved on the spot thanks to the training in my regiment in the earlier days.

There was a semi-furnished Reliance container inside the church compound, which was meant for me. We always learnt to stay with the men, therefore I declined that offer. I stayed in the tented camp with the rest of them. No arrangement existed for toilets and bathing. Army life had taught us that proper hygiene and sanitation was the first thing we attended to in an established tented camp. We dug army field latrines in a secluded corner and provided hessian screens. We used to eat in the open verandah at the sides of the church. A community kitchen and some tables had been placed by the padre for feeding everyone who stayed in the vicinity. As it was getting warmer, the fly menace became more unbearable and we decided to shift. We were on the lookout for hiring some buildings which had been repaired and made available for our offices. Satish Sinha went looking around and got a few leads. In the meantime, after cash doles were dished out to everyone by the Government. In addition to rescue and relief, the Government announced a 50:50 public-private partnership for rehabilitation. We also contributed by purchasing rations for the church to return their hospitality. The Keshubhai Patel Government was replaced by Narendra Modi, who was very keen on immediate action. CARE had the same philosophy on public relations as the armed forces, the relief & rehabilitation measures taken must stand out prominently, let your villagers speak about it. I realized that we must be at the forefront in the press/media when the CM visited my adopted villages.

I used to leave the camp every morning with some old CARE hands like Patel, Pawan Kumar or Chalapathi to take me around to the three talukas, they had already worked in during the rescue and relief. Each one knew their villages backwards and could be relied upon for their advice. I endeavoured to visit a maximum number of villages every day, get to know their problems and apprise them of our offer. i.e., the public-private partnership with the Gujarat Government for the reconstruction of their entire village had taught me that time spent on recce is never wasted, there were no shortcuts on visits to ground, maintaining an aide-memoire of names/places, the local problems and reports required to be made. There were some 10 villages each in Anjar and Bhachau and 12 in Rapar under us. In about three weeks, the interaction was so intense that I had come to know all the sarpanches' names and their mobile numbers.

Villagers are very worldly-wise and could give you very practical tips on how to cut costs. You have to be a patient listener most of the time. The local population of Kutchis comprised upper caste like Patels and Darbaris 13% and 9% respectively 20% Muslims and remaining the SC/ ST population of mostly Kolis and the Rabaris, the shepherd and cattle herding group. Casteism played an important role. A Patel and Darbari considered themselves superior to others. In earlier days, when I had my first exposure in Rann of Kutch in 1965, a Kutchi was a Kutchi and it didn't matter whether he was a Hindu or a Muslim. Times had changed now with Muslims being allotted land by the panchayats on the periphery or one corner of the village. The Muslim

Wakf Board had now come out into the open, supporting the Muslims of Kutch with promises of better financial rehabilitation packages from Saudi Arabia. This led to a conflict of opinions even in the old Hindu-Muslim villages whether to opt for the government package of public-private partnership or not. Invariably the Muslims wanted to go out to Wakf Board instead of us. We had a hard time trying to convince the panchayats that what we were offering is in their interests. We had in house discussions on the various caste wise alignments and were careful not to create problems for ourselves on this issue. Once again, my Army's secular background helped.

Another problem that existed was that a uniform compensation amount had been worked out by the government officials based on the size of the house damaged by the quake. There were villagers who owned bigger houses who felt. cheated. In Rapar taluka, on the contrary, being the highly marginalized community, most of the houses were thatched huts, of temporary nature. The government had given very little compensation to the villagers. They were expecting pucca houses as compensation, which meant that we would be building their houses almost free of cost with no government compensation. With all these problems, we went around the 32 villages explaining to panchayats how the scheme will work. Villages would take days to decide to go into partnership with you in the hope of bargaining for more. Some even wanted "in situ repairs" by the government without partnering with anyone. We had to display an infinite amount of patience and perseverance while dealing with villagers, there was no alternative.

The next problem was the house itself. Several designs were suggested by various builders, designers, architects and other agencies. We shortlisted a uniform 30 square metres (325 sq ft) to all villages, (costing around Rs 97,000) irrespective of their entitlement from the government packages. Every panchayat was in dialogue with me for the house design. Some did not want attached toilets and were more in favour of community toilets away from the houses, which was agreed to. We had a husband-and-wife team from CARE France who had some experience in the field of sanitation and had agreed to design the community toilets in the villages. They had brought very contemporary toilet designs, which were being used in South Africa and some Sahara countries. When we tried to fit in the designs, we discovered that they are unsuited to Indian conditions. In interior Gujarat, in villages, there was virtually no electricity at all. Even if it was there, being at the end of the feeder, with a voltage of 120 volts, the WCs would never work. When the villagers saw the models, they laughed at us. We sent this couple to Delhi to see the Sulabh International latrines, which required no electricity. When the villagers agreed to install these, we gave the go-ahead. The community toilets had 12 sets with partitions provided, exactly like the army field latrines and two covered water reservoirs on each side were provided. The community highly appreciated the design and there were no problems thereafter. For us in the Army, this is nothing new.

Our office functioned from Sanskar Nagar from two adjoining flats. There was a mess that came up in one of the rooms temporarily. We also looked around for accommodation for living for all. Hiring was done and our staff was asked to shift. Seeing a vacant plot alongside our building we requested the owner to give it on short term lease, for our camp mess. The mess in the building shifted to the camp below and all problems were sorted out. The tented camp is not everyone's piece of cake. It required help from the local Army unit to help us set it up. I had taken up a flat next door for my living. At Bhachau, we looked around for hiring a piece of land of approximately 2000 yards area where our field office could come up. I then spoke to one of my friends for prefabricated huts from Udaipur which could come up very fast on cemented plinths. Our consignment of six huts arrived after the cemented plinths were properly cured and ready. Construction of two big office huts, one field mess and three huts for staff living was complete with a week. Furniture, fixtures and fittings took another week and the field camp at Bhachau was ready by June 30. We received furniture for one school building at Anjar, which arrived at Kandla Port. Another consignment of refined oil for the villages also arrived. We had a very good liaison with the Kandla Port Trust and were able to take possession of the stores immediately. We needed railway containers for our site offices which were collected from the railways at Gandhidham for ten major sites. We needed to construct *aanganwadi* centres and we got some NGOs to do it for us. What we suggested to Action India, an NGO run by the veteran actress Nafisa Ali that we needed to model the same on the lines of *bashas* of the NE India. Sure enough, there was a trainload of bamboos along with my old friends from Lunglei who trained the local labour to make *bashas* on cemented plinths. These *bashas* were an instantaneous hit as they withstood the ravages of the stormy weather as well and lasted much more than their life expectancy. My stint in Mizoram came in very handy. Even today some of the locals are using bamboo top construction, for cattle sheds and animal shelters.

We satisfied all conditions of the Gujarat Government, on the formal allocation of the village to our project, the village resolutions in our favour, and the individual house owner's signatures on the social contract. The modalities of payment by the Government after the first payment and the role of gram panchayats/rehabilitation committees were worked out. Debris removal was one great problem that I could not manage despite my best efforts. Eventually, we paid Rs 6.5 lakhs for six villages for debris removal by private parties using their JCBs and manpower. We submitted our papers to the Collector and got moving. Some news even filtered down to the CM, Narendra Modi and in meetings with NGOs, he made it a point to monitor our progress, during the NGO meetings.

Now coming to the raw materials and their dumping. We arranged steel rods by placing orders on SAIL, which arrived in railway wagons and had to be lifted from Gandhinagar or Ahmedabad. Villagers were very apprehensive about reconditioned steel coming from Alang and made it very clear that only SAIL steel was acceptable. The government had established single-window clearance for cement permits initially but later it was opened for free sale at an exorbitant rate of Rs 151 per bag. We got Re 1 reimbursed for every bag returned. When you order cement in lots of 50 lakh bags, it is a substantial saving. Cement bags and steel rods were placed centrally at Bhachau and Rapar subsequently. For cement, we ensured covers to be made so that moisture of Kutch does not ruin the cement. After the construction picked up, there were no problems with storage even during the rains.

My knowledge of tendering and negotiations with the shortlisted parties was based on what the Army taught me, as a Station Commander. Three contractors were shortlisted for the reconstruction activities by my team, later approved by the Project Management

Committee at New Delhi. One was an Ahmedabad firm, one Bombay Electric Supply and Transport Company and the third one a local small-time contractor from Bhuj. Negotiations by Mr KS Agarwal, the civil engineer, brought down the price of each unit to Rs 97,000. Five hollow block making machines purchased from two suitable vendors from Pune and Chennai were installed at selected locations on a commercial basis. Micro entrepreneurs selected from amongst the villagers were afforded loans and were responsible to provide at least 20% of the total requirement of cement blocks used in the construction. These machines began to provide a livelihood to the local population. We had proper Quality Control & Assurance at work, the daily checks by site engineers, testing labs to check the quality of construction material in addition to mobile checks by the NCCBM/state engineers. There was also monitoring by the village committees and by the house owner himself.

We selected Nilpar, a small hamlet of 35 households situated in Bhachau taluka, 2-3 km off the Rapar Kharoi Road, as the pilot project for our construction. It was the villagers' trust in the government that helped us to get their resolution first. Nilpar was amongst the worst affected villages during the quake in terms of the destruction of buildings and public infrastructure. All 35 houses, the primary school, five temples and the community hall were destroyed. A groundbreaking ceremony on 20 May 2001, was done by the Collector Mr Harsh Chhibber, IAS sometimes in the first week followed by the first phase of our construction process. Maximum publicity of the event was arranged and we got very good press coverage. Five houses were to be constructed initially with our design, and the foundation work commenced. A few days later, I was asked to stop work because the villagers felt. that we were not providing seismic columns at the corners and three-band protection which JP Industries at Kankhot, a nearby village, was providing. After protracted negotiations with the villagers, we were able to convince them of our good intentions and our design was accepted. When five houses were nearing the lintel stage, we started laying the foundation on eight more houses. Simultaneously, the excavation work on ten more and the debris clearance and marking of the remaining twelve commenced. We gave every house owner a signed copy of the house design and the work schedule targets. The entire village acted as good conscience keepers and wanted to know the why and what of the construction process. Earning the faith and goodwill of the villagers was the key to our success.

As a leader who had just embarked into the corporate world, PR is one great quality that was an invaluable adjunct. We arranged tours from other villages from Rapar and Anjar to see our pilot project. Word went around very fast and we were approached even by those villages which were not adopted by us but were with other rehabilitation support agencies. I did not accept this as it was unethical to enter others' domains. Twenty-one more resolutions followed but in bits and pieces. Our regular interaction with the community strengthened advocacy exposure of the villagers to media, TV and radio besides meeting the various NGOs/UN agencies and government agencies, which had made them worldly-wise and conscious of their rights. I took a calculated risk that all construction would be complete in three months. We handed over the first lot of completed houses to the owners on 24 July 2001, including the one donated by Mr Frank Wisner, the ex-US ambassador. The ceremony was a big affair with

Mr PM Sinha - Chairman Pepsi, Mr Chiryu Amin - Chairman FICCI and Mr Tom Alcedo - Country Director CARE India in attendance. There was big fanfare with massive media coverage. Selected donors and some Gujarati NRIs (Shri Bhiku Bhai Patel) from North Texas, USA attended.

We had set a target of 2500 houses in the first nine villages which had submitted a resolution in our favour. In these nine villages, other than Nilpar, we had selected a model house, which we constructed first. This model house was constructed to demonstrate our sincerity and commitment to the villagers. The house was modelled with us, using the same three-band protection. My team of cluster engineers worked day and night to complete Phase 1 by 30 November 2001, again anticipated and the calculated risk picked up in the armed forces, gave the required fillip to the project.

We had already constructed a pre-fabricated field camp at Bhachau which was liked by everyone. Similar structures were required at Bhuj, Anjar and Rapar Blocks. Suddenly, without even consulting us, the Government of Gujarat delinked Health and Education from the adoption scheme. All community infrastructure buildings were taken away from us and allotted to other organisations, in violation of the partnership agreement. This left us only with Livelihoods which came under the CARE and Disaster Emergency Committee of the UK and other NGOs. Despite protests by us, there was no change in the government's decision.

As the Project Director in Gujarat, we realized that Livelihood activities have a great role to complement the reconstruction activities, with the broader aim of increasing family incomes. We needed to gain access at the village level, and involve the whole community for the work to succeed. Initiatives taken by us took a holistic approach within this umbrella. Livelihood activities are community-specific and are demand-driven. They proved their worth as the confidence-building measures with the communities, where our work was in progress. The biggest hurdle was the funds which were difficult. to come by initially. Mobilizing a proper team within CARE to play a pivotal role and lack of clarity were big hurdles. Until we evolved a concept on how to work with state-level NGOs like SEWA and NID, it was always a non-starter. We accepted an Agricultural Development offer, in which we provided the seeds and tillage assistance for small and marginalized farmers. The repairs to water harvesting structures, facilities for water storage, irrigation and drinking purposes were damaged during the quake, followed by the Enterprise and Micro Insurance, for disaster proofing the local rural economy. In addition, five more machines were provided for block making, and a Business Resource Centre was planned to be established in nine villages for traditional handicraft restoration. We also trained new masons, electricians and carpenters as a part of Reconstruction Related Training. The whole game of restoring the shattered economy was heavily based on livelihoods restoration.

Unlike many aid projects that focus on rebuilding infrastructure by hiring expensive builders and designers, high profile engineers and architects of national standing, the Project Management Committee chose a person like me, the Project Director with absolutely no knowledge of rehabilitation and reconstruction work along with project team of 42 members, which had no professional standing worth its name. My team delivered the goods, especially in the reconstruction of 7500 earthquake-resistant houses in 30 villages. We also worked on diverse tasks such as management, logistics and administration and information services. We also worked full time to assist people in rebuilding their lives and livelihoods. The very fact that I am still in touch with some sarpanches, Hasmukh Thakkar, my ex-secretary, Jayenendra Rathore and a few more of the same team in Ahmedabad, has added years to my life. We also got a taste of what it is to work for the state government. You would be lucky if a decision is taken in good time and when taken, you can never discount the possibility of its rollback.

I had hoped to serve in Delhi after my retirement for various reasons, firstly there are prospects of finding a reasonably decent job. Secondly, I had to attend to my wife. who had been operated on for carcinoma which required regular follow-ups and reviews and thirdly, my children required that I do not move anywhere out of the NCR area because it would mean additional commuting for them after touching Delhi. CARE India had promised me during the interview that I would have my office in Bhuj but I would be called every month for briefings/debriefings. For the first few months, this requirement was complied with but after some time it was given a go by. My frequent visits to attend to my wife were posing an additional burden on them. When I requested for my transfer to Delhi after completing the project there were airy-fairy replies, there was a position in Vijaywada available after the Andhra cyclone where I could be adjusted. I declined the offer and looked around for leads at Delhi as a consultant. New Zealand High Commission selected me for the post of consultant to the Trade Commissioner to promote their business in Gujarat, Maharastra, Andhra, Karnataka and Tamil Nadu. It was a very cushy job within the confines of the High Commission and there was a lot of value attached to my advice. I was reporting to Mr Peter Healey, the

Trade Commissioner and there was another New Zealander, Mr Peter Price who was the coordinator. We had excellent rapport within the newly constituted team which was expected to grow further after we visited these states. Peter and I made several trips to Gujarat, where my old contacts with the administration helped. Fletcher Challenge Forest of New Zealand provided two earthquake resistant, cyclone proof temporary shelters on a no-cost basis at Kotda (Anjar) and Rapar (Taluka Office Compound) during Sep 2001. Our site offices functioned from these two shelters. Dimension wise, Kotda shelter is 100 sq. feet and Rapar shelter is 300 sq. feet. Both shelters have been visited by the local community whose opinion was dead against wooden structures and there was nothing we could do to change their mindset.

Despite being vulnerable to the ravages of fire and requiring ongoing maintenance to resist decay or rot, New Zealand Trade Commissioner felt. timber offered lighter materials for transport to the construction site, ease of construction and greater flexibility. Timber was also resistant to earthquakes, but the villagers in Gujarat found it hard to believe. When we said brick, stone and reinforced concrete quickly succumbed to the movement of the earth, flexible timber framing will survive, the villagers just laughed. They rejected the New Zealand offer for reasons of not being earthquake resistant, little protection against heat and cold, flimsy walls, windows, doors and flooring, high cost and limited utilisation of shelters. We had suggested them for primary Schools, primary health centres and sub-health centres, shop kiosks/internet/cyber cafes, community centres cum religious halls for meetings in small villages.

Going into the details of what was being offered consisted of a heavy timber structural frame designed to support the complete load of construction on the 325 sq ft cemented plinth with light timber claddings and linings. New Zealand had a ready supply of timber and the need to create a large number of houses relatively quickly and cheaply, made the offer quite tempting. The lesson learnt is that it is all very well to plant new ideas on wooden structures but it is very difficult. to change the mindset of villagers. After seeing our pre-fabricated structure at Bhachau, every villager felt those were better suited for local Indian conditions. A similar offer was made to Andhra Pradesh but again, it was the community that rejected it outright. Now after almost four years of non-stop work in Gujarat and Andhra Pradesh, I thought I needed a break. When I got back to Delhi around mid-August 2004, there was a mail waiting for me from Chesterton Meghraj & Co.

Entry into Corporate World

My next foray was in the field of property/facility management by joining a subsidiary of Chesterton Meghraj Properties Limited, a real estate company, in 2003. My old colleague from the Artillery, Lt. Col. Ashutosh Beri, had launched a new company called Workplace Management & Consultants Private Limited. Beri had entered this field after seeking premature retirement from the Army. He had gone through the mill, was involved in market surveys and research work for the last five years. He had faced numerous challenges in the emerging field and had gained valuable experience evolving maintenance strategies for all types of buildings. He had realized that professional management services in the maintenance of various types of buildings are the need of the hour. The development of various types of buildings in the real estate market went far beyond private houses, residential colonies and government offices buildings. Private property owners, sometimes back, thought it a waste to spend anything on maintenance, which resulted in decay, unplanned fiscal outlays reducing the life and value of the properties.

The new entrants into the realm of properties were commercial office buildings, residential complexes, shopping malls, golf courses, country clubs, call centres and hotels which were developed by real estate developers and leased/rented out to various individual corporate houses to get a greater bang for the buck, it is not the immediate return you get, it is the sustained overall comfort, quality and preservation of resources, in the long run. The people's perception on how the support services in these built. up environments have to run smoothly, has undergone a sweeping change. Mounting infrastructure costs, rapid technological advances, improved quality of life and standards and increased safety and security threats, have all called for better management of resources. Now you can see why some malls fail to attract crowds.

While facility management is the provision of services to the building owner who is providing space to various individuals. It includes operation and maintenance of the entire building infrastructure, based on the needs of the client. It includes corporate house buildings for their use, golf courses and hotels. Property management is the complete total management of building premises on behalf of the owner. It may include commercial office buildings leased/rented out to individuals, residential complexes and shopping malls. It took me some time to understand the difference. Seeing the vast scope of services that I could never have imagined earlier, I had to first acquaint myself with what my company was providing pan India and in the NCR. The most obligatory was the electrical services provided in all malls, call centres, corporate buildings including the lifts, elevators, escalators, ACs, AHUs, and chillers. The second next obligation is the building management systems which is the heart of all services including fire protection systems, water management, energy management & audio-visual equipment. The third is the personnel required to be trained in housekeeping, hazard cleaning/glass cleaning, security, pantry services & catering management. You can continue adding more services like transportation services/ambulance/car hire, horticulture & landscaping, pest control & rodent services, front office, mailroom operations, key & locker, headset, car parking & conference room management. The list is endless and one can see that it is a real slog for anyone from the armed forces making a late entry into the field, like me. Add the word "management" to each problem area and you are quite safe.

In facility management, the value-added Services are add-ons, not paid for by the client which sets you up as better than other companies in the same trade. We decided that the EME style analysis these days like life concept, advice on annual maintenance contracts/warranty, preventive maintenance, periodic audits/checks, good documentation, adherence to user manuals, safety drills & cost-cutting measures always impresses the good clients. When I asked Col. Beri how he managed to keep adding services we are not even sure of doing it. He explained that to be one up on our competitors we have to include some services unknown to others. That's where we would score over others. In this trade, we need to find someone to do all these value-added services. These are big names but small little things adding value to our services.

For my experience, Col. Beri sent me to study various types of sites. The first one was a commercial building Gold Souk in Gurgaon which was still under construction and nearing the fit-out stage where our client needed assistance to formulate some policy for the smooth functioning. The first written work we produced was in consultation with the company heads. The idea was to assist them in various designs and architecture of the interiors, show windows for presentation/display of goods, for sale. As consultants, we encourage tenants to create innovative and exciting storefronts and interiors. In addition, we set up a Facility Manager's office on the first floor making full use of the limited space provided by the owners. RP Singh, our Electrical Engineer and I took charge of all the Electrical & Mechanical services which included AC equipment, pump room, lifts, fire station and the power supply system and DG sets. We selected a contractor who provided the trained staff for Housekeeping and Security agencies and put them on the job. We now got down to operation and maintenance as per the SOP which was readily provided by Col. Beri, totally made afresh for this site.

When the site had stabilized, Col. Beri asked me to join him at the Unitech House where our HQ was located. This handling of the site operations for almost three months was the foundation on which I built. up my knowledge of facility management. Maintenance of various equipment in my regimental service like charging sets and generators, vehicles like jeeps and *jongas*, and cleaning with the use of gadgets was not something new for me. My keen interest and on the job experience also helped in understanding the schedules given in the various manuals. I learnt the value of crisis management and escalation ladders when I was asked to resolve a crisis later which developed in Sahara Mall, around 10.30 pm after a storm. A huge hoarding with its structure anchored to the building top floor by steel posts collapsed and fell on six clients' cars, parked outside damaging them. Claims for damages were made but I got hold of the workers immediately to remove the hoarding to enable cars to move out. We tactfully accepted reduced responsibility for the damage but attributed this to an act of God over which we had no control. Every car owner was assisted by us in presenting the claim to the insurance companies and our own company's liability disappeared.

My company entered into a partnership with Unitech and we were given the responsibility to maintain all Unitech buildings. I was assigned the duties of Head Quality Control in the new vacancy created for me specifically. My team comprised a bright youngster Arun Mishra, a former marine engineer and an architect summer job intern, Madhavi Jain and the Office Manager from the managerial staff. The CEO felt. that to lead and operate an organisation successfully, it is necessary to direct and control in an organised, systematic and transparent manner. We felt. the need to enhance the company image by obtaining accreditation of ISO 9001-2000. We had repeatedly emphasized to our employees that the Total Quality Management System must focus on customer satisfaction as its paramount requirement. All our employees in Head and Regional Offices, call centres, corporate office buildings, shopping malls and residential complexes must be involved. The leadership and decision making provided to it at various levels helps to create a mutually beneficial relationship which is most important in the service industry. I was nominated by the CEO, Lt. Col. Beri to attend a week's Quality Audit course on ISO certification with the KPMG and gained invaluable experience on ISO 9001-2000. Arvin Advisory Services Mumbai was appointed as our consultants. They formally commenced Gap Analysis for Head Office and four regional offices in April 2005 During their second visit to NCR Region further were inputs obtained including our Head Office, In addition, they have visited the regional offices and sites at Bangalore and Mumbai before I commenced the audit. I audited all regional offices, the majority of our sites of call centres, malls, corporate offices and residential complexes to get things going. Most of the forms & data that were already available in the company were incorporated. There was no escaping the fact that I had to write all the quality manuals, all by myself. The contents of these documents are still with the successor company, maybe under a different company name now, related to manuals/SOPs on Procedures, Systems, Flow Charts and Checklists & Forms.

We commenced the process of quality standardization in all regional offices and all four types of sites in NCR, Kolkatta, Bangalore and Mumbai. We have made a good start at Highland Park at Kolkatta, Garuda and Sigma Malls at Bangalore. where we modelled the sites according to the preparation and tried out Quality Procedures and Systems. Implementation checks of processes in the NCR Region, Mumbai and Bangalore were done independently by Arvin Associates. All SOPs and Quality Manuals above had to be slightly remodelled on the lines suggested by Arvin Advisory Services and issued to sites for implementation. We were awarded certification for ISO 9001-2000 in Sept 2005, I was personally congratulated by Mr Romesh Chandra,

Chairman Unitech and Mr Anuj Puri, CEO Chesterton Meghraj for the hard work put in for obtaining this certification. It is more like getting a fitness for war in the case of Army units. A certificate issued by KPMG has great value. I have retained all the soft copies of all documents with me. Several old colleagues and friends in the facility management field have approached me for the same. Col. Beri and I have spent long hours preparing these documents and I feel giving these away on a petty remuneration is unethical.

Col. Beri asked me to take over the Business Development portfolio in addition to Quality Control. It is here that the credit must go to the man that places so much trust in you that you don't feel the pressure of work. First, I was to take over as Head Western Region temporarily from PK Singh, who had just resigned. I was offered this post on increased remuneration but I declined. We were also tasked to select a suitable person for the post within my stay of over one month. We both had a wonderful time, as I warned to move with my family for a longish stay. We both enjoyed the hospitality of my nephew Anuj and his lovely wife Smita and their two girls along with my sister Meenakshi. I carried out the audits of all Mumbai sites of WPM like five Runwall Townships which were residential complexes, Nirmal Group Township besides Phoenix Mills, R Mall and a few more. It's amazing to see how the Phoenix Mills project is a multi-user development over 1.2 million square feet in Lower Parel, Mumbai. The project involves three components retail, commercial and entertainment in various stages of development. The mall is part of the redevelopment of an old textile mill, which had stopped functioning in 1993 and was lying closed for years. It was quite a task but I managed to convince one of our employees from Bangalore to permanently relocate there.

As the Head Transition team, we were asked to proceed to Chandigarh to take over Dell Management Services. Earlier, we were a part of Col. Beri's team that made the presentation to their CEO, Col. Mehra, an old-timer with tons of experience in call centres. We were selected based on the excellent presentation by the team and our impressive company profile. Our company with just 2-3 years of its existence in the field of property/facility had a total portfolio of 9 million square feet of offices, retail and residential property under management, including Unitech's Signature Towers, Palms residential, Business Parks, Info-Centre, Trade Centre, Techno Park, Power Grid Corporation of India Limited as well as other facilities including Sahara Mall, Call centres of Dell & NIIT and ITC. We had a significant presence in Gurgaon, Kolkata, Bhubaneshwar, Mumbai, Nasik and Bangalore. We had a 50;50 partnership with Unitech which was doing well. A new office in Hyderabad was about to be set up at that time. This facility was to function as a call centre as well as Dell's Corporate office. Having got their very stringent requirements in mind, we took our contractors for electro-mech and housekeeping along. We were able to shortlist the security organisation which Dell had already done but their personnel needed briefings and training. After a week's stay at Chandigarh, my transition team was able to take over the site completely. To give you an idea, we worked on a transition plan a month in advance, prepared draft SOPs, manuals and Quality documents, identified building systems, worked out Electro-Mechanical requirements and the model to be adopted for process delivery. This was followed up by my visit to the site. We had to discuss the organisational structure and deployment plan based on the data collected during my visit. After discussion with Col. Beri and Finance, the budget was approved and the team was nominated as stand by. All this took about three to four weeks. The crash program for one week that followed included the preparation and submission of preventive maintenance schedules for all equipment. In addition, the technical audit to conform to the agreed scope of work given out by Dell and the scrutiny of all annual maintenance contracts had to be done. All other aspects like contract execution, staffing and training schedule, customer service desk, building operations and maintenance systems were complied with. The software for accounting was also installed. It was a nightmare completing all these requirements in the beginning and then catering for new client's requirements, which invariably kept adding. After completing the transition at two or three sites, there was no looking back.

We kept on adding one site after another in Calcutta, Pune, Bangalore Indore and NCR as well. We submitted proposals, the moment we got a lead, that a new site was coming up. PowerPoint presentations were readied and the financials were discussed in-house between the three of us, Head Commercials, Head of Operations Vinay Talwar, and of course Col. Beri. We were able to bag new sites and also renew contracts in the existing sites. At one stage we had a combined tally of almost 150 sites all over India with great chances of new ones coming up. We were involved with the taking over with the transition team at Bangalore for Garuda Mall. Luckily, I had taken up accommodation in the RSI, which was close to the Garuda Mall. Arun Mishra was staying with me and the others were in lodges close by. Garuda Mall is 5 lakhs sq ft is one of its types, with a mall and a five-star hotel combined. The owner, ex DG Police Retired, had his relatives running the place, who had massive requirements. We positioned our Southern Regional Head, Mrs Smita Padekar, a hard-core electrical engineer who was of great help. We hired one marine engineer, Mr Reddy as our Facility Manager. I executed the transition plan exactly the way I had done for Dell and it was a matter of immense satisfaction that we returned to Gurgaon within 10 days after the site became operational.

We were back in Bangalore again within two or three months, this time for something not so pleasant. There were serious technical problems as I learnt from Mr Garuda himself, after waiting outside his office for two hours. First, pertained to the failure of one of the lifts in the hotel, where one of the local MLA's family had been trapped for half an hour. He attributed this failure to bad maintenance. He had also been threatening to get an arrest warrant issued for the arrest of the company's CEO or me in his absence. Second, was the RO plant in the hotel which had packed up, again due to bad maintenance. Guests fell sick when they drank bad water. He had penalized the company Rs 16 lakhs for both the lapses and wanted us to vacate the site within one week. After hearing him, there was no point in justifying anything as he was seething with anger. The Army had taught me no negotiating skills, my strength lay in my tenacity and the never give up attitude. Creative ideas come to you when you are not afraid of failing. It was worth the risk and I tried a de novo approach to the problem.

First, we had to get our facts straight. There was a lot of adverse publicity but this occurrence did take place. I sat down with Head Southern Region Head, Mr Reddy and one engineer Mr Javed and wracked our brains for finding some solution. I had been given a mandate by Col. Beri that I had to resolve this somehow, and not lose the site. I requested Mr Garuda and his entire board to join me for dinner at RSI Bangalore the next evening. He declined but his board members accepted my invite. We also treated the members to drinks & dinner and did not utter a word but formally apologized to Garuda management on behalf of the company. We requested them for their support but they never committed. Mr Reddy luckily ran into a friend of Mr Garuda who said he would put in a word to save the contract. The next day, I again called on Mr Garuda and requested that we be given one more chance to perform. I planned to replace the complete team and stay there indefinitely and oversee things myself, to which he appeared amenable. The truth was the sexual harassment of our lady Head, which one male relative of the owner had resorted to. She too said that she did not feel comfortable working with him. We did not want to ruffle feathers and solved this problem by moving her to Western Region and bringing in a new set of personnel moved from other local sites in Bangalore. We were stuck for almost three weeks in Bangalore to save the contract and our fine was reduced to Rs 4 lakhs thanks to Mr Garuda. My perseverance was appreciated by everyone and most of all by Col. Beri and Unitech's Romesh Chandra. They gave me a raise in salary of over 1.5 lakhs per annum, which I hadn't even asked for.

My team also paid a visit to Calcutta for taking over a site HI Land Park, a residential complex. Eastern Region was under a lady, Mrs Sushila Mukherji, who had good links with the local bureaucracy which was running Hi-Land Park. The problems we faced there were much more because the labour unions are very strong. We also carried out the pre-ISO certification technical audit and found that there were serious gaps that needed the attention of Col. Beri. We also had a team get together at Fort William Club where I was staying. More sites were promised by the Eastern Region Head but there were problems as usual with personnel and manning. Next on the list for taking over was the Treasure Island Mall in Indore. This was our first foray into MP and I had accompanied Col. Beri, about two months earlier for the presentation. We had met Mr Manish Kalani, a very enlightened young entrepreneur who had grandiose plans to launch more malls in MP and we assured him of our support in his ventures. As a start, we provided Arun Mishra and a team of two electricians and one housekeeping supervisor free of any charges, during the fit-out stage to help them go ahead. When our turn came for me to lead the transition team, to take over the mall, it started with a lot of problems. Instructions from Col. Beri were to sort out the problems at my level. While Manish Kalani and Avnish Hasija, the Site Manager were okay to work with, it was very difficult. to deal with the Kalani elders who tended to treat everyone like their menials. I had selected the best Army officers for the jobs of Senior Mall Manager, Col. Ravi Batra, my good friend, who at my insistence joined. I had also requested Lt. Col. Vijay S Patil, my old colleague from 17 Para Field Regiment to join me. Both left due to foul and intemperate language used by senior Kalani. I then requested Manish to get their people to man both these positions. Arun Mishra was finally selected by them for the post of Senior Mall Manager. The Mall functioned well under their new team leaders from the Police. I stayed for a while for about 10 days during which I was able to visit Mhow and meet our very dear friends Sivinder and Tripta. As always, they are such a delightful couple who have endeared themselves to our family. It's a joy to be with them anywhere and exchange laughs. We are indeed fortunate to have such good friends.

My next tour of duty was Pune, which was of special interest to me because of my old association with NDA and also the fact that my older sister had chosen to settle down here with her son Pankaj at Clover Highlands, near NIBM. My team visited Aamby Valley City, 75 km from Pune, near Lonavala owned by Sahara India. The city spans over 10,600 acres that are nestled amidst the mighty Sahyadri mountains connecting it with Deolali hill ranges. Aamby Valley City offers almost all recreational amenities, like an 18-hole golf course, five-star restaurants, water and adventure sports. We realized that this being a huge township by itself requires all services like Deolali/Mhow cantonment, Amby Valley has massive vital technical installations like powerhouses, step-up stations and power supply which need to be operated daily, maintained and serviced as per schedule. The neat and aesthetically laid out township and the facilities are mind-blowing.

Sahara Parivar was looking for an agency with credentials like ours. because this is not their core competency. In my experience as the station commander at Amritsar, Ganganagar and Mhow, this was nothing new for me. Municipal services like roads & pavements, effluent treatment plants and solid waste management had also to be taken care of. After a second visit, we made a final presentation incorporating our complete core competencies and how we would like to maintain and operate Aamby Valley City. Some of the suggestions made by us during the presentation, I still remember having said that we would ideally divide the site into zones of smaller areas under one Central Grid, for efficient management. A central control room having a dedicated telephone number for registering complaints from the users. Maintenance control centres shall be established in various zones for immediate attention for maintenance related issues. A dedicated quick reaction team shall be ready for each zone to attend to the complaints within 5 minutes. A call centre can be used as a hub for all kinds of maintenance complaints, task allocation, task completion and customer feedback. I also got an offer in writing from Sahara Management that our company WPM could also consider providing an administrator for the Amby Valley administrator, in our financial package (to replace one Brig. Sircar who had just resigned) throwing hints at me to relocate. Professional ethics and loyalty to my organisation learnt from the Army, foreclosed this option.

We also visited another site close by near Talegaon Dabade, JCB Manufacturing Pvt Ltd, when we were around in this area. My team carried out the site survey with one Col. Moses and made the presentation after two weeks. We now had plans to upgrade the office at Pune to full branch level with a full staff comprising one Manager Operations & office executive. We also decided to maintain continuous liaison with JCB Manufacturing Ltd., Pune by Regional Head (WPM), Mumbai. We made preparations for regular site visits and had wanted to commence the selection process for the vendors, equipment tools & tackles which included aerial delivery platforms, spares & consumables, landscaping, water harvesting, catering set up and maintenance of the guest house. We had taken action to resolve grey areas, areas of non-convergence of views and basic differences. We tried our best to analyse the strict final criteria/key deliverables on our agenda for implementation. We had developed a viable support plan & had planned to implement it vigorously after approval. Once again, we made a financial bid for Rs 15 lakhs per month but we were outbid by another local party who quoted much less, after studying the details of implementation given by us.

By now, I had gained valuable experience with client's requirements, generally spelt. out in RFIs in very seemingly ambiguous language, but one site visit would clarify everything. The submission of proposals, participating in meetings with clients, discussing service delivery and financials were at my fingertips. Electromechanical services, the type of engineering services, the housekeeping services and the type of machinery and the landscaping services were also learnt. The calculation of the common area maintenance charges was on the top of my agenda and I learnt this from our Head of Operations, Mr Vinay Kumar Talwar. There were many thumb rules which I learnt from these two gurus of Facility/Property Management Ashutosh Beri and Head Technical, Vinay Kumar Talwar. It used to be a great embarrassment sometimes, to answer questions on my technical qualifications. I can now say that hands-on experience matters more than degrees/diplomas. A stage had now come where I could work out the sinking fund charges for every site on a per sq ft basis, the evaluation of maintenance and operational charges, the electrical loads, the comprehensive insurance charges and even the façade cleaning charges, all by myself. Both these gentlemen were ready to share all the details based on their experience, you only needed a person who was keen to pick up all the knowledge. I also slogged very hard to gain the confidence of these two gentlemen, to share this kind of exposure.

During my stay in Sector 22 Gurgaon, I also kept in touch with my old Commanding Officers under whom I had the privilege of serving, retired Generals KK Hazari, Harjit Talwar and Lt. Col. OP Khanna. Col.

Khanna dropped in one day with a request for my help in locating a gentleman by the name of Gurmit Singh who had settled in the newly constructed Celebrity Homes in Palam Vihar. He told me that Gurmit was his tenant in his house, who had duped him of some six months' rent. I drove down to Celebrity Homes with the Colonel and finally located Gurmit Singh in one of the flats in F Tower. Gurmit apologized and paid the Colonel his dues by a cheque, which bounced. After a few days, he turned up again at my house for help. We visited Celebrity Homes again at the same flat. This time we got the cash out from him and the matter was closed. I had noticed earlier that the flats were a very decent size and reasonably priced. I asked Gurmit if I could show his flat to my wife in the evening. When Manju saw the flat, her first reaction was good, but with the rider. She was not prepared to go beyond the third floor as I knew her vertigo would come in. In the meanwhile, the landlord had increased the rent after four years which I thought was justified. We had seen independent bungalows, 500m plots and townhouses but nothing like what we saw in Celebrity Homes. Children were happy that we had dropped the idea of a bungalow after Yogesh Sharma had a massive burglary in his bungalow. Our friend Admiral Ravi Vohra and a few others also were keen to move out to a flat.

The next problem was the funding. I had to raise 60 lakhs in one go, where I could barely raise around 30 odd lakhs. Housing loans were difficult. for retired people but with my salary from WPM and a certificate (still serving) from Col. Beri, I could get the loan after massive paperwork. Now comes the crunch issue, the loan repayment terms. I took a lot of help in running around for an NRI loan from Mr Avinash Mathur, my daughter in law, Aviti's father who knew the loopholes well and is gifted with better-negotiating skills. NRI loans are to be paid in dollars but could afford high monthly premiums those days, for almost 10 years. At the first available opportunity, I disposed of the Dwarka flat to liquidate the loan of 50 lakhs for the present flat. With the spare money, I could also invest in a studio apartment in the same complex. I will always give Avinash all credit for pushing through this deal with all his perseverance and tact. I had kept quiet throughout when he negotiated the deal with the HDFC.

As I was nearing the end of my tenure, on account of reaching 65 years of age, as the Head Business Development & Quality Control, the total number of WPM and WPM (NCR) facility/property management was 75 and the total area came to approximately 17 lakhs sq ft in. We were still going strong with the large number of IBM sites coming up, especially in Chandigarh, Pune and Hyderabad. We also tried very hard to get into The India Exposition Mart, a massive kind of permanent trade centre of around 20 lakhs covered space cum exhibition halls and vacant grounds slated to come up in Greater Noida. My team visited the place and prepared a very effective proposal of around Rs 13 crores over three years, which was the highest proposal ever quoted by me. We went through the tendering process and qualified for the contract The presentation at the Vasant Kunj office was made by Col. Beri and myself. We were competing with companies like ILFS, CB Richard Ellis, Knight Frank, DLF and many others. Remarkably Col. Beri stood his ground and almost bagged this prestigious contract till some political interference and pressure on the management, came to our notice. ILFS had been given the figures quoted by us and they undercut us by a few lakhs only to beat us in this game. We felt sorry to lose out but I understand later ILFS ran into losses from which they could never recover. Next was the entry into Ansals Mall at Ludhiana, which I headed the transition team to take over. We would have run into losses, had we not liaised with the local electricity board officials and found out that the power breakdowns were almost 8-12 hours daily which the management had failed to inform. It was an inherent trait in all my engineers to go into minute details, even if I was sitting with the management, they would find things for themselves. I was fortunate to head such a devoted team of engineers, managers and workforce.

The biggest satisfaction that I drew was my involvement with a golf course for our partner Unitech in Karma Lakelands, Gurgaon, located 28kms away from the International Airport, spread over 260 acres of prime land. This project was conceived for development as an exclusive up-market leisure complex comprising of villas, chalets, lifestyle retirement village with a five-star hotel with almost all recreational facilities like health, spa and club around a 9-hole golf course. WPM had a major role to play in its progressive development and operations. I had the experience of the Golf Secretary in Tactical Wing School of Artillery Deolali of 1983-84 where we had converted the age-old browns into greens. I also laid out a nine-hole golf course at Lalgarh and also resurrected one at DSC Centre at Kannur. To me, this was just the challenge I wanted. Most of the work on the layout, construction and designing, water bodies and the irrigation system was already complete and only the property management was expected of us. We strategized the property management plan integrating the municipal services, the technology, processes and systems for running a golf resort. In addition, I learnt a lot about various turfgrasses and their maintenance. Playing on this par 33 course with friends was a great pleasure. Col. Ravi Rana, our manager, had looked after the course very well.

I think Col. Beri and I made a formidable team and I learnt a lot from him. In my send-off at the Bristol Hotel, I could see a bit of sadness in Col. Ashutosh Beri's eyes. He had wanted me to continue but the partnership with Trammel Crow and later with Jones Lang Laselle had forced his hands. The trouble with Indian owned companies is that some family members are always planted in the company to oversee their interests. Mr SK Khanna, Head HR was placed precisely for this job who fixed the retirement age at 65 years for everyone except himself. The excuse given was that the Americans wanted to post their key personnel in a job performed by me. I left without a fuss and received numerous offers from those I had worked with. I had to take a good break and this opportunity could not be missed.

On my return from Australia, my good friend Vinay Kumar ensured that I continued my relationship with WPM by joining a subsidiary, Proform Facilities Pvt Ltd. I thought I had had enough of the all-India image and now needed to confine myself to NCR. Rajinder Sethi had worked with me in various places and his offer, which I thought was a good idea. Sethi was also assured of a working relationship with JLLM, the successor company of WPM. I felt. very secure with him and joined the new company as its CEO, in the same field of facility management on the same terms. Without wasting any time, both Sethi and I prepared a comprehensive brochure for Proform Facilities which included Manh Sneh Corporation being run by Mr Manoj Yadav, his partner. We established ourselves in DLF Phase 3 and commenced work at American Express in Udyog Vihar. Though not a big contract, we provided Electro-Mechanical services, housekeeping, pantry and photocopier services for one year. We submitted a reply to a tender document and were invited for a presentation by Delhi Metro Rail Services. This was seven days a week contract for cleaning and housekeeping services at all DMRC stations/two depots and the mechanical wagon cleaning operations. In my presentation, we emphasized fully mechanized cleaning and housekeeping operations using biodegradable and eco-friendly chemicals and reagents. The metro management listened very carefully and we were shortlisted. A Bank guarantee to the tune of Rs 1.25 crores was submitted. We were the lowest quotation and on the verge of bagging the contract. There was some technical hold up and the contract was stalled for a month. After a month, DMRC ordered fresh tenders for some unknown reasons and refunded our bank guarantee. We resubmitted our tender at the same rates but were never invited for making a presentation, possibly due to tip-off by the management to quoting lower than us. Such things happen in semi-government organisations when you try to avoid giving bribes.

We were doing well and managed to get a few more sites such as Galaxy Mall, Cosmic Kitchen, Iffco Tokio and Indigo Airlines for security, electromechanical services and housekeeping. The contracts were relatively small and the profits were very marginal because of cut-throat competition and the regular increases in minimum wages in Haryana and Delhi. Whenever we got a fresh contract labour department officials were waiting for their share of the contract. We made presentations for facility management in Delhi for Chinmaya Mission, IDSA, Rajiv Gandhi Bhavan, Diwan Chand Imaging Centre and Mool Chand Hospital without success and at

Ghaziabad, we bagged Shipra Vista, Indirapuram and Shipra Apartments, Vaishali. We also bagged interGlobe Technology and Oracle sites in NCR and Virgin Atlantic cargo at Delhi airport. There were several sites in Global Business Park and some like Gold Souk already with us. In about a year we had managed about 45 sites and were planning to expand to Jaipur and Alwar where some new malls and residential complexes were coming up. We also tried to get one residential and mall at Calcutta but were let down by our WPM representative there. I had also kept fulfilling my duties as a resident in Celebrity Homes right from the time I purchased a flat here.

After returning to India, on 4th Nov, I rejoined Sethi and continued in my old assignment. We were finding it very difficult. to retain our sites because of the regular minimum wages increases and the cut-throat competition in facility management. I requested a lower degree of involvement in the outside touring and presentations. There were presentations to be made at Anandpur Sahib, Bikaner House, Commonwealth Games, and Kabul Airport, For the last one, I did not volunteer despite repeated requests and allurements. We had two trips to Anandpur Sahib (*Virasat-e-Khalsa*) and we submitted tenders for electromechanical services, heating ventilation and air conditioning, not ordinary housekeeping but that of 500 years old Sikh relics requiring technical expertise and security. This was a massive contract and we were shortlisted along with Col. Beri's JLLM. As we could not provide the bank guarantee of over Rs 2 crores, I opted out of the contract. As for Bikaner House, we secured the contract without any problems. In the Commonwealth Games contract, we were in danger of being led up a garden path because of vested interests. We decided to remain out for very good reasons.

Assignment Celebrity Homes

We were back in India by 14 Jan 2010, after a holiday in Australia. I had another assignment waiting for me in our complex, the Celebrity Homes. Right from the day of entry in Celebrity Homes, there was a running battle between two groups who were hell-bent to ruin each other by trading charges of petty corruption. Even after one group handed over Celebrity Homes to the other in 2008, the organisation was functioning without any controls because it had no clue on how to handle the RWA. Before I could even get over the jet lag, I was given the news that I have been appointed the Secretary Celebrity Homes Residents Welfare Association, in absentia. While being humbled at the confidence reposed in me, I learnt that there were problems with the builder and his partner who was carrying out the facility management duties. Sethi had paid me for my leave period and therefore I could not let him down. I told him I would be able to do one job only and therefore offered to resign, which he declined to accept. I told him I would be available to him anytime if he had a requirement. There were pending issues with DHBVN regarding electrical loads being charged arbitrarily fixed by Ansals to fleece us. I met my coursemate and fellow DS from Wellington, Gen. Lohchab who was the Director DHBVN and apprised him of the problem. He straightaway reduced the electrical loads by almost 50% and the matter stood resolved. The next problem was the continuance of the RWA Committee even the General Body decision to hand over, on the plea that the court case against Cosmos Builders was still pending. I was stunned to see a parallel RWA conduct a meeting after our RWA meeting on 25 April 2010, when the President & the Treasurer announced that the duo had met the Chief Secretary Haryana during their visit and they had been assured a favourable outcome of the case, which was incorrect. To add insult to injury, when I pointed this out to them, one of them threatened libel. It was not difficult. to conclude why these two had got together. We also could not help noticing that in a highly polarized society, how one bad fish can sully the waters.

In the meantime, the Pro Fac Facilities arbitrarily increased the Maintenance charges by almost 20% and that too, with retrospective effect from Oct 2009. I apprised the new President that Pro Fac Facilities had no justification for this increase and residents were communicated not to pay. We had a meeting in the meanwhile with Pro Fac which was very inconclusive and full of insinuations. After exhausting all our energies to explain that we would accept this increase but not with retrospective effect, our talks fell through. In the meanwhile, I was able to obtain a copy of all the documents submitted by Ansals to DTCP whereby our association stood approved. It is a pity that we refused to take over when Ansals had offered to hand over in 2006, on the plea that we had insufficient knowledge of management. To my horror a letter of 2006 signed by our President was shown to me, to corroborate. I paid Rs 500 from my pocket to obtain from the Registrar, the copies of all five declarations made by Ansals from July 2002 to May 2008. Ansals claimed that they handed over the declarations earlier, we found these much later with the RWA, dumped in one corner. It was also amazing to know that a large number of people including the President himself were not even owners of their flats because they had not paid the registration to the government for the transfer of property from Ansals.

Having got a very clear idea of the Haryana Apartments Ownership Act and Rules, I explained the same to one senior defence official who had promised to support me to oust Ansals. The meetings we held endorsed their faith in us to continue. We had made it a point to work selflessly for the organisation which is our own home. We gave an ultimatum to Ansals to hand over the site to us by 30 June 2010 and clear out by that date. Luckily, we contacted the right person from Ansals, who was located in Palam Vihar, the ex-CEO SFML who was fully in the picture. There were a lot of negotiations required which we were able to push through. Towers were promised Rs 43 lakhs as a refund of Sinking Fund, Suites Rs 4, 99,000 and an additional Rs 6 lakhs for running the Condominium. There was an anomaly in Maintenance Charges wherein Suites were being charged Rs 3.40 per sq ft against four Towers Rs 1.50 which was resolved by us. All equipment would be handed over in 'as is where is' condition on 30 June 2010. There were frequent power failures and only one functional generator which also was working on 50% load. Security Deposit was also agreed to be handed over to the residents directly by Ansals. Club and Swimming Pool were non-functional and required extensive repairs and the Swimming Pool required a license fee of Rs 1 lakhs to commence operations.

We were required to submit complete paperwork for one water softening plant that had to be installed, which was already paid for. We had no funds, so we had to resort to taking six months' advance of maintenance from residents, which too was opposed by one or two residents. In the meanwhile, we officially lost the much-touted court case against Cosmos Builders, for which some of us had paid two instalments of Rs 10,000 each. What hurts you is the misuse of funds pointed out by the audit whereby golf green fee, fictitious lawyer fee, travelling expenses to Chandigarh and refreshments paid out of the RWA Account. After handing over the original receipts as proof from various entities to the person concerned, we decided to close this case with great difficulty. Whatever was left in the Legal Fund was transferred to the successor Condominium. We had to take legal advice from Advocate, Mrs Madhu Tewatia, for drafting a legal agreement for the handing over of the buildings in the complex to us, which is still pending. We have only obtained the responsibility of maintenance of common areas, which came to us on 30 June 2010.

We found the Condominium Bye-Laws already submitted and approved by Director Town & Country Planning. What was required was a written set of rules and regulations for day-to-day functioning and delegation of powers, the opening of accounts and preparation of inventories handed over by Pro Fac. We had requisitioned the services of Aastha Engineering to take over all electrical equipment right from the takeover point of DHBVN. The various electrical fittings such as GO Switch, mains reading meter, circuit breaker, two transformers, the HT/LT. panels, UPS and AMF to the various risings/meters in the basement were all in shambles, for lack of maintenance. Both generators were lying off-road for want of spares. Mr Raj Verma, our engineer, found the generators oil sumps full of thick sludge, at the time we took over from Pro Fac. Lifts were mostly nonfunctional and then the firefighting equipment had never been tested leave alone being certified fit. (Imagine if there had been a fire). We had also asked for all the built. drawings and sanctions approved by DTCP. In the peak summer, July 2010, we started the process of how to keep systems going without interruptions. i.e., electrical including generators/transformers, lifts and water supply. We prayed to the Almighty not to put our fire system to the test till we have made it serviceable. For long term measures, I requested my old friend Col. Beri of JLLM to help us carry out a complete technical audit of the complex which was done for me without any payment. I retain a copy of that report even now.

Now I must bring to your notice how the complex functioned before 30 June 2010. Ansals had a Facility Manager and a team of electricians, firemen, housekeepers, office boys and a security team. There was no maintenance of any equipment worth its name, ever carried out. The basement was full of junk stores locked by the contractors. There were certain malpractices, which a builder must never adopt in any site, now seen as sales gimmicks. First, provision of an emergency circuit in each flat and villas, in which one light and one fan point were unmetered and therefore, free of cost. This was misused by some residents who got the electrician to place the entire flat/villa on an emergency circuit. The meters were tampered with in most cases and were located inside the villa, against the latest orders of DHBVN disallowing that. When we got the first DHBVN bill for June 2010 was Rs 7.75 lakhs, left unpaid by Pro Fac. We were able to recover Rs 6.00 lakhs, which meant a difference of Rs 1.75 lakhs on electricity alone. It takes no rocket science to know that these are not transmission losses but losses due to theft of power by our residents. I was able to pinpoint the location of tampered/unserviceable meters and houses fully on unmetered emergency supply. Some of the residents involved in these unethical practices were some senior defence officers and RWA office bearers. Some residents had refused to pay power backup charges of Rs 20,000 saying that they do not want it. There was a huge list of defaulters of maintenance and electricity charges, not only closed flats/villas but residents occupying and not paying upfront. There were neither serviceability certificates from the authorities nor the maintenance contracts for lifts or generators and fire services. Overhead water tanks on the roofs were rejoined to make one common supply in each house and not two earlier.

Parking was usurped by our residents like spoils of the Bangladesh war and many cars of those who did not even own a flat here, were parked, including one of a resident from Palam Vihar. No Deed of Apartment had been executed by any resident to establish ownership under Haryana Apartments Ownership Act 1983 and Rules. This is not all as far as the behaviour of the civilized and educated residents of this high-end society. One resident refused to park in the basement but chose to do it under his flat behind the Tower security. One lady banned the entry of all maintenance staff into lifts because she saw them ogling at her. The same woman regularly brought a cycle rickshaw full of groceries right up to the lift. One couple locked a portion of the common area for their children's bikes, a table tennis table and other personal stores. Ansals, after handing over maintenance charge to us, locked the Sales Office which they wanted to demolish, being an unauthorized construction. They also locked four shops on the ground floor which were claimed by the one resident to have been sold to her. In all meetings where residents were requested to be more disciplined and conduct themselves as per social norms, residents almost came to blows with each other and ended up with free use of expletives and abuses. Blank threats to my life were made in public which I never took seriously. Hate mails and other tactics were freely exchanged by some erratic residents. There are some "high ranking individuals' ' whose sole job was to incite violence and goad other residents to file court cases against the management. I was in a very tricky situation when an elderly policeman from PCR Van, which had entered the complex, came to our temporary office in the Celebrity Club billiard room. He looked at me and asked if I was the Secretary. When I confirmed, he told me there is a complaint of "outraging of modesty" made by a lady from F 503 against you. I remembered that person in the morning, throwing tantrums on the illegal power backup charges, and walking away in a huff. When the police officer summoned her, she arrived and he asked her, "Madam, I am not so well educated in English, but what you have said does not behove a lady from a good family to express it, this way. I don't know Secretary Sahib. He doesn't appear the type to outrage anybody's modesty. Tell me what exactly do you want?" She again stomped out saying that even the police had been bribed, she now has no complaint, in that case.

A daughter of a prominent resident with a friend insisted on swimming in the pool in an improper attire when checked by the guard, told him to buzz off. One lady called the PCR van because I had prevented her son from playing football on the lawns. Policemen who came left after telling her not to call 100 for such small things. The same person at the behest of our fellow resident, had me summoned by the SHO at the Palam Vihar Police Station at 9.30 at night, several times on charges of misbehaving with children and preventing them from playing in the lawns. A resident of Garden Homes, a senior defence official, fought a battle with us to prevent his meter from coming outside his house because he was the culprit who stole maximum electricity. The last point was a case filed by the same lady in People's Court against the Board of Managers that we had forcibly changed the electrical meter of her house without her permission. I attended several hearings and the case was finally decided in our favour. I do not wish to bring in any more episodes but all I can say is that I had my hands full and could not attend to calls from my old company, even once.

First, we took it upon ourselves that we will get everything going as best as we could within the financial constraints. We asked Ansals to immediately transfer Rs 58.99 lakhs being our money. This was again offered but not accepted by our successors. All drawings and official allotment of parking to residents be given with diagrams. Plans were executed correctly, complete renovations to the Celebrity Club and Swimming Pool were done by them at their cost, all AMCs and serviceability certificates from various authorities of electrical, lifts and fire equipment were obtained. We put our heads together and got going with the move of one old 500 kva generator from the basement to the outback along with the other generator, removed the emergency circuit of all residents permanently to prevent pilferage, changed electricity meters after bulk purchase of new tested ones, metered the complete supply going into EWS and obtained payments from them. We also made a parking management plan be invoked in phases starting within Suites, Towers and Garden Homes and generated income. The Deed of Apartments was made mandatory for all residents, power backup charges of Rs 20k for towers and Garden Homes and Rs 10k for Suites was put into effect. Residents Handbook was prepared and issued. Social functions in the Club were initiated every month. All contracts for Electro-Mechanical, housekeeping and horticulture are decided by a board and vendors selected. ESI, PF of all Condominium employees be paid directly and not by a contractor on payroll management. We made sure that our Board of Managers were unencumbered and there was not one occasion when someone pointed out a conflict of interest.

We now have a good taste of the way our young nouveau riche behave, it does not matter whether they are civilians, IAS officers or airline pilots formerly from IAF or Generals or for that matter, ordinary shopkeepers/ property brokers. Elections are manipulated by self-seeking individuals, who would manipulate hook or by crook to get into positions of power for petty gains. I am reminded of what Churchill said in 1946 before our independence

> "Power will go to the hands of rascals, rogues, freebooters; all Indian leaders will be of low calibre & men of straw. They will have sweet tongues and silly hearts. They will fight amongst themselves for power and India will be lost in political squabbles".

Celebrity Homes residents didn't have to wait long to prove it. We have a heterogeneous crowd, some with scruples and some without. We have to learn to live with them in the same environment. Ansals had not been good administrators and the residents had never been exposed to the discipline and controls in a gated complex and were quite used to their free lunches, which we, the veterans, were not prepared to give. We, the veterans, have ensured that we put the Condominium on a good foundation for the succession by a younger Board of Managers. There was a concerted effort on our part not to create personality cults or take undue advantage or perks of our position by billing it to the Condominium. With that in mind, we all resigned prematurely from our positions on 5 November 2011, so that those who claimed to have had better managerial expertise and felt left out, could be given a chance. We now see the Board functioning with sound financial backing for which we laid the foundation, experience and skills provided by the first management and with an altogether different approach. The fact remains that fundamentals are so strong that no new organisation can undo the changes we initiated with a sense of permanence, be it under HAO Act 1983 or HRRS Act 2012. The regular change of vendors/contractors, review of the annual budget, adherence to a more efficient SOP on Finance with reduced financial powers and cap on unnecessary expenditure would go a long way in paving the road to a better quality of life.

Corporate Sector & Solid Waste Management

I was offered a consultant job by Ambience Group for six months on a handsome salary which I accepted. During this period, I used to visit all their malls and reported directly to their Senior VP who had worked under me at WPM. I met the Mall Manager Roy Peter, who was keen to leave and start a new venture with Memios LLC of USA, engaged in Solid Waste Management. Peter and I, both resigned and started our new company Alpha Tech Facilities & Services Pvt Ltd with our office at Gurgaon. We prepared all the company profiles and registration and other formalities before being introduced to Mr Dan Mckenzie, their CEO at Delhi. We got the authorization for Alpha Tech to represent Memios in India as their sole agent. The next step taken was to co-opt Gen. Vinay Shankar, who I knew quite well, to join us as our Chairman. We then had a series of meetings with one Anil

Goswami who also brought in Sudhanshu Mittal, a local politician, to join the company.

Memios LLC USA is one of the leading companies which offers sustainable waste management solutions based on pyrolysis conversion technology. Memios LLC USA proposes to invest in India by a joint venture partnership with my company Alpha Tech to cash on the opportunity thus created.

What is Pyrolysis Conversion Technology?

- Pyrolysis is a conversion technology that chemically decomposes organic materials by heat in the absence of oxygen. It has been in use for 100 years and has been heavily used in the chemical industry and other industrial applications. Pyrolysis has been used to produce charcoal from coke, activated carbon, methanol and other chemicals from wood, coke from coal; convert biomass into synthesis gas/biochar, cracking of medium weight hydrocarbons from oil lighter ones like gasoline and turn waste into safely disposable substances.

- The benefits which are likely to accrue from this technology are no initial capital costs to be borne by us. Power generated is available for commercial use in the national electricity grid. Carbon credits are obtained from low emissions, no greenhouse gases and other atmospheric pollutants. Usable by-products require no segregation of garbage. The space requirement for a plant is only 500 sq metres. Eligible for incentives offered by the Government of India.

We had agreed to retain 51% shares with us and offered 49% to Mittal and Anil. With this understanding, I invested Rs 3 Lakhs of my own money for my 7.5% sweat equity and requested my friend Sivinder to invest Rs 5 Lakhs. Most of the investment was done by Mittal and the office shifted to Connaught Place. We started functioning with me as the CEO and Director, Peter as the Managing Director and Vinay Shankar, Goswami and Mittal as Directors. First, we had to verify whether the waste to energy plant existed in South Carolina and what were its capabilities. Four of us took a business trip to Charlotte, South Carolina to see their solid waste management plant in operation. The team comprising Sudhanshu Mittal, Roy Peter, Anil Goswami and self, went around seeing their project. I was never convinced about the efficacy of the project right from the beginning. They explained the blue flame burning at one corner of the plant was to run the prime mover of the turbines to produce 4 MW of energy from 100 tons of garbage. The garbage I saw was some kind of wood beaten into pulp and nowhere near the classic garbage from the Indian community bins. They explained that after initial shredding the garbage, it would assume the same form, on which I had expressed reservations. Next, we also saw another project in the Houston Hospital on Pneumatic Waste Transportation and were fully satisfied with its efficacy. When we returned, we got an MOU ready for Memios LLC USA but there were too many unresolved issues when we discussed with Goswami and Mittal on the shareholdings. Anyway, we started a market survey involving various municipalities and boards, all types of building complexes and townships. We prepared the Statement of Purpose for seeking finances for funding operations for the first six months in a joint venture partnership offered by Memios LLC and Alpha Tech. A comprehensive proposal was covered as a presentation and prepared single-handedly by me as follows:

In India, increased urbanization and the unplanned population migration from rural to urban areas has led to slums formation and an exponential increase in garbage/waste generation. The situation is very alarming as most municipalities and civic bodies are unable to cope with it. It is a very familiar sight to see huge garbage/waste dumps on the roadsides lying un-disposed; mostly rotting, with horrible stench emanating from it. Landfills which were in use earlier as dumping grounds, either is full to the brim or not financially viable. To get an idea of the wastes generated, there are municipal solid waste, industrial waste, medical/hospital waste, construction & debris material, tyres, wood/green waste, biosolids/sewage & sludge in treatment plants, animal /agricultural waste, packaging material, paper and hazardous waste chiefly glass, electronic/electrical items and cables.

We thought huge opportunities exist in the management of municipal solid waste. Competing technologies in the world market today, use pyrolysis, gasification, plasma arch and combustion techniques. Garbage/waste treatment plants, where functional today, suffer from the drawbacks such as being very expensive in capital costs, occupy a lot of real estate, require waste segregation techniques and the effluents/by-products generated are difficult to dispose of. Therefore, garbage/waste disposal is now a live problem both in rural and urban areas.

The Essence of Memios Partnership Proposal

Before the joint venture agreement was signed, our good performance during the next six months would be imperative. A good performance would be to demonstrate our capability to install and operate the Memios plant first at two locations. In the present arrangement, Memios USA is prepared to reimburse our share of profits to us which was about 25% of the total Rs 2,000 per tonne of solid waste being charged by us as a processing fee. The State Electricity Board would have bought the power at competitive rates and paid us accordingly. See the benefits and the profits. Garbage got removed at a cost, got processed to produce power and solid carbon, processing cost and cost of power received from the State Electricity Board. A win-win situation for all, as everyone shares profit according to an agreed percentage.

Our targeted areas for Installation of Memios plants were residential communities/townships, Commercial and Industrial properties, hospitals, airports and shopping centres & malls. My presentations to at least 12 Chief Ministers/Ministers for Urban Development and other politicians like Farooq Abdullah and his son, Omar were well received but everyone wanted a donation to party funds, in advance before the contract was issued in our favour. This donation was upwards of 10 crores and above.

Future of Fresh Business Start-Ups in India

All new startups those days when FDI was only 49% or below. The plant itself cost upwards of $ 3.5 million which required a funder. We got one first from Canada but when he saw the ease of doing business in India in 2012, he started laying down more stringent conditions. Under the slew of incentives announced by the Government, we would be in a position to liquidate the loan in 12-13 years. No organisation was prepared to give us the lease of land for the plant for more than 5 years at a time. We needed a tranche of $0.5

m for the organisation in the first month to commence followed by the remaining $3m in six months.

After our trip to the plant at Greensboro, internal problems started with disagreements on funding and shareholdings. Mittal also wanted his wife and son to be co-opted in the company in some capacity. Peter and I had travelled to almost every nook and corner of the country and made at least 25 presentations in state capitals like Goa, Patna, Lucknow, Calcutta, Pondicherry, Bangalore and Chandigarh etc. We found Mittal tightening his hold by defaulting on payments of my salary whenever I proceeded abroad for a vacation to either Australia or USA on the plea of financial crunch. We also moved out from Connaught Place to Laxmi Nagar in one of his office buildings which were lying vacant. Thanks to Mittal's rigid insistence for majority shares (51%), we lost a golden opportunity to start a pyrolysis plant in India. I lost over Rs 8 Lakhs on the entire deal. (Rs 3 lakhs personal investment plus Rs 5 lakhs from Sivinder). We also consulted Gen. Vinay Shankar after this development. He was very emphatic that he would form a new company minus Mittal and his partner, for continuing the partnership with Memios LLC.

We registered afresh as Swamukt Waste Energy Pvt Limited. and established an office in Vasant Kunj and proceeded as planned. We shortlisted engineers and MBA graduates from Pune and were all set with all the proposals sent to various institutions. We also found a funder, from the UK a certain Mr Neelan, a Sri Lankan Tamil, who was heading a British furniture chain Pharma, who released the first tranche of $100,000. We got the deals from various organisations like DC Jhajjar and Poona Cantt Board but lost out on the funder again because Mittal threatened them and got the deal scuttled. No Indian bank would give us a loan of Rs 5 crores without collateral and we had none. Dan Mckenzie came out with another proviso that Swamukt needs to put in $100,000 as the returnable earnest money deposit, The vendors supplying the waste to energy plant worth over 2.5 million had to be paid in advance, which would be adjusted later when the funding came through. Both Gen. Vinay Shanker and Brig. CS Sandhu had contributed a combined Rs 75 lakhs. I arranged a loan of Rs 10 lakhs from Ramesh Apte to make up the shortfall and stood a guarantee for the same.

We should have raised eyebrows on the earnest money deposit to Memios LLC USA because it was never discussed earlier. We had some tenders returned by various organisations, out of which we were returned Rs 4 lakhs to Ramesh Apte. We suffered the forfeit of our earnest money with Memios with a net loss of Rs 15 lakhs by me. With my Dignity and Honour intact, I paid back my friends their full investment from my pocket after borrowing from my son, Rohit. The fact that they accepted not a penny as interest, speaks highly of them as well. I am very happy that I chose to retain my good friends like Sivinder and Ramesh who had invested at my behest. It is my strong conviction that we, the defence officers must never venture into business with unknown civilians. Never invest your hard-earned money in any venture, irrespective of future returns. Everyone outside the civvy street, especially the politicians and the bureaucracy, is out to fleece you.

Reunions, Get-togethers and Jubilees

"You don't stop laughing when you grow old, you grow old when you stop laughing."
George Bernard Shaw

Reunions are great opportunities to share memories, rekindle old friendships and exchange light-hearted banter, which may be even resorted to leg-pulling as I said earlier. For us, in the uniformed community, reunions or get-togethers or jubilees are universally accepted as "in things" sporting the same tie/scarf, regimental associations, sporting institutions/clubs. What amazes me is the irrepressible spirit of our great 23 NDA course, now between ages 78 to 80 years. We have been getting together on 23 December every year at Delhi for our reunions and no end seems to be in sight.

The credit for organizing these functions from the very beginning goes to our late course mate Colonel Lalit Roy, Nikku Gill, UBS Kohli and Rattan Gaba. Subsequently, the entire burden fell on the broad shoulders of Lt Gen Prakash Suri, who has done yeoman's service in "keeping the flock together". Chandigarh Chapter organized by Lt Gen Gurbaksh Sihota is also functioning admirably. Why I say that the course spirit is "irrepressible" because our course has always held get-togethers at Delhi & Chandigarh regularly and added the famous Southern Sojourn at Chennai on 27-29 Jan 17, Chandigarh Meet on 23-24 Dec 17, Eastern Sojourn at Kolkata on Feb 18, Pune Meet on 23-25 Feb 19 and Goa Meet on Sep 19. This liveliness and vibrancy have no ceiling, it is just the joys of reuniting with old friends to enjoy life to the fullest. Agreed for us the time is flying past at a great lick and we continue to lose our dear course mates in regular succession, but it doesn't change the attitudes of the remaining die-hards from the 23rd course who are unwilling to lose pleasant memories of our association. Also look at our mates and their ability to withstand the challenges of distance and time to come from Bangalore, Hyderabad, Kolkata, Chennai just to renew old bonds of friendships.

With coursemates CD Puri and GS Bal

Echo Squadron

Natarajan, Essen, Chatterjee, Arren and self at Kolkatta

Golfers at Chandigarh

The mega event of the course (which we could not attend, being away overseas) was the Golden Jubilee Reunion (GJR) Dinner was held on 20th Dec 2012 at the Manekshaw Centre in great style. It appeared to be the most appropriate location for such a momentous event. All those who attended the event appreciated the décor and the ambience of the venue. We had a record attendance of 105 coursemates and spouses. It was very heartening that so many of our coursemates from distant locations took the trouble of participating in the GJR festivities. The finale was the wreath-laying at the Hut of Remembrance at NDA Khadakvasla by six of our stalwarts, which included Essen Guptan, Partha Sen and Chand Dev Puri. It indeed speaks volumes for the spirit of the "Terrific Twenty Third". Yoga Shivir for fitness freaks, under the aegis of Veterans Defence Forces Group of Col. RS Gaba, arranged at Haridwar from 22 to 24 Oct 18, was highly appreciated by everyone.

Like all courses which pass out from the IMA Dehradun, we too celebrated the Golden Jubilee Anniversary of our commissioning from the School of Artillery, Deolali on 30 June 2013. We were just forty-five of us gunners from the 380 odd who had been commissioned from Deolali. Some emergency commissioned officers had left us after six to eight years of service to the nation. Simultaneously, our batch mates from the Armoured Corps and Infantry got together at IMA Dehradun, Engineers at CME Kirkee, Signals at MCTE Mhow, ASC at ASC Centre Bangalore, EME at EME School Baroda got together for this poignant occasion. For us Gunners, the bulk of the spadework was done by Gurbaksh Sihota and Natarajan. We reached Deolali for the celebrations on 29 June 2013 from various places all over India, where we had decided to settle down. Whenever course get-togethers of this kind take place even in IMA, everyone is accommodated together as a course, irrespective of rank. Much to our disappointment, the General officers from the course chose to be accommodated in the VIP rooms in the messes while the rest were accommodated in two bunches in Captain's accommodation in the messes. That was no camaraderie, friends!!!

The first evening was a course get together in A Mess, where we introduced ourselves at the podium, as a couple by turns. All of us between the age bracket of 69-72 years, needed to brush up our memories. Some of us had not met each other for some time five decades and some retired earlier than the rest and a few had not met for the five decades. It was great to see the back slapping and the camaraderie. One and all were behaving like youngsters and regaling each other with anecdotes of the years gone past. We had also taken great pains to invite two of our very distinguished instructors and their ladies as our guests. Maj. Gen. & Mrs YK Kapoor and Maj. Gen. & Mrs RP Chadha honoured us with their presence, which was highly appreciated. Regrettably, no other instructors could be present, I guess, most have already passed away. Our course get-together for a photograph in the lawns of B Mess followed next. Manju and I visited all the houses we had lived in our postings at Deolali and Nasik and were delighted to see them well maintained as usual. We were invited for dinner night at the Centre Mess which was a grand affair with the band in attendance. This occasion coincided with what would have been our pipping ceremony at the Chetwode Hall. Jogi and I did try a Chetwode slow march of sorts, through the Artillery Centre Mess, when the band played Auld Lang Syne. The next day was some optional events like a round of golf or a visit to Shirdi which was extremely well organized. We played hosts also at a function at the Temple Hill Institute where we had invited the Commandant and his team. There were about 35 couples who attended this get together.

For those whom we had met in service, the names like Raghuvanshi, DK Bhandari, Mediratta, Roshan Sharma, Jogi Kahlon, Gurbaksh, Nat, Minoo Panthaki, Joginder, PC Reddy, Billoo Verma, Manjit, Satya Dev, and Harbans Chaudhry, ring bells. It was a great pleasure to meet with our spouses, exchange notes on grandparenting and renew old acquaintances once again. Others included some we had never had the pleasure of meeting in service and were meeting for the first time in five decades, like Pardaman, Arun Kumar, Bhatta, Makhan Singh, Devinder Dewan, ID Bhardwaj, Kohlatkar, Luthra, Manohar Sethi, Talwar, Gurmeet Khurana, KC Verma and their spouses, were those who graced this occasion. It is possible that during our pre-commission course I did not meet a few others from our course. I remember meeting them for the first time in my life, our friends like Ashok Sehgal, DS Uppal, Prahlad Toro, Ram Nath and DIG (BSF) Majgi. The very sporting Mrs Rita Gulati represented her late husband Kirti, our Twenty Third course football blue from Kilo Squadron NDA. Kirti had passed away some seven years back. We take this opportunity to pay our respectful homage to our June 1963 Gunner coursemates and spouses, who are not with us today. It has been a privilege to pass out together from our alma mater. With the festivities coming to an end on the third day, we all departed from Deolali carrying very pleasant memories of our Golden Jubilee.

Golden Jubilee Reunion at Deolali

Paratroopers aging gracefully

    The armed forces have always accorded the place of honour to units for their single-minded devotion and dedication during battle. It is an honour to be commissioned in the highly decorated 17 Parachute

Field Regiment which won its Honour Titles in 1948 (Zojila) and 1971 (Poongli Bridge). Those officers who have served in this unit during wars will understand what it takes to be a part of the Honour Title Day or the Platinum Jubilee celebrations. The Platinum Jubilee of 17 Parachute Field Regiment, the show case of these attributes was celebrated from 31 Jan to 2 Feb 2016 at Agra Cantt. Amongst the galaxy who graced the occasion were our old 2IC, the nonagenarian, Lt Col SS Sant, who had come on the wheelchair from Chandigarh to meet us. A series of very star-studded functions beautifully organized by the generation next were the highlights. What followed was the finest days of my newly raised 12 Air OP Flight, where I had won a Mention in Despatch during 1971 operations in the Rajasthan Sector. I am also privileged to be the second Commanding Officer of 141 Field Regiment which won the Honour Title KARGIL and the COAS Commendation for their outstanding performance during Op Vijay.

Can anyone ask for more?

At the 17 Para Field Regiment Platinum Jubilee

At the Platinum Jubilee of 17 Para Field Regiment in Agra

This 75mm pack howitzer in the foreground was lost during the 1962 war and recovered from China after 28 years

Cardinal Gun at the 17 Para Field Regiment Officer Mess

141 Field Regiment Battle Honour day celebration

The Soliloquy

Random Thoughts

I have introspected the way I have led my life. Few well-wishers, the straight speaking Maj. Gen. Shyam Behari Lal Kapoor, who was my immediate superior at DSSC Wellington once remarked, "Dabbu, I have followed your excellent career graph while you were in service. Although you have all the requisite qualifications required for promotion, I am sorry to say that you have not prepared yourself for higher ranks". As an honest and forthright man, I thought about it and made some pertinent observations. Like others in my service, I too had my dreams and desires. I was born with a destiny, which I knew nothing about. Had I known what was destined for me beforehand, I may have taken life on a different course altogether. As a young boy born and brought up in a small town like Dehra Dun, I nursed the dreams of becoming an Army officer just like the ones from the Indian Military Academy who looked so good to me. Life in the armed forces was a dream and was a desire of every youngster in those days. Dreams were not illusions; they were very realistic and capable of being achieved. I desired what I dreamt about. I had not placed hopes on my destiny to take me places as I knew that I have to work hard. I dreamt well and not beyond the realms of reality. I knew that I need to dream of achievable goals. For dreaming well, I need to motivate myself first, lead a simple, uncomplicated life, yet not so simple as to be gullible. I had learnt from my father "'Aspire to be the best in your profession and not worry about the results". I developed the highest regards for my CO, Lt. Col. Harjit Talwar (known in the regiment as Tally, later Maj. Gen.) who told me a few things. Some were the virtues of a true gentleman which Tally always quoted based on Cardinal Newman's sayings:

"A true gentleman carefully avoids whatever may cause a jar or a jolt. in the minds of those with whom he is cast: all clash of opinion, or collision of feeling, all restraint, or suspicion, or gloom, or resentment, his great concern being to make everyone at their ease and home. He has his eyes on all his company, he is tender towards the bashful, gentle towards the distant, and merciful towards the absurd; he can recollect to whom he is speaking, he guards against unreasonable allusions or topics which may irritate: he is seldom prominent in conversation and never wearisome. He has too much good sense to be affronted by insults, he is too well employed to remember injuries and too indolent to bear malice. He is patient, forbearing and resigned to philosophical principles: he submits to pain because it is inevitable to the bereavement. After all, it is an irreparable end to death, because it is his destiny. He may be right or wrong in his opinion, but he is too clear-headed to be unjust; he is as simple as he is forcible and as brief as he is decisive". Frankly, I have yet to find a person of similar credentials in the Army, other than Tally.

Tally visited me at Amritsar in 1990 during my command of the brigade, his views on *sharafat* which he said, were ingrained in the best of age-old Indian culture of dignity & honour. The placing of national interests foremost, Army's and the unit before your own were something of a dichotomy, he felt. In the era of increasing opportunism, careerist/sycophantic brands of officers have led to fallen standards of integrity and self-esteem. Providentially our men are not yet affected and the indomitable spirit of our jawans and youngsters has not let us down in wars and low-intensity conflicts.

None of us from good backgrounds should sell our souls for a good ACR knowing fully well that all promotions to the next rank are dependent on reports and not necessarily on merit or qualifications. We need to have a strong backbone and guts to oppose mindless orders. One must serve with dignity and honour and maintain self-esteem.

Dignity & Honour

I have this quote from Shakespeare, which lies in front of me:

> My honour is my life, both grew in one
> Take honour from me and my life is done.

Of course, the worst humiliation you can face in the armed forces is to be branded a "coward" in battle. You cannot buy dignity and honour later. Going by my Regimental History, I respect Tally and Tiger Behl, the silent witnesses in Namka Chu, for their valour that went past unnoticed. Some others did not distinguish themselves, so well. The fog of war is sometimes responsible for covering up actions, both of valour and cowardice. The godly virtues of dignity and honour are so well embedded in me by my regiment, that it would be impossible to desert in the face of the enemy unless you succumb to your base instincts. Things cannot get worse than cowardice!

I have found these age-old concepts of Dignity and Honour to be enormously helpful in learning how to conduct myself professionally and socially in civil life also. I feel regardless of who you are, what organisation you belonged to and what your achievements were, you deserve to be treated with dignity and honour. I felt motivated to achieve what looked like a very daunting task, in the worst of times in Gujarat. I made sure my subordinates too, were treated with Dignity and Honour. Honour is built on the dignity that an individual should adhere to, the word *izzat* sums up everything. This word did function to keep my conduct above board to maintain my honour. When acting in an honourable manner, I treated my men with the same dignity and respect and did my best to fulfil what the organisation had ordained me to do.

Now coming to my tryst with Dignity and Honour (or *izzat* for me) in the Army, these are priceless and sacrosanct. It was a privilege to hold a commission in the Indian Army and I understood, accepted and fulfilled all the obligations and commitments expected of me. I learnt to stand on my feet and be judged on my merit based on what the superiors thought of me. I understood to uphold the values of Dignity with *izzat* instilled in me. The tryst would be truly redeemed with the restoration of self-esteem and *sharafat* which are ingrained in our Indian culture of honour and integrity. No organisation in this country gives you so much Dignity and Honour as the Indian Army even after retirement. It is rather surprising that the organisation, using its full powers, chose to deprive me of my Dignity and Honour by posting me to inconsequential appointments, instead of utilizing my services, where both the service and myself could benefit.

Art of Command

What I learnt from Tally and Sushil Mathur is that you must give your subordinates more than what you can get out of them. There should be no reason to deprive anyone of anything especially career prospects, livelihood and leave. Truthfulness and dependability are as important as valour in battle. The element of trust in all relationships is crucial. Be accessible to your men, let there be no communication gaps. I have always accepted that a good soldier is made of mindful obedience and not mindless obedience. You can afford to disagree with your seniors but do not become disagreeable.

Today's Army is much better (on paper) than what it has been in my service. The art of command states that it is not the exclusive preserve of a privileged few senior officers. Sometimes, senior officers' authority trumps logic and accuracy because original research for them is a big "no-no". Even now, there are no born commanders but with experience, new commanders can be groomed with superior qualities. These are trust, professional ethics, devotion to duty before self, compassion and care of the men entrusted to you. In my entire service career, the professional ethics I learnt from my seniors, were unquestionable. Even the parchment commission signed by President Radhakrishnan addressed to me, lays importance on ethical character values, and states: "I, reposing special trust and confidence in your fidelity, courage and good conduct, do by these presents constitute and appoint you, Dinesh Mathur to be 2nd Lieutenant in the Indian Army from the 30th day of June Nineteen Hundred and Sixty-three.

Sycophancy

This ingrained quality is now slowly but surely pervading in all aspects of Army life, at the cost of moral courage. This is because our senior officers in the "No mistake" syndrome are averse to hearing anything other than hunky-dory. We have to be ruthless against sycophancy before it becomes an invitation to disaster in the form of sustained and avoidable mediocrity. There is also a need to place more reliance on demonstrated verifiable professional competence rather than on "spoken reputation" only. If we have a good look at the career profile of our senior ranks, most of them are from the select lot of ADCs, Dy MAs/MAs to senior officers. There have been instances of sycophantic behaviour established which prompted Gen. Sunderji to write a DO letter to all officers in 1986 to guard against such tendencies. Things have only got worse now with personal biases and opinions, regional clannishness, the colour of the lanyard and regimental affiliations. Last but not the least, I can speak about myself, that I avoided hitching my wagon to the rising stars of the moment. in deference to the advice of some of my worthy seniors.

Loyalty & Integrity

I have always followed the mantra below:

"An ounce of loyalty is better than a ton of cleverness. If you belong to an institution, speak well of it. If you want to damn, get out and damn to your heart's content. A strong wind will, one day, blow you off and you'll never know the reason why".

Anonymous

Loyalty is a two-way street. When you expect unstinted loyalty from your men, they too expect you to be loyal to them. In other words, their lives in battle, career interests, rights and privileges need to be protected by you in return for what they give you by way of placing their lives in your hands and carrying out your orders.

Loyalty to the organisation is different from individual loyalty to the superior officer. Where there is a conflict between individual and organisation loyalty, I would rather go for loyalty to the organisation, even if it means sacrificing my self-interests. The very fact that I did not choose to adopt the route followed by some of my colleagues to go to court indicates my unstinted loyalty to the organisation. As a Brigade commander, I looked for loyalty to the country, the organisation and the brigade/unit rather than to me personally. Integrity again is quantified along with loyalty. People who remain within their privileges, are fair, compassionate and care about the values, beliefs and feelings of others fit into the integrity of the highest order. People who flaunt perks and privileges, cannot rise above prejudices/personal biases and opinions, regional and regimental affiliations usually fail the integrity test. The quantification of this quality for ease of computerization is wayward as you can either possess this attribute or not, and nothing midway.

Strategic/Tactical Wisdom

Contrary to popular belief, strategic/tactical wisdom is not intrinsic to the human mind. There are no born strategists/tacticians. Brilliant strategists acquired these traits by learning and practice. It is all a question of mental faculties; some officers develop these in service and contribute to the organisation while in some, they remain stunted even while rising to the ranks of Generals. It is these latter gentlemen who are parochial, petty-minded, unsure of themselves, vindictive and always looking for ways to get ahead with props because they are under-confident to deliver the goods themselves. Unfortunately, there is also a new trend. The emerging breed of "die-hard" pseudo professionals feel that strategic concepts were their exclusive preserve. Others, even those who had exposures in high altitude, counter-insurgency areas and deserts cannot claim to speak/express opinions because they had not foot-slogged enough. What could be a game-changer now is the creation of the organisational environment in which fresh ideas/out of the box thinking is encouraged. What would become inevitable then, is that the entire business of war is handed over to the right brand of professionals.

Nam, namak aur nishan

This ethos inculcated in the 17 Para Field Regiment formed the basis of my life in the armed forces. We were taught that the reputation of the country and the Regiment mattered first. Next, was the fidelity of the salt. (*namak*) partaken by us, like *amrit* for the Sikhs. Lastly, the colours of the Regiment (our guns) must never be allowed to fall into enemy hands even if it means your sacrifice in the process. All these qualities are enshrined in our constitution and apply to all citizens of our country also, but who cares. No better example of valour, if I take the names of Harjit Talwar and Amarjit Behl in the battle of Namka Chu in 1962. The retrieval of the lost guns of 1962, much later, shows the indomitable spirit of the Regiment.

Befittingly, on retirement, my complete set of uniforms including green SD and blue patrols with my medals were presented to my regimental quarter guard. The physical manifestation of *naam, namak, nishan* (reputation, fidelity, flag/standard), is my uniform. I take pride in calling myself a double winger, a paratrooper and an aviator and each of my uniforms are born of acts of bravery and sacrifice in the line of duty, recognized or otherwise, I couldn't care less.

Moral Courage

This critical factor in our service career is very intrinsic in its value, despite the changes in rank and appointment. While physical courage is an instinctive reaction, moral courage is a different kind of courage. It is more deliberate and calculated to stand up for your belief in what is right, particularly when it is contrary to what your seniors believe is right. It is very individual based and when exercised by senior officers, does motivate the juniors to do things likewise. Though the caveat is that the senior must set the example for junior to emulate, what happens is that at lower ranks we pontificate, when we reach the higher ranks, we forget to practice what we preached earlier. Like my mentors, in my command of both Brigades and as the independent Deputy Director General of the DSC, I practised what I preached.

If all seniors possess moral courage in ample measure, the risk to the career down the line would diminish. Being an infectious commodity, it would be the accepted norm that everyone accepts. The existing environment frowns upon such displays of moral courage which are at variance with what the next senior has propagated. Therefore, it surmises that higher the rank, greater the need for moral courage. Though this quality is sometimes inborn, it is also cultivated by upbringings in good units, which produce leaders who display good personal examples.

The Working of the Military Secretary's Branch

Before 1969, the MS Branch worked on the age-old system of qualitative assessment which was devoid of quantification, as it exists today. The selection process by and large was fair, representations against ACRs were very few and the recourse to legal proceedings was even less. The reporting in ACRs was brutally honest and frank. The reporting officers had the guts (moral courage) to look the ratee straight in his eyes and call a spade a spade. Most officers aspired to command their *paltans* and anything above was considered a bonus. There has always been the more aspiring and career conscious, or if you wish to call them ambitious officers, with expectations/desires to climb the professional ladder. Nothing wrong, they had to work hard for it. This trait has become very apparent from the rank of Brigadier upwards, which itself is a healthy sign.

After 1969, the MS Branch implemented the computerized system of the evaluation of the officer's performance and potential based on a 9-point rating scale. A pen picture and the recommendations for promotion and future employment were added to the bare numerical skeleton, to give it a complete personality. I can emphatically state that all policies evolved were in the larger interests of the organisation while keeping individuals interests also in mind. Ideally, the assessment of any ratee's performance can be best judged during actual combat, where results would speak for themselves. The closest we can get to combat conditions are in the low-intensity conflicts in the J&K and the NE. In all fairness, a Commanding Officer in high altitude areas must have some incentive added for the degree of difficulty, over his peers in peace stations. Likewise, majors serving under combat conditions on the Siachen Glacier must receive some credit over those serving in Central India. All these issues had been nicely resolved by the system and one didn't have to look back. The efficient manner in which the appraisals, selection/promotions system, postings and cadre reviews are handled has been rightly acknowledged by the civil services, police forces and even the Tata Consultancy Services. Some of our tried-out processes have found favour in these organisations and adopted them with suitable modifications. The MS Branch model has been designed to be the fine-tuned structure, manned by highly professional and competent officers. These carefully selected officers with a strong moral fibre and above-board integrity, also possess a great sense of dedication. Over the years, they had evolved clear cut policies capable of execution. bringing in its wake, maximum satisfaction levels.

In a democracy, socio-political issues will first impact the most effective and cohesive institutions like the armed forces. The demands for cost-cutting on the Chiefs to reduce flab, cadre reviews and the like are nothing new. Thus, every Chief is faced with this predicament as well as some unresolved problems left behind by the previous incumbent. So, in the best of intentions, an attempt is made to find yet another formula that would improve the credibility and also, be in the best interests of the organisation. Where officer cadre is concerned, the functioning of the MS Branch straightaway comes into focus. In my opinion, the problem per se does not lie with this carefully designed, time tested and robust system. The bigger malaise which has led to the state as it exists now could be summarized as follows:

- There is always an ongoing debate on whether the open or closed system for ACRs is good or is there something better than this? It is not only the debate alone that is harmful but also the vacillation in the policy. The closed system has been tried out at least twice. All I can say is that the closed system had engendered a new breed of higher reporting officers, lacking the moral courage and guts to face the officer, to show him his actual performance. They further resorted to couch the ACR in such terms that it cannot be called adverse and yet the grades and the recommendations were so lukewarm that the ratee's career stood no chance in the comparative merit. The closed system created more problems than it could solve, as it became a tool in the hands of unscrupulous initiating officers to protect their turf. For very good reasons, we are now back to the open system as the damage done by the closed system has been realized. Let's hope, this closes the chapter of closed systems, once and for all.

- The substitution of the well-tried out 5-point rating scale for the Brigadiers and above by the 9-point rating scale also defies logic. This again is tantamount to creating a situation where the reporting officers have discretionary powers of using a higher gradation for those they want to promote and a lower one for those they don't. Technically, it again cannot be called adverse but lukewarm all the same. What was wrong with the good old 5-point rating scale to warrant this change?

- The severe dilution of the brutally frank and factual assessment norms in ACRs of the past era has given way to inflated reporting, more by the fears of complaints. By rating every officer above average or outstanding has overburdened the system. There is also an added fear for the ratee that honest & strict assessments project a distorted image of running an "unhappy team" to superior officers. We, as officers holding responsible appointments, have become increasingly parochial, biased and vindictive. We have been poor examples for our juniors to follow. While pontificating ethical values at lower ranks, when we reach the top, we tend to brush these aside for our petty interests. To prevent masking of performance, it would be worthwhile to introduce a Ratee

Achievement Chart, as an Appendix to the ACR to be completed by the ratee, to be seen by all reporting officers in the chain. Sometimes, we need to highlight our achievements which may go past unnoticed inadvertently or otherwise.

- The misplaced sense of loyalty to one's arm or service is fast overtaking the overall interests of the organisation. This has led to a new "tribal" culture exacerbated at times by common bonds of old school ties, clannishness/regionalism and being fair selectively, only to those we have had the opportunity to serve with earlier. Subjectivity in reporting induced by the relationships or proximity to senior officers from the same regiment, caste or regional denomination is generally taken care of, by the system. The need exists to restore the old system of red tabs (now could be star ranks) not belonging to any arm/service, with only IA transcribed after their names. The wearing of colourful lanyards, pouches and hats could be confined to respective regimental functions only. Added to this, the case of conflict of interests came to the fore, when aspiring Colonels of the Regiments inflate the assessments of their regimental COs, in a quid pro quo, to earn the coveted position. The selective and unilateral grant of waivers and redressals by senior officers in the hierarchy as special favours or exceptions is basically to circumvent the well-known selection process.

- The creation of separate streams for command and staff (only) for Brigadiers and above had also been tried out before and shelved. The creation was necessitated more on the dictates of expediency rather than on efficiency, as it was believed that the concept, though elitist, was a halfhearted measure. It had only succeeded in creating three distinct categories amongst officers. One, the favoured command "charm" stream, two, those left outside as the "supplementary" staff stream, and those remaining in their respective arms & services appointments, awaiting empanelment into staff stream. Foreign armies too, have realized, "Where and how, was the much-vaunted thinking brains of the army to be applied?" There have been no wars for the last three decades for our commanders to gain vital operational experience, to execute doctrines. At best, there is only a low-intensity conflict to substitute a full-blown war. Be that as it may, now that the start has been made in the creation of the full-fledged command and staff streams, let there be no reversion/vacillation again. In the "closed class exclusivity" of the command stream, we need to guard against the possibility of engendering commanders with insufficient staff exposure and in the staff stream, of staff officers with no exposure to command functions. We could now consider the introduction of a purely specialist General Staff Course in the War College Mhow, based on an open written examination (like Staff College Entrance) for outstanding Colonels/Brigadiers for the eventual empanelment into the General Staff. The course modalities including the stiff selection norms, course content and duration could be worked out under Indian conditions, rather than replicate the course run by the General Staff Academy in the foreign armies. The selected officers could be groomed for command appointments for providing continuity in strategic planning at the national level, experience and expertise, so vital for the direction of military operations. In this way, we avoid on the job training before an officer learns the ropes in military operations/intelligence.

Now coming to the MS Branch and its "in house" remedial measures to curb subjectivity in reporting. Thankfully, these actions to protect the career interests of the officer have a universal acceptance. The sections dealing with cases of deflated/inflated reports should continue their task of effacing the report deflated/inflated as hitherto fore. What could be considered as a long-term measure for the removal of this malaise is the follow-up action against the defaulters, who have so far gone scot-free. Where the default. is unintentional, say technical reasons, (inadequate knowledge, infrequent or intermittent personal contact) a chance to correct their assessment could be given to the reporting officer. Where the default. is deliberate, a show-cause notice be given to the defaulting reporting officer and the effacement, inflated/deflated, made by the MS Branch. Three repeated defaults should debar a reporting officer from these duties and endorsements made in his dossier for life. Coupled with the deflated/inflated report action, in all fairness, the ratee could also be informed that such an action has been taken to clean up his report.

The MS Branch also takes "in house" remedial actions to provide relief to ratees when any award of censure or counselling is administered, without a show-cause notice. These remedial actions need to be applied universally. If the award itself is against justice and fair play, then why empower a select few in the hierarchy to commit the same mistakes? The complete removal of such an award would enhance the transparency, credibility and image of the MS Branch.

At present, three looks are given to each officer for promotion to the next higher rank. This has contributed to the dilution of standards and is not in the interests of the organisation. If we reduce the number of looks to two only, it would be more in the interests of the organisation. I don't think a radical change can take place in the career profile to qualify for the third look.

Some of the promotion policies followed in the quantification of reports was based on the present to previous merit ratio of 70:30. The performance in the last two/three reports should have more importance attached to it. When we do away with the previous merit altogether, the past performance on professional courses, gallantry awards, field service is ignored and this serves as a disincentive for career courses like HC and HDMC. These policies must be spelt. out in detail and in advance. The system of communicating to the ratee, his OAP vis a vis the batch OAP could continue. This system had worked quite well for almost three decades till the aberrations started creeping in. The recourse to tampering with well-tried out policies to sort out short term problems and the circumvention of the well laid down processes/norms arbitrarily, has not gone off well. It would be in the interests of the organisation to revert to the old tried out system or somewhere close to it. As an added safeguard, we need to evolve a code of conduct, to establish an environment of ethical visibility and continuity of policies by laying them down in writing. The US Army Manual FM 22-103 "Professional Ethics at Senior Levels", could provide the framework.

MS Branch policies have far-reaching consequences and deserve a longer shelf life. The officer holding the appointment of the Military Secretary is also answerable to the entire officer cadre of the Indian Army and must never succumb to pressures by anyone in the hierarchy or outside it. To undergo the necessary transformation in this decade, the MS Branch needs to carry out a comprehensive review of all its officer cadre management policies, for bringing about qualitative changes in transparency in its functioning. We need to study the policies of various foreign armies, purely for comparison and adaptation of strong points under the Indian environment. We also need to involve the stakeholders in the policy formulation, i.e., the officers from the field formations. Therefore, a study group drawing officers from the various field formations and the IDSA and CDM could carry out an in-depth analysis of the organisational effectiveness, review of existing management policies for selection for promotions, career progression, career courses and appointments, duration of tenures and miscellaneous aspects, review upgradations in cadre review (even suggest those requiring down gradations) and suggest overall improvements in the functioning of the MS Branch. The study could also bring in fresh minds from leading human resources management companies like the TCS and L&T. Despite reading some of the indictments of the MS Branch by the Armed Forces Tribunals, I feel it is still the best bet for managing this huge officer cadre (50k) of the Indian Army.

Quest for Equivalence with Bureaucracy

In any democracy, the executive decisions are implemented by the civil servants, indirectly implying that the civil authority is supreme. We from the armed forces cannot be equated with any other service. Keeping in mind the service conditions, making the career attractive and the early retirement to maintain a young profile, a military edge was given right from independence onwards. Our distinguished Chiefs like Gen. Thimayya and FM Manekshaw maintained that we were a special class by themselves and needed to be treated as such in matters of pay and perks. It is a pity now, the moment an officer gets posted as a Maj. General and above in Army HQ or attends the NDC course with the civil services officers, he aspires to look for equivalence with the IAS.

Gunners and General Cadre

Before my commissioning, I had heard of arms and services in our army. Arms were Infantry, Armour, Artillery, Engineers and Signals. There were support services like ASC, Ordnance, EME and others. Artillery, engineers and signals were the supporting arms. This was later changed to combat arms and combat support arms. Nobody at IMA told us at the time of opting for our choice of arms, that this distinction exists. There were some unofficial changes introduced in the aftermath of the Henderson Brooks Committee Report regarding officers from the services not being considered for higher command of formations for various reasons. This restriction did not apply to officers from supporting arms and till 1971 there was no such thing as a general cadre. As a gunner, we are integrated as forward observation officers with the infantry which in some cases provides an opportunity to command an infantry company in a war as it happened in my case. I had the opportunity thrust on me, of assuming command of C Company 2 Para after the company commander Lt. BR Parab was killed during the night attack on Ichchogil Canal on 16 Sep 1965. There have also been many instances where artillery OPs have been killed while leading troops in an attack. To say that you all do not face the danger and privations as the infantry is taking a step back in contemporary warfare.

Being a thoroughbred gunner who fought his way into the Artillery even in IMA Dehradun, I had been taught to maintain the highest regimental standards throughout my service and had served with true regimental spirit and honour. Regimentation has been closest to my heart and I had promoted the esprit-de-corps both as a regimental and a Brigade Commander. Being brought up throughout the Para Brigade environment, we learnt to think 'out of the box' and contribute to the organisation without fear or dread. We need to remember that you have to perform far better than your peers in the Infantry and other arms, this commences from the first all arms course you attend.

Why did we accept the General Cadre in the first place? By sending out our best officers to the General Cadre, have we not diluted standards in our Arty Brigades.? Gunners traditionally display higher standards of professionalism, spectacular capabilities and the ability to bring about the wanton destruction of will, spirit and morale of any enemy. This was even acknowledged by the COAS after the Kargil war 1999. There is a need for dispassionate analysis of the future battlefields where we are considering the employment of Integrated Battle Groups under a corps and doing away with all division HQs including, of course, in the new Arty divisions. Is it not a fact that fire planning is a supported arm responsibility? So, to make this concept work, is it not possible to give the experience of Arty Brigade command to selected infantry and armour officers? What is so technical about Arty Brigades, to make it an exclusive preserve for gunners? In the era of integrated battle groups, artillery commanders should also have the flexibility to accept infantry or armour units in the composite battle group and perform the same task. Likewise, some artillery units could be allotted permanently to the integrated battle groups for better flexibility. Modalities could be worked out and the concept is validated on the ground. Integrated battle groups with artillery, engineers and signals back up are like mini divisions, after shedding the intermediate link. Likewise, a logistics brigade, with five or six logistic modules to support the integrated Brigades could also be thought of. This may sound a bit revolutionary but a start can be made with the placing of a highly qualified gunner Deputy Commander in those composite artillery Brigades commanded by infantry or armour officers. The recourse to more self-propelled artillery and its bold and audacious use, direct firing by field guns called forward, would optimize the combat power of the battle groups and indirectly enhance the image of artillery.

Concept of Artillery Support in Future Operations

We have perfected the outdated Russian concepts of World War II in the artillery wherein massed fire distribution technique is accepted as the panacea to all problems of neutralization of enemy defences by fire assaults. We accept that area neutralization can be temporary and lasting (not permanent) depending upon the quantity of ammunition and the duration of fire assaults. If we have a 155 mm indigenous regiment firing one round gunfire rate normal (1) for one minute, one round @ Rs 1 lakh, it would cost Rs 18 lakhs. The cost of neutralization of one sq km objective area for a two-up Brigade attack, which also is for 30 minutes duration, by six medium regiments (100 guns concept) would require a colossal amount of ammunition hence at a massive cost to the exchequer (Rs 32.40 crores).

Success in future wars will ultimately cover a vast spectrum of conflict with increased emphasis on information and cyber warfare with force multipliers like unmanned aerial vehicles especially drones, EM spectrum and satellite imagery. This would form part of all the battle groups, regardless of its composition, against our two adversaries on the Northern borders, we are likely to be confronted with heavily fortified and cemented sangar type defences which would require to be softened up before the physical assault. by infantry all arms team. Against that we would be better advised to go in for long-range direct firing or self-propelled guns with smart precision/laser-guided top attack Krasnopol type ammunition to replace the artillery guns of today. The latest surveillance and target acquisition mean including UAVs must also be co-opted. With the advent of swarm technology, multiple targets seeking precision-guided drones either fired from a gun or released from a standoff aircraft would precede the physical assault. by infantry/armour. The components of air defence, engineers and signal EW groups would continue to be grouped with them. In the mountains, as it happened in Kargil 1999, it would be normal for guns, both self-propelled and towed to move up to deliver direct fire assaults on fortified positions. The key lies not in tactical nuclear weapons or Agni, or Prithvi or Brahmos but reliance on cost-effective technology. A mix of armed drones fired by a gun or released from an aircraft, multi-barreled launchers, missiles and guns could decimate the objective before infantry or armour assaults go in. Just don't think, covering fire and move is the only basis of tactics today. This fixed mindset must go, sooner the better.

With the enemies knocking at our Northern and NE borders today, it would be prudent to avoid distinctions between the two types of Brigades and go flat out in protecting/defending one's turf. Artillery Brigades are performing well in low-intensity conflicts without the use of gun support. Now is the time to rise above such man-made differences and discard them for something better. Do you think you need a general cadre when the distinction between Brigades is removed, once and for all? Better to get rid of the distinction and have a fresh rethink on artillery support to promote inter arms cohesion.

Contributions to Various Publications

I am reminded of my friend, a serving officer whose wife exhorted him that he had to write an article for a military journal because all his coursemates have done so. In her wisdom, she averred that your professional standing and competence were always on display and a status symbol for a lifetime. Hot topics like Why the Army must have an Aviation Corps, Employment of Attack Helicopters, Employment of Independent Light Batteries and Strike Corps operations were the current topics then. When the friend explained the quandary, he was in, I told my friend not to worry about all this because the top-down structure of the Indian Army, does not encourage all functionaries in the chain of command, to pen down their military thoughts, and rejects them for reasons of security. As it is, most field commanders abhor anything written, and tend to label good ideas appearing on paper, as the works of paper tigers. Instead, ARTRAC and the vast array of training centres/institutions such as the DSSC & War College are vested with the sole responsibility to write manuals and papers. When these are approved in Army Commanders Conference, it is only then, they become accepted doctrines. Sometimes back, writing specialists or gladiators as they came to be known, were those who qualified on courses abroad. They are also commissioned to reproduce foreign army manuals under Indian conditions, but this was possible only if he had managed to smuggle out their classified army doctrines. Gladiators, being thoroughly indoctrinated by the foreign academia richly endowed with the gift of the gab and good connections with the top brass, often display their new-found prowess, with faithful reproductions of what you call today, the cut-paste jobs. The system has neither the time nor the patience to tap more on the experience of battle-tested soldiers. So, I told my friend to relax, tell his wife not to worry and forget it.

Analysing further, our hierarchical pattern of functioning does little to encourage critical thinking or thinking 'out of the box'. Most of the doctrines and tactical concepts that emerge are from the after-action reports and the analysis of the last war. There is a wide gap between the professed desire and what happens, as there is no credit for innovation and adaptation. Field commanders, today, from Brigades upwards are too busy punching tickets to surge ahead. Our critical thinkers are branded mavericks and are the first ones to be eliminated. A suitable climate just does not exist for critical thinking skills and most Brigade Commanders only wish to know the fads of their divisional and corps commanders. Our senior commanders also advocate the concept that tactics are the exclusive preserve of senior-most officer present whose tactical thoughts, if propounded earlier, must be prominently displayed on sand models/training rooms giving rise to the troubling assumption that, "Rule 1. The Commander is always right. Rule 2. If he is not right, Rule 1 applies". The mere fact that not one new tactical thought has germinated in our Army in the last fifty years is should send a chill up the spines of the powers that be. What has contributed to this poverty of thought is never going to be analysed by the top brass of our Army.

The only time I felt. free to write about my stint as Col. GS Coord DSSC Wellington was when I had to write scripts for the Commandant on current doctrinal issues which meant injection of new ideas and not hackneyed themes. Both Generals I wrote for, would heckle me if I wrote something unrealistic or impractical. When the US Army War College team came to give us a presentation on 'The Airland Battle' I had to slog for days to get the basics myself and then reverse engineer/adapt it to the Indian battlefield scenario, so that the Commandant could establish the tie-up for the presenters. I remember the US team General commenting that your Commandant had already covered their subject so well that he had nothing left to speak. There were more occasions when the Commandant spoke, like while introducing a subject of guest speakers or presentations or even while summing up all important exercises and wargames. Later, during my tenure as the Dy Commander of an Infantry Brigade, every operational/non-operational paper/plans/ presentation was prepared by me and the only credit my Brigade Commander gave me, was in saying, "When you have a Dy Commander so highly qualified, why should I work"

Later during my command of the Arty Brigade, the SOP written by my team for the Security of Cantonments is still valid as a master document in Western Command, which is open for verification. There was so much to learn from the corps wargames prepared by me under the guidance of our Corps Commander. I was fortunate to command an Infantry Brigade in semi-desert terrain and have put my experiences down in writing a training note on Forward Zone Battle forming part of the corps doctrine in my time. After retirement, I have made it a point to attend a selected lecture on national security at USI, CLAWS and ICWA. ICWA had also offered a fellowship for a doctorate on Sino Indian border Dispute for three years but I thought, enough was enough. I did try to pen down some of my thoughts but found it very difficult. to penetrate the glass ceiling of established military analysts. Try hard as you may, every newspaper editor has contacts with the upper echelons of power in the armed forces and civil services. They keep known people on their payroll who are already commissioned to write on contemporary subjects. Many of my articles were rejected on grounds of "too many articles received on the same subject or too long or condense it to 1500 words and resubmit. In some cases, my articles are published by papers carrying my ideas but under a different name, cases of clear plagiarism, which is so difficult. to prove. I have accepted this with a smile and have decided to voice my opinion selectively on national security matters unmindful of whether anyone listens to me or not. Most of my analysis is coming out true. I hope to review national security matters being discussed in the media, in our overall core interests. I have attended many seminars/interactions with some leading think tanks like the Institute of Defence and Strategic Studies Singapore, University of Queensland, RPI New York, Washington State University and Georgia State University who have respected my views. My unstinted loyalty and support to the country's resurgence and its armed forces would continue. Some of my contributions, written over some time, after retirement as discussed in the articles which follow.

Kutch Revisited

Published: August 2001

Our military special carrying 2 Para Battalion group including 49 Para Field Battery moved on 'white hot' priority to Ahmedabad and further, on 9th April 1965. Finding ourselves parked inside a railway siding at Gandhi Dham, early next morning, our move under Maj. Prem Chandra commenced almost immediately thereafter. Our destination was the gateway to Rann, Khavda. Rann of Kutch lay just six km north of it. Having set up a tented camp for the night, mess established with Krishna More to serve us drinks before the hurried meal we retired for the night. Early next morning, BC and the two OPs Bunny Khanna and the newcomer Mehandru were briefed by CO 2 Para for the impending task. OP Khanna was staying back as the BK to tie up the local administration.

We were raring to go into action for Operation Kabaddi.

Khavda, a sleepy oasis of hundred-odd houses made of mud-brick with thatched roofs, four or five sweet water wells and some trees, which provided shade, lay on the dust track to the Rann. Few good houses that existed were promptly requisitioned by us and the shady area cordoned off for the battalion headquarters

and the helipad. Water was drawn from camel operated Persian wheels. Water pumps and electricity weren't heard of. Not surprising, our portable water pumps were seen by the locals as curios and treated as veritable shrines for visits.

Tall bearded, in their traditional attire donning tall turbans Kutchi menfolk greeted you wherever you went. Women in colourful dresses carrying babes in arms, heavily bedecked with silver jewellery from heads to ankles. Both locals and the Army learnt to cohabit peacefully, without incidents, despite sharing water points, rest areas and the same animals for load carriage. We also realized that it is fun living in tents. But for a few days only. Briefings after briefings followed, we endured them all.

The word "Rann" is derived from Sanskrit "Irina" which means salt. waste. Locals believe Rann was the raised portion of the sea bed and navigable lake during Alexander's time in 325 BC. Rann is now a vast salt. encrusted wasteland. Higher pieces of rocky ground called "Bets" also exist, in which luscious scrub like grass grows in abundance. We loved driving jeeps on the Rann, at speeds unimaginable those days. We also hated driving one behind the other in convoys, at "camel speeds" with fine salted dust blowing into your eyes. Absence of landmarks, only quarter-inch maps available, coupled with harrowing tales from those getting lost, imposed a caution on our journey to the next halt, Mori Bet. Reaching late in the evening, we were off to our action stations at Biar Bet and Point 84. By the end of April 1965, Pakistan's test war in the Rann was over, long before it was even fought. What a disappointment!! We now had to fight another enemy. Boredom.

Watching the sunrise in the early morning chill and quietude in the Rann can be bracing. Ample time to admire the fauna as well. Herds of graceful chinkaras, wild asses and rabbits abound in these areas. Many had seen the Army for the first time and did not feel threatened. As for the birds, Gujarat is India's only known flamingo breeding ground and is a staging area for the "endangered migratory lesser flamingo flying vast distances to destinations northwest Africa. This graceful avian being, whose name means "flame-coloured", the pink flamingo species are deeply vibrant beauties. Ornithologists the world overcome to study their behaviour, habitats, foraging activities and mating displays. The salt. marshes attract flocks of these pink birds flying in the blue skies from October to June every year. The flamingos remind me of life's mysterious beauty and their excited calls and intricate dances earn them the honour of Gujarat State Bird. Vipers and scorpions were also in plenty. If one was not careful while putting on your boots, you could be in for a surprise.

Locals informed me that in the fifties, nine wild asses were trapped and sent to Saharanpur for breeding mules for the Army. Being very stubborn cousins and propagators of brahmacharya, they chose not to multiply in custody and died unmourned with unblemished characters and gave no chance to the Army. This experiment has not been tried again and the wild asses population has dwindled to a bare 700 now.

Never in my life did I see so many camels of all shapes, sizes and hues. A good number had saddles fitted with leather *mashaks* or water carriers. Kutchis indulge in camel yarns which are impossible to believe. Newborn baby camels arrive standing and follow their mother long distances within two hours of their births. Most of us believe in the phrase "as stubborn as a mule". I can say with some experience that, in stubbornness, camels beat a mule hollow!!

During afternoons, if you chose to drive instead of a siesta, you could see mirages all over. The fly population here by day proliferates dramatically and disappears at night. It was a common sight to see people lunch inside mosquito nets. Melville woke up after a siesta in the afternoon inside a sand dune. Yes, inside a sand dune, that's what he told the BC. 11 Field party at Vigokot was another great affair. Imagine climbing on top of their Officers Mess shelter to do para roles. Both Harry Srinivasan and Butch agreed that our wild youngsters were to blame for breaking the shelter into pieces.

Flaming red sunsets at 7.45 pm, again are a sight to watch every evening. Wind speeds of 15-20 knots kept the evenings very pleasant when we dined together in our battery mess. Someone tried his hand at parasailing, using a plywood skid board hoisted by a parachute and ended up breaking his femurs.

Bittoo Gill's promotion party on 30 June 65 was an unforgettable affair. Lightning accompanied by a squall warning as predicted was delightfully ignored as we concentrated more on backslapping, camaraderie and dirty jokes. Camels braying and running helter-skelter was too insignificant to notice. With happiness all over, the gala evening did not last long. A sudden cloud burst followed and, in a few minutes, the Rann was a vast expanse of water with us floating inside. It seems, when moist winds blow from the sea during May- June, their moisture got absorbed by the hygroscopic salts of the Rann. Water thus formed, had oozed and collected below earth's strata. Consequently, the entire Rann had got filled with saline water in two or three days. Now augmented by the rain, the incoming waves from the Arabian sea and the freshwater drained out by the local Luni River, wreaked havoc. It was like being shipwrecked!!

OPK and I perched on bets, located our submerged tents, jeeps and trailers with long camouflage net poles in good time. Next problem was to move these to the bet. Fishing for own belongings inside bunkers followed. Some had to be given up as bad losses, like my Sony transistor. Ropes and tow chains helped us recover vehicles but could not be started. It was well past midnight and a few hours nap would help, we thought. The following morning found us looking skywards as our Commander Brig. Nambiar in an MI4 helicopter spotted me for a supply drop. We stood on the bonnets of the vehicle, slapping our empty tummies in an SOS. Down came a gunny bag containing some puffed rice, KitKat chocolates, kraft cheese and a jerrican of drinking water. Propelled into action by this manna from the skies, we now turned our attention to our vehicles and succeeded in recovering two of them. Others two were started and driving back to the headquarters, in this condition was a task by itself. After an enforced halt. at Khavda. We left for Bhuj, the next day.

At Bhuj, we got the much-needed respite in our tented camp near the Fort. Shopping in Bhuj town was possible only on weekends. Local shopkeepers accepted cheques without any fears. Kutchi silver jewellery being very exquisite and cheap was extremely popular and in demand. Someone informed me that smuggled gold was also available but that did not bother us. We did see a few single storey concrete buildings such as the District Collector Coelho's office, two good cinema halls, a civil hospital and some private houses. Besides this, the two of Maharao's palaces were too heavily guarded for anyone to enter. The majority of the construction was single-storey stone construction. We attended a nice dinner hosted by Neeru Hegde's cousins. We visited Mandvi and Kandla, which had very primitive port facilities those days. Our BC Prem, no shikari like Jagga, managed to kill a partridge with the windscreen of his jeep. Anjar, Bhachau and Rapar, my adopted villages today. were big mud-brick villages where we halted once on our long convoy drive. By now the trains were laid out at Gandhidham for us to move back to the sweltering heat of Agra in mid-July 1965, ending our brief sojourn in the Rann.

Development activities in the Rann and the discovery of Dhola Veera, an Indus Valley equivalent of Harappa in India, by the Archaeological Survey of India in 1992 added to the interest now being taken. Ambitious efforts to reclaim the Rann from the Arabian Sea, on the lines of what Israel and the Netherlands have done by treating the hygroscopic soil with chemicals is laudatory. Salt is the main product and it is believed that once the Rann is flushed of the insoluble salts, it would produce tons of agricultural products as well. Development projects, construction work and electrification have now gone on for years, despite being in seismic zone 5. The perceived threat from Pakistan hastened all construction activities in the district, regardless of mother nature's warnings. Soon, the mud bricks were replaced by multi-storey structures, cantonment and the existing airfield improved to take on IAF fighters. All caution in construction was thrown to the winds.

For me, the turn of events in the last 36 years has taken a full revolution. I was back to Bhuj, again on the same date, 9 April 2001 as Director FICCI CARE Gujarat Rehabilitation Project, which was a coincidence. With the daunting task of reconstructing 10,000 houses in the three talukas, facing me. I have no doubts that will be met by my team with all the resources at my command. All this is due to my previous Kutch connection. It would be on the same lines as what my fine Regiment did in April- July 1965. Now I have the finest partnership of this millennium backing us, the world's biggest NGO CARE and the finest corporate body FICCI. With the community's help and cooperation, we hope to bring joy and happiness to the lives of Kutchis again.

Chinese Perceptions on Border Territorial Disputes and Their Relevance in Indian Context

Published: June 2008

Introduction.

China has common land frontiers with North Korea, Russia, Kazakhstan, Kirgizstan, Tajikistan, Mongolia, Afghanistan, Pakistan, India, Nepal, Bhutan, Myanmar, Vietnam and Laos. Small wonder that the Communists, on coming to power in 1949, recorded 119 border problems with its neighbours. Against India, what was essentially a semi ratified Indo Tibetan border problem, became a full-fledged Sino Indian border dispute. China's insistence on restoring its historic frontiers has played an important role in spelling out its national interests in today's environment, where geopolitics tempered with dynamic and pragmatic concepts is more relevant than historical claims. What is worrisome now is whether China's national reunification program would override other factors such as its international image, economic growth and domestic political & cultural development. China's recent enhancement of its military capabilities, unambiguous claim over Arunachal Pradesh & Aksai Chin, transgressions across the line of actual control and scant regard for the international border (McMahon line) while professing friendship cooperation and unhindered trade with India, are signs which can only be ignored at our peril.

Chinese Tally of Known Border Disputes

China's known historic claims and border/territorial disputes with its 15 neighbours and maritime adversaries are not discussed. Only significant treaties are discussed in brief. China attributes the following disputes to history:

Russia

- Greater NW China was seized by Imperial Russia under the Treaty of Chughuchuk in 1864. Today, these are parts of the Republic of Kazakhstan, Kirghizstan and Tajikistan.

- Greater NE China comprising Vladivostok first in 1859 under the Treaty of Aigun and then in 1860 under the Treaty of Peking lost to Imperial Russia. Sakhalin Island is divided between Japan and Russia. Pamirs lost to Russia in 1896.

- The Kuril Islands acquired from Japan lost to Russia in 1945 under Yalta/Postdam Agreement.

Great Britain

- Pamirs also lost to Britain in 1896.

- Nepal was annexed by Britain in 1896.

- Sikkim was occupied by Britain in 1889.

- Bhutan lost to Britain in 1865.

- Assam was forcibly ceded to Burma in 1826.

- Burma lost to Britain in 1826.

- Andaman & Nicobar Islands ceded to Britain.

- Malaya lost to Britain in 1895.

- Thailand placed under Anglo-French forces in 1904
- NEFA lost as a result. of aggression to Britain.
- Sulu Islands lost to Britain.
- Hong Kong was forcibly extracted on lease for 100 years.

France

- Amman lost to the French in 1885.
- Thailand placed under Anglo-French forces in 1904

Japan

- Senkaku Islands and Taiwan lost to Japan in 1895.
- Sakhalin Island is divided between Japan and Russia.
- The Ryukyu Islands lost to Japan in 1879.
- Korea was declared independent but annexed by Japan in 1910.

The Philippines. Sprattley Islands are occupied by the Philippines.

Vietnam. Border delineation disputes, Gulf of Tonkin & Paracel Islands.

Burma Kachin State, Rivers Irrawaddy/Salween basins and two other areas

Laos. Adjustments are required on its porous borders with China.

North Korea. Mt Paektusan area.

Portugal. Macao, a Portuguese trade settlement for almost 3 centuries, made an overseas province in 1844 in an agreement with China annulled in 1928.

Resolved Border Disputes/Treaties

Sino Nepal Boundary Agreement 1960. This was signed on 21 March 1960 between Chou En Lai and BP Koirala to delineate the border between Nepal and Tibet Autonomous State. The Chinese laid claims on Mt Everest but agreed to accept the North face only given strong & persistent Nepali claims to it as Sagarmatha which was their religious deity. The framework of the agreement was on the much-hyped Panchsheel and high watershed principles, more or less conforming to the Mc Mahon Line running from Burma-India - China tri-junction to Nepal.

Sino Burmese Border Treaty 1961. The Chinese accepted the McMahon Line based on the principle of a high watershed between Burma and China as the legitimate border with minor modifications. China had made very modest territorial demands and gained very little territory. Why China considers this treaty as a model, needs to be examined in greater detail. It is possible the Burmese Government had two aims in mind, viz to seal its borders in the Kachin region bordering China against its insurgents and also get China to mop up its Nationalist Chinese gangs which were still active in that region.

Treaty with Pakistan. In this treaty, Pakistan ceded 2700 sq km of Shaksgum Valley in Pakistan occupied Kashmir to China, way back in 1963. Except for a clause on Kashmir dispute outcome, it is technically, this is an invalid treaty as Pakistan had merged this area into its Northern Areas and not POK.

Treaty with Russia 1990s. During the ideological rift with the Soviet Union in the early sixties and later, serious border clashes took place.

Both sides claimed three islands in the and Argun rivers. Till 1995 no agreement could be reached as both sides maintained their positions. Taking advantage of the dissolution of the Soviet Union, China's tough stance paid off and the disputes were resolved in its favour. The border treaty was signed in 2004.

Treaties with Kazakhstan, Kirgizstan & Tajikistan. Treaties signed with Tajikistan in August 1999 on border delineation, Kazakhstan in October 2000 on sharing of river waters and Kirgizstan on boundary demarcation in November 2000. These were directed to address China's concerns on cross border terrorism in its Turkestan province coming from the Muslims in Central Asian republics.

Sino Viet Nam Border Treaty. Disputes included the land frontiers of adjoining provinces and the territorial waters demarcation in the Gulf of Tonkin and ocean rights and interests over the Nansha Islands and their adjacent waters. These issues came to the fore when the Soviet Union allied with Viet Nam. China then undertook its ill-fated punitive operations against Viet Nam's intervention in Cambodia in 1979. Later, China and Vietnam signed the land border treaty and maritime agreement in December 1999 and December 2000, respectively.

Sino Laotian Treaty on Border Regime. This was signed in October 2001 for better border management and included very minor border adjustments.

Sino Mongolia Treaties. Though border delineation was not a major issue, the Soviets influence was worrisome for China. She pushed through the signing of a boundary agreement in 1988 before the Soviet collapse and signed two more bilateral agreements in 1994 and 1996, basically to wean the country away from Russian influence. The last one signed in April 1996 for Enhancing Military Mutual Trust is aimed at prevention of cross border terrorism, especially of Muslims, which China perceives as a big threat, and assistance in coal mining in Mongolia.

Sino Bhutan Agreement. Direct talks with Bhutan commenced in 1984 and sixteen rounds have taken place. Some issues such as border trade, cultural visits and peace and tranquillity on borders have been ensured but no formal treaty has been signed. Indo Bhutan treaty of 1949, which makes India responsible for Bhutan's defence, is always questioned by China.

Hong Kong & Macao have reverted to China on the expiry of the leases/agreements with Britain and Portugal respectively.

Unresolved Border Disputes.

India. The unresolved border disputes with India (Aksai Chin, Shakghum Valley, Arunachal Pradesh) are the direct result. of non-acceptance of the high watershed principle as the frontier between India & Tibet. It is pertinent to note that in the case of Burma (Myanmar), China accepted the McMahon Line as the border between Burma & China up to India- China - Burma tri-junction and applied the same high watershed principle to define its borders with Nepal, again along McMahon Line; yet it chose to leave two large gaps, to apply a different set of parameters when dealing with India. The reopening of claims on Sikkim by China cannot be entirely ruled out.

Others. China is yet to resolve its disputes on Spratley Islands with the Philippines and Paracel Islands with Viet Nam. China still considers Taiwan a part of China but has accepted one nation two systems status for it. Though China has not yet taken up issues with Japan on Kuril & with Russia on Sakhalin Islands In the recent past, it has not conceded that the issues are settled.

Chinese Approach to Resolution of Border/Territorial Disputes

General. Commentaries from media sources and official statements on the political strategy evolved for resolution of border/territorial disputes, bring out cogently that there were recurring themes and keywords which were hints for smaller neighbours to resolve boundary disputes with China quickly before time ran out. Political leadership under Chou En-Lai played a very significant role. As a part of a larger Chinese design, Nepal was rewarded with aid for signing the treaty and to wean it away from India. New China News Agency, a tool of the Government improvises a clever, manipulative and purposeful approach for the execution of defence policy.

Identification of Disputes & Cartographic Aggression. By the end of 1950, China had indicated its intentions on the undetermined boundaries it controlled. The first step was to commence cartographic aggression. Some maps reproduced were originated when Nationalists were in power and some new ones depicting boundaries well beyond their established frontiers. To buttress its stake in the neighbourhood well documented territorial claims were made. The first step was to annex Tibet and started laying claims to Taiwan, Hong Kong and Macao. All border problems were raised by China itself and not the other party to the dispute.

Status & Validity of Earlier Treaties. China questions the legality of treaties signed with imperialist powers in the 19th and early 20th centuries and refuses to be bound by earlier territorial agreements. Admittedly, international norms do allow abrogation of perfectly concluded treaties when both parties agree and not unilaterally. Therefore, a need to examine unilateral abrogation, de novo can be ascertained from as International Court of Justice. It is very unlikely that China would accept its final decision. China's interpretations/understanding of translations of various principles such as high watershed principle, definitions of "mutually acceptable comprehensive settlement" and "border dispute" is not a problem of their understanding of the English language but hardened attitudes.

Chinese Strategy

We notice that some trends/lessons emerged from how border disputes have been resolved so far. This could form the framework of future negotiations with China.

- The concrete outlines of a new treaty have always been based on China's proposals. Therefore, China adopts a tough line and floods the media and the target country with Chinese claims, proposals and counter-proposals.

- All claims based on historical facts are prepared in a very painstaking manner by a special military cartographic department. Chinese archives have preserved all documents and they have been utilized very well to suit their designs. It used the most potent European concept of sovereignty for furthering its interests and ambitions in Tibet. A new geopolitical scenario required the creation of viable Sinkiang & Sichuan states out of unwieldy

Greater Tibet which in any case was an autonomous but integral part of China.

- The emphasis appears to be on the signing of new bilateral treaties to replace the delegitimized ones or modified drafts of old ones. One can be sure that a basic framework of every new treaty is already kept ready.

- China believes that better bargaining comes from a position of strength. For that to happen, China has an infinite amount of patience. It waited for 42 years for it to assume a position of strength visa vis the Soviet Union to push through and force a decision to resolve its border disputes in the Amur River region.

- China also believes in the testing of patience and reactions of its adversaries before launching its forces into an all-out war. Against Soviets, it first threw broad hints by serving a notice that it had intentions to terminate the Sino Soviet Treaty of Friendship of 1959 prematurely. Having massed its troops on Sino-Soviet border, it stalled the Soviet's move to open a front against it and then launched its punitive war against Viet Nam based on USSR's inaction. It was a clear diplomatic victory for China for total abrogation and no renewal of its unequal treaty.

- China wishes to deal with smaller neighbours first, tackle bigger ones later. China reserves the right to punish nations that she perceives as weak and may have to resort to punitive operations having limited objectives. Once limited objectives are achieved, the bilateral dialogue is to be continued again, till an agreement is reached.

- If the party to a border dispute is an adversary or a country perceived as a potential threat to China's security and economic interests, the Chinese would maintain a tough line to achieve moral, physical and psychological ascendancy in a prolonged no war no peace status. It believes massive buildup of forces and logistics infrastructure in target areas as well as the display of economic clout in the region would extract sizeable concessions for itself.

- State organized protests, virulent media propaganda and rallies against foreign missions form part of China's overall strategy. China spends good intelligence money in hiring supporters/overseas Chinese population to storm foreign missions, subvert opinions in target areas and may go to the extent of even organizing hoodlums to counter-protests against the government as was done against public outcry abroad during Olympics torch rallies.

- Deng Xiao Ping in the late eighties, to enhance China's world image publicly exposed its adversary, USSR as being just a "paper polar bear". This was crude diplomacy, though the first indication that the Soviet empire was threatened by internal dissensions; the state itself was an economic disaster and a collapse was inevitable.

Possible Model for Territorial Claims War.

Setting for Conflicts. Chinese Military Commission of which President Hu Jin bao is the Chairman is having second thoughts on fighting long-drawn military conflicts as an instrument of state policy.

A short swift conflict that has no chance of ending in a stalemate is preferred. China, at present, would prefer to launch its operations differently in three stages. First, is the consolidation stage when China has gone about creating a peaceful environment around its claim's periphery, executed various safeguards to its territorial integrity and built up confidence amongst locals in the target area. The next stage, the shaping stage, would endeavour to shape events in the region and wrest the balance of power including military buildup in its favour. Finally, in the "mean business" stage, it would create strategic imbalance and instability in the region by an economic blitzkrieg and diplomatic/political manoeuvres. Against India, its first stage along our Northern & NE borders may be already over and the second stage may have just commenced. This could be followed either by a short and swift military campaign or an economic blitzkrieg or both.

Economic blitzkrieg. China does not believe in large scale attacks on military or strategic targets but instead has opted to neutralize adversary's financial, banking institutions and commercial establishments as well as administrative infrastructure nodes such as hydroelectric powerhouses, dams and water supply and telecom networks by a massive & continuous cyber intrusion. China may be engaged in excessive silting of the Parachu River joining the Sutlej to render Nathpa Jhakri and Bhakra Nangal ineffective and damming/diversion of waters of Brahmaputra & Ganges Rivers in Tibet. Assuming Chinese business establishments would already have established links with Indian business houses, the computer codes would be cracked and viruses would be inserted over the complete establishment. Some varsities, R&D organisations and semi-government links including NGOs would also be targeted to confuse us into believing these were little pranks. Timing of the real economic offensive would be carefully disguised in times of preoccupation, such as national calamities and general elections. This stage may be, yet to follow

China's Vulnerabilities in Changed International Environment

Global Economics. World events of the last two decades also played their part in changing the Chinese psyche chiefly the disintegration of the erstwhile Soviet Union and the emergence of the United States as the sole surviving superpower. There are no two opinions on the fact that China had its share of successes too but its opportunist streak is evident. Despite accusations against China of unfair trading practices the world over, the US chose to make long term trade investments in China. China balance of payments position now is well above the $225 billion benchmarks of March 2006 and has increased even further, which makes the financial institutions in the US heavily dependent on cash flows from Peoples Bank of China instead. What an ironic situation today, watching the recessionary trends in the US economy in return for huge investments in China! The time to act to correct this imbalance is now, especially in the wake of the galloping crude oil prices & world food crises, the recent setbacks to the Chinese economy by the earthquake and the Olympic Games.

Authoritative Capitalism. The Chinese economy may have seen phenomenal double-digit growth due to massive American investments, state-driven economic measures and corporate governance and infrastructure which has been improving with time. China has got this version of capitalism even before getting some semblance of democracy. Though such a version of capitalism defies all economic theories, it has accelerated the immediate growth rate. In the long run, however, China's growth rate may slow down after 2010.

Tibet's Future. Now, China could claim that the situation has changed in the last three decades. Its logistics are in place, Lhasa – Golmud railway line is through and Lhasa – Gormo oil pipeline is in place and traffic on its Western Highway is passing unhindered through India's Aksai Chin. China has acquired the capability to mount massive military operations up to three armies of 12 infantry divisions which could be easily sustained from the Tibet launch pads, all directed towards its potential trouble spots. China's forcible control of Tibet has made this possible. Tibetan protestors/rallies against the Olympic Torch run world over and the repressive actions by the Chinese in Lhasa confirm Beijing's nervousness in handling this tricky issue of its sovereignty over Tibet. European Union & American pressures, pacifist world backing the Dalai Lama along with its dreams of superpower status may now force the Chinese to come to terms with him. One thing is certain, the fruits of the Chinese economic boom are not coming to Tibet and this could be the start line for any counterstroke from the western world.

Recommendations for Own Approach

Review of National Interests. Both India and the West have contributed to legitimizing China's illegal occupation. The British withdrawal from the subcontinent ignored the balance of power which shifted towards Communist China. India's decision not to help the Dalai Lama, when the Chinese forced him to sign the 17-point Treaty of 1951 also was incorrect Things have changed dramatically with the emergence of India as a strong power in the East of Suez., China's perceives the beginning of the second cold war with the possible collusion of India and the US. We have been provided with a window of opportunity to give a de novo look to our national interests. Tibet holds the key to the resolution of India's long outstanding border disputes with China. For this India must persuade the world to recognize the Dalai Lama as the Head of State of a legitimate Tibetan government, China's preoccupations in Tibet and Xianjiang, the presence of newly independent Islamic states on its frontiers in Central Asia would make it think twice before it makes another move against this powerful alliance.

Resolution of border & river waters disputes. The talks have gone on for twenty years plus and an ineffective treaty of peace and tranquillity has been signed. There is no progress reported whatsoever during the last meeting. Such tardiness can only come when there is no deadline fixed for the outcome of the result. of talks. Therefore, a need exists to lay down the upper time limit for bilateral talks which could then be taken on by an UN-appointed arbitrator whose decision should be final and binding on both sides. Appeals from both sides could be made to the International Court of Justice, the jurisdiction China Hague whose territorial would have to recognize first. The issue can be resolved within a stipulated period with UN influence. Likewise, we must contest the Chinese actions in Tibet to dam, silt. and divert river waters in the International Court of Justice.

Victims of Aggression Principle. Everyone talks of Arabs being victims of aggression but what about India? If we are victims of the Chinese aggression of 1962, what steps has the government of the day taken to recover lost territories in Aksai Chin and Shuksgom Valley and across the LAC in Arunachal Pradesh? Have we reviewed our national interests and reminded our political bosses that to safeguard our national interests, it is vital to recovering lost territories? It is legitimate for any self-respecting nation to do so. Egypt did so in 1973 against Israel. Every Pakistan army officer takes an official vow to avenge the 1971 defeat. One of our Army Chiefs had the temerity to comment that the actualities on the ground do not favour us and this would be an unrealistic goal to achieve, even for the next 20 years. Well, if we haven't recovered lost territories so far, we are a nation with a defeatist national pride and we do not deserve to keep this territory anyway. Some other measures as discussed in the next three paragraphs:

- **Counterclaims in Chumbi Valley**. Day after day, we react to Chinese claims on the Tawang tract of Arunachal Pradesh being part of the Greater Chinese empire. So timid is our reaction that even our Prime Minister deliberately avoids visiting Tawang to not antagonize the Chinese. We seem to have forgotten that Chumbi Valley in Tibet was once a part of the British empire till 1907 when it was sold for 75 lakh rupees to appease Tibet. Using this territory, the Chinese can drive a wedge through Siliguri Corridor to dismember Eastern states from the rest of India. Therefore, Chumbi Valley was and will remain vital for our national defence. A counterclaim must be established on the same token as the Chinese claim on the Tawang tract. If we do not recognize the sale by the erstwhile powers to Tibet, our claims over Chumbi Valley would appear legitimate. Once we have decided on its return, we should be bargaining for Tawang Tract in exchange for Chumbi Valley.

- **Buildup in Ladakh.** Aksai Chin by all accounts is with China now. Do we accept this as a fait accompli or contest the Chinese claim or contest the claim and interdict/prevent the use of Western Highway to China? For the last option, it may be too late now and would create a near-war situation. We do not need a thumbs up from China to contest the Chinese claim on Aksai Chin and position more troops in a forward posture in Ladakh ahead of the so-called LAC (a creation of China we do not recognize), create logistics infrastructure to maintain these troops in that area, re-commission Chushul, Fukche, Leh and Daulat Beg Oldi as forward air bases. We could later move the International Court of Justice for contesting Chinese claims in this area. We stand 50-50 chances for getting the territory back by arbitration. Even if arbitration goes in our favour, would China vacate Aksai Chin? If we lose, it has been already lost and you can rest assured that the Government of the day will not fall. Very few people are aware of the fact that we lost 350 sq miles of Northern Rann to Pakistan in the arbitration. We need the political will to take this step.

- **Legal Status of McMahon Line.** We signed the Simla Agreement of 1914 accepting the McMahon line along with the high watershed principle as the border between Tibet & India to which Tibet is a party (on behalf of China). China did not sign this treaty because it did not agree to the Sino Tibet borders and not Indo Tibet border. The legal status of this treaty needs to be ascertained from the International Court of Justice, (more so because of the Sino Burmese & Sino Nepal agreements) and Tibet (China) must honour it.

Delimiting Spheres of Influence. China had been fomenting insurgencies in the northeastern states earlier and providing party to party support to Maoists/Marxists. China has armed Pakistan, is busy building a naval facility at Gwadar on the Makeran coast and has provided nuclear and missile technology beyond doubt. Have we achieved anything by sponsoring China's case for admission to the UN and getting its position as a permanent member of the Security Council in the seventies? Agreed that Nehru had erred in his assessment of the Chinese aggressive designs and failed in the resolution of border disputes. That was !950s and early 60s, it is 2010 now. Today, our geostrategic experts/think tanks should review our national interests afresh and suggest new foreign policy initiatives on the Track 2 approach, different from the one that existed in the sixties.

- China is going the whole hog wooing the African states, SE Asia countries and Central Asian republics. Can India outsmart China on the diplomatic plane to provide massive economic assistance programs with better technology and relief programs as a long-term investment in these regions? We should only build up goodwill and not expect anything in return?

- West had advanced numerous reasons for the balkanization of Yugoslavia, which apply here too. In addition, the right of self-determination and the repression of the minority Tibetans by the majority Han Chinese in their own country are other valid reasons for Tibetan autonomy Agreed, there would be repercussions in J&K, where China may ally with Pakistan to seek the right of self-determination for the Kashmiris on similar lines. That is to be expected. Sino Pak collusion has done enough damage to India and their retaliation to the grant of autonomy to Tibet cannot be worse than that

- We need to improve the demography of border areas opposite Tibet by settling our ex-servicemen from hill tribes like Garhwalis, Gurkhas, Kumaonis and Dogras and plainsmen from Assam. Some of this has already taken place due to the migration of Bangladeshis and locals from the borders to urban areas.

Formation of Regional Alliances & Agreements.

- Strengthening of bilateral cooperation between alliances such as SAARC and ASEAN Regional Forum (ARF) and Asia Pacific Regional Cooperation needs to be initiated to block China's unhindered entry into Myanmar. ARF has both India and China as dialogue partners but China has enlarged and strengthened its position in the member countries chiefly Myanmar. ARF must issue directives to restrict China's trade unless it improves its WTO malpractices and human rights records.

- UN efforts to bring about a peaceful transition to democracy in Myanmar should be encouraged along with a massive reconstruction program under SAARC especially in the wake of the recent cyclone. This is a window of opportunity for India as well and must be exploited. US must restrain China from entering SAARC countries. Membership of SAARC to Myanmar must receive top priority.

- Nepal must be weaned away from China's influence by fresh initiatives from India to the Maoists. China has vested interests to cultivate them. Our transit treaty with Nepal needs to be renegotiated and China's long-term investments in Nepal should be neutralized by a SAARC initiative.

- Central Asian Regional Security Forum to be revived to include Turkey Iran, Afghanistan and newly independent Muslim republics such as Kazakhstan, Kirgizstan & Turkmenistan. Our diplomacy to keep Iran on our side should bear fruit now with the reward of observer status for us. The US must be persuaded to change track on Iran policy on the same lines as North Korea. India could broker an attempt to bring the US and Iran together to pave way for reconciliation.

- (Pacific States Organization to include Taiwan, Japan and South Korea and US & Canada with observer status for ARF, India & Australia is possible to counter China's designs in pursuance of its territorial ambitions.

World Trade. China has been accused of unfair trade practices such as dumping consumer goods in Europe in violation of laws, broad-based intellectual property thefts, industrial espionage and the artificial subsidy in the value of yuan against the dollar. What the US expected on China's entry into WTO was the dramatic increase in exports of its products and services in the largest emerging market in the world playing with the same trading rules as the other members of the WTO. Today, grave violations of WTO rules, burdensome red tape, discriminatory policies cum protectionism and language problems and loss of jobs haunt the American business especially the medium and small entrepreneurs. Only giant multinationals like Boeing and Cargill appear to have benefited from bilateral trade with China. This calls for a review of China's membership in WTO and imposing economic/trade sanctions. Federal Reserve too, has to evolve a workable solution in such a manner that it clears the balance of payments deficit, putting China's galloping economy on hold and bringing the US economy back on rails.

Leverage of Global Warming. China's polluting industries are the ones making consumer goods and machinery for the developed world. This year China is expected to replace the US as the biggest producer of greenhouse gases in the world. Such an unbridled pace of industrial development should be checked by the world body in terms of the Kyoto Protocol. Developed countries of Europe, Canada and the US should be persuaded to limit the import of Chinese goods on this account unless China improves its polluting records not merely carbon credits scores.

Leverage of Beijing Olympics. The creation of disturbances during the Olympic torch run has at best been of limited nuisance value but has brought the Chinese repression measures in Tibet to the fore. World sports bodies should not have allotted Beijing as the venue in the first place. Any boycotting of the opening ceremony by France, Germany & US heads of states too will have a minimal effect on the Games. Till China resolves the Tibet problem, all human rights issues and does not improve its track record on WTO matters all future allotment of sporting fixture venues to China should be held in abeyance.

Indo US Military Cooperation. We have an advantage of a growing economy that lost out to the Chinese on globalization. Here is a good opportunity to strengthen ties with the West and the US at China's expense. The signing of a civil nuclear agreement with the US, expanding economic cooperation in Africa & Asia Pacific to checkmate China and restoration of the balance of power in South Asia would appear logical. Modernization of strike forces for high altitude operations and containment of terrorism in this part of the world should be high on our agenda. The use of naval power projection in the Indian Ocean to ward off Chinese influence would also assume importance. Indo US Military Cooperation would automatically take care of the imbalance in South Asia caused by Sino Pak collusion.

Conclusion

China, the "international pariah" of yesterday, flouting norms of internationally recognized behaviour, is getting away with the behaviour reminiscent of rogue states like Uganda and Libya. It is a strange paradox that the world body accepted China as a permanent member of the Security Council, even when China is unwilling to accept the jurisdiction of the International Court of Justice? Nations that do not honour international courts/treaties/agreements and violate all known codes of conduct are a threat to fellow members of the UN and the entire world. We now need to evolve a workable global strategy against such nations, leverage world opinion and apply sanctions/pressure/impose war reparations where nations have used force to achieve territorial gains. In a civilized world, all bilateral issues could be better resolved by the International Court of Justice in a specified timeframe rather than allow misplaced national interests and history, an excuse to restore frontiers. It is pointless quoting defence expenditure of totalitarian regimes like China & Pakistan in real terms while comparing it with India. Most figures quoted are fudged and are, therefore, unreliable. China has spent three times India's expenditure every year, in the last decade. Going by this yardstick, it is not unusual to read about China's military modernization, which brings forth successful conduct of anti-satellite tests, an aircraft carrier under production, acquisitions such as SU 30 fighter bombers, midair to air refuelling aircraft, MIRVs, SLBMs, development of Hainan Island in the South China Sea as a nuclear naval base and closer home, the acquisition of a naval base at Coco Islands off Myanmar coast for eavesdropping on India's missile programs.

China is again back to a sino-centric orientation and India is on its hit list. This also does not augur well for other countries in the South Asian region. We need to replace the third world blinkered mentality with x-ray vision binoculars of an emerging power. All Chinese moves in Tibet must be countered by the completion of our offensive and defensive preparations & upgrading our logistics infrastructure in Ladakh, Uttarkhand, Himachal Pradesh & Eastern Sikkim & Arunachal speedily. Apart from taking countermeasures against a possible ecoblitz, we also need to have a look at satellite imagery, surveillance bases and intelligence network in our border areas and harden our cyber and C4 I network against hacking and other forms of intrusions. Having acquired the capability to hit the Chinese hinterland with the Agni III, the existing nuclear asymmetry can be rectified only if we muster the political will to sign the civil nuclear agreement with the USA at the earliest.

Of Chinese Diplomacy and War

Published: December 2014.

Introduction

The recent visit by Chinese President Xi Jing Ping has brought back memories of *Hindi Chini Bhai Bhai days* when the Republic of India and the Peoples Republic of China concluded the famous Panchsheel Agreement and very similar agreements on trade and commerce. Sixteen MOUs signed on 18 Sep 14, pertain to exchange & cooperation in various fields, including trade & exports promotion with a notional investment of $20 billion. Chou En Lai, well into his third term then, in 1960 also sent out a terse message to PM Nehru, also in his third term. Now, President Xi, (pronounced as she), in his first term has sent out a message to PM Modi, also in his first term. Another striking similarity is in the careful timing of the border standoffs in the Ladakh Sector, i.e., Daulat Beg Oldi Sector in 1962 and now in Demchok - Chumar areas.

Inferences from Sino Indian stand-Off in Ladakh

The latest standoff sends out a strong coercive message to India; firstly, India must accept border delineation without preconditions. Secondly, recent talks between President Xi and PM Modi and agreements on trade imbalance removal, fresh capital investments and military cooperation, are conditional on peaceful resolution of border issues. Lastly, the PLA always stage-manages incidents on LAC in Aksai Chin & Arunachal Pradesh. to focus on its vital interests.

Now, after PM Modi's visit to Japan & the US and the communiqués that followed, makes it is amply clear that the world order cannot afford to neglect its strategic concerns on China's rapid emergence as a superpower and a viable threat at the same time. Chinese obsessive sino-centricity and its strategic concept of a regional people's war under modern conditions makes its position unassailable, akin somewhat to the Middle Kingdom of the past. China still believes countries on its periphery, like India, Japan, ASEAN states being, weak nations, can always be bullied into submission by coercive diplomacy. Strictly speaking, the definition of the periphery in geographical terms did not bother the US earlier, but it does so now. China's thrust into the South China Sea & its abiding interest in the Indian Ocean now provides the catalyst to Indo US cooperation in the Indian Ocean.

After the reprieve in Demchok - Chumar area, it would also be interesting to see what approach China adopts against ongoing massive street rallies by students in Hong Kong and Macao to reverse its decision to screen candidates first direct elections slated for 2017. Its oft-repeated statements professing democracy and rule of law as pillars of economic prosperity and social stability would be severely put to test.

The genesis of the Sino Indian border problem

Our Army Chiefs from Generals Cariappa to Thimmaya had warned the Government from time to time about the existing Chinese threat, but were brushed aside by the Nehru- Menon combine and other bureaucratic advisors, who lulled the nation into complacency. Our national leaders were busy creating friendly feelings amongst Indian people towards the Chinese, not realizing that the "nation of opium eaters" were in fact, a reborn nation after Chiang Kai Shek was overthrown by the Communists in 1949.

China immediately claimed large tracts of Indian territory in NEFA, Uttar Pradesh, Himachal Pradesh and Ladakh, as her own. White papers were compiled and published by both sides. Issues both controversial and non-controversial in each other's favour. These found their way in various government organs/media, then also very active, viz, NCNA and Radio Peking. Having first recognized Tibet in 1951, as an integral part of China, we also earned China's gratitude by the voluntary withdrawal of our mission at Lhasa, two post offices and the trade posts at Gyangtse and Yatung besides the company-sized force operating in Tibet to guard our trade routes. All this, kind courtesy to our ICS/IFAS (Indian Frontier Administrative Service) and IB advisors to the PM.

The revolt. of Khampas in the mid-fifties, in southern and eastern Tibet, rattled the Chinese. The terrain in Eastern Tibet afforded greater opportunities to China than Western Tibet which favoured India. China badly needed to develop Western Tibet land communications through Aksai Chin linking Lhasa with all important towns. viz Taklakot, Gartok and Rudok. In effect, this new road could link Sinkiang to Western Tibet and nullify the overriding advantages which India enjoyed here. Western Highway was opened amidst great fanfare in Sep 1957, a function attended by both our Charge d 'Affaires and military attaché' to Peking. Aksai Chin received a small mention in the Indian Parliament "as a place where not a blade of grass grows".

The escape of the Dalai Lama from Lhasa and his subsequent arrival in India on 01 Apr 59 precipitated matters. The defence of Himalayan borders was then handed over to the Indian Army. A tinge of bureaucratic control was evident in deployment orders such as 'to occupy as much territory as possible to prove India's possession' and 'not to patrol beyond 200 yards of their posts'. Besides creating confusion, it also resulted in penny packet deployment Where local commanders changed this aim "to stand fast and fight till further orders" or act as the situation demanded, the troops put up a resolute fight.

Lackadaisical Approach of Policy Planners

The brutal truth is that we never consider long term national interests while adopting a pragmatic foreign policy. The British were good strategists who had envisioned the grant of some sort of practical autonomy for Tibet under China, which went hand in hand, to maintain peace and tranquillity on India's northern and northeastern borders. We, Indians as successors, did not understand the nuances of a new Sino Indian border instead of the Indo Tibetan border we inherited from the Brits. Terms such as "highest watershed along Karakoram Range or Mc Mahon Line were never accepted by either the Nationalists or the Communists.

India must be rueing its three decisions on national interests; one, not to come to the Dalai Lama's help in 1951 when he was forced by the Chinese to sign the 17-point charter, two, sponsor China's case for admission into UN and third, the one-China policy, it followed. Tibet always held the key to the resolution of long outstanding border disputes with China, sadly, it is not even thought of. History has now repeated itself taking one full circumvention of over half a century. Those who do not learn from past lessons, are destined to repeat the mistakes of the past?

Basic Shades of Chinese Diplomacy

Present-day diplomacy is nothing but negotiation, persuasion and conciliation for promoting your vital interests and opposing interests of others which are detrimental to us. Both India & China subscribe to these processes, knowing fully well that when diplomacy fails, war results. Chinese leaders like Chou En Lai and Deng Xiao Ping held similar views.

Behind this process, preparations for war including a strong modernized army, development of strong state power based on stable institutions, strong economic foundations and the search for new allies is an ongoing process. China has exhibited its instruments of state policy of negotiation, persuasion and conciliation, with infinite patience, with a caveat, if you do not accept our terms for trade and commerce, we (China) being five times your economy in global terms, we will ruin your economic progress. The next stage is coercion, or tougher economic pressures, threat to use force to recover lost territories or even launch punitive operations, similar to 1962 and against Viet Nam in 1979.

Present Military Scenario in China

President Xi Jin Ping, a renowned hardliner on national security with an assertive stand on China's place in Asia, is the powerful Chairman of the Central Military Commission. Now in his first term, his national interests lie in adopting a defensive posture that projects power across the Pacific/straits and face regional rivals like Japan. To get it, he means to strengthen China's naval and air forces, to get the combined land, sea and air branches to work in close coordination, the way advanced Western armed forces do.

China's military budget has grown to be the second-largest in the world, 2.5% of GDP, behind that of the United States, with the new acquisitions "There cannot be modernization of national defence and the military without modernization of the military's forms of organisation, there is an ongoing reform of leadership and command systems, force structure and policy institutions", he was quoted as saying.

PLA today, is structured around seven powerful regional joint commands, originally set up to defend the country against invasion from Russia and to uphold the party's domestic control. Xi convened a senior leadership group in March 2014 to oversee reforms in which five task forces have been created to examine specific issues, on training, force reduction, political indoctrination, rooting out corruption and improving the way the military manages its logistics infrastructure.

After reforms, the new Chinese military that is likely to emerge by the end of 2020 (after one more aircraft carrier is ready) will be much more focused on confronting Japan, India & Viet Nam, perceived as a threat to China, on account of their long outstanding land border/territorial waters disputes.

China's prime strategic maritime interest is centred on Japan's alliance with the US. Indo US improved ties in the Indian Ocean are also a matter of concern for China. In furtherance of its territorial claims in the East and South China Seas, reunification with Taiwan and sea lanes protection in the Indian Ocean, the Chinese Navy is today, going in for a massive revamp.

Indian Responses

In the early fifties and sixties, India had become extremely wary of China's cartographic aggression all along the unresolved 4,057-km LAC and now, with over 600 intrusions by PLA, in the last three years, nothing has changed. What is evident is the brazen military assertiveness in all the three sectors of the LAC – Western (Ladakh), Central (Uttarakhand, Himachal) and Eastern (Sikkim, Arunachal). In Ladakh DBO and Nyoma sectors as well as Trig Heights and Pangong Tso Lake and Demchok & Chumar. Though Chinese troops usually go back after marking their presence, now they are increasingly coming deeper and deeper into our territory intending to stake claim to disputed areas. Indian responses to the Chinese intrusions, at best have been positive improvements in a defensive posture in 1989, some 17 rounds of inconclusive border talks, the conclusion of a Peace & Tranquility Agreement, numerous written protests on intrusions and flag meetings at brigadier level, which have proved inconclusive.

Possible Chinese Actions

Under this premise, peoples war may be conducted in the garb of usual armed provocations/intrusions with grazers', culminating into regional offensives with maximum use of special forces & rapid deployment forces. Now with improved railways and Lhasa - Gormo pipeline laid in Tibet and its present force levels this is possible. Speed of operations is crucial, intending to finishing unfinished business before UN-sponsored cease-fire becomes effective. Operations could assume the following form:

- Capture contiguous areas up to the claim line in the DBO sector and, simultaneous with regaining control of heights overlooking Chushul village and Spanggur Gap. These actions provide the much-needed depth to Western Highway in Aksai Chin and tie-down Indian troops in Ladakh before they consider an offensive.

- Move and occupy Tawang Tract and capture areas up to the claim line along with interdiction of Siliguri Corridor from Chumbi Valley side to sever the line of communications to NE before mountain strike corps has a chance to mobilize for the counteroffensive.

Suggested Indian Counter Measures

Some measures which merit the attention of our defence planners on strategic, economic and social/cultural planes are as follows:

- Internationalise efforts at restoration of status quo on Tibet to pre 1950 status. We need to accord immediate recognition to the Dalai Lama and the Kalon Tripa (PM) Central Tibetan Administration at Dharamsala as the legitimate exiled government of Tibet. Recognition must be arranged from other countries as well. Revival of Tibetan cultural centres/institutes/seats of learning and medicine in SAARC countries must go on. We need to assess the Chinese reactions in detail before making this move.

- We need to establish consular facilities in Lhasa and Gartok on a reciprocal basis. China must agree to our establishing trade centres at Yatung, Gyantse and Gartok on the Silk Route planned by China.

- Forge economic and military ties with US, Japan, Australia, Taiwan, South Korea, Viet Nam, Myanmar, ASEAN Regional

Forum and Asia Pacific Regional Forum. Maintain equally balanced relations with BRICS and Shanghai Convention.

- We need to discreetly wean away SAARC counties from Chinese influence by fresh initiatives and massive reconstruction aid programs.

- Develop closely-knit cooperation with Pacific Rim & Indian Ocean Rim countries for sea lanes protection under US control, to keep the Chinese influence in check.

- Real-time intelligence set up in Ladakh and NE has improved but a lot needs to be done in space/cyber security including hacking of computers, river water damming and satellite imagery for real-time intelligence.

- Completion of all road construction and logistical infrastructure projects right up to the border.

- Ensure security of Siliguri corridor by staking a claim on the strategic Chumbi Valley, a dagger-like slice of the territory on the Indian side of the watershed, which was mistakenly ceded by the British to Tibet. It may be noted that a Chinese military advance of fewer than 100 km would cut off Bhutan, part of West Bengal and NE states with over 50 million population. This could be part of a package deal with China.

- Cleverly exploit Chinese weaknesses in compliance with World Trade Organization norms such as its dumping policy, global warming and pollution record and other violations/irregularities/non-adherence to the Kyoto Protocol. Also, exploit its Human Rights and labour laws violations.

- We should also issue stapled visas for Tibetans, Uyghurs and Mongols from Inner Mongolia on the lines of the one issued by China for the residents of J&K or Arunachal Pradesh.

- We should position a full-fledged IAF complement in the NE that would imply the creation of infrastructure such as advanced forward airfields and helipad on priority. We must reach out north of Mc Mahon Line to interdict bases/PLA infrastructure in Nyingchi Prefecture /elsewhere in Tibet.

- We should pursue efforts under UN aegis to declare the Himalayas as a Zone of Peace with complete demilitarization in Tibet, Myanmar, Bhutan and Nepal. and geographically contagious areas in India.

- Attempt peaceful restoration of the century-old trade links, economic, cultural and religious interaction between India and Tibet. Aim to make the present Indo-China borders softer and more porous.

Therefore, without sounding like a prophet of doom, it would be naive to accept the opportunity to trade with China without adequate safeguards. It is imperative to constantly develop our capability be it conventional or nuclear, improve logistics infrastructure and adopt an aggressive defensive posture along the LAC, even as we seek a peaceful resolution of boundary problems. Tibet holds the key to our future relations with China, even if it means a reversal of our earlier stand on Chinese suzerainty, now with limited autonomy.

Sino Indian Standoff – What Next?

Published: June 2019

Our long history of repeated border clashes or border intrusions or transgressions has been a major flashpoint in Sino-Indian relations, in the aftermath of 1962. The Chinese have successfully managed to prevent India from building any major infrastructure on the Indian side of the border, while they have built. an extensive array of military infrastructure on their side, commencing with their Western Highway on our territory Aksai Chin. Reduction of seven military regions to five theatre commands and the merger of Xinjiang and Tibet into one Western Theatre Command has already taken place. Airfields facing Ladakh, Hotan and Garunsa, are now operational with a squadron each of J7 and J11 fighters and much-improved ground facilities. The airlift capability for inter theatre move confers the capability to build up to eight divisions in a time frame of one month. The Gormo Lhasa oil pipeline is also operational. Beijing's decision to aggressively patrol along the Indo-Tibet border should be seen from the perspective of China's grand strategy of grabbing as much territory as it can, in the garb of protecting its interests, territory, and sovereignty.

All along the 4057 km LAC, especially the fresh claims on Galwan Valley has now reached a very critical stage. Any misperception, miscalculation, or error along the tense border could easily escalate into a full-blown conflict. Thirty years of the same map to map alignments and varying interpretations of the LAC have agreed out of reach of both sides. The paramount fact is that China is already in possession of large chunks of our territory; so, what is there to negotiate for? In Ladakh Sector, the LAC runs up to the line where the Chinese forces had advanced in 1962. In the Middle Sector, it marked the extent of fictitious Chinese territory and also the line that marked the limit of their administrative control as it existed in Nov 1959. In Arunachal Pradesh, except for Thagla Ridge and Longju, the LAC ran through the entire length of the territory and not "up to where the Chinese reached in 1962". It is a different matter now, that the entire Arunachal state is claimed as Southern Tibet and Sikkim merger not accepted.

Incidentally, the term Line of Actual Control in the negotiation of border disputes was coined by Mao Tse Tung in his three points charter of 24 October 1962. The inflated territorial claims advanced by Communist China right from the beginning was based on the misplaced notions of disabling India's military to bring about political upheaval. Times have now changed and those ideas do not stand the scrutiny of logic especially when land warfare has become more complex, fluid and subject to greater influences. One expected after six decades of the previous engagement and RMA introduced, that the Chinese Army now would be more professional and civilised, it sadly isn't. The doctrine propagated by the National Defence University Beijing has introduced the notion of "shock and awe' above anything else. In the age-old Chinese strategy, two very critical components of "Shi" are, deceiving others into doing your bidding for you and waiting for the point of maximum opportunity to strike. Western Theatre Command now thinks that the opportunity to flex its muscles to implement China's grand strategy is now. Force build-up is now complete, administrative echelons have been topped up and the troops mobilised in the guise of an exercise, which brings "Shi" in their favour.

This leads to questions about our preparations. Our defensive preparations must also have been completed. Nothing unusual because, whenever, there is a buildup in rear areas, reported by various means such as the satellite imagery, it must happen. From all accounts, the road to DBO is a very sensitive issue for both sides. In addition, perceptions about the LAC may vary but the fact remains that defensive structures on our side of what we perceive as the LAC had been constructed, in violation of all the agreements which held good so far. The realization must now have dawned on the powers that be how myopic their vision was to stall the raising of the mountain strike corps, for lack of funds. Nothing stops us from completing its raising and positioning it now, as an existential threat or a possible deterrent Thoughts of our armchair strategists like, "making it costly for the Chinese to transgress across the LAC", do not apply to a country that can sink trillions into BRI and other ventures across the globe. What then should be our modus operandi to stop all the incursions/transgression by the Chinese? Every meeting will bring forward more claims of the interpretation of this magic word "LAC", because claims based on negotiations are hard to prove, especially to an adversary who is still nursing the ambitions of a Middle Kingdom. Therefore, some new thoughts need to be injected into our mindset if we are to end this ongoing impasse.

Our foreign policy needs to be transformed into a more dynamic one, implying that diplomacy must prevail to establish order in the region before it turns into a conflagration of unforeseen dimensions. A "balancer", maybe the US, to establish an equilibrium of power must be kept in the picture from the beginning. We need to take up the border dispute to the International Court of Justice at The Hague, for arbitration for acceptance of Mc Mahon Line as the border accepted by China, as in the case of Myanmar and Nepal. We have nothing to lose, as we have already lost Aksai Chin in Ladakh and may lose some more chunks of our territory in HP, UP and Arunachal, if we lose the case. Remember, we lost 800 sq km of Rann of Kutch in 1965 when ICJ gave 90% Rann to us and 10% to Pakistan. Before all that happens, as a layman, our defensive posture could aim at the following:

- Complete mobilisation alert of the three services in a graduated response, including manning of the coastline from the Arabian Sea to the Bay of Bengal, land frontiers and our skies.

- Defensive measures against hacking are taken by all likely targets against enemy cyber-attacks and espionage. Hardening of the cyber, EM spectrum, C4I networks, government, armed forces, railway and civil aviation networks

- Protection arranged against enemy anti-satellite weapons launched to bring down own satellites and imagery of the specific battlefield areas.

- Preventive measures taken against the use of river waters as a weapon of war.

- Strengthening our surveillance bases and intelligence network in the border areas.

- Some measures like augmentation/acquisition of equipment, ammunition and armament stores is an ongoing process along with production lines being stepped up.

A need for long term foreign policy that matches China's economic and military strategy is established. To achieve both these goals, we cannot go it alone. So, we have to enter into alliances. Alliances grow out of a consciousness of well-defined common interest. We have identified some of them with the US and with Russia, our old alliance partner. We need to assure both US and Russia that our maintaining ties with them are not at the cost of the other. We need to restore the old equilibrium and wean away Russia from China and Pakistan by settling all irritants with Putin. Our core interests point towards an observer status in the Collective Security Treaty Organization of Central Asian Republics with Russian support. As far as Afghanistan is concerned, we need to prevail on the US to work for a better deal with the Taliban. We need to work with both the US and Iran to bring them back to the negotiating table and restore the nuclear deal. To all countries in our immediate neighbourhood including Pakistan, we need to emphasise that our support to the US in the challenges it faces in the world order, must not be misunderstood. A strong U.S.-India partnership in defence and economic cooperation and the activation of the U.S.- Australia-India-Japan Quadrilateral must graduate to the next level of co-locating its forces in India within a stipulated time frame.

The possibility of improving ties with Central Asian Republics merits special attention. Tajikistan shares boundaries with China and Pakistan and it abuts Afghanistan's Wakhan Corridor into China.

Tajikistan is just about 20 km from Pakistan-occupied Kashmir across the corridor and could provide India with a strategic edge and vital intelligence on China & Pakistan movements in POK along the Karakoram Pass and towards Siachen Glacier. Tajikistan is also a member of the Collective Security Treaty Organisation (CSTO), along with Russia, Armenia, Kazakhstan, Kyrgyzstan and Uzbekistan. It may require a green signal from the CSTO to allow Indian military operations from Ayni. India has spent approximately US$70 million to renovate the airbase and has a contingent of the Indian Air Force and the Border Roads Organisation. Efforts must be made to convert this as a military base in Ayni to gain a strategic foothold in Central Asia and keep a check on China and Pakistan. Moscow's influence and clout will play a vital part in the decision making and India should expect some concessions from President Putin especially after RM's recent visit to attend the Moscow Victory parade. Our ties with Vietnam, the Philippines and Taiwan must be renewed with the exchange of intelligence and assurances, given that both countries are also fearful of Chinese military power. Special emissaries to the African countries, West Asian countries including Israel, Myanmar and all Mekong basin countries would prove beneficial in the long run. We may also consider the creation of the East Turkestan Uighurs government in exile and provide some support to them clandestinely. We must also grab the opportunity of our position in the UN Security Council to get a resolution passed declaring the Himalayas as a zone of peace.

Grappling with the Dragon

Published: September 2019

Just as the Doklam standoff last year, was the direct response to India's opposition to China's Belt. and Road Initiative, it is no rocket science to know that the events in Galwan Valley are closely linked to the Road Darbuk Shyok DBO (DSDBO) More ominously, India had openly declared its intention to attract manufacturing away from China, now that the country appeared vulnerable to the coronavirus epidemic and the growing trade tensions with America. Besides the ban on 59 Chinese apps, India is well on its way to cement its strategic relationship with the Quad. The writing on the wall is very clear. China continues to see India as a major obstacle to its global plans. India's strong message appears to have been well received - a lot of water has flown through the Galwan River since 1962.

But do you expect a dragon to stop breathing fire!

Confabulations at various levels both at the theatre and NSA level for "disengagement" have been in full swing. As brought out by this author earlier, what are these negotiations for, for whose benefit? The aggressor had forcibly occupied our territory in 1962 and then withdrew 20 km unilaterally just because of the logistics problems he would have to face and the Himalayan passes closing made him a sitting duck for the US and IAF then. Did he mark those areas on the ground where his attacking troops reached on 21 November 1962 to foist a claim of a so-called LAC? What is the sanctity of this imaginary line when there are differing perceptions for the last 58 years? As it is, China has no respect for international laws, world opinions and agreements. The Chinese language itself is a complex secret code, many words sound the same and, in any case, they never keep their words. Puns and misunderstandings abound. Hopefully, the disengagement, if reduced to writing like the previous ones, is in one language only, the English vernacular.

Coming to status quo and status quo ante. I suspect there is more to it than what meets the eye! The Chinese will never agree to the status quo ante because going back to April 2020 would nullify all the "nibbling" actions it had done. Was it just to get a glimpse of this brand-new road alignment DSDBO? By disengagement and status quo, China has sent us back 1.5 km into our territory and it had come 2 km into our territory in the Galwan Valley. If the policy of buffer areas as propounded in East Ladakh is accepted the way it is, we would be overall losers by about 0.5 sq km in each of the seven hot spots. Though, very small in comparison to what we have already lost in Aksai Chin, about 32000 sq km, but a loss is a loss. I think the gains for China are not commensurate with the deployment and the efforts that had been put in. Globally they have made more enemies. What then, were their aims here against defences so well guarded? The whole action was initiated first in Sikkim and then in Ladakh. Treacherous as they are, the Chinese must be massing troops elsewhere, going for our well-known vulnerabilities.

As far as China is concerned, she is fighting a "calculated war". Whether it is a trade or a territorial claim or a war on Covid 19, it may not have the wherewithal to tackle all at the same time but has made serious miscalculations on shi. Sun Tzu and Mao Zedong have, both emphasized more deception than on any other military doctrine. They also believe in the ancient 36 Stratagems for world domination, which consists of 6 chapters, each chapter consists of 6 stratagems. The essence of these flowery maxims has already been brought out in some form or the other, earlier. That the Chinese have infinite patience and believe that by surprise and deception will one day win wars without firing a shot, is no brainer. Though western writers have given the Chinese larger than life importance to the nine elements of their strategy, it would, however, be prudent to examine each element critically.

- Never lose sight of shi. Right now, they may agree it is not in their favour.

- Establish and employ metrics for measuring relative strengths. We do the same in an appreciation of the situation and have computer matrices to war game it. Need to complete all military, civil, cyber and cyberspace, including hardening of EM spectrum, against attacks.

- Steal your enemy's ideas and technology for strategic purposes. It is part of our strategic intelligence acquisition including satellite imagery from our allies to maintain surveillance. Nothing new in that as it is an ongoing process.

- Manipulate your enemy's advisors. Maybe alluding to our allies, especially Israel and the US, who should have already planned something in the overall scheme of things including space and maritime interests of the free world.

- Be patient, maybe even decades, to achieve victory. They have waited for almost 58 years and have deliberately not settled border disputes but have grabbed Aksai Chin which has virtually put paid our claims and road DSDBO is troubling them

- Military might is not the critical factor for winning a long-term competition. Diplomacy also pays dividends. China is busy weaning Nepal and Bhutan from our sphere of influence to make SAARC redundant. Our diplomatic overtures in Central Asia, SAARC, Quad and with Russia must be intensified.

- Recognize that the enemy will take extreme, even reckless action to retain a dominant position. We may have done that in 1962 but not this time.

- Induce complacency to avoid alerting your enemy. National preparedness cannot be ignored by us. No elaboration is required.

- Always be vigilant to avoid being encircled or deceived by your enemy. Intelligence reports both our own and from our allies must be credible and timely.

Let us hope that these nine elements of the Chinese strategy and the 36 stratagems, however deep they sound, are soundly taken care of whilst the negotiations are on and in the planning for the management of our borders. It is time to do away with the LAC and replace it with the Line of Control (LC) properly delineated on maps and marked on the ground, on lines of what we did with Pakistan. The step-by-step approach adopted for disengagement should be wrapped up with the delineation of the LC. Similar exercises must be done in the Central and the Eastern Sectors as well. With war being a distant possibility, we must not let down our guard and go flat out in preparing ourselves for war, if forced on us.

Some may argue that in the present imbroglio, we have fallen into a trap carefully laid by the Chinese by the huge expenditure on mobilization that has taken place to counter the Chinese transgression from May 2020 onwards. Well, the expenditure on defence forces is the price we pay for maintaining our sovereignty and territorial integrity. Posterity will never forgive us if we allow a repeat of 1962. It is now expedient to ramp up our preparations at the national level to meet this threat on our borders along with the ensuing war on Covid 19. We know what our defence planners would do in all sectors, so no elaboration is required. More emphasis should be laid on what is happening in Xinjiang, Tibet and Yunnan which means a rethink of our strategy to counter the expansionist dragon in its den on the diplomatic plane.

What is worrisome is the divisive tendencies particularly of the oldest opposition party affecting national cohesion and unity.

Afghanistan, its sectarian divisions, and international stakeholders

Published: Aug 2021

The challenge has returned, to where it began. Afghanistan's reputation as a 'graveyard of empires' stands fully validated, where both superpowers made forays to a place where even "angels fear to tread" and achieved results of no significance. Traditionally too, it has never been a stable country with consistent administration under a single authority.

As the Taliban - fresh from their victory over the US-backed government forces - intensify efforts to formally take over power in Afghanistan, an analysis of the broad divisions in the country on ethnic and sectarian lines and their role against the Taliban resurgence would be instructive. Equally interesting and diverse has been the response of the international stakeholders spread across the region, and even beyond. Both the domestic and the international factors are crucial, as they together are likely to give shape to the new internal dynamics in Afghanistan.

Pashtuns - Areas around Kabul to its northeast, the Badhakstan province and parts of the south, were loyal to Hamid Karzai, the ousted former Afghan president, a Pashtun, who headed the High Council for National Reconciliation, along with Abdullah Abdullah (Tajik), who led the High Council for National Reconciliation (HCNR), and Gulbuddin Hekmatyar (Pashtun), a two-time Prime Minister.

All five Pashtun factions had strong militias but chose to avoid combat with the Taliban, possibly on some inducement/promise of uninterrupted opium production later.

Tajiks - After the Northern Alliance ceased to exist, the north, especially the famous Panshir Valley, was the most peaceful region of Afghanistan. Tajiks are loyal to Hamid Karzai but opposed to Uzbeks. They did not assist the Afghan National Defence Security Forces (ANDSF) and dispersed. The Taliban's success in neutralizing the Tajiks was mainly due to the unpopularity of the Ghani regime and Karzai's waning influence because of the rivalry with Abdullah Abdullah.

Uzbeks - Mazar-I-Sharif province has a militia bordering Uzbekistan loyal to former Vice President Gen. Abdul Rashid Dostum, a pro-Communist controversial figure who controlled five provinces. He chose to remain abroad and returned to avoid combat in Mazar-i-Sharif. His Uzbek militia did not assist ANDSF for fear of antagonizing the Taliban.

Hazaras - The Bamiyan province bordering Iran has its warlord Mohammad Karim Khalili, leader of the Shiite Hazara party coalition, controlling a large swath of the Afghan interior and a sizeable pro-Iran Shia militia, opposed to both Uzbeks and Tajiks. Iran has denied support to them and the militia appears to have offered little resistance to the Taliban and surrendered in its three provinces.

These four main tribal power centres in Afghanistan, each with suspect loyalties, are faction-riven and influenced by the countries in their neighbourhood.

Tribal rivalries have made the country difficult to govern. Each group maintains its armed militia ready to quarrel with its rivals and unwilling to submit to any central government. In addition, Afghanistan is an arena for its neighbours to play out their rivalries. If the President is a Tajik and his government Tajik dominated, it may become a source of alienation to the Pashtuns.

Both Karzai and Ashraf Ghani had even alienated their tribes and made little effort to extend the writ and security of their governments beyond Kabul.

Going by history, agricultural and dairy produce was just enough to sustain the population in good times but now the situation has changed. Most of the food items are imported. When the warlords were left to govern their respective areas controlled by them, they found it more lucrative to cultivate poppy instead of cereals. Poor farmers, eking out a living growing opium, were contributing to the wealth of the warlords, who with drug traffickers funded the Taliban insurgency by supplying large stocks of weapons captured from the warlords' warehouses.

The areas between Jalalabad and Kandahar, inhabited by the Pashtuns, is the rich agricultural belt that also produces the bulk of opium. The power vacuum created by the warlords and the drug traffickers enabled Taliban and Al Qaeda to make fresh inroads in places, which once were liberated by the coalition forces.

In both the Tajik North and Pashtun South there is a realignment of power centres after the Taliban's resurgence. Their militias have dispersed and they could lose their control in their respective areas of influence if they remain in hiding for too long. They would want to reassert their hold; in case the Taliban is unable to consolidate its hold in Kabul. Simultaneously, they would like to continue in their 'narcotics for weapons' trade, if not disturbed by the new regime.

Current situation

The US - The US has a right to bring the war to a close as the Soviets did, but not in the manner that it turned out to be. The intelligence and planning could have considered the safety of all those who sacrificed so much to help them achieve their aim. Be that as it may, the US is now more preoccupied with the evacuation of its embassy in Kabul after the exit of all the forces. Additional troops to evacuate stranded US diplomats and citizens have arrived.

A core group of American diplomats who had planned to remain at the embassy in Kabul was being moved to a diplomatic facility at the international airport. The US warnings to the Taliban to allow uninterrupted evacuation appear to have been well received. The US has warned the new regime of its obligations to the UN Charter and human rights including women.

Taliban - The Taliban blitzkrieg has thrown all things out of gear as evacuation plans appear to have been hastily contrived. Even the Secretary of State Antony J. Blinken has acknowledged that the offensive had moved faster than US officials had expected. He admitted that despite two decades of war with American-led forces, the Taliban have survived and thrived, without giving up their vision of creating a state governed by a stringent Islamic code.

If records are any indication, the declarations and assurances by the top Taliban leaders of the safety of minorities and women's rights and other issues, have no meaning. The Taliban would return to its repressive measures, impose Sharia laws, deny citizen's rights, and control the media.

Pakistan - Pakistan's contiguous borders with Afghanistan, based on the designs of the 19th Century British colonial administrators, stand disclaimed by the opposite parties and to this day are disputed. What Pakistan fears most is that the unified Pashtun tribal belt, across the disputed Durand Line, would be detrimental to its sovereignty.

In its quest for a deep state in Afghanistan, Pakistan PM Imran Khan had a pre-condition - Ghani should quit - which has been done now. Their support for "good Islamic militants" in Afghanistan, such as the Afghan Taliban, the Haqqani Network and the Lashkar e Taiba, is nothing new.

It now remains to be seen how Pakistan moves forward to bring the "Loya Jirga" (Special legal assembly in Pashtunwali, the traditional code of laws of the Pashtun people) in the peaceful transition to a Taliban-led government. Pakistan would not want Karzai's presence at the National Council for Reconciliation, as he is perceived to be an Indian supporter.

Iran - The pro-Iran Hazara Shias fear the fundamentalist Sunni Taliban takeover and have the full support of Iran's Supreme Leader Ali Khamenei. Iran's active involvement has been subdued by the present US sanctions. They did not provide arms and safe sanctuaries to the anti-Taliban factions in the adjacent border provinces.

It appears an understanding has been reached with the Taliban that anti-Shia operations would not take place in the future. Iran has established relief camps on the borders, for screening Afghan refugees entering Iran.

Russia and Central Asian Republics - Geography confers this region with limitless options. It remains a potential tinder box, its vast natural resources have given some of the state's significant bargaining power with all those who have stakes in the region. The Central Asian republics of the former Soviet Union have a treaty with Russia - the Collective Security Treaty Organization - and hold their views (read Russia's) on the border situation with the Taliban resurgence.

China - The Wakhan Corridor - a narrow strip of territory in Afghanistan, extending to China and separating Tajikistan from Pakistan - has its geostrategic importance for both China and Pakistan in their trade with Central Asia. It also provides a route for Uyghur rebels to move into their safe sanctuaries in Afghanistan. The Taliban claims control of the vital passage from China, inhabited predominantly by the Tajiks, who support the East Turkestan Independence Movement (ETIM) from its very inception. China badly needs to plug its escape routes to safe sanctuaries in Afghanistan and is prepared to seek an understanding with the Taliban very soon.

China's interests in Afghanistan also lie in its ambitious global infrastructure project Belt and Road Initiative. With the Taliban coming to power, a road through the slender Wakhan Corridor from Xinjiang province to Kabul and then on to Peshawar – the capital of the Pakistani province of Khyber Pakhtunkhwa - complements the existing corridor to Gwadar, a port city on the southwestern coast of Pakistan's Balochistan province, that enhances the trade and its rare earth mining prospects in North Afghanistan.

India - Pakistan has checkmated India to some extent, though the Taliban has recognized India's role in the reconstruction projects and Salma Dam. It is well known that groups like the JeM, LeT and IS are an adjunct to the Taliban and would expand their training facilities and camps in Afghanistan for expansion towards the South. The obvious target would be India through Jammu & Kashmir.

In the present scenario, wait and watch would be the best policy for the recognition of the regime, status of development projects/activities and the exodus of refugees. Some contingency planning must already have taken place.

Inside Afghanistan

Published: Aug 2021

The quest for the establishment of a broad-based, gender-sensitive, multi-ethnic, and fully representative, independent Afghanistan has eluded the world powers once again. Afghanistan is back to square one, to its pre-war status of a possible base for jihadist non-state organisations.

The country has once again fallen under the sway of a resurgent Taliban, after two decades. It threatens to create a Greater Pakistan, with an adjunct Islamic Emirate of Afghanistan under the patronage of Jallaluddin Haqqani, Gulbuddin Hekmatyar and other radicalized elements like Al Qaeda, LeT and Hezb e Islamic Group.

Afghanistan has ceased to be the geographical buffer between the Iranian plateau and Central Asian Republics, coveted both by Russia and British India, in the past. It now provides the much-needed 'strategic depth' to Pakistan.

Operation Enduring Freedom launched by the US-led coalition forces for the location and elimination of Osama bin Laden in later 2001, and the withdrawal of the coalition forces, starting July 2021, are now history. To be fair, the US has given top priority to its national interests. It helped raise a 350,000 strong and fully equipped Afghan National Defence Security Forces (ANDSF), revamped the police and civil administration and was rebuilding Afghanistan. Yet the Taliban succeeded in toppling the government of Afghan President Ashraf Ghani.

This was not a war between nations; it was a war among the Afghans. At one end were the insurgents, the indigenous Taliban, who after 2001 had melted into the countryside with their regime toppled. At the other end was ANDSF, raised specifically to deter the Taliban from an insurgency by isolating them from habitation areas and preventing them from gaining control in the provinces.

What the Taliban regime may do

The history of successful counter-insurgency operations around the world has shown that the victors would be those who maintain cohesion and prevent themselves from being isolated. In this case, the Taliban deserves full marks for establishing bases and gaining control in the rural areas, whereas the ANDSF personnel either deserted or fled from their posts or surrendered The trump card had been played with finesse by Pakistan, through its simultaneous support to the US and the Taliban.

The Taliban has learned a few lessons from its earlier stint in power. They were extremely surprised to achieve their goals without much resistance. In their recent avatar. they will not want to be seen as international pariahs. They would not waste time in assuming responsibility and announcing key portfolios.

They may now opt for a clean break with al-Qaeda to secure international acceptance and recognition. However, that does not imply that Al-Qaeda would abandon them. Al-Qaeda, IS and other radicals would easily embed their cells unseen within the outlying areas in the present chaotic situation and re-emerge at a time of their choice.

Generally, the Taliban can be expected to build its credibility with the world and its citizens, deliver services and administer justice effectively, following the constitution. The Islamic Emirate of Afghanistan could exist only on paper.

Pakistan's future role

Pakistan too has learned some lessons. Pakistan appears to have negotiated a quid pro quo with the Taliban to reject new US bases on its soil in exchange for the Taliban's assistance in tackling the Tehrik-i-Taliban.

Pakistan would avoid any mention of the Durand Line, which may resurrect old differences. Its deep state has been achieved and the turn of events has proved that the decoupling of Pakistan from the Taliban is not going to be easy.

World powers may now seek Pakistan's assurance to keep their ally, the Taliban, under control. The fear of economic sanctions such as the Financial Action Task Force (FATF), more barriers in trade and financial inflows, .and the declaration of Pakistan as a terror state, would keep the Damocles sword hanging on Pakistan. Logically, the dissolution of the Haqqani Network and the Quetta Shura should follow next.

Afghanistan has always been a simmering pot of tribal violence. The militias of the various tribal factions did not come to the rescue of ANDSF primarily because the regime was also the most corrupt, inefficient, and unable to govern. Tribal affinities, loyalties and habits die hard. Tribals, especially in the North, Northwest and South, love possession of weapons and are forever looking for ways and means to procure and use them on every available opportunity.

If a Taliban administration is unable to build its credibility, provide effective governance, bring in reforms and control narco-terrorism, it would just need a spark to ignite passions in tribal regions for a Greater Tajikistan and Pashtunistan, leading to the de facto partition of the country, here again, neighbours like Russia and Central Asian Republics, China and Iran could play a decisive role.

Afghanistan on a global stage

The free world appeared to be in deep slumber when Doha talks were deadlocked, a vacuum was created by the sudden exit of coalition forces and the Taliban onslaught that followed.

Rather than issue calls for more infructuous United Nations Security Council meetings and issue resolutions and communiqué on its future status, it is now time to allow the Afghans to settle their issues themselves, once and for all. But can they?

As and when the stability is restored, subject to the successor regime's requirements, there should be an UN-sponsored multi-national development assistance plan for massive reconstruction, civic actions to restore democratic institutions and confidence in the present regime. The restoration of law and order, good governance in both urban and rural areas, capacity building and destruction of poppy cultivation could then follow. Afghanistan remained neutral during both World Wars. What stops it now from becoming one, guaranteed by the five powers?

Who knows when the world powers would sink their differences against the common enemy of terrorism and deny the establishment of an Islamic Emirate of Afghanistan? Who knows if the US can resolve its mutual differences with Iran and work for peace efforts in the Middle East? Who knows when the US will settle all issues with Russia, and may conceivably partner with Russia in a strategic alliance to force China to abandon its South China Sea claims?

Sounds a bit utopian, but it is within the realms of possibility in the present era of alliances.

Social & Spiritual Aspects

My father's advice before I left for NDA still resonates in my mind. To be the best in your profession was not going to be easy. I had to first complete the training in two academies before I could even think of buying myself a drink or even venture near a cigarette. I had maintained the strict *gurukul* concept in mind throughout the first four years. When a bit of financial stability did come in after we received our arrears of first pay in October 1963, the blueprints of my peace station life began to emerge. In a large family like ours, my father still had one daughter to marry off besides two of his sons yet unsettled. Nobody would ask you for money but it is your assessment of the situation which told you that it was your responsibility to chip into the family kitty, which would be most welcome. Father was determined to see that at least one of his three engineer sons, could pursue his studies for MS and PhD abroad now that most of his commitments were over and he still had a few years to retire. He did nothing to change me or my approach to life, not even advised me on anything later.

I was guided by the events of the day to make decisions very early in life. Firstly, the only source of income I knew would be my salary alone, which was quite comfortable those days. None of us in the regiment had a flamboyant lifestyle, smoked or drank in excess because the moment your wine limit was exceeded you were administered a reproof by the Second in Command. Take my word for it, it kept you on a tight leash. Like it or not, an austere lifestyle fitted in well in my persona throughout. The other choice I made was that I would work extremely hard to the best of my abilities for a life of fulfilment and duties, regardless of the fruits as enshrined in Bhagavad

Gita. The hard drive of our minds is endowed with spirituality if one is not attracted to power, position and wealth. Spirituality ensures respect for professional ethics and morals, seeks to restrict desires and keeps our baser instincts in check. The joys of spiritual transcendence also require a lot of sacrifice and commitment both in terms of your attention and time. I did not seek a path of glory or exceptional valour as neither it came my way nor did I go out of my way to seek it in combat. There was a right mix of transcendence put in my life whenever I saw my deeply religious mother always praying for my safety during the wars I was involved in. Prayer worked like therapy for her. In a way. I noticed that the hard choices made by me as a 19-year-old have stood me well in life. For me, the joy of living life full size, the Dignity and Honour you enjoy, performing your duties well without fear or favour and the fulfilment of my goals brought me lasting happiness. It is now that I feel I am ready for more transcendence when all my professional & family commitments and duties to society have been completed. I am happy, not to be a public figure or a celebrity or basking in my old glory and valour. More importantly along with the transcendence, it is also the time to enjoy the love, joy and laughter with family and friends, work selflessly for the nation and its well-being and influence some sections of marginalized society towards better living. I don't think we can be more satisfied with life than now.

After my full tenure in the Army spanning almost four decades and a stint with FICCI CARE at Gujarat, I had taken a conscious decision not to run around for assignments outside NCR. I had an offer to proceed to Dilli East Timor, the tsunami hit Andhra Pradesh and even Chhatisgarh for research work on Maoist insurgency. I declined all as there was a requirement to set up a house somewhere. We preferred Gurgaon to Noida as we already had invested in property earlier in Gurgaon. For quite some time Manju stayed alone in the huge house which was provided for her by the NGO CARE. I decided to settle finally at Gurgaon because there was Manju's follow up treatment which I had so far ignored. Besides, the children dreaded the prospects of commuting down to Dehra Dun every time they came home for a visit. We had made good friends in our neighbourhood and also with our friends around. Kiran Sharma and Manju and Pradeep Misra were amongst good friends. Rohit's wedding was celebrated from our bungalow No 446 in Sector 22 and all my friends helped me out during the wedding by way of one/two rooms, transport and of course their company.

It started in Brig. Kultar Singh's house, one fine evening over a drink. Kultar and I had served as Directing Staff together at DSSC Wellington and were regulars for golf along with neighbours Pradeep Misra and YD Sharma. We decided to play together at the newly commissioned Air Force Sports Complex at Gurgaon four times a week with a possible another round at Delhi. As we teed off very early, I could still make it to my office around ten in the morning. On days when we had visits, I had the flexibility to decline and this paved way for the expansion of the foursome, into a full-fledged golf kitty with no stakes but a pot luck meal once every month by rotation. It was great fun with excellent eight couples whose spouses were avid golfers and another two who weren't, making a total of ten couples. We had even thought of applying for a stay together in one of the new HUDA colonies but that didn't take off. We had a few get-togethers in our bungalow in Sector 22 and also one at Celebrity Homes. We decided that our golfer friends needed a house warming party in 2006 and we were overjoyed with the response and the presents of this great group. Over a while, we noticed that our Golfers group was getting enlarged with the entry of the 61 Commission group which we were avoiding, all through. We, therefore, took a conscious decision to exit from this group and join another golfers group here in Celebrity Homes. This group comprising AM Dheeraj Kukreja, AVMs Ajit Singh, Jagjit Gandyok and Vicky Chopra is doing very well and we are enjoying each other's company in the monthly get-togethers for dinner of five or six couples. We are in total harmony and will soon restart our dinner every month by rotation which COVID 19 has thrown in disarray. We also had a DSOI kitty group for couples and another musical one called Mehfil. Both groups besides the Ladies Club and kitty group keep us very busy. Socially we are busier after retirement than when I was in service.

Golf has restarted with vengeance now!! We play on Mondays and Fridays every week. If an opportunity presents itself, I do try and make it to Army Golf Course where I have been playing for the last 32 years. During my posting at Army Headquarters, I was in the regular four-ball of Vice Chief Chandra Shekhar and we enjoyed immensely then with small stakes of ten bucks, ten-twenty in our parlance. Invariably we were quits at the end of the month, Being a gentleman's game, we stick to the rules of the golf laid down by Royal & Ancients and the local club rules. I am happy to note that our foursome plays without stakes here at Gurgaon because the aim is to enjoy each other's company as well as the game. I also had the pleasure of playing Top Golf while in Atlanta last year. This is a different concept with the primary aim of entertainment and socializing. What an impressive locale in Atlanta downtown with 150 tee-off points on a huge three-tier building, brightly illuminated which has a place for corporate events, birthday parties, bachelor or bachelorette parties, corporate events, date nights, or just a night out with friends, and everyone will have a great time fueled by food and drinks all the time. You can select the holes you want to play and earn points for the closeness to the pin. There is a time stipulation involved, you can select the various packages for the slot fee to be paid in advance. Top Golf is here to stay.

Coming to social life in the Condominium. As stated earlier, when I arrived here, the atmosphere was very vitiated. The small community was divided into two distinct groups with the usual fence-sitters and few others who were either instigators or the *tamashbeens*. It's a pity that the finest society having the ambience of the best-gated complex in Gurgaon is full of young and arrogant residents who are used to the *wild west* lifestyle, have no respect for seniors and therefore, do not accept the concept of community living. I do hope, as these young residents get older, they would be able to understand what respect is and what it counts for. The management and maintenance of our complex is first an individual and then a collective responsibility. Stress was laid on individual awareness, knowledge of bye-laws and guidelines/rules laid down for community living and smooth operation of all services/facilities. What followed next was the selection of the team of dedicated residents who have a flair for concerted hard work to seek community goals and have no personal stake or conflict of interest. It is a sad state of affairs that very few residents take interest in condominium affairs to select the right people for running the management now. There are no such things as community service or concerted hard work to seek community goals and control of expenditure. I feel that joining the Board of Managers is like being vaccinated for Covid 19, still elusive but once is enough. The herd immunity (in the form of community service) yet not visible, may take years. Be that as it may, both of us are fully conscious of the fact that our choice of friends must narrow down to a few trustworthy and dependable ones. Like all other communities, there are fair-weather friends who you need to guard against.

The uniformed community continues to grow smaller in numbers every year. From my old coursemates and colleagues, a few have departed and those with us are the people who matter to me. Those who have departed were also as good but their lives were destined for greener pastures ahead of us. We both realize that the road ahead continues to be full of medical challenges like bad knees, asthma and respiratory disorders, cardiovascular blockages, brain atrophy, cancer and dementia. We have to maintain a positive attitude, exercise regularly to defeat them, if not, learn to live with them also, in this very complex. We are lucky to have good friends in Mukta & Lalit Chawla, who were the first couple to welcome us here in early 2006 and are very hospitable hosts. Others include our very respected planter and good friend Sardar Saran Singh and his complete family, the dashing couple Ashok & Abha Bhandari, the evergreen Monty Kochchar, the scholarly Professor Bharat and Yukti Gupt, the witty Arun & Madhulika Kumar, the soft-spoken Malik Yash and Vijay Kapoor, the information warrior Maj. Gen. Sukku and his pride Lalita Kapoor our oldest friends, the very effusive Prem and Yash Bhajanka, the happy go lucky couple Gopal & Shan Bagai, the very serious RK & Shobha Jain, ever-smiling Lalit & Seema Bajaj, the great Vipan and Simi Gulati, evergreen Satish

& the young as ever, Saroj Mehta, not forgetting the always smiling Simarjit (specifically for his contribution to the Condo) and his businesswoman wife Seema and finally our great friends AP and Indira, all very dear in every sense. We are fortunate to have Dr Madhu Rana in our midst, a multi-talented and spirited lady. To add, our dear friends from the uniformed fraternity; a galaxy of retired Generals, four to five Air Marshals and the one and only Admiral, the towering persona in Ravi Vohra and his lovely wife Rashmi; all members of our DSOI kitty, which as of now stands discontinued. We used to meet regularly every month and are all very fond of the wise counsel and friendship prevailing in this group.

One of our very good regimental friends who later joined the civil services, we got to know them here only, but they deserve a special mention. In Ashok and Jaishree Jain, we found a very warm-hearted, affectionate and steady couple. Ashok is in his new avatar as the practising Supreme Court Senior Advocate fought my cousin's case and saw it to its logical conclusion. He has been like a brother to me and what humility means, you got to see in this great couple. He celebrates his birthday with me on 10 December every year. On our Golden Anniversary, on the actual date 20 October last year, he held a party in our honour at his residence, just because they could not be present in station on 28 December 2019 due to a long-standing commitment in the family. Their sincerity and friendship is something we will always cherish throughout our lives. Ashok Jain had served as the President of this Condominium with great distinction, sense of commitment and dedication, albeit for a short duration with impeccable credentials and a very clean record. He has brought us into the Mehfil get together every month which we all are yearning to get back after COVID-19.

We had the good fortune to connect with a few families of relatives in Celebrity Homes here. Shri Katyayani Dayal. I had met first time during a meeting organised by Mr Lalit Chawla who felt that his advice on how the RWA should function was enlightening. When I met the quiet unassuming man, I was struck by his sincerity and singleness of purpose. He advised that we should assert our rights and be prepared to take over responsibilities from Ansals rather than complaining about how Ansals were functioning. On our front, we had developed a great regard for Shri Katyayani Dayal who attended our granddaughter's party in 2007 and met all his friends in my family especially Ranjit, a Member Railway Board and Mahesh who was the Chief Mechanical Engineer Northern Railways. There were other relatives who he knew well like Dr Prem and Ravi and Jyotsna, my niece married into their family. The family reunion was complete and I was always a welcome guest at Dayals. Whenever we went to call on them, it was generally accepted that Uncle would insist that we leave after dinner with them. They are such a loving family that we held Uncle Dayal in high esteem as he resembled my father in some ways. Whatever, Uncle Dayal said was law and I took all his directions literally like my father. Even when he was sick, he had asked his younger granddaughter Pooja to give me a call because he had placed a lot of faith and knew I would never let him down. He passed away very suddenly in 2009 not before we realized that our best friends in the complex were the Dayals family. Uncle had his last meal with us being with him at his residence; had also asked his daughter in law Poornima to get me a drink. I then mildly requested that I would love to have one with him later when he gets well. We treasure our relations with Rishi and Purnima Dayal very much and we are proud of our nephew Arjun Swarup, now married to their lovely daughter Radhika. That is not the only reason we are so fond of them; they are a class apart and a very caring couple. It is to their credit that we find in them a lot of good and genuinely healthy friendship.

I realize we are now both 75 years plus senior citizens ageing gracefully and we need to accept that getting old is a reality which we need to embrace and prepare for. We should be grateful to God for allowing us to continue to be a part of the elite 3%. I have no experience in the exploration of old age as I am treading for the first time. In the complex, hidden and emotional world of the elderly. I meet some elderly who speak to me as though they are speaking to a youngster and they seem to know everything. When saddled with the specifics about ourselves, we are completely ignorant and unprepared when it comes to getting old and the road that lays ahead of them. The harsh reality has dawned on me that we have already bid goodbye to the generation before us, to some of our peers as well as the generation next. This means that our lives continue to keep getting lonelier by the day. Hence the tearing hurry to learn to live in this world, in solitude. Every day I spend a few hours all by myself in my study with some hobby or interest to keep myself occupied. Sudoku, or a crossword puzzle, a sketch/drawing to copy on an easel with some paints and brushes. Some old photographs albums to clean, replace some photos missing/misplaced ones, reignite passions on old ones with the better half, are my latest interests. The biggest treat of the day is the early morning video calls to grandchildren abroad, getting down to their level, sometimes playing the fool and getting witty answers from them.

My expectation level from the service has also come down with age. I do not expect any favours from anyone and would treat any help given by anyone as a bonus. The Regiment of Artillery is so big now that they can't attend to every retired officer. Your regiment possibly may be the only one that would remember you only if you maintain contact with them. I have overcome the urge to be envious or grumpy when not offered a drink by anyone during our get together on raising days in the local artillery mess. I have accepted this with a smile and will never grudge a present-day senior being served ahead of me.

We are extremely fortunate to have Col. KV Kuber, in our midst, whose vast and thorough knowledge of Srimad Bhagwad Gita and its teachings. Thanks to his exceedingly well-prepared presentations, he has generated a lot of interest among the residents. We began our spiritual journey in May 2018, with an exposure to the Gita, an hour each week. We also discussed Kunti's blessings to her sons, the Pandavas, to wage this righteous battle at Kurukshetra. We dwelt on the *Dhayanam*, the meditative song, recited before discussion on the various events that led to the war. *Dhyanam* is important because it gives a view of the battlefield where two armies had lined up, the greatness of warriors of both sides, idealisation of the supreme deity, Sri Krishna. It also inspired us to read the Gita.

The concept of the righteousness of the cause with the blessings of Sri Krishna was espoused. This played a crucial role for a smaller army of the Pandavas pitted against the bigger army of the Kauravas with those of his brothers hundred sons. The arrayed armies, the inspections, the visual description with war room briefings on both sides and the roaring of counches on both sides mark the beginning of the first chapter. On an inspection of the battlefield, Arjuna displayed negative signs indicating his unwillingness to fight. Kuber gave us a very fine exposure to the central theme of the Gita to do one's assigned duty with diligence without hankering for the fruits of action. The dilemma one faces on the battlefield and the doubts faced by Arjun were answered by Sri Krishna. The daily problems we are confronted with are very similar. We had completed just about done 10 verses in the third chapter when Covid 19 struck in March 2020. We are temporarily in limbo but we hope to resume as soon as we can.

The spiritual journey I have now embarked upon is to seek maximum knowledge about meditation and how to be a good human being. I also had the pleasure of going through Autobiography of a Yogi by Swami Yogananda, so thoughtfully presented to me by Uncle Dayal. I found the contents enlightening and inspiring. I am learning to meditate based on the Kriya Yog as advised by the Swamiji in his book, which is very easy and practical. The entire transcendence aims to quieten the mind, control and focus one's thoughts on a plane of higher consciousness, oust anger by breathing exercises, chanting Gayatri Mantra, concentration on breathing. Words also, cannot substitute the experience and understanding in real terms. Mental gymnastics sometimes gets the better of me; makes me feel that I am taking great leaps on a spiritual journey, but the harsh truth is I was merely removing the cobwebs in my mind where the biases, professional differences and prejudices picked up over the years, are still obstacles. That was my realization after years of contemplation and the intellectual quest of spiritual pursuits. It is only now that I am sure that there is nothing to be gained in retaining this "mental baggage", that I started to experience joy and happiness in all my actions.

I cannot claim to have achieved a lot but it has made my life better. Along with all this literature, we have had the benefit of regular visits by our family friends and gurus, Mr Gamini and Surangini Marapana. They are one of very affectionate and the finest couple we have ever met. We had the good fortune of meeting them in Sri Lanka in 2000 during our visit there. We have been receiving a lot of advice and wise counsel from this noble and selfless couple who we hold in great reverence and respect. I do read Buddhist literature which has made me a far better human being than I was. Vipassana Meditation is what I have liked most because it is so easy to practice once you understand the essence behind it.

We have great reverence for Hanuman Chalisa, Lalita Chalisa, Meher Baba's Parvadigar and Praschatap prayers, Durga Shapshati and the teachings of Buddha through various literature presented by Marapanas. Some of the teachings expressed in all literature are an eye-opener for me. I will also not hesitate to follow some good teachings of other religions and scriptures, which do not preach violence. My faith and beliefs are unaffected by this additional delving, which I find are nothing but equivalents of my religion.

Epilogue

Serving in the Army with a fearless attitude fortified by Dignity and Honour, I still walk erect with my head held high, this being the leitmotif of my success. Having a mind of my own, I tried very hard to maintain my identity. I did keep myself firmly grounded to humility (*aukat*), to embedded moral and family values (good *sanskar*) and professional honesty, which, fortunately, are intrinsic only in our Army life today.

I think have provided interesting glimpses of my varied experience while in service which are truthful and honest. I am not one of those who hates to tell the truth. My motivation in putting my experiences down on paper is far from settling old scores. I am writing these solely as a very concerned army officer with unimpeachable integrity and loyalty. I had my visions of this great Indian Army which I hold so dear. I do hope some of my experiences bring about a mid-course correction in the lives of those who choose to read them.

As I have stated in the Prologue that I have neither displayed extraordinary valour or bravery nor have I done anything so spectacular for others to write about, I took it on myself to narrate my experiences in uniform and outside it, as nobody would bother to write about me, after I am gone. There were great opportunities that came my way, but I think I did not grab them. Well, that's the way I am, and if one is not prepared to compromise on his beliefs and principles, the profession of arms is not for him. My wife, Manju tells me I am aggressive and outspoken, which probably went against the grain. Yes, I asserted myself with conviction, whenever it was necessary, but aggressiveness no, because I had no props, and my mentors were not those, who would support me for my wrongdoings.

Nothing in life is without meaning or is entirely coincidental. During my daily prayers and meditation, I have tried out the time-tested technique of forgiveness, which has worked wonders for me. The great secret of forgiveness is that once you have forgiven, it is unnecessary to repeat the prayer. It is only through forgiveness that we can erase someone else's wrongdoing and keep our slate clear. It is no use holding others responsible for ruining your career because whatever wrong happens to you, is God's desire in the form of retribution for your past life's Karma. Whoever has harmed you in this life, is now the instrument or the medium through which God desire is conveyed and needs to be accepted. The interplay of planetary configuration with Karmic determination, popularly known as the imponderables of fate or destiny or luck, whatever you may call it, is responsible for the occurrence of this strange phenomenon in the Army. It is not uncommon to find many officers possessing excellent professional qualifications and experience, truthful, trustworthy and dependable in battle, unable to reach the rank they deserve. The "mediocre" serving under more benevolent commanders from the same arm /service or group, unsteady in battle, thanks to "lady luck", get to positions where they hardly fit in. Like all other vocations, in this great Army too, we serve under those who tend to assume the mantle of self-anointed messiahs/surrogates for seniors for dispensing justice and fair play, on the protagonists like me. It is these antagonists who harm others' professional careers while procuring the best from their superiors.

I have led my life on my terms and it has been a very rewarding one; full of professional achievements as unit & Brigade commanders, altruistic joy in the success of my coursemates and subordinates and last of all, the attainment of the personal goals I had set for myself and the family. Without my lifelong and loving companion, Manju's help, we could never have enjoyed this enchanting and beautiful world we live in. We have travelled the world over and met such adorable people everywhere, some of whom are now great friends, in our exclusive circle. What can be more satisfying than to see my four grandchildren with moral values and *sanskars* firmly embedded, blossom into responsible citizens of this global village, with the minimal supervision of their caring parents. I am reminded of the famous lines from HW Longfellow:

> The lives of great men all remind us
> We can make our lives sublime,
> And, departing, leave behind us
> Footprints on the sands of time.

To my dearest family, we both love you all dearly for what you had given us in our lives.

My parting advice is to leave nothing for 'later' because in waiting for later, we can lose the best moments, the best experiences, the best friends and the best family.

The day is today ... The moment is now ...

CPSIA information can be obtained
at www.ICGtesting.com
Printed in the USA
LVHW082333070522
718112LV00005B/360